MINDFUL AMERICA

MINDFUL AMERICA

The Mutual Transformation of Buddhist
Meditation and American Culture

Jeff Wilson

OXFORD
UNIVERSITY PRESS

OXFORD
UNIVERSITY PRESS

Oxford University Press is a department of the University of Oxford.
It furthers the University's objective of excellence in research, scholarship,
and education by publishing worldwide.

Oxford   New York
Auckland   Cape Town   Dar es Salaam   Hong Kong   Karachi
Kuala Lumpur   Madrid   Melbourne   Mexico City   Nairobi
New Delhi   Shanghai   Taipei   Toronto

With offices in
Argentina   Austria   Brazil   Chile   Czech Republic   France   Greece
Guatemala   Hungary   Italy   Japan   Poland   Portugal   Singapore
South Korea   Switzerland   Thailand   Turkey   Ukraine   Vietnam

Oxford is a registered trademark of Oxford University Press
in the UK and certain other countries.

Published in the United States of America by
Oxford University Press
198 Madison Avenue, New York, NY 10016

Library of Congress Cataloging-in-Publication Data
Wilson, Jeff (Jeff Townsend), author.
Mindful America : the mutual transformation of Buddhist meditation
and American culture / Jeff Wilson.
pages cm
Includes bibliographical references and index.
ISBN 978–0–19–982781–7 (hardcover : alk. paper)—ISBN 978–0–19–982782–4
(ebook)—ISBN 978–0–19–938357–3 (ebook)   1. Buddhism—United States.
2. Awareness—Religious aspects—Buddhism.   3. Awareness.   I. Title.
BQ732.W55 2014
294.3′42117—dc23
2013046420

9 8 7 6 5
Printed in the United States of America
on acid-free paper

CONTENTS

ACKNOWLEDGMENTS

I would like to thank those who read portions of the manuscript or attended presentations on this research, including the participants in the 2010–2012 cohort of the Young Scholars in American Religion seminar at Indiana University–Purdue University Indianapolis; participants in the Religion, Food, and Eating in North America program unit at the American Academy of Religion; and students and faculty at the University of Virginia, University of British Columbia, and University of Lethbridge. I am also thankful for the comments of two anonymous reviewers, and the hard work of Oxford University Press, especially my editor, Cynthia Read. The librarians at Renison University College and the University of Waterloo were kept busy with my constant requests for materials. I'm very grateful to have had their support. Portions of this material—particularly selections about mindful eating in Chapter 4—appear in my essay "Mindful Eating: American Buddhism and Practical Benefits" in *Religion, Food, and Eating in North America*, edited by Ben Zeller, Marie Dallum, Reid Neilson, and Nora Rubel (New York: Columbia University Press, 2014). I thank the editors and Columbia University Press for permission to include elements of that essay here.

A second group of persons to whom I owe a debt are the thousands of Buddhists and practitioners of mindfulness who have welcomed me to their gatherings since the 1990s. Of particular importance were the Vipassana and Zen groups at the Ekoji Buddhist Temple of Richmond, in Virginia. Although this is not a work of ethnography, my time in the field for other projects definitely impacted the observations and interpretations I make here. Thank you for your hospitality.

Finally, I must acknowledge the many people who had to sacrifice in order that I could complete this work. First are my undergraduate and PhD students, who at times had less of my attention due to deadlines. Also, Renison University College granted me an early half-sabbatical that contributed to completion of this research and required the school to cover my duties, for which I am grateful. Second, and more directly, is my family, who had to put up with many lost opportunities for fun (and chores!) while I plugged away at this manuscript. My thanks to my children for leaving me alone to work at some times and for not leaving me alone at others, so that I had many sanity breaks from writing in order to draw, wrestle, tell stories, and play. And especially I thank my wife who served as a sounding board for my ideas and provided the essential support without which this project would simply have been impossible.

This book is dedicated to all who suffer in America and who seek solutions through mindfulness.

MINDFUL AMERICA

Sitting in the waiting room at the Pocono Medical Center in the Pennsylvania mountains, a young woman picks up *Spirit of Women*, a national medical publication designed to provide women with health care info, improve family health, and increase patient loyalty to the hospitals that distribute the periodical. As she turns to the article "How to Lose a Pound a Week Without Feeling Like You're on a Diet," she learns that one of the biggest calorie traps is mindless eating. "The solution is to be mindful: You can get pleasure from food and eat less when you pay attention."[1] On that same day, the *New York Times* Best Sellers list includes numerous books recommending mindfulness, including *Relish: An Adventure in Food, Style, and Everyday Fun* by Daphne Oz; *The Omni Diet: The Revolutionary 70% PLANT + 30% PROTEIN Program to Lose Weight, Reverse Disease, Fight Inflammation, and Change Your Life Forever* by Tana Amen; *Daring Greatly: How the Courage to Be Vulnerable Transforms the Way We Live, Love, Parent, and Lead* by Brene Brown; and *Clean: Overcoming Addiction and Ending America's Greatest Tragedy* by David Sheff.[2]

Meanwhile, South Carolina congressional candidate Mark Sanford is talking with Yahoo News during a ride to an event. Three years earlier he started a daily meditation practice during a rough patch in his political career. As he describes it:

> I come from the Christian faith. That's my faith tradition. But what I do like about Buddhism is the idea of being present...I think that that's missed in Western culture, where we're so busy looking a week out, two weeks out, a month out, a year out and we're hurried and we're busy. And I think if there's any one thing I learned from that year

I spent on the farm in the wake of getting out of office and just having a very, very quiet year, is the importance of stillness and quietness. And that extends beyond just the physical location. It extends really into the moment of, Are you really with that person or are you thinking of the next thing you've got to do? So I do like very much that part of Buddhism. I think it's right."

The next day Sanford is elected to Congress.

In Santa Monica that evening, about forty people are listening as Dr. Melvin G. Belzer, professor in the Department of Psychiatry and Biobehavioral Sciences at UCLA, coaches them in the basics of mindfulness meditation.[3] This is just one of the six-days-a-week programs offered by the UCLA Mindful Awareness Research Center; people who don't live in Southern California can participate through the Center's online courses. For younger people who want a more active style of meditation there is Inward Bound Mindfulness Education, whose teen retreats will run at wilderness sites throughout the western United States during the coming summer.[4] Members of the tech-savvy business crowd are already looking forward to gathering in September in New York City for the Wisdom 2.0 Business conference, dedicated to exploring "how to create business environments that inspire mindfulness, innovation, and engagement."[5] On the more traditional front, the Buddhist monks and nuns of Magnolia Grove Monastery in Mississippi spent the previous day chanting and practicing silent meditation, as they joined thousands of other American Buddhists across the country in observance of a monthly Day of Mindfulness.[6]

These are just a tiny portion of the mindfulness activities going on in the American springtime of 2013. This book examines the diverse ways in which the Buddhist-derived practice of mindfulness meditation has been applied to facets of American culture. Over the past three decades, mindfulness has gone from being an obscure Asian religious technique to a widely touted panacea and a serious money-making industry. A government survey in 2007 found that more than 20 million Americans used meditation for health reasons; and Americans spent $4.2 billion on mindfulness-related health practices in 2009.[7] The Mindfulness Research Guide listed 420 research articles on mindfulness in 2010, and in 2012 the Center for Mindfulness in Medicine, Health Care, and Society listed 820 mindfulness-based health practitioners in its database.[8] That same year, an average of 550,000 Google searches for the keyword "mindfulness" were performed each month.[9] Mindfulness has been the subject of articles or reports by ABC News, CBS Sunday Morning, CNN, *Cosmopolitan*,

Elle, Fox News, *Good Housekeeping, Huffington Post, Ladies' Home Journal, Marie Claire*, MSNBC, National Public Radio, the *New York Times, O: The Oprah Magazine, Parents, Psychology Today, Reader's Digest, Redbook, Self, Time, Prevention*, the *Wall Street Journal*, WebMD, and *Woman's Day*, among many, many others.[10] Major American businesses provide their employees with mindfulness training, including Target, Aetna, Hearst Publications, eBay, General Mills, Ford, Facebook, and Kaiser Permanente.[11]

We now have advocates for and practitioners of mindful eating, mindful sex, mindful parenting, mindfulness at work, mindful sports, mindful divorce lawyers, mindfulness-based stress reduction, mindfulness-based addiction recovery, and on and on. Recent years have seen best-selling books on mindfulness by members of Congress, Google engineers, and psychotherapists, and articles on mindfulness in Christian and Jewish magazines. Mindfulness is being taught in the public schools, the hospitals, and now even to the military.[12] Today mindfulness is touted as a cutting edge technique said to provide everything from financial success to mind-blowing female orgasms. *Mindful America* explores how mindfulness came to be applied to so many nontraditional concerns, how it has been changed and reconceptualized, and how it both relates to American Buddhism and is increasingly the property and fascination of non-Buddhists.

An important guiding thesis for *Mindful America* is that this is actually how Buddhism moves into new cultures and becomes domesticated: in each case, members of the new culture take from Buddhism what they believe will relieve their culture-specific distresses and concerns, in the process spawning new Buddhisms (sometimes, crypto-Buddhisms) that better fit their needs. My focus throughout, therefore, is on the specific practices necessary to make the product of a foreign time (premodern), culture (Asian), and religion (Buddhism) available for widespread application in contemporary American society. The hope is that this will be a pioneering first study of a particular major Buddhist influence on present-day American culture, and that it will also serve as a case study for how myriad non-Western religious practices are rendered appropriate for mainstream appropriation.

For this reason the chapters are organized around *processes* of adaptation, rather than discrete case studies of particular mindfulness applications and their historical specificities. Chapter 1 is the most historical section of the book, as it examines some of the mediating forces that have brought and continue to bring mindfulness to the United States. Chapter 2 shifts to look at the ways in which mindfulness's traditional Buddhist context is eroded away, a process of mystification necessary to make it available for a wider range of new American pursuits. The most important of these pursuits is the topic of Chapter 3, where we see how mindfulness has been taken up by the medical and psychology industries as an important new tool for their own ends. Chapter 4 is concerned with how mindfulness moves further into the mainstream of American society, serving average American needs in the everyday middle-class American life. Chapter 5 explores the marketing strategies that are used to bring Americans to mindfulness, and how mindfulness is used to make money in connection with various products, including mindfulness itself. The final chapter looks at the moral aspect of mindfulness: for many Americans, mindfulness provides a sense of values and a way to not only reconnect with the sacredness of life but also to potentially save the world itself. In the postscript, I consider some frames of analysis—primarily drawn from the study of American religious history—that can help us make sense of what is going on in the American rush to mindfulness.

Practical Benefits in Buddhist History

Buddhism is old. With approximately 2,500 years of history so far, Buddhism is one of the longest-surviving of our large religious traditions. This venerable age can tempt commentators to depict Buddhism as an ancient, conservative force, a relic from a time and place totally dissimilar from our own. But one of Buddhism's enduring insights is precisely that all things change, and Buddhism has managed to reach such a respectable age only by countless changes geared to make Buddhism relevant to evolving circumstances. In particular, when moving out of northern India into a large number of culturally distinct Asian regions, Buddhism was aided in its penetration of new societies by long-term processes of creative adaptation, especially by reconfigurations that allowed Buddhism to provide concrete benefits that each new culture desired. The changes taking place in the mindfulness movement today are a continuation of premodern practices of selective adaptation and modification that provide relevance to Buddhism for previously non-Buddhist societies. At the same time the incredible speed with which new developments are occurring within the mindfulness movement is one of the unique aspects of the encounter of Asian and Western cultures in the fast-paced, competitive, capitalistic, globalized world we now inhabit.

Examples of cultural adaptation based on practical benefits in Asian Buddhist history abound. Buddhism's early patronage in China often came from rulers who appreciated the teaching that the buddhas and Buddhist gods would provide supernatural support to kings who protected the monks and made monetary offerings for the creation of scriptures and images. Many of the scriptures that advance this idea were written in China, not India, suggesting that this was part of an adaptive strategy to make Buddhism fit the needs of Chinese patrons. A prime example is the *Sutra on Perfect Wisdom for Humane Kings Who Wish to Protect Their States*.[13] Written in China during the mid-fifth century C.E., this widely used sutra promised material prosperity and continuous power as a reward for helping Buddhism to flourish. It also provided concrete tools to deal with calamities that potentially faced the nation. Whenever kings had to deal with drought, plague, or enemy armies, they could have the sutra performed as a way to ward off these dangers. The Buddhist sutra literature, thus, took a place among the preexisting Chinese constellation of hybrid religious and political texts of the Daoists, Confucianists, Legalists, and others who melded supernatural, ritual, and governmental concerns. By adapting to local concerns and desires, Buddhism found a niche for itself, and from there it eventually became indelibly interwoven into Chinese religious practice.

Likewise, in the Japanese situation, Ian Reader and George Tanabe have identified the importance of *genze riyaku*, meaning this-worldly or practical benefits, in the spread, domestication, and continuing patronage of Buddhism.[14] Aristocrats, monks, merchants, and peasants all participated in Buddhism as a way of acquiring practical benefits to be enjoyed in the present life. The worldly benefits most often sought by Japanese Buddhist practitioners have been health, love, business success, protection from harm, and the bestowal of children. Old traditions were adapted to better provide these benefits, and new practices were created to pursue them. One of the best places to observe this practical orientation in the Buddhism adapted to Japan is in its material culture, which overruns with amulets, lucky charms, magical symbols, fortune-telling devices, and the like. These objects have been used by people at all levels of society, forming a truly common type of Japanese Buddhism. Though they have undergone modifications in the modern world, the general patterns of this-worldly benefits have remained remarkably intact from those of premodern times. Consider, for example, the lucky charms for sale at a Japanese Buddhist temple in Figure I.1. These represent the basic wishes that average Japanese people go to Buddhism to fulfill. We see amulets on sale promising safety on the roads, success in school, easy childbirth, recovery from illness, receiving employment, fulfillment of wishes, health, family happiness, business prosperity, and protection from evil.

This pattern repeats itself in modern America, but with a twist. Americans on the whole are disinclined to look to Buddhist magical items and ritual

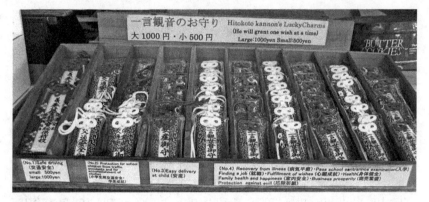

FIGURE I.1

services for their benefits—instead, they turn to Buddhist meditation, which more easily fits into prevailing scientific worldviews. Mindfulness has managed to reach into nearly every institution of American society—churches, schools, hospitals, law enforcement, prisons, courts, military, media, pop culture—because it has been subjected to the specific processes that I describe in this book, and thereby transformed so that it delivers cultural benefits desired by Americans. The alterations of Buddhism that I discuss in *Mindful America*, therefore, represent both departures and continuance at the same time. They are transformations of the tradition, to be sure; but they are also playing out a larger pattern that has always occurred, and which must occur if Buddhism (or, really, any religious tradition) is to integrate successfully into a new host culture.

Local and Global

The mindfulness movement is truly international in its scope. It is the product of a global circulation of monks, meditation teachers, books, articles, television programs, Internet websites, and everyday practitioners, Buddhist and otherwise. Its channels run from Asia to the West and back again, with important advocates in Europe, Australia, Canada, and elsewhere. The process of transformation is dialogical and takes place partially in Asia, with new developments subsequently exported to the West. It is important to always keep in mind this international dimension of the mindfulness movement. In the current era, it becomes harder and harder to find significant religious phenomena that are *not* transnational in some noteworthy way. And this has caused us to reassess how we tell the history of the past as well, as with such new perspectives suddenly the past seems more global and interconnected than once was acknowledged.

The transnational aspect of the mindfulness movement is apparent whenever we look at any particular manifestation of mindfulness. For example, a prominent group in this book is the Shambhala community, founded by the Tibetan exile Chogyam Trungpa. Shortly before his death, Trungpa moved his base of operations from Colorado to Halifax, and a core group of about 500 highly committed Americans relocated there in the several years to either side of his passing in 1987.[15] These American expatriates long served in some of the most important administrative and teaching positions within the Shambhala organization in Canada. Long-time Trungpa disciple Barry Boyce—born and raised in the United States, formerly the senior editor of *Shambhala Sun,* and today the editor-in-chief of *Mindful*—is an example. Nova Scotia is also the site of Gampo Abbey, a major Shambhala-affiliated monastery, which is home to Pema Chodron, an expatriate American nun who is one of the most popular Buddhist figures in the West. Today the mix of Americans and Canadians in Nova Scotia Shambhala organizations is more balanced than before, but Shambhala continues to attract or recruit Americans to Canada to practice and/or work in its institutions. Many others are second-generation American-Canadians, who combine American cultural forms passed down from their parents with Canadian culture absorbed from their birth country. Publications such as *Shambhala Sun,* most of whose subscribers are in the United States, are therefore examples of binational Buddhist organizations that escape easy definition as either wholly American or wholly Canadian. Consider, for example, that *Shambhala Sun* authors regularly comment on American culture and politics, but rarely refer to aspects of Canadian society. For some researchers, this neither-quite-fish-nor-fowl situation might prove frustrating; for myself, I view such fuzzy borders as opportunities. American society includes millions of people not born in the United States; billions of consumers of American cultural products live outside the United States; American citizens live in nearly every country in the world, and many travel or stay for extended periods of time in multiple foreign countries with ease and frequency; many religious traditions, organizations, and people are bi-, tri-, or multinational in their identity or reality, with American being only one component of their totality. All of these are, from my point of view, part of the story of American religion, and therefore appropriate for inclusion here. With this hermeneutic choice I do not intend to be imperialistic in my definition of Americanness, but just the opposite: in the 21st century, our narratives of American religion and culture should actively decenter the geographic United States and the official-U.S.-passport-wielding individual in order to consider the larger scope of Americanness and all its locations of production, enactment, consumption, and contestation. The same is true for works on Canadian religion, Mexican religion, and so on.

Even in the gigantic intersecting web of flows that researchers on contemporary culture study, there are particular centers where most of the development and exportation of particular phenomena takes place at certain points in history. Here, I concentrate my discussion on mindfulness phenomena in the United States, because it is a particular strength of my own training, because currently and for the preceding few decades it appears to be both the largest creator and the most eager consumer of new trends in the mindfulness movement, and because I believe there is value in case studies that illuminate international trends by examining them through the lens of particular local instantiations. We learn about two things at once in such projects: the transnationally diffuse *and* the culturally specific. International movements are always impacted by the local conditions in which real people participate in them, and today most places and phenomena are impacted by flows of people, ideas, materials, and power from sites well beyond their own neighborhood—it is at the intersection of such levels of scale that, I feel, many of the most interesting projects await for us to pursue. Despite the particular focus on the United States, *Mindful America* should prove useful to people who wish to study this movement in Europe, Asia, Canada, Australia, and elsewhere. I hope it will be of service to those who wish to keep a broadly international scope in view, without concentrating on any particular country, as well as those conducting firmly emplaced projects that consider aspects of mindfulness that manifest in very specific locations.

In looking at the transnational mindfulness movement from the vantage point of the United States, we can see how cultural and political particularities unique or especially strong in America have affected the development and practice of mindfulness, and we can gain a case study whereby to examine mindfulness elsewhere in a comparative fashion. Often, it is America that exports new trends in mindfulness to Asia, as recent research in South Korea and other countries has demonstrated.[16] The United Kingdom, Canada, and Australia in particular have notable mindfulness publishing activities, but even collectively they do not equal the annual mindfulness book or article production of the United States alone. In the pages that follow I focus my attention on works by Americans (be they natural-born or naturalized), residents or frequent visitors to the United States, and, less centrally, others whose works Americans consume in an especially active manner. The approach is to look at mindfulness in America while glancing further whenever appropriate, to discern the networks in which American mindfulness is embedded. I feel this offers the opportunity to tell a rich story with both nuance and wider utility.

It is reasonable to ask, what is the mindfulness *movement*? As I use the term, it refers to the widespread and growing collection of people who practice (and, especially, those who actively promote) techniques of awareness derived originally from the Buddhist cultures of Asia, which are typically grouped under the label "mindfulness" in 21st century America. Exact definitions of mindfulness differ sometimes within the movement, and no strong attempt to define mindfulness will be attempted here: on the one hand, freezing a movement into a single instantiation artificially solidifies what is an active, ongoing process, and on the other hand, the point of *Mindful America* is not what mindfulness *is*, but what various practitioners *say* it is, and how they employ it.

Is mindfulness religion, and is the mindfulness movement a religious movement? The answer, I argue, is "sometimes." Religion is not a phenomenon that exists neutrally in the world—it is a label applied variously by different people and by the same people at different times. This is true of its alleged opposite, "the secular," as well. Likewise, terms such as "scientific," "superstitious," "traditional," "modern," and so on are not mere statements of fact. The approach of *Mindful America* assumes such labels to be more than dry descriptors—they are markers of value employed strategically by agents in ways that reveal further patterns of value and preference. Thus when an author speaks of the scientific, nonreligious practice of mindfulness, he or she is not stating a fact: he or she is making an argument, one impacted by such variables as race, education, cultural background, professional training, intended audience, and more. The same is true for the author who insists on the religious, Buddhist, or other nature of mindfulness.

A Personal Reflection

One of the main things that draws me to the study of American Buddhism is the opportunity to be a pioneer. That's a frustrating but also tremendously fun and exciting situation. When I began *Mourning the Unborn Dead* (my book on Buddhist post-abortion rituals being used by American Buddhists, Christians, and others), a handful of scholars had noted in passing the existence of such rituals, but no one had actually studied them.[17] Likewise, when I produced *Dixie Dharma* (my book on American Buddhist regionalism and Buddhism in the South), a few researchers had acknowledged that Buddhism existed in the South and varied from place to place in America, but there was no systematic work that investigated what those differences might be or why they might arise.[18] And with this book on mindfulness, I find myself on the frontier again. Mindfulness is everywhere, and few scholars of American Buddhism would fail to note its presence. Yet no one has focused their gaze exclusively and at length upon the phenomenon. We've been offered a few tantalizing tidbits— a look at Mindfulness-Based Stress Reduction (MBSR) and New Thought similarities in Wakoh Shannon Hickey's intriguing PhD dissertation, ethnographic work at the Cambridge Insight Meditation Center as part of a larger sophisticated work on Theravada Buddhism in America by Wendy Cadge, a perceptive but mostly descriptive chapter on Insight Meditation by Gil Fronsdal in a book now fifteen years old, a few pages in David McMahan's *The Making of Buddhist Modernism*, and Anne Harrington's *The Cure Within*— but no main courses.[19] Here I make a first attempt at providing a full meal of mindfulness for scholars to chew, savor, critique, and hopefully eventually surpass. This project carries forward many of the interests first explored in my earlier books, such as the role of non-Buddhists in adapting and spreading aspects of Buddhism, the impact of Buddhism on wider American culture, the influence of American religion and culture on the practice of Buddhism, and the race, gender, and class dynamics at play within American Buddhism.

Because many people have opinions about mindfulness and the way in which Americans are using it, it seems useful to provide some comments about my own position. I am neither an advocate for nor an opponent of mindfulness. I do happen to be a Buddhist but am drawn to study mindfulness because of its prominence in the United States and its status as a rich site for exploring religious and cultural transformation, not because I have any investment in mindfulness itself. I was first introduced to mindfulness in gym class as a public school student in the early 1990s, and I have practiced countless hours of mindfulness as part of my fieldwork at various Buddhist sites in the United States, Canada, and Japan since the later 1990s, but do not have a personal mindfulness practice; in the same way, I have said untold numbers of Christian prayers during site visits for other research, but do not pray as a Christian when at home. At no point in this book do I address or attempt to tackle the issue of whether mindfulness actually *works*—that is to say, whether it delivers any of the benefits suggested herein by my subjects, from nirvana to weight loss. I have no idea whether it works, and it is not a question I am interested in answering. There are many studies that suggest it does work; there have also been criticisms of some of those studies (and criticisms of the criticisms, etc.). For my purposes here, it simply doesn't matter whether mindfulness works: what matters is that various Americans *assert* that it works, and those assertions and applications are a very interesting example of cultural encounter and transformation that tell us something about ourselves in the early 21st century.

My interest is in the dynamics that play out when two or more cultures meet, and I look to religions as my topic because they are both impactful and fascinating—and I focus on Buddhism specifically as my most common test case because it is the system I know best. The encounter of cultures always results in ironies, absurdities, innovations, conflict, exaggeration—and sometimes profundity as well. You will find them all here. Mindfulness is far too large and complex a phenomenon to be reduced to any simple statement or value judgment. No matter where one stands, when looking into the mindfulness movement each observer is likely to find elements that strike him or her as crass, others that appear exploitative, things that are deeply moving, developments that seem genuinely positive, and phenomena that may be outright dangerous. He or she will encounter saints, sinners, charlatans, and ordinary folks just trying to get by. But the determination of the quality of any given mindfulness book or the character of any particular mindfulness advocate or application is a decision that can be reached only by each subjective reader, and different readers will come to different conclusions. I have my own reactions; in fact, I have multiple reactions, because the same mindful applications and authors have at times struck me as vulgar and at other times as profound in the process of examination and reexamination during the course of research and writing.

In this book, I do not attempt to push a hard sell for any particular viewpoint on any particular part of the mindfulness movement, or the movement as a whole. The mindfulness movement *is*, and because it is, we must each grapple with its manifestations and draw our conclusions. I seek not to be an advocate or a critic of the mindfulness movement, but a chronicler and analyst. The role specific task for the scholar of religious studies, as I understand it, is to investigate those profoundly complex, beautiful, horrifying, socially impactful cultural systems that we have labeled religions—and when confronted with cultural products that partially or primarily operate outside the sphere of specific religious systems yet nonetheless manifest in some ways like religions, to turn the tools and insights gained from investigation of formal religious traditions to the service of illuminating such phenomena further.

That is the approach of this book, which contains history but is not strictly speaking a tightly argued historical work, and is informed by the perspectives of people in the mindfulness movement but is not an ethnography. Both such projects would be worthy, and there are a great many other possible approaches to the slippery diversity of the mindfulness movement. *Mindful America* is an exploration of the mindfulness phenomenon, concerned with large-scale trends observable within the movement, and the forces at work in such trends. My primary method has been to immerse myself deeply in the literature of the mindfulness movement itself, looking for trends and following storylines as they presented themselves. The actual body of evidence consists of hundreds of published books, an even greater number of articles, and electronic media (blogs, tweets, bulletin board posts, etc.) numbering in the thousands; the most important of these are contained in the bibliography at the back of this book. It is my hope that this first book-length treatment of the mindfulness movement by an outside researcher will serve as a jumping off point for many other projects that reflect the interests, perspectives, and strengths of other scholars, and that take the weaknesses, missed opportunities, and blind spots of my approach as fodder for further illuminating this important cultural development.

1 MEDIATING MINDFULNESS: HOW DOES MINDFULNESS REACH AMERICA?

Mediate: to occupy an intermediate or middle position; to be between; to form a connecting link or a transitional stage between one thing and another

—*Oxford English Dictionary*[1]

"One day in my early thirties, I found myself sitting in a quiet circle in a room while a woman at the front struck a metal bowl with a wooden dowel and told us to listen to the sound with our full attention," wrote Kiera Van Gelder in the spring 2012 issue of *Buddhadharma*, one of the main American Buddhist magazines.[2] "She had us follow our breath as we inhaled and exhaled, and gently reminded us to let go of any thoughts that arose. All these exercises were part of what [the instructor] called 'mindfulness,' and we did them doggedly week after week." A reader could easily be excused for imagining that Van Gelder was describing her experiences in a Buddhist monastery, but in fact she discovered mindfulness in a totally different kind of setting. "In time I'd understand they were practices done daily in thousands of Buddhist communities, but my entranceway to the Buddhist path was not through a sangha. It happened when I was a patient at a mental hospital and my teacher was a psychiatrist, not a lama."

At the same time that Van Gelder's article appeared, Gretchen Rubin's *The Happiness Project* was firmly ensconced on the *New York Times* Best Sellers list, where it had been sitting for an entire year (it ultimately spent 121 weeks on the list during 2011–2013). As Rubin explained, she had been living a hectic life in New York City when she looked out the bus window into the rain and realized that something wasn't right. "I wasn't as happy as I could be, and my life wasn't going to change unless I made it change. In that single moment, with that realization, I decided to dedicate a year to trying to be happier."[3] The book narrates her adventures in the pursuit of happiness, month by month. As she related, friends kept telling her she should study Buddhism if she wanted to become happier. To that end, she dedicated October to exploring mindfulness, but she just wasn't interested in pursuing formal meditation. Instead of doing silent, seated mindfulness practice, she experimented with snippets of mindfulness practice in various ways, such as through keeping a food journal and reading about Buddhism. Despite her reluctance to meditate, she affirmed that mindfulness calms the mind, elevates brain function, improves the present experience, reduces stress, and soothes pain; it also can help break bad habits. As she succinctly told her readers, "It makes people happier, less defensive, and more engaged with others."[4]

The experiences of these two women illustrate important facets of the mindfulness movement in modern America. Rather than in a Buddhist context as might be expected, these non-Buddhist women encountered aspects of Buddhism in very non-Buddhist spaces.[5] For Van Gelder, it was in a hospital that she was introduced to mindfulness as part of a treatment to deal with serious mental health issues. At first she didn't even know that her practice derived from Buddhism. For Rubin, the incentive to do mindfulness came from meditating friends who wanted her to be happy but weren't trying to convert her to a new religion. She didn't engage with Buddhist practice communities directly and in fact decided that mindfulness and its reputed benefits could be accessed without doing any sort of traditional meditation. And the hundreds of thousands of non-Buddhist Americans who read her book encountered mindfulness at an even greater remove from Buddhism—through the pages of a pop advice memoir penned by an agnostic of Christian heritage.

How did we get to this point, where mindfulness apparently can exist entirely outside of Buddhism, and non-Buddhists can teach other non-Buddhists about Buddhist-derived mindfulness to gain control over mental illness, achieve self-fulfillment, and sell books, with nary a mention of the idea of pursuing nirvana? Is this the way that mindfulness was understood in the past? What is mindfulness's historic relationship with Buddhism, anyway? By tracing some of the history of how mindfulness was mediated from premodern Buddhist Asia to its many expressions in contemporary America, we can discern the multiple ways in which Americans encounter mindfulness, and consider what effects occur when Buddhist practice is disseminated via these different pathways. We can also begin to note the incredible complexity of the mindfulness movement's American ecosystem—for lack of a better term—which includes everyone from ascetic monks hidden in the wilderness to secular New Yorkers, and everything from traditional silent retreats to the self-help section of Amazon.com.

Translating Mindfulness

The beginnings of American interest in Buddhism are usually dated to approximately 1844, the year that Edward Salisbury read his "Memoir on the History of Buddhism" to the American Oriental Society and the Transcendentalist journal *Dial* published Elizabeth Palmer Peabody's translation of an extract from the Lotus Sutra.[6] From there it was a long time before widespread attention to Buddhist meditation developed, even among those Westerners sympathetic to Buddhism, and longer still before significant numbers of Americans actually began to try their hand at it. From 1844 until well into the 20th century, the term "mindfulness" played little or no role in the emerging American fascination with Buddhism. For the first century of American interest in Buddhism, the conversation was dominated by an interest in Buddhist belief systems, ethics, and the personality of the historical Buddha, rather than practice. When practice was raised, it was often by Buddhism's opponents, who painted the mainstream practices of devotion as idolatry and evidence of Buddhist Asia's fatal backwardness in comparison with the modern Christian West.

How then did mindfulness finally enter into the American Buddhist vocabulary? Mindfulness is an English word, and can be slippery in the way it is employed to translate or designate specific meditation techniques. Other word choices exist for all of the terms that have been translated as "mindfulness," and indeed they have been used at various points in American history. Eventually, mindfulness became especially attached to the Pali term *sati* (Sanskrit = *smrti*), but it took decades for it to emerge as the clear favorite translation, and even today there is ambiguity in many usages.[7] This fluidity can frustrate linguists, but as I argue later in my postscript, it is one of the key characteristics allowing mindfulness to become so widely appropriated and applied in American culture.

Today "mindfulness" is well established as the preferred translation of "sati," as a survey of translations from the past half century will readily demonstrate.[8] Sati literally means memory or remembrance. In its usage as a technical Buddhist meditation term, it usually also implies awareness, attention, or alertness. References to it can be found scattered throughout the Indian Buddhist canons and their commentaries, and naturally also in translations of these texts into various Asian languages. There are a number of texts or usages, however, that are particularly important in relation to sati in the modern period. Classical textual presentation of sati comes to us in the West primarily from the *Satipatthana Sutta*, the closely related *Mahasatipatthana Sutta*, and in its specifically breath-oriented practice, from the *Anapanasati Sutta* as well.[9] Sati is also generally important because of its place as the seventh step (*samma-sati*, "Right/Correct Mindfulness") on the Noble Eightfold Path, which constitutes the fourth of the Four Noble Truths.[10] These truths/path are one of the key formulas for basic Buddhism and appear in virtually all introductory discussions of Buddhism in the West, regardless of sect or cultural affiliation of the author. Sati also appears in a few verses of the *Dhammapada*, a traditional collection of aphorisms that early on became one of the most popular of all Buddhist texts in the United States, a status it retains to this day. The *Satipatthana Sutta*, *Anapanasati Sutta*, and *Dhammapada* all exist in Mahayana forms, but their translation and use in America are overwhelmingly based on their renditions in the Theravada scriptures, preserved in the Pali language—these are the versions typically employed even by Mahayana American commentators. There are also major post-canonical texts that contain monastic commentaries on these texts, such as the *Visuddhimagga*—this commentarial literature was extremely important in the premodern period, but is often eclipsed in English writings by a quasi-*sola scriptura* mindset that tends to prefer using writings attributed to the Buddha without significant pre-20th century elaboration (but comments by modern-day writers are typically welcomed).

How did mindfulness come to be the preferred translation for sati, and what phases can we detect in the usage of the terms "mindful" and "mindfulness," particularly in the United States? A quick examination of selective English-language sources related to Buddhism is instructive. In 1853 the British Methodist missionary Robert Spence Hardy, one of the pioneering figures in the English-language study of Buddhism, defined sati/smrti variously as "the conscience, or faculty that reasons on moral subjects; that which prevents a man from doing wrong, and prompts him to do that which is right" and as "the ascertainment of truth."[11] This definition hardly carries any of the usual sense of memory, though it does relate to the idea of awareness as the faculty of discerning reality. In 1870 F. Max Müller, one of the most important of the 19th century Orientalists, allowed his translation of the *Dhammapada* to appear in a book by Henry Thomas Rogers. Müller translated sati variously as "watchfulness" and "well awake," again neglecting the sense of remembrance.[12] In 1871, Henry Alabaster, an employee of the British Consulate General in Siam (Thailand), rendered the seventh step (samma-sati) of the Noble Eightfold Path as "correct memory."[13] This errs to the other side, failing to indicate what is being remembered or that remembrance relates to the activity of meditation.

One of the most influential English-language Buddhist texts of the late Victorian era was Col. Henry Steel Olcott's *Buddhist Catechism*, first produced in 1881 and reprinted innumerable times since. Olcott was one of the most important Americans involved in Theosophy, an eclectic new religious movement based on American and European metaphysical religion, Hinduism, Buddhism, and other sources. He was also a major figure in the anticolonial Buddhist revival in Asia. Olcott did not use the word "mindfulness" anywhere in his catechism. Instead, he rendered the seventh step of the path as "Right Memory."[14] The first significant American translator of Buddhist texts was Henry Clarke Warren, a reclusive scholar associated with Harvard University. In 1896 he published a version of the *Mahasatipatthana Sutta* in his *Buddhism in Translations*, the first such opportunity that American English-language readers had to be exposed to comprehensive teachings about sati. But Warren chose not to translate sati as "mindfulness." Instead, where later translators would talk about the "four foundations of mindfulness," he used the term "four intent contemplations."[15] In 1907 Paul Carus, editor of Open Court Press and another of the towering early American interpreters of Buddhism, described the seventh step of the eightfold path as "right self-discipline."[16] After more than fifty years of investigation, the turn of the 20th century came and went without much hint to Americans interested in Asian cultures that something called "mindfulness" might play a major role in Buddhism.

This does not mean that mindfulness wasn't being employed to translate sati, only that its use therein was not yet common and "mindfulness" was not yet understood to be an important element of Buddhism in the West. We have the Pali Text Society, particularly Thomas William Rhys Davids, to thank for both of these eventual developments. Like many of the British Orientalists, Rhys Davids was employed as a civil servant in Asia before launching his career as a scholar. He founded the Pali Text Society in 1881, dedicated to studying and publishing on Pali (and therefore to understanding Theravada Buddhism). In the same year he delivered a series of lectures on Indian Buddhism for the Hibbert Trust, founded by prominent Unitarian Robert Hibbert to promote liberal religion. Very occasionally, Rhys Davids used "mindful," implying cautious awareness, in his Hibbert lectures, apparently as a translation of the word sati.[17] This infrequent use continued for decades. For example, in 1886 he translated samma-sati as "right mindfulness" in the book *Buddhism: Being a Sketch of the Life and Teachings of Gautama, the Buddha*. But he also used the translation "four earnest meditations" for what Warren had called "four intent contemplations" and later translators would call "four foundations of mindfulness."[18] So the translation of sati had not yet been set firmly in Rhys Davids's mind. In 1890 the Society produced his translation of the popular post-canonical text *The Questions of King Milinda*. One of the question-and-answer exchanges begins thusly: "The king said: 'What, Nâgacena, is the characteristic mark of mindfulness?' 'Repetition, O king, and keeping up.'"[19] The brief dialogue that follows implies that continually keeping one's mind abreast of the unfolding of events leads to confident knowledge and self-control. Buried in a long and diverse text, the few pages related to sati are among the first instances of Pali Text Society use of "mindfulness" beyond mere mention of the concept, but they fail to draw a reader's attention to mindfulness as anything particularly important to the Buddhist tradition. Likewise, Albert J. Edmunds, a British-American Orientalist who also belonged to the Pali Text Society, used mindfulness to translate sati in his 1902 version of the *Dhammapada*, but the term appears so infrequently that it does not signal a major Buddhist teaching or practice. [20]

This began to change by the end of the first decade of the 20th century. The Pali Text Society produced its own, fuller translation of the *Mahasatipatthana Sutta* in 1910, which soon superseded Warren's version. Translated by T. W. Rhys Davids and his wife Caroline Augusta Foley Rhys Davids, it continued his earlier precedent of using "mindfulness" for sati, which now had become his preferred translation. Thus what in 1886 he had called the "four intent meditations," he now called the "Fourfold Setting up of Mindfulness."[21] The other authors of the Pali Text Society followed his lead. For example, in 1926 and 1927 Robert Chalmers, the former governor of Ceylon, used "mindfulness" for sati in his translations of the *Satipatthana Sutta* and *Anapanasati Sutta*, as did Isaline Blew Horner in her own translations of these suttas in 1954 and 1959.[22]

The Pali Text Society's translations were widely circulated and influenced the entire lexicon of English-language Buddhism throughout the 20th century. They decisively cemented "mindfulness" as the most preferred translation of sati over other possibilities, such as memory, remembrance, contemplation, or meditation. Simultaneously, they established different translations for other words that easily might have been rendered as mindfulness. For example, the word *appamada* (Sanskrit = *apramada*) means recollection, heedfulness, earnestness, or watchfulness, and thus is very close to the sense of mindfulness.[23] Among other places, appamada appears in the second chapter of the *Dhammapada*. But T. W. Rhys Davids decided on "diligence" as the translation for appamada instead of mindfulness, and that usage has been continued by most subsequent authors.[24]

Of course, today some authors still use mindfulness to indicate Buddhist terms or concepts other than sati, especially if the writers in question are not themselves specialists in the translation of Indian technical vocabulary. For instance, sometimes one can find authors who use mindfulness in reference to *vipassana* (Sanskrit = *vipasyana*).[25] Vipassana means insight, and because such insight is often developed in the course of mindfulness of the act of breathing (*anapanasati*, "mindfulness of breathing"), many commentators conflate vipassana meditation in general and mindfulness. Complicating things further, this type of breath awareness is common in the Japanese Zen practice of *zazen* (literally, "seated meditation") and thus "mindfulness" has been increasingly used to describe zazen, or even just Zen meditation and attitude generally, by English-speaking Americans. Similar breath-attention techniques are found in Tibetan and other forms of Buddhism as well, and they too are now generally lumped in as mindfulness practices. And at least one prominent interpreter of Buddhism to America used "mindfulness" to translate *samatha* (Sanskrit = *shamatha*), meaning concentration, tranquility, or calming.[26] These other uses of the term mindfulness correspond more or less to the period since the dramatic rise of the mindfulness movement, so we can say that the movement has had both the impact of making sati far more popular than it once was and of influencing how forms of Buddhist meditation other than sati are understood and talked about.

The Practice of Mindfulness Meditation Prior to the 20th Century

Today mindfulness is a common topic of discussion among Western Buddhists and Buddhist sympathizers, relatively few of whom are ordained monks or nuns. In our egalitarian and consumer-based culture of privatized religious practice, this does not strike us as noteworthy. But historically speaking, this is an extreme departure from the norm. Prior to the 20th century, few everyday Buddhists would have even heard of mindfulness practice, much less read texts on it or engaged in it themselves.

Looking back to Buddhism's development in Asia, we find that mindfulness meditation has been practiced primarily by ordained monks and nuns, as part of a much larger package of mutually supporting practices and beliefs, and ordinarily was associated with world renunciation and the pursuit of nirvana. Mindfulness meditation techniques developed within early Indian Buddhism are recorded in various classic scriptures (such as the *Satipatthana Sutta*), which attribute them to the historical Buddha. Indeed, there are Buddhologists who feel that it was mindfulness-related techniques—such as vipassana generated by awareness of the fourfold foundations of mindfulness—that represented the primary meditative innovation of the Buddha, as other forms of Buddhist meditation have clear antecedents in pre-Buddhist Indian religious practice. The specific method most associated with mindfulness within American Buddhism is that of simply mentally observing and noting changes as they occur within oneself or in one's environment. Most often this is directed toward the breath. There are two favored techniques, as explained by Joseph Goldstein, one of the most prominent Buddhist meditation teachers in America: "Awareness of the breath can be practiced in one of two ways. When you breathe in, the abdomen naturally rises or extends and when you breathe out, it falls. Keep your attention on the movement of the abdomen, not imagining, nor visualizing anything, just experiencing the sensation of the movement. Don't control or force the breath in any way, merely stay attentive to the rising, falling movement of the abdomen."[27] This technique is especially favored by practitioners, such as Goldstein, who have connections to the Mahasi Sayadaw lineage of Burmese mindfulness meditation.

Goldstein continues: "The alternative is to be aware of the breath as it goes in and out of the nostrils, keeping the attention in the area around the tip of the nose or the upper lip. Maintain the awareness on the breath much as a watchman standing in a gate observes people passing in and out; don't control or force the breathing. Simply be aware of the in and out breath as it passes the nostrils. It is helpful in the beginning of practice to make mental notes either of 'rising, falling' or 'in, out.' This aids in keeping the mind on the object."[28] This second technique is actually the more common and traditional. Awareness of the breath through attention and noting is expanded eventually into mindfulness of thoughts, feelings, and actions generally. For example, if a thought arises in the mind about something, one merely notes "thinking" and tries not to react to the thought in any particular way. Similarly, if one commits an action of some sort, such as yawning, one mentally notes "feeling urge to yawn... raising hand to cover mouth... opening mouth... yawning... closing mouth... lowering hand."

There are alternative styles in other forms of Buddhism, but usually they are variations on a common theme, not completely different approaches. For example, the second technique offered by Goldstein is very similar to how basic breath meditation is often taught in various Mahayana forms of Buddhism, such as Zen. In addition, some beginning Zen meditators are instructed to count each breath until reaching ten, at which point the counting starts over again at one. And in the Soto lineage of Zen—which was eclipsed in early Western interest in Zen but began to rise to a very important position in the 1960s with the arrival of prominent Soto missionaries—formal noting is discouraged in favor of bare attention that lets thoughts and sense impressions come and go like the wind, neither clung to nor ignored.

Whatever the exact details, like all silent meditation techniques, these formal practices of awareness historically have not been widespread among the mass of regular lay practitioners in Buddhist countries. But—as an early type of meditation that likely traces back to the historical Buddha himself—mindfulness has existed in some form in most traditions of Buddhism, and thus has always been at least a dormant resource waiting to be called forth to meet new situations.

In the *Satipatthana Sutta* the Buddha is depicted teaching his monks a variety of methods for maintaining awareness of the body and mind. In the opening paragraphs, the sutta describes the purpose of mindfulness practices: "Monks, this is the direct path for the purification of beings, for the surmounting of sorrow and lamentation, for the disappearance of pain and grief, for the attainment of the true way, for the realization of Nirvana—namely, the four foundations of mindfulness."[29] In this classic presentation mindfulness is taught to the monks, not the general Buddhist community, and it is clearly associated with traditional transcendent monastic concerns, such as nirvana. Mindfulness meditation is to be pursued as a way to disengage from clinging to the everyday world of suffering and turn toward a rigorous discipline, resulting in breakage of the cycle of rebirth. Diligent mindfulness produces high-level trance states known as *jhana* (Sanskrit = *dhyana*).[30] The Buddha specifically recommends applying mindfulness to the body (breathing, posture, actions, physical impurities, disintegrating corpses, etc.), sensations, states of mind, and various Buddhist concepts, including the Four Noble Truths.

This is the framing that mindfulness techniques receive in the traditional commentaries of Buddhist lineages over nearly the entire sweep of Asian Buddhist history, regardless of lineage or location. Mindfulness is presented as a strenuous, lifelong task, one that occurs within a framework of renunciation and detachment: the practitioner seeks to acquire eventually the bliss enjoyed in peaceful meditation, rather than to enjoy the activities of daily life via mindful attitudes. Mindfulness implies caution, heedfulness, and ambivalence toward the world in general and the object of one's mindfulness specifically; in this traditional framework, mindfulness operates as something that puts distance between oneself and one's experience, so that one ceases to be troubled by it. In the premodern Theravada tradition, it was decidedly not a process of inhabiting the present moment so that one connects with the immanent wonder of the sacred.

The importance of meditation within Buddhism gradually declined over time, as scholar monks and liturgical specialists gained greater status within the sangha. By the 10th century c.e. the techniques for applying mindfulness to gain insight (vipassana) had mostly died out in Theravada Buddhism. Many centuries passed until in the modern period—beginning in 18th century Burma and slowly spreading into Thailand and Sri Lanka in the 19th century—small, mostly marginal revivalist movements appeared.[31] These new vipassana movements based their techniques on textual, especially canonical, sources rather than unbroken meditation lineages, relying especially on new readings of the *Satipatthana Sutta* to reconstruct what they believed to be proper Buddhist meditation. These movements—which, unlike mainstream Buddhism, believed individual insight meditation practice to be the key to proper Buddhist practice— slowly grew, and as they developed they often became allied with other modern reformist streams that sought to revitalize monastic discipline, strengthen the soteriological primacy of nirvana, adapt to evolving scientific knowledge, and make Buddhism relevant to practitioners in colonial and postcolonial settings.[32]

Compared to Southeast Asian Theravada, the trajectory of meditation was not particularly different in the history of East Asian Mahayana and Central Asian Vajrayana Buddhism: meditation primarily was confined to the monastic community, where it was often not a central concern, especially outside of the few large training monasteries. Though few Buddhist monks or nuns would have objected to the idea that mindfulness was a legitimate Buddhist practice, it was far from the sine qua non of Buddhism, and those practitioners who did engage in meditation frequently pursued techniques other than sati-type mindfulness, such as koan or visualization. Beginning in the 19th century in East Asia and the 20th century in Central Asia, small revitalization movements began to appear in reaction to the changing world situation of Western colonialism and imperialism. As in the Theravada countries of Southeast Asia, such movements sometimes stressed the importance of meditation practice, including techniques that focused on awareness rather than concentration or visualization (this was particularly true for reformers of the Zen schools in Japan, some of whom visited Southeast Asia in their quest for resources with which to transform Japanese Buddhism).

Collectively, these reformist movements were clearly minority streams within their own cultures. But they had zealous and often articulate spokespersons, many of whom spoke from the authority of their own experiences with meditation. With their concerns over Buddhism's place in the contemporary world, and modified, less ceremonial forms of individualistic Buddhist practice, they would prove unusually appealing to Westerners exploring Asian culture. It was from this meeting of modern-minded Asian meditators and Western seekers fascinated with Buddhism's potential as an alternative philosophy and spirituality that the mindfulness movement would eventually emerge.

Mindfulness in America Prior to the 1970s

The critical turning point for the mindfulness movement as such was the 1970s, but it could begin to come into its own at that time only based on seeds planted in the previous decades of the 20th century. During the first seventy-five years of the 20th century, American Buddhist awareness of mindfulness techniques grew slowly. Such awareness was generated and cultivated by a number of sources. First were the translators and Orientalists, such as the Pali Text Society, whose increasing volume of publications made ever more of the Theravada Buddhist canon available to readers in the West. Some of the Western readers of these volumes became interested enough to travel to Asia, in some cases even choosing to ordain as monks. Second, clustered around such transnational associations as the Pali Text Society, the Maha Bodhi Society, the Buddhist Publication Society, and the nascent vipassana movements, a global network of like-minded Asian and Western Buddhists and sympathizers began to develop. At its heart were a relatively small number of modernist Buddhists, with monks from Burma, Sri Lanka, Great Britain, and Germany often having the most important roles, and a number of prominent laypeople from these and other countries also playing a part. A glimpse of the heterogeneity of such networks can be seen in the Burmese monk Mahasi Sayadaw's book *Practical Insight Meditation*. As he describes in his preface: "The Venerable Nyanaponika Mahathera [German] put this translation into final literary shape after attaining confirmation of his valuable suggestions. U Pe Thin's [Burmese] translation was revised by and improved upon, as to style, by Miss Mary McCollum, an American Buddhist lady. She practiced Satipaṭṭhāna meditation under the guidance of Anagarika Munindra [Bengali] at Burmese Vihara, Bodh-Gaya, Bihar, India. Anagarika Munindra stayed with us for a considerable period. He sent her revision to us for perusal and approval. When done, it was forwarded to the Venerable Nyanaponika Mahathera. This book is therefore, the co-ordination and combined publication of the aforesaid two translations, with my Preface added thereto."[33]

These practitioners and publications oriented toward Southeast Asian Buddhism were in turn a subset of the larger 20th century conversation on Buddhism, which often included Japanese, Chinese, American, and other clergy and laypeople. Though individuals sometimes had preferences for one type of Buddhism or another, information on any type of Buddhism was at such a premium and opportunities for fellowship among Buddhists in the West so rare that Westerners tended to consume Buddhist publications (and ideas) regardless of their sectarian sources. Meanwhile, Asian Buddhists from across the continent and of every tradition engaged in dialogue and exchange, assisting one another variously with methods for revitalizing Buddhism, for resisting Western imperialism, and for competing with and borrowing from Christianity and other religions. In this environment, information on Theravadin mindfulness practices appeared alongside perspectives drawn from the Japanese and Tibetan esoteric traditions, the East Asian Pure Land schools, stories of the Chinese Zen patriarchs, and often quite a bit of Theosophical and other quasi-Buddhist material.

Much of the work of promoting mindfulness fell to monks associated with the vipassana movements. Lineages springing from two famous Burmese meditation masters, Ledi Sayadaw and Mahasi Sayadaw, became especially important.[34] Monks and the occasional layperson associated with these lineages established new centers in Asia for teaching Buddhism to the public at large and pioneered the dissemination of difficult sati-based practices to laypeople. They popularized and commented on classical mindfulness-related texts; many of these texts and their commentaries were translated into Western languages, particularly German and English. Through this process sati was promoted to the West by such monks as the Sri Lankans Soma Thera and Walpola Rahula, the British Nanamoli Thera, and especially the German Nyanaponika Thera. Beyond dissemination of printed materials, monks also visited Europe and occasionally North America to teach meditation for limited periods. Though of low initial impact, the infrastructure for what would eventually become the Western mindfulness movement was being laid.

Works of this period continued the traditional framing of mindfulness as a renunciation practice undertaken for the pursuit of nirvana. A classic example is Soma Thera's 1941 *The Way of Mindfulness: The Satipatthana Sutta and Commentary*. According to Soma Thera, mindfulness "is the only satisfying way for the seeker of truth when the diffuseness [papañca] of the external world with its thin layer of culture, comfort and allurement, ceases to be interesting and is found to lack true value."[35] As mindfulness is not suited to the ordinary person, he claims that "it is strenuous whole-time work, and only resolute hearts in whom the consciousness of life's suffering runs deep, could hope to pursue it to the end, the attainment of Saintship."[36] Soma Thera insists that the practitioner of mindfulness must read and understand classic Theravada texts, and that the training is best undertaken in solitude under the guidance of a master meditator.

Soma Thera's approach was the most common one during this period. There were hints of a broadening perspective, however, that appeared from time to time. Two monks in particular provided works that pointed toward the direction that mindfulness would eventually take in America by the 20th century's end. The most important mindfulness figure for the West prior to the 1970s was Nyanaponika Thera. A German Jew who fled Hitler and ended up taking ordination as a monk in Sri Lanka, Nyanaponika stands out because he went further than his contemporaries in suggesting that mindfulness could improve the world and ordinary life, because he wrote many of the most influential texts on mindfulness for Westerners during this time, and because he forthrightly asserted that mindfulness was itself the heart of meditation. His training included a period of instruction under Mahasi Sayadaw.

Nyanaponika's most famous work was *Satipatthana, The Heart of Buddhist Meditation: A Handbook of Mental Training Based on the Buddha's Way of Mindfulness* (often shortened simply to the declarative title *The Heart of Buddhist Meditation* in its many later editions).[37] Nyanaponika announces on the first page of the book that "This book is issued in the deep conviction that the systematic cultivation of Right Mindfulness, as taught by the Buddha in his Discourse on Satipaṭṭhāna, still provides the most simple and direct, the most thorough and effective, method for training and developing the mind for its daily tasks and problems as well as for its highest aim: mind's own unshakable deliverance from Greed, Hatred and Delusion."[38] Nyanaponika's assertion that mindfulness is for the daily tasks and problems of life (as well as for ultimate conquering of the "three poisons" that results in nirvana), is remarkable in its clarity and confidence for its time. He continues on the same page with the even broader claim that "Right Mindfulness is, in fact, the indispensable basis of Right Living and Right Thinking—everywhere, at any time, for everyone. It has a vital message for all: not only for the confirmed follower of the Buddha and his Doctrine (Dhamma), but for all who endeavour to master the mind that is so hard to control and who earnestly wish to develop its latent faculties of greater strength and greater happiness."[39] This sort of rhetoric reframes mindfulness as not just for Buddhists, and not just to reach nirvana, and promises benefits to be enjoyed by ordinary people who engage in it. These benefits, he states at various points in the book, include mental clarity, freedom, energy, well-being, happiness, quietude, balance, self-control, the avoidance of rash words and actions, and perhaps even salvation of civilization from impending war and disaster. Here we have the tentative beginnings of a practical benefits approach to mindfulness.

Yet, we are still very far away from the way mindfulness is promoted today. Nyanaponika always talks in abstracts: he describes a process—paying attention to your thoughts will help you avoid negative behaviors—but doesn't specify any particular applications of mindfulness to daily life or provide concrete examples of persons assisted in their tasks and problems by mindfulness. He always associates mindfulness with renunciation, and exalts the pursuit of nirvana over other reasons to engage in mindfulness. When he talks about meditation in everyday life, his concern is that one's rigorous mental training not be disrupted by necessary mundane chores, *not* that mindfulness can enhance regular activities. He considers mindfulness extremely difficult to carry out in non-retreat settings, and despite his magnanimous gesture to non-Buddhists, he repeatedly belittles Christianity and always contextualizes mindfulness with a complicated framework of Buddhist technical terms and concepts. Overall, it is clear that Nyanaponika still believed mindfulness to be a Buddhist practice, for Buddhists (preferably monks), to be pursued in quiet settings away from the bustle of modern life, for the purpose of mental mastery and the eventual transcendence of this world. And if some laypeople, including non-Buddhists, develop greater clarity and moral self-discipline through exposure to mindfulness, all the better.

The other significant figure for this time period was Walpola Rahula, a Sri Lankan monk whose 1959 book *What the Buddha Taught* became near gospel for many Buddhists in the West. Written while he was studying at the Sorbonne after eight years' residence in the West, *What the Buddha Taught* reveals Rahula to be most interested in presenting Buddhism as a rational, humanistic religion that uncannily fits with modern times. He therefore cherry-picks from the Buddhist tradition elements that best demonstrate this ideal. The second-to-last chapter takes up the subject of meditation, or as he phrases it, "mental culture."[40] Here Rahula especially stresses the importance of mindfulness, stating that the *Satipatthana Sutta* is "the most important discourse ever given by the Buddha on mental development."[41] Rahula launches into a series of instructions on mindfulness of breathing designed for Westerners, with suggestions such as sitting on a chair instead of in the lotus position. Following tradition, he begins by stressing the transcendent direction of mindfulness: "This exercise of mindfulness of breathing, which is one of the simplest and easiest practices, is meant to develop concentration leading up to very high mystic attainments (*dhyāna*). Besides, the power of concentration is essential for any kind of deep understanding, penetration, insight into the nature of things, including the realization of Nirvāṇa."[42] But then Rahula takes another, significant turn: "Apart from all this, this exercise on breathing gives you immediate results. It is good for your physical health, for relaxation, sound sleep, and for efficiency in your daily work. It makes you calm and tranquil. Even at moments when you are nervous or excited, if you practice this for a couple of minutes, you will see for yourself that you become immediately quiet and at peace. You feel as if you have awakened after a good rest."[43] He continues from there to comments on remaining mindful during all one's activities, and stresses the importance of the present moment. "One who lives in the present moment lives the real life, and he is happiest."[44]

Here we find most of the elements of the mindfulness movement, though still in infant form. Rahula asserts that many practical benefits can be gained from mindfulness, including health, relaxation, calm, and even work efficiency. His assertion about the present moment leading to happiness is very this-worldly, and while suggesting rigor he takes pains not to frighten away Western laypeople. In the popular 1974 revision of *What the Buddha Taught*, Rahula added an extensive selection of bits extracted from the Buddhist canon—this included portions of the *Satipatthana Sutta*, boosting the place of mindfulness in the book. But there are still elements of the later mindfulness movement that are missing from either version. Rahula believes these benefits come from mindfulness of the breath, not mindfulness of specific activities. There is mindfulness performed while working here, but not yet mindful work. The mental and physical benefits to be gained are extremely vague and relate to basic life satisfaction—applications of mindfulness are not yet finely tuned instruments to be applied to very specific activities for very particular ends. Still, compared to older approaches, we are well along the path to developing an everyday mindfulness orientation as an option for those interested in Buddhism. That this is a Buddhist practice for Buddhist persons, according to Rahula, is clear. From the title of the book to the way nearly every page is drenched in technical Pali terminology, mindfulness is very much a Buddhist concern, not something for all people, except to the extent that—as a good apologist—he feels everyone really would be better off becoming Buddhist.

Small Pieces of the Puzzle

The evidence suggests that the pool of Westerners initially attracted to mindfulness teachings during the first half of the 20th century—whether framed as world-transcending or otherwise—was not large. For the average American interested in Buddhist meditation, this was mainly a community of textual communication through journals, letters, books, and pamphlets. Actual practice communities anywhere in the West were small and mostly confined to a few metropolitan areas. Thus instead of intensive training in ideal circumstances under a meditation master, those Americans who did dip their toe in the waters of mindfulness typically did so alone. Mindfulness was just one practice amidst the many types offered by Buddhism, and outside of the few large organizations such as the Buddhist Churches of America (which did not promote meditation), practices were still generally limited to the reading of books and discussion of Buddhist ideas.

For Americans not born into the religion, the attraction of Buddhism usually wasn't mindfulness, but rather its alternative worldview and the way Buddhism allegedly combined pacifism and ancient purity with a modern scientific sentiment and freedom from dogma. This phenomenon is clearly displayed, for example, in the pages of *The Golden Lotus*, one of the primary American Buddhist periodicals of the mid-20th century. In the April–May 1958 issue, the editor complains, "Curiously enough, one of the Buddha's most helpful admonitions is certainly not prominent in Buddhism today, if not exactly forgotten. It may be found in the sutras as 'smrti', and in the Buddha's words as reported by his followers, but not easily discovered in contemporary Buddhist writings."[45] In England in 1965, Christmas Humphreys, one of the preeminent mid-20th century English-language interpreters of Buddhism, found a similar situation: "The few of us monastically bent by temperament are happy to meditate all day; a large number of us are quite unimpressed with the need for it...Not long ago I watched a provincial Buddhist group, already well established in the study of first principles, just fade away when a bhikkhu assumed control and made them meditate instead. Long periods of sitting may be right for Zen in Japan and for neophytes in Burma and Tibet, but the Western mind is differently framed."[46] It seemed that the time was not yet ripe for widespread engagement with mindfulness.

However, in postwar America many small pieces of the supporting structure for the emergence of the full-blown mindfulness movement were nonetheless coming together. Higher education exploded after World War II as the G.I. Bill for veterans and then the Higher Education Act of 1965 helped to send ever more Americans to university. The growth in education coincided with the creation of formal religious studies departments, many of which included teaching on Buddhism in their curricula. Among the favorite works adopted as textbooks were *What the Buddha Taught* and *The Heart of Buddhist Meditation*, whose straightforward titles, modern perspectives, and accessibility to the intelligent nonspecialist made them staples for college syllabi. At the extreme end of this phenomenon, some professors even began to assign mindfulness practice to their students as a way to understand Buddhism from the inside. For example, Professor Donald Swearer studied mindfulness with Nyanaponika Thera in Sri Lanka, and in January 1969 after returning to the United States, he led a class of twenty-eight Oberlin College students in a four-week workshop on Buddhist meditation. The students spent two weeks performing mindfulness of the breath for ninety minutes each day; read the *Satipatthana Sutta, The Heart of Buddhist Meditation*, and other works; and also spent two weeks performing Zen meditation.[47]

Buddhist groups, though still small in number, were growing. In 1965 Congress repealed the racist immigration laws established between 1882–1924 that had kept Asian immigration to a minimum. Soon large numbers of Thai, Vietnamese, and other Buddhist immigrants would arrive and begin establishing their own religious institutions. In 1966 the Buddhist Vihara, America's first Theravada temple, was opened in Washington, D.C. Interest in Buddhist practice was growing among native-born Americans as well, spurred by all of the above factors, the Beat and then counterculture search for alternatives to mainstream Cold War American culture, and the arrival of missionary-minded Buddhist teachers in the West. These new Buddhist teachers, many of them trained in the Zen traditions, did not tend to stress mindfulness as such. For example, the published works of Robert Aitken, Philip Kapleau, and Taizan Maezumi—three of the most important Buddhist missionaries in the United States—contain almost no use of the term mindfulness, and when they very occasionally employ the word "mindful," they usually mean it in the sense that other Americans did, as a generic word indicating caution rather than a technical term for a form of Buddhist meditation. The most prominent use was in Shunryu Suzuki's 1970 watershed book *Zen Mind, Beginner's Mind*, which toward the end contains a brief chapter (fewer than three pages long) titled "Readiness, Mindfulness"—hardly a call to arms for mindfulness's place in American Buddhism.[48] But if mindfulness per se was not a common term for many of these missionaries, they did value Buddhist techniques of awareness, and through the groups that they founded a nascent meditation-oriented American Buddhist infrastructure began to grow.

The psychology industry, which would eventually become a major vehicle for the mindfulness movement, was also sinking deep roots in American culture, such that by mid-century psychological perspectives had become part of the basic worldview of contemporary Americans. Though mindfulness meditation wasn't yet on the radar of American psychiatrists and psychologists, the works of Japanese scholar (and frequent resident of the United States) D. T. Suzuki had spread interest in how psychology might benefit from dialogue with Zen Buddhism. Suzuki, it should be noted, did not typically use the words mindful or mindfulness in his writings.

American military and political involvement in Southeast Asia brought ever more Americans into contact with Buddhist cultures, and the rise of commercial jet aviation made travel to Asia easier and more attractive for those with relative means. Westerners had already created a genre of travel literature related to exploration in remote Asian Buddhist lands, often with a focus on Tibet. For the first time works began to appear that focused on Western laypeople and their attempts to master mindfulness meditation in Southeast Asia. Pioneering among these was *An Experiment in Mindfulness*, published in 1958 by British Rear Admiral Ernest Henry Shattock.[49] He trained with Mahasi Sayadaw in Burma, where he took up mindfulness practice as a way of achieving relaxed quietude in order to deal with the tension-inducing business of modern life. Shattock's book was eagerly read by Western Buddhists and alternative spiritual seekers, such as Henry and Ruth Denison, who were inspired to go to Asia in search of meditation training. Ruth Denison later became one of the founding figures of the mindfulness movement in America. Shattock's book was followed not long after by the Australian Unitarian and lawyer Marie Beuzeville Byles's *Journey Into Burmese Silence*.[50] The first significant account by a woman involved in mindfulness training, it described her training in the vipassana tradition of Ledi Sayadaw. Americans made their foray into the genre in 1971, when John Coleman published *The Quiet Mind*.[51] Coleman was a CIA operative assigned as an advisor on security matters to the Thai government when he began investigating meditation, which led him to train with U Ba Khin, a major lay disciple in the lineage of Ledi Sayadaw, in Burma. These books provided a Thervadin mindfulness counterpart to the accounts of travel and training in Tibet and Japan that had become popular. They helped attract young Americans to Burma and Thailand who sought adventure, spiritual sustenance, or both. Whether traveling privately or through programs such as the Peace Corps, more Americans began showing up at Southeast Asian meditation centers.

Collectively, these disparate elements—the growth of higher education; the creation of the religious studies discipline; the rise in Asian immigration; the founding of American meditation-oriented Buddhist centers; the countercultural revolution; the popularity of psychology; the deepening political, military, and cultural entanglement in Southeast Asia; and the publishing of mindfulness travelogues by Western laypeople—would all contribute to the success of the mindfulness movement in America.

From Roots to Trunk: The 1970s

Important as it all may be historically, everything prior to the 1970s is merely prelude to the main story of how mindfulness came to America. This was the decade when the seeds sown by a small number of Orientalists, Theravada monks, Buddhist laypeople, travel writers, CIA agents, and fellow travelers began to sprout. When the decade opened, mindfulness was a marginal practice within Western Buddhism, associated with a handful of books and pamphlets, most of them by Asians or Europeans. By the end of the decade, the major players in American mindfulness were all in place, and permanent institutions dedicated to the promotion of mindfulness were beginning to make their mark. The center of the mindfulness movement was shifting toward the United States, which would soon emerge as the dominant player in the mindfulness game.

In particular, three sources for mindfulness teaching appeared in 1970s America that would become the most important wellsprings of the American mindfulness movement. The first was teachers trained in Asia in the vipassana movements who began offering workshops and retreats for native-born lay Americans. The second was the modernist Vietnamese monk Thich Nhat Hanh, who would soon exert an intense gravitational pull on almost all forms of Buddhism in America, as well as crossing over to become one of the most recognizable Buddhist representatives—along with the 14th Dalai Lama—to non-Buddhist general audiences. The third was Jon Kabat-Zinn, a doctor and scientist who found new ways to apply and market mindfulness outside of Buddhist contexts.

Buddhism as a worldview apprehends all phenomena to be part of a ceaseless, beginningless chain of cause-and-effect that ultimately involves all things in the universe. Such a view does not truck easily in pat origin stories. But Westerners raised on a diet of Hollywood fare and ideas related to the Genesis narrative of the Bible are slow to give up on the concept of clear storylines that begin at a specific point. If we were to indulge such a sensibility, a fine starting point for the mindfulness movement in America might be the summer of 1974, in Boulder, Colorado, at a Buddhist summer school for hippies and alternative spiritual seekers established by a flamboyant exiled ex-Tibetan monk. In the mid-1970s Chogyam Trungpa was one of the most important Buddhist teachers in the United States, especially for those inclined toward the Tibetan tradition. Famous for his excesses—womanizing, drunkenness, pretensions of royalty—as well as an undeniable charisma and often uncanny ability to adapt Buddhist monastic ideas to the rebellious countercultural spiritual hunger of the contemporary West, Trungpa is among the most complex and colorful figures in American Buddhist history. In 1974 Trungpa was living in Boulder, Colorado, where he ran the Rocky Mountain Dharma Center. He decided to create a summer school named the Naropa Institute, which would draw intellectual and spiritual types from around the country to participate in a diverse curriculum.[52]

Trungpa, Ram Dass, Allen Ginsberg, John Cage, and others taught and performed at Naropa that summer, but for the story of mindfulness in America the most important participants were Jack Kornfield and Joseph Goldstein. Born into American Jewish homes at the end of World War II, both had encountered Buddhism in Thailand while working for the Peace Corps. Kornfield went on to ordain as a monk in the Thai forest tradition, and Goldstein studied mindfulness in India with Anagarika Munindra, a lay teacher trained in Burmese vipassana. Both eventually returned to America. Trungpa invited Kornfield to teach at the Naropa Institute, while Ram Dass invited Joseph Goldstein, and when the two met in the Boston area in the lead-up to the summer school, a momentous partnership was forged. Their mindfulness classes at Naropa were popular, and Kornfield and Goldstein began to tour the country offering meditation retreats. In 1976 they opened— with two other young Buddhist Jews, Sharon Salzburg and Jacqueline Schwartz—the Insight Meditation Society (IMS) in Barre, Massachusetts.[53] In 1981 Kornfield moved to California, where in 1988 he founded Spirit Rock Meditation Center. IMS and Spirit Rock became powerhouses for the teaching of mindfulness meditation, cultivating a large number of students and teachers and nurturing an expanding network of affiliated groups across the United States. Along with other Americans influenced by the vipassana movements who returned from Asia to teach in the 1970s—such as Ruth Denison—the Insight Meditation Society's teachers inaugurated a vibrant stream of mindfulness-oriented meditation in America. Though the styles of these teachers are diverse, they actually represent different manifestations of only a few particular strands within modernizing Theravada. These lineages mostly originate with Ledi Sayadaw (who taught the layman U Ba Khin, who in turn taught the lay teacher Satya Narayan Goenka) and Mahasi Sayadaw (who trained the lay teachers Anagarika Munindra and Dipa Ma). Kornfield, Goldstein, Salzberg, and Denison trained with Mahasi Sayadaw; Goldstein, Salzberg, and Schwartz studied with Munindra; Goldstein and Schwartz were trained by Goenka; Salzburg and Schwartz studied with Dipa Ma; and Denison trained under Khin. Furthermore, Mahashi Sayadaw, Munindra, Dipa Ma, and John Coleman (who trained with Khin) all served as visiting teachers at IMS.

From the beginning the IMS teachers sought to balance tradition and adaptation in their presentation of mindfulness to the West. On the one hand, they were explicit about their grounding in the Theravada tradition, and retained many elements of the retreat-oriented training they received in Asia. Spirit Rock showed more flexibility in inviting teachers from non-Theravada traditions, but insisted they had to be paired with teachers from the vipassana lineages.[54] On the other hand, a conscious attempt was made to downplay chanting, ceremony, and many aspects of Buddhist cosmology and belief.[55] This does not necessarily mean that the teachers did not themselves appreciate such things, but they perceived them as potential obstacles to American students. Spirit Rock also went much further in integrating Western psychology into Buddhist mindfulness training. Kornfield earned a PhD degree in clinical psychology in 1977 and many of the other teachers he invited to Spirit Rock were likewise involved in psychology or psychotherapy in some way.

While the lay teachers from the vipassana lineages were seeking to transmit their training to a new audience in America, a crusading monk from the Vietnamese tradition was planting new roots in Western soil. Thich Nhat Hanh was already familiar with Western society, having studied and taught at Princeton and Columbia Universities in the early 1960s. He befriended Dr. Martin Luther King, Jr. and was a frequent writer and speaker in the West on the Vietnam War. Hanh and his monastic colleagues pioneered a Buddhist "third way" that sought to distinguish itself from either the Communist or capitalist opposing sides in the war. He was given asylum by France in 1967 and was officially exiled by Vietnam in 1973 following the signing of the Paris Peace Accords. As he began to rebuild a place for himself outside of Asia in the mid-1970s, he started teaching meditation to Westerners, which he previously had not done. In his teachings, Hanh emphasized the practice of mindfulness paired with a dedicated engagement with the world. This struck a chord with many people in the West, especially the United States, and became the basis of one of the largest networks of practitioners.

Hanh represents a different branch of Buddhism than the one the vipassana teachers drew from. Like most Vietnamese Buddhists, he is associated with the Mahayana form of Buddhism. Usually referred to in English as Zen Master Thich Nhat Hanh, he is a lineage-holder in the Thien tradition, which shares common roots with Japanese Zen. Thien is not fully identical with Zen in the Japanese mode, however, and one of the most important differences is the relative influence from Theravada traditions. Vietnam is a border area between Mahayana East Asia and Theravada Southeast Asia and thus draws on both regions. The Theravada influence on Hanh appears specifically in the attention that he gives to mindfulness exercises such as those found in the *Satipatthana Sutta*. One might say that he tends to emphasize Theravada-type mindfulness exercises, but with a Mahayana, especially Zen, interpretation. Like the monastic founders of the Burmese vipassana movements, Hanh was already a reform-minded modernist Buddhist in Vietnam prior to his exile, having been influenced by earlier reformers such as the Chinese monk Taixu.

The first indication that Hanh would soon rise to become the most important figure in Western Buddhism—outstripping even the 14th Dalai Lama in terms of direct influence through number of students taught and the degree to which terms and concepts he has coined or emphasized ("engaged Buddhism," "interbeing," "mindfulness," etc.) impact the very language of contemporary Western Buddhism itself—was his 1976 book *The Miracle of Mindfulness*.[56] With its affirmative mindfulness-based title, deceptively simple and cheerful prose, and clear instructions on applying mindfulness to everyday life, this book set the template for the dozens of books Hanh has subsequently published. Frequently republished and still in print, *The Miracle of Mindfulness* immediately established Hanh as a voice to pay attention to. Hanh has since published more than 100 books in English, most with Parallax Press, which was established in Berkeley in 1986 to disseminate his teachings.[57] He has also built a massive network of practice groups known as the Community of Mindful Living—at the end of 2012 the Community listed 357 official affiliated groups in the United States alone.[58] He is one of a handful of true "celebrity Buddhists" in the West: he appeared on the cover of the bimonthly *Shambhala Sun* ten times between January 2000 and January 2013, more than any other figure, and has been repeatedly interviewed by Oprah Winfrey. Although based in southern France, Hanh has toured and taught in the United States nearly every year since his exile.

The third important source for the mindfulness movement is Jon Kabat-Zinn, whose influence in its own way rivals or perhaps exceeds that of Thich Nhat Hanh. The descendent of an Eastern European Jewish family that moved to the United States at the beginning of the 20th century, Jonathan Kabat came from a highly intellectual background. His father, Elvin, was an internationally recognized immunochemist, and his father-in-law, Howard Zinn, was a famous historian and activist; Kabat-Zinn studied at the Massachusetts Institute of Technology, where he encountered meditation when Zen missionary Philip Kapleau came to speak.[59] Kabat-Zinn studied mindfulness meditation with Thich Nhat Hanh and other Asian Buddhist teachers, including Seung Sahn, founder of Providence Zen Center. Seung Sahn arrived from South Korea in 1972, and soon gathered students from the non–Korean-American population who were interested in Son, the Korean version of Zen. Kabat-Zinn helped found the Cambridge Zen Center (in Seung Sahn's tradition) and went on to become a meditation teacher himself. He also trained at the Insight Meditation Society with teachers such as Kornfield, Goldstein, and Salzburg, and eventually Kabat-Zinn taught his own courses at IMS.

But whereas Seung Sahn, Thich Nhat Hanh, and the IMS teachers were explicit about teaching within a Buddhist framework, even if one significantly altered to appeal to American culture, today Kabat-Zinn works outside of formal Buddhist tradition and has often downplayed the connection between mindfulness and Buddhism. With a PhD degree in molecular biology, Kabat-Zinn has worked to apply mindfulness within a scientific rather than a religious frame. In 1979 he founded the Stress Reduction Clinic at the University of Massachusetts Medical School. There he developed a new technique he initially named Stress Reduction and Relaxation Program (SR&RP), but eventually renamed Mindfulness-Based Stress Reduction (MBSR). The core of MBSR is an eight-week course of training for patients who wish to apply mindfulness to their stress and pain. As Kabat-Zinn explains in his best-selling book *Full Catastrophe Living*: "The SR&RP is based on rigorous and systematic training in mindfulness, a form of meditation originally developed in the Buddhist traditions of Asia. Simply put, mindfulness is moment-to-moment awareness. It is cultivated by purposefully paying attention to things we ordinarily never give a moment's thought to. It is a systematic approach to developing new kinds of control and wisdom in our lives, based on our inner capacities for relaxation, paying attention, awareness, and insight."[60] Kabat-Zinn and the legion of teachers who have been trained to lead MBSR sessions believe that mindfulness confers concrete health benefits, and when practiced alongside traditional biomedicine and psychotherapy it offers a powerful antidote to many ills faced by modern Americans. Studies based on his research are routinely referred to by advocates of the mindfulness movement as evidence that their practices are not simply religious fantasy, but scientifically proven techniques with natural, measurable benefits. New forms of therapy, such as Mindfulness-Based Cognitive Therapy, have arisen from the combination of Buddhist practice and Western psychology that he has helped to foster.

With the Insight Meditation Society and associated teachers, Thich Nhat Hanh, and Jon Kabat-Zinn all operating by the end of the decade, the 1970s were the decisive turning point for the mindfulness movement. Though mindfulness would not go big time until the end of the century, all the pieces were in place, and further elaborations were really just developments of trends that were established by the time Ronald Reagan took office. Within the Buddhist community, mindfulness's stock was slowly rising, but it was still not generally seen as *the* Buddhist practice, and ideas about mindfulness had not fully coalesced around sati-type awareness techniques or their application to specific components of daily life. An illustration is Chogyam Trungpa's 1976 publication *Garuda IV: Foundations of Mindfulness*.[61] Trungpa's discussion of mindfulness is markedly different from current framings and understandings. For Trungpa in 1976, mindfulness is a beginning technique that leads into other, more advanced, more effective forms of meditation and Buddhist practice. The term mindfulness as a referent is not yet fully solidified, as he sometimes uses it to refer to various different meditation forms, such as samatha, a type of single-pointed concentration.[62] Mindfulness is for him entirely associated with traditional Buddhist goals and is applied to the mind, body, and moment-to-moment experience. He never suggests applying mindfulness to eating, sex, work, parenting, school, or other mundane activities; there is no implication that it would enhance or improve such activities; and mindfulness is not treated as having therapeutic value or scientifically demonstrable medical benefits.

Mindfulness, from Obscurity to Fame: The 1980s and Beyond

During the 1980s, the currents of mindfulness outlined so far in this chapter slowly percolated through the United States, initially confined primarily to actual Buddhist centers, in-group publications such as *Inquiring Mind* (the journal of the Vipassana community) and *Mindfulness Bell* (the journal of Thich Nhat Hanh's Community of Mindful Living), and New Age bookstores. Older works on mindfulness—such as those by Nyanaponika Thera—were reprinted, and Parallax Press appeared in 1986 to publish and market the works of Thich Nhat Hanh. Popular early titles from Parallax Press included *Being Peace* and *The Sun My Heart: From Mindfulness to Insight Contemplation*, as well as slightly more traditional texts such as *The Sutra on the Full Awareness of Breathing: With Commentary by Thich Nhat Hanh*.[63] There were virtually no publications on mindfulness in the 1980s by non-Buddhist authors, and even among the Buddhist authors those books that used the word mindfulness in their title were nearly all by Thich Nhat Hanh or writers with a connection to the Theravada tradition.

IMS, Spirit Rock, and their many affiliates were new lay-driven lineages derived from Theravada Buddhism. More traditional monastic-led Theravada was also spreading in the United States. The first Thai Theravada temple, Wat Thai in Los Angeles, opened in 1971. Over the coming decades scores of Theravada temples opened across the country, usually associated with a particular ethnic group, such as Thai, Sinhalese, Burmese, Khmer, or Laotians. Some of these temples—especially if they were influenced by the Asian vipassana movements—offered mindfulness sessions for lay people, including interested practitioners from European or other non-Asian backgrounds. Often these activities were on a relatively local and ad hoc basis, but some of these monks attracted a sizable meditation-oriented following and became well-known teachers in the larger Buddhist community. A good example is Bhante Henepola Gunaratana, a Sri Lankan monk who came to the Washington, DC Buddhist Vihara in 1968 and began to publish a few small works on mindfulness in the 1980s.

The first handful of studies of mindfulness as applied to various psychological interests began to appear as theses and dissertations during the 1980s. Meanwhile Jon Kabat-Zinn and his MBSR colleagues in Massachusetts were developing models for teaching meditation to non-Buddhists in secular, usually medical, environments. Most early MBSR instructors were themselves Buddhists or directly involved in formal Buddhist practice. Results of scientific studies carried out with the use of MBSR were published in relevant journals—for example, in 1985 Kabat-Zinn was lead author on an article in the *Journal of Behavioral Medicine* titled "The Clinical Use of Mindfulness Medicine for the Self-Regulation of Chronic Pain."[64] Some people were starting to take notice: for instance, Joan Borysenko included a chapter drawing on Kabat-Zinn's mindfulness work in her best-selling book *Minding the Body, Mending the Mind* (1988).[65]

Mindfulness was still mostly seen as a Buddhist practice and goal, but some authors (including Kabat-Zinn in *Full Catastrophe Living*) began talking in much greater detail about how precisely mindfulness could be applied in everyday life—this was the genesis of the first ideas that would lead to the specificity of mindful eating, mindful sports, and so on. Such developments came about because of several factors. First, enough time had passed that American meditation teachers' practice had deepened and informed many of their activities, not just formal meditation sessions while seated or walking in the meditation hall. Second, because the demand for meditation training came almost entirely from laypeople who had little interest in full renunciation and monastic ordination, teachers continually searched for ways to make mindfulness relevant in the actual normal lives of their students. And third, by the end of the 1980s many of the wave of Baby Boomer Buddhists were settling down into families and mainstream-type jobs, as the influence of age and the Reagan era shifted the dominant cultural icons from hippies to yuppies. Naturally, these people began to apply their training to their newly middle class, often suburban concerns.

Mindfulness began to go big time in the 1990s. Buddhism experienced a flourishing of public attention, brought on by multiple factors. One was the Chinese occupation of Tibet and its place in the Hollywood media, as represented by movies such as *Little Buddha* (1993), *Seven Years in Tibet* (1997), and *Kundun* (1997). A second was the 1991 founding of *Tricycle: The Buddhist Review* (the first truly nonsectarian mass market American Buddhist magazine) and the redesign of *Shambhala Sun* as big, glossy, professional magazines for the newsstand and general readership—approximately half of the readership of these magazines did not identify as Buddhist. Mindfulness teachings and authors were present from the beginning: *Tricycle*'s first issue included a teaching by Thich Nhat Hanh, its second issue offered a teaching on mindfulness of the body by Spirit Rock teacher Sylvia Boorstein, its third issue once again had a commentary by Thich Nhat Hanh, and the fifth issue contained an essay on the retreat experience titled "Mindful to the Quarter-inch."[66] The rise of big chain bookstores such as Borders and Barnes & Noble provided Buddhist publishing houses with more options for selling their wares, and by mid-decade the advent of the Internet and especially Amazon.com made their potential reach ever wider. American Buddhist publishing houses were also becoming savvier about marketing to non-Buddhist audiences. In 1992 Wisdom Publications published Bhante Gunaratana's *Mindfulness in Plain English*, which quickly became a standard text for American Buddhism. Buddhist books that were not on mindfulness specifically, but included discussion of mindfulness practice—such as Sogyal Rinpoche's 1992 *The Tibetan Book of Living and Dying*—became bestsellers.[67] Thich Nhat Hanh's publication of books accelerated, and Buddhist traditions in America—such as Japanese Zen and Tibetan Buddhism—that had not made much use of the terms "mindful" and "mindfulness," began increasingly to frame their own teachings with such vocabulary and concepts.

Following coverage of Mindfulness-Based Stress Reduction by Bill Moyers on his 1993 PBS special *Healing and the Mind* (and the book by the same title), Jon Kabat-Zinn and MBSR became nationally famous. Kabat-Zinn's books on mindfulness—such as his 1994 *Wherever You Go, There You Are: Mindfulness Meditation in Everyday Life*—now became bestsellers themselves, and he was a regular interviewee on television and in print.[68] The MBSR process was taking on a franchise model, with new centers appearing around the country either for the dissemination of MBSR or strongly committed to MBSR as part of a broader program of holistic medicine. A good example is the Duke Center for Integrative Medicine, part of the Duke University Health System in Durham, North Carolina. Founded in 1998, it offered MBSR as the Center's first public program.[69] Other similar initiatives, often at university-associated hospitals, spread MBSR to many new regions of America.

By the end of the 1990s, a critical mass of Buddhist meditation groups, Buddhist publishing houses, Buddhist periodicals, and the Internet coalesced to give Buddhism a prominent place on the American religious landscape and an influence far beyond the numbers of actual Buddhists would suggest. Buddhism became popular enough that authors began to sub-specialize, producing the first works not simply on mindfulness but also on mindful applications: mindful eating, mindful driving, and so forth. Buddhists realized they could market the health and other effects of their meditation, and non-Buddhists started paying attention. The primary model of the mindfulness movement began to shift from the quasi-monastic, periodic extended retreat model to the firmly embedded practice of mindfulness while in the home and at work, 365 days a year. This also enabled mindfulness to move from the property of experts honed over a lifetime of meditation practice toward ordinary, often new practitioners and their enthusiasm for a new way of life, unregulated by the old guard.

Mindfulness was also starting to catch on outside of Buddhism. One of the first important extra-Buddhist phenomena was the development of mindful sports. Phil Jackson, coach for the internationally popular Chicago Bulls basketball team, described in *Sacred Hoops: Spiritual Lessons of a Hardwood*

Warrior (1995) how he used mindfulness with stars such as Michael Jordan and Scottie Pippen. As he explained, "When players practice what is known as mindfulness—simply paying attention to what's actually happening—not only do they play better and win more, they also become more attuned with each other...the real reason the Bulls won three straight NBA championships from 1991 to '93 was that we plugged in to the power of *oneness* instead of the power of one man, and transcended the divisive forces of the ego that have crippled far more gifted teams."[70] Soon mindfulness was finding its way into the training of other teams, and trickling down to the streets and neighborhood courts where regular kids who idolized Michael Jordan tried out meditation as a way to "be like Mike."[71]

The 2000s then were the crossover decade for mindfulness. It went from being a popular practice in Buddhist circles to being a popular practice available to all spiritually inclined Americans, or even those simply looking for relief from their stress. MBSR was flourishing in hospitals and a critical mass of therapists had developed under the influence of mindfulness-based techniques such that practices, books, and branded forms of mindfulness therapy appeared. Mindfulness was now a basic part of the spiritual vocabulary of North America: authorized by science, endorsed by Oprah, marketed by Buddhists, appropriated by self-help gurus, it appeared in such a tidal wave of publications and applications that it seemed that everyone was doing mindfulness, in every conceivable situation, without any need to announce one's commitment to Buddhism to do so. Mindfulness's mainstream success is represented in three different phenomena: the explosion of books with "mindful" or "mindfulness" in the title, the widespread appearance of mindfulness techniques in books with no outward connection to mindfulness, and the proliferation of trademarked mindfulness brands.

Often works in the first category—those with mindful or mindfulness in their title—were written by people marketing themselves based on medical or therapeutic credentials, rather than traditional sources of Buddhist authority, and were expositions on how to apply mindfulness to some specific activity or problem in life. Examples include *Mindful Recovery: A Spiritual Path to Healing from Addiction* by Thomas Bein, PhD and Beverly Bien, MEd (2002); *Grieving Mindfully: A Compassionate and Spiritual Guide to Coping with Loss* by Sameet M. Kumar, PhD (2005); *The Mindful Way Through Depression: Freeing Yourself from Chronic Unhappiness* by Mark Williams, PhD, John Teasdale, PhD, Zindel Segal, PhD, and Jon Kabat-Zinn, PhD (2007); and *The Mindful Path Through*

Shyness: How Mindfulness and Compassion Can Help Free You from Social Anxiety, Fear, and Avoidance by Steve Flowers, MFT (2009).[72] All of these examples emphasize the alphabet soup of letters after the authors' names on their covers and fall within the self-help genre. Books in this category do not intend to teach Buddhism; often, Buddhism is barely mentioned. A number of distinct subgenres emerged, such as mindful eating (e.g., *Eating Mindfully: How to End Mindless Eating and Enjoy a Healthy and Balanced Relationship with Food*, 2003), mindful relationships (e.g., *Mindful Loving: 10 Practices for Creating Deeper Connections*, 2003), mindful parenting (e.g., *Momfulness: Mothering with Mindfulness, Compassion, and Grace*, 2007), mindful education (e.g., *The Mindful Teacher*, 2009), and mindful work (e.g., *Inner Productivity: A Mindful Path to Efficiency and Enjoyment in Your Work*, 2009).[73] There was also a proliferation of niche publications outside of the established subgenres (e.g., *Mindful Knitting: Inviting Contemplative Practice to the Craft*, 2004).[74]

A counter-phenomenon that also demonstrates mindfulness's growing strength is how it appears in books that are not otherwise ostensibly about meditation or awareness. Examples include *Great Sex for Moms: Ten Steps to Nurturing Passion While Raising Kids* (2002), *Clinical Sport Psychology* (2006), *The Structure House Weight Loss Plan* (2007), and *The Marriage Checkup: A Scientific Program for Sustaining and Strengthening Marital Health* (2009).[75] Mindfulness had become so omnipresent and available that non-Buddhist authors could appropriate it at will for any number of projects—it was now simply another on a long list of tools that any turn-of-the-millennium American might have at their disposal.

Finally, the glut of mindfulness books, combined with the American penchant for self-promotion and entrepreneurship, resulted in the creation of branded mindfulness programs and techniques as authors sought to carve out unique spaces for themselves in the increasingly competitive market of the mindfulness movement. From a certain viewpoint, MBSR was the first of these, but it wasn't until the 2000s that this became a common phenomenon. By the end of the decade there were many examples, such as Jurisight® ("the mindfulness-based teaching developed specifically for law students and lawyers"), Real World Mindfulness Training™ ("The secret: instead of 'working' on mindfulness, start 'playing' with it instead!"), and Mindfulness-Based Mind Fitness Training™ ("mental armor" for military personnel).[76]

Conclusion

One important element of this history to note is the manner in which mindfulness moved ever further from being the exclusive property of Buddhist monks. Second, we can notice that mindfulness progressively came to be applied to new concerns, and that its earlier nirvanic-orientation faded. Third, we see the proliferation of media and genres in which mindfulness is discussed and represented. Mindfulness publications today can be broken into several categories, including: (1) texts on Buddhist mindfulness by Buddhist clergy, (2) texts on Buddhist mindfulness by laypeople, (3) mindfulness articles in general-audience Buddhist magazines, (4) self-help mindfulness texts by Buddhist authors, (5) self-help mindfulness texts by non-Buddhists, and (6) mainstream media reports on the mindfulness movement. Each new iteration reaches a larger and more diverse audience, expanding the cultural penetration of the mindfulness movement.

Though technically separate, these three phenomena (loss of monastic control over mindfulness, practical uses of mindfulness, and new media channels for mindfulness dissemination) occurred as related developments. It is important also to note, however, that new developments do not necessarily eliminate older forms. The oldest texts are still in use; monks are still teaching about mindfulness; Buddhists are still using sati to achieve nirvana; and of course there is nothing to prevent one from pursing mindfulness for both this-worldly and other-worldly ends. But these older patterns came to share the conversation with ever more voices in a swelling cacophony of mindfulness communication, with the earlier forms pushed to the relative edges as the great mass of discussion, publication, and practice comes to be located in non-monastic, non-renunciatory contexts.

It is no longer necessary to fly to Asia, go on an extended silent retreat, attend a Buddhist temple, or even read books by Buddhists in order to learn how to do mindfulness. Those who seek out meditation can just as easily pick up *The Complete Idiot's Guide to Mindfulness* (2008).[77] Even this effort is hardly needed: with nearly every single day bringing a new story on mindfulness somewhere in the mainstream media, and mindfulness spreading ever wider in the universities, schools, hospitals, and therapists' offices of the nation, mindfulness seems to be nearly unavoidable. Barely a twinkle in the eye of T. W. Rhys Davids in 1910, today mindfulness is, quite simply, everywhere.

2 MYSTIFYING MINDFULNESS: HOW IS MINDFULNESS MADE AVAILABLE FOR APPROPRIATION?

Mystify: to involve in obscurity; to obscure the meaning or character of

—Oxford English Dictionary[1]

It was natural for veteran mindfulness teacher Andrew Weiss to draw on his long personal history with Buddhism when he set out to write a meditation manual. Ordained in both Thich Nhat Hanh's Order of Interbeing and the White Plum lineage of American Soto Zen, he had also studied in the Theravada and Korean Son Buddhist traditions. Weiss co-founded a Buddhist meditation group in the Boston area and taught mindfulness meditation regularly to the general public. Not surprisingly then, his book *Beginning Mindfulness: Learning the Way of Awareness, a Ten-Week Course* (2004) used such Buddhist elements as the five lay precepts, Tibetan teachings on tonglen meditation, and the *Sattipathana Sutta*'s teaching on the fourfold foundations of mindfulness. These and other Buddhist tools were discussed at length to provide a systematic program for personal mindfulness practice—*Beginning Mindfulness* is nothing if not a thoroughly Buddhist book.

Yet, Weiss worried that his book might turn off potential readers who had qualms about Buddhism. Therefore, starting on the second page of his introduction, he set about alleviating the fears that he imagined non-Buddhist readers might have. First, he downplayed Buddhism's status as a religion: "The teachings of the Buddha, in their earliest and original form, are remarkably free of doctrine. While they embrace the same fundamental truths that are present in all the world's great religions, they offer no religious creed for people to believe in ... The Buddha is not a god or a being to be worshipped."[2] Next, he stressed that mindfulness practice would not interfere with any reader's own pre-commitments, religious or otherwise: "You do not have to become a Buddhist to practice mindfulness in a nonsectarian context. You can be a

Christian, a Jew, a Hindu, or an agnostic and still practice the Buddha's teachings on mindfulness without any conflict."[3] He illustrated this by referring to his own Jewish roots, claiming that mindfulness teachings actually enhanced his Jewish identity, as he asserted: "I find that I can practice them without having to abandon my ancestral spiritual roots, without giving up one iota of who I am. If anything, as I practice mindfulness, my sense of who I am and my connection to my spiritual roots become clearer and clearer."[4]

Though Weiss's approach to mindfulness was explicitly Buddhist, his agenda, apparently, was not. In Weiss's understanding, practicing mindfulness was not the same as practicing Buddhism—they were two different things that could be disaggregated from each other. Ultimately, it was more important to Weiss that Americans read his book and begin meditating than it was that they read it and become practitioners of Buddhism like himself. With this as his goal, mindfulness's Buddhist origins might even be a hindrance, and so he headed off potential resistance by downplaying the possibility that Buddhism presented a threat.

By the time Weiss wrote *Beginning Mindfulness*, his assertions about mindfulness's easy accessibility to Jews, Christians, and agnostics were noncontroversial. They were echoed by countless other books and articles written by Buddhists and non-Buddhists alike. Nonetheless, when we swap in other practices from different religious traditions, it becomes clear how remarkable Weiss's assertions actually were. For instance, eyebrows would likely be raised if an American author wrote a book about beginning rosary practice, stressing that Christianity merely embraces the teachings found in any given religious tradition, that the early Catholic teachings are free of doctrine, that the Virgin Mary is not an object of religious devotion, that saying the rosary does not conflict with Hindu or agnostic belief, and that it had made him a better Jew. Something about Buddhism made it available for appropriation and radical recontextualization, an availability not shared by most other religious practices in America.

This chapter examines the strategies and possible motives whereby Americans alter, diminish, obscure, eliminate, or simply ignore the historic connection between Buddhism and mindfulness, and considers some of the various implications of such practices. I call this process mystification, by which I mean that mindfulness's roots in Buddhism are made less overt in order to further various agendas. These tactics have helped to make Buddhist-derived mindfulness extremely popular in the West, increasing the audiences who can potentially benefit from mindfulness practice, as well as increasing the pool of Buddhists and non-Buddhists who can benefit financially and otherwise from teaching about mindfulness. The results are significant changes in how Buddhism is understood and represented, what mindfulness is held to be, and who is empowered to speak about and for Buddhism and its practices.

Reinterpretation of Buddhist Cosmology

Mindfulness in its original context existed in a complex, self-reinforcing web of Buddhist cosmological, devotional, philosophical, psychological, ecclesiastical, and soteriological concepts and practices. For instance, the *Satipatthana Sutta* references concepts such as Buddhahood, monkhood, nirvana, the four noble truths, and transmigration through the round of rebirths. These in turn relate to nearly every aspect of premodern Buddhist worldviews. In such views, people exist temporarily as human beings during their present lifetimes. But human existence was just one among many possibilities: each living being experienced life after life after life (and death after death after death) in a beginningless, endless cycle of change and suffering. Intentional moral and immoral actions activated the force of karma, which led to good or bad fortune, and determined whether one was reborn as a deity in one of the heavenly realms, a demigod, a human, a perpetually hungry ghost, an animal, or a being in one of the many purgatorial "hell" realms of torture and punishment.

Wherever one was born, it was only temporary, as each life would come to an end and be followed by another in a new situation, ad infinitum. The only possibility for escape from such ceaseless movement through the mortal world of suffering was achievement of nirvana, reached by following the difficult teachings of the Buddha and best sought through the monastic institution. Nirvanic release was achieved through strenuous efforts, including overcoming our mistaken sense of a core, essential selfhood, and gaining the ability to see through and resist the temptations of the demonic god Mara who frequently plagued meditators. For those still far from nirvana, devotional activity directed toward the Buddha and monastics helped to accumulate spiritual merit, and hosts of serpent people, spirits, cannibalistic ghouls, chimeric monsters, and other supernatural beings populated the world, some as protectors of righteous Buddhists and others as potential threats that could be warded off through Buddhist practices. This panoply of practices played out against the backdrop of thousands upon thousands of world systems throughout the universe, each filled with beings living, struggling, and dying because of their failure to fulfill the Buddhist path. Buddhist mindfulness was a way to confirm these beliefs about the self and the world, and provided access to rebirth in the highest heavenly realms should one fail in the quest to achieve total release in the present lifetime.

All of this presents a potential problem for those who wish to promote mindfulness activity in the United States. American culture and religion have multiple roots, but for the large majority Buddhist concepts are unfamiliar, if not bizarre or even threatening. Although the United States has diversified and multiculturalism has become a cherished value for significant portions of the populace, xenophobia is a strong historic trend in American society, expressed variously as fear of foreign cultures, distrust of non-Christian religions, and prejudice toward nonwhite racial groups.[5] Christian and Jewish teachings have sown distaste for religious systems that include figures other than the biblical God, especially those that include statues or images that can be interpreted as idols. American culture promotes a strong sense of personal self, with religious teachings about an eternal soul and psychological reinforcement of healthy egoism. Western notions of time tend to be linear and teleological, and reincarnation-type beliefs—though on the increase—are not mainstream. At the same time, there is also backlash in many quarters against religion in general as authoritarian, backward, and delusional. In some cases this drives a retreat into personal spirituality, while for others it results in either hostility or simple indifference to religious concepts, practices, institutions, and ways of thinking.

Given these general patterns in American culture, a Buddhism that holds to more conservative views toward Buddhist cosmology and related ideas is unlikely to attract significant converts—indeed, it may face opposition from both competing religious groups and secularists. Thus many feel it is imperative that Buddhism be reinterpreted or presented in ways that are not too challenging to preexisting American norms and mores. If Buddhism can be reduced to a narrow set of ideas and practices, or those preferred practices can be shorn of connection to Buddhism altogether, all the better for those who wish to promote mindfulness. Not surprisingly, then, in the contemporary American mindfulness movement, most or all of the fundamental context for Buddhist mindfulness practice tends to be reinterpreted, minimized, or left out.

One common tactic for reducing the difficulty posed by Buddhist concepts is to render them in psychological, metaphoric, or symbolic terms. Buddhist cosmology is a particularly common target for such strategies. For example, hungry ghosts play an important role in Buddhism. They are one of the six forms in which a person can be reborn after he or she dies. These beings are depicted as simultaneously emaciated and possessing distended, empty stomachs. Their necks are narrow, such that they have great difficulty swallowing food and water to feed their incessant hunger. Normally invisible, they haunt the human world, gathering near people in the hopes of choking down an errant morsel. Food that does manage to reach their stomachs often turns into flames, further increasing their suffering. Buddhist commentaries stress that rebirth as a hungry ghost is one of the direst possible states—only life in the hellish realms of punishment is worse. Buddhists are warned not to commit karmic offenses, especially those involving excessive craving and attachment, lest they fall into the body of a hungry ghost after death, and dedication of merit to the ghosts in order to relieve their suffering is a common ritual of Zen in Asia and most other forms of Buddhism.

In the mindfulness movement, hungry ghosts are reinterpreted. From frightful, pathetic supernatural entities that crowd about us unseen and slavering, they become metaphoric images of our own mental states of desire and need. They are especially common tropes in such applications as mindful addiction recovery and mindful eating. For example, in *Cool Water: Alcoholism, Mindfulness, and Ordinary Recovery* (1997), William Alexander claims "I had become a 'hungry ghost'—the mythic creature with an enormous belly and pinprick mouth, cursed with an insatiable thirst. The thirst was too great. There was not enough liquor or valium to slake it."[6] For Alexander, his addictive craving was so intense that he poetically described himself as a hungry ghost—he did not mean to imply that he was actually a restless spirit, or that such creatures existed in any literal sense. They are "mythic" creatures, not scientific realities. Likewise, in *Eat, Drink, and Be Mindful* (2008), Susan Albers described the concept of the hungry ghost, but wanted to make sure her audience didn't mistake her. "The ghosts are a metaphor. They represent people's inability to make themselves feel better by fulfilling their physical urges and desires…We are all very much like hungry ghosts."[7] She then provided an exercise for self-reflection, titled "Your hungry ghosts (or feelings)." All of the popular mindfulness movement authors who talk about the hungry ghost realm locate it only in the present, in one's own mind, rather than in a supernatural posthumous state. They don't suggest that readers must be wary lest they be actually reborn as such creatures, or that they should engage in rituals to dedicate merit to them.

It is not only the hungry ghost realm that can be interpreted in this psychological manner. In her article "The Middle Way of Stress," Judy Lief rebrands the six realms of existence in the Buddhist tradition as "Six Patterns of Stress."[8] The god realm becomes "the stress of perfectionism," the jealous god realm becomes "the stress of the rat race," the human realm becomes "the stress of insecurity," the animal realm becomes "the stress of habit," the hungry ghost realm becomes "the stress of never having enough," and the hell realm becomes "the stress of eternal warfare."[9] In each case, the realm is not an actual place or metaphysical state of existence, but a psychological state fueled by particular fears and attachments. To deal with these stresses, one should be mindful, because "a primary mind-training tool is mindfulness practice, through which you learn to settle your mind and to tame its wildness."[10]

The demon-god Mara also receives similar treatment. Mara is a fearsome opponent of the Buddha, who alternately tempts and attacks him in the traditional stories. He stalks Buddhist monks and nuns, disrupting their attempts to reach nirvana and sometimes possessing their very bodies. All of the realms of samsara, from the heavens to the hells, are said to be under his control, and all the beings within them. Yet when writers of the mindfulness movement speak of Mara, he becomes downright banal. "Mara is the personification of things that get in the way of Right Understanding," explains Ronna Kabatznick in *The Zen of Eating: Ancient Answers to Modern Weight Problems* (1998). "Mara is the force that takes you out of the present by enticing you with something else, like a fantasy of the future (e.g., an urge for a bag of potato chips) or a longing from the past (e.g., the muffins you had last week). Mara comes in many forms: fear, anger, resistance, or as general unwillingness to look at what's true."[11] The Buddha's arch-nemesis is converted from a deadly form of evil into one's own negative emotions. Mara's minions fare even worse: "When Mara strikes, you feel like you're being attacked by a ruthless army. The expression *the armies of Mara* depicts this image. First you are attacked by *desire*. All you can think about is french fries."[12] From an overwhelming horde of roaring monsters and devils, Mara's army is rhetorically transformed into fried potatoes.

Removal of Monastic Context

As discussed in the previous chapter, mindfulness in Asian Buddhist history was a monastic practice, preserved, taught by, and typically practiced by ordained monks and nuns. Not surprisingly, the modern revivers of vipassana practice and the practitioners of mindfulness who first publicized it to the West were Buddhist monks. They were the ones who had custodianship of the Pali or other ancient scriptural sources and direct access to teachers with many years of practice to provide instruction. They did not have family or business concerns to pull them away from time devoted to meditation, and culturally it had always been assumed that meditation was a practice primarily for the ordained sangha. Laypeople participated in Buddhism through devotional activities and support of the monks; meditation was quite rare among the general Buddhist populace prior to the 20th century, and though of increasing interest, is still not the dominant mode of religious practice among laypeople in Asia.

What we see with the mindfulness movement in America is the gradual transfer of authority from monks to laypeople. This does not mean that no monks are involved in promoting mindfulness; major mindfulness advocates include Thich Nhat Hanh, Bhante Henepola Gunaratana, and others. But whereas English-language promotion of mindfulness was dominated by monks for most of the 20th century, today lay voices far outnumber monastic ones. As this phenomenon has grown, there has been an accompanying shift in the way that mindfulness is framed, often losing its connection to Buddhist concepts, morality, renunciation, and eventually Buddhism itself.

The movement away from monastic authority over mindfulness progressed through several overlapping phases, which can be clearly seen in the evolving history outlined in Chapter 1. First there were monks in Asia— including Asians and ordained Westerners—who taught both ordained and lay students. Some of these monks, such as Nyanaponika Thera and Walpola Rahula, began to write and publish English-language books on mindfulness for the general public, not just monastic consumption. These works began to attract Western students who traveled to Asia and either ordained or practiced within a semi-monastic communal retreat setting, where they had to adhere to Buddhist precepts.

Eventually, these students returned to the West, where most of them eventually took up lay life once more. But though they had ceased to operate as monks or nuns, they did not forego the role of teacher. Rather, they created many of the first important mindfulness-based Buddhist communities in America and elsewhere. Examples abound, such as Ruth Denison and Jack Kornfield. A new role model emerged: the deeply trained Western lay teacher, who had acquired experience through traditional modes of practice but now offered mindfulness in a new setting (America), to a new audience (lay Americans on retreat), and with a new allure (the ability to relate culturally and socially as fellow Americans with children, mortgages, and jobs, and to deliver the teachings in impeccable native English). These were teachers who were neither truly monk nor lay, as they had experience with both sides of the equation and could marshal insight based on both roles. Their teaching charisma was fundamentally based not on their having passed through the ritual of ordination or their adherence to monastic discipline, but on their ability to provide concrete instruction in mindfulness that could be followed by other laypeople. In other words, they possessed not a symbolic charisma rooted in their traditional role, but a pragmatic charisma established through the practical application of their message.

From these returned lay teachers came the next evolution. These teachers now taught American laypeople who never traveled to Asia, and who infrequently or never interacted with full monastic Buddhism. Though the instruction was explicitly Buddhist, and most often delivered in a retreat setting or regular practice group, much of the Buddhist cosmology was downplayed. This happened in part because Westerners were not always convinced of it in light of modern science and Western cultural ideas. John Coleman spoke for many when he admitted being "disheartened to think that so many who live by the Buddhist faith seemed, if I understood his teachings at all, to miss the point. His message, surely, was that the truth lies within the self, that the aim of those who live by his word must be genuine enlightenment by *transcending* all the gaudy nonsense of ritual and sophisticated forms of worship."[13] Here Coleman attempts to be faithful to the Buddha precisely by disclaiming aspects of Buddhism that he rejects—this isn't a denial of Buddhist practice but a sifting in order to present an improved Buddhism.

Another reason for the relative lack of Buddhist cosmological notions and devotional practice was because the focus was always on the practical details of mindfulness meditation itself, and therefore the lion's share of time was taken up with delivering instructions for practice. It should also be noted that silent retreats were one of the most common modes of mindfulness dissemination in the 1970s and 80s, and in a situation where no one is talking, naturally little overtly Buddhist content is dispensed. A second generation of lay teachers swiftly began to emerge who had mainly or only practiced Buddhism in America, had personal exposure to only limited selections of Buddhist tradition, and were taught either by a mixture of missionary monks and lay Americans, or only by other Americans.[14] Jon Kabat-Zinn is one among many examples of this type.

As the mindfulness movement grew in popularity, it added new monastic voices, but not at nearly the same rate as those of new lay spokespersons and advocates. Ordination was not widely available in the United States, but this did not present a particularly important problem. Americans were coming to believe that ordination was not necessary for mindfulness training, nor was expensive travel to Asia. Indeed, if mindfulness could be practiced in one's native language and country and without fully giving up one's normal life, there seemed to be few incentives for pursing ordination. For some, monks ceased to be honored role models. Instead, the monastic institution came in for criticism, as Americans imagined it as stultifying, backward, foreign, or extraneous. Observe how author Janet Taylor removes authority from anyone except the empowered individual American self—especially foreign monks in robes—in the opening paragraphs of her book *Buddhism for Non-Buddhists: A Practical Guide to Ease Suffering and Be Happy* (2012):

> This is American Buddhism. This isn't about wearing strange robes. This isn't about speaking in a different language... This is about how you show up in your life right now. **In this moment.** This is about you being who you were born to be. We may have 98% of the same DNA with each other, but we are each as unique as a snowflake... This is about learning to experience you, and the world around you in a radically different way. American Buddhism is not about being Buddhist. It's about using the practices of Mindfulness, Meditation, and Visualization to ease suffering and be happy... The Buddha was this man who emphasized that he was just a regular guy, not a god or anything special, except that he was "awake". He encouraged anyone hearing his teachings to not believe him just because he said it. Question these teachings! Try them out! See if they work for you!... The Buddha taught that EVERYONE has the potential to awaken, to be fully present and to live abundantly in each moment... We all have this incredible potential for happiness, because there is innate goodness within each and every person... If you find a thought, a practice, or an action that adds value to your life, keep doing it. If not, toss it aside. **Buddhism is the opposite of many other "isms", because you are enthusiastically encouraged to think for yourself.**[15]

Such reorientations arrogate further authority to the lay teachers and repeat culturally familiar scripts originally derived from the Protestant–Catholic antagonism that contributed to the intense privatization, spiritualization, and anti-institutionalism of much of modern American religion. Others maintain their rhetorical respect for the ordained sangha but rarely pay it more than lip service, further demonstrating the traditional context's irrelevancy. Through practices such as these, lay teaching and lay practice became normalized, with monasticism the exotic, exceptional context for mindfulness.

With the abandonment of monasticism eventually came the diminishment of the retreat model. Retreats are still being held, to be sure—in fact, nearly every day of the year there is a Buddhist mindfulness retreat going on somewhere in America—and the expanding number of retreat centers serve as engines helping to drive the mindfulness movement. But the center of gravity has shifted away from the frequent, multiday retreat model for most mindfulness practitioners. The first generation of lay teachers trained in retreat contexts in Burma, Thailand, India, and other parts of Asia. They imported this model to the United States and have perpetuated it, but today most mindfulness discussion is about how to practice mindfulness while performing the regular tasks of one's lay life. Lay lifestyles are not merely grudgingly accepted as not necessarily in conflict with the pursuit of mindfulness; rather, lay life is increasingly valorized as the proper or best place to carry out mindfulness practice. This is a significant change from the earlier point of view. Even monks who were relatively enthusiastic about the possibility of Western lay participation in mindfulness practice, such as Nyanaponika Thera, recognized that retreat was necessary as a regular practice. For example, in *The Heart of Buddhist Meditation*, Nyanaponika asserts: "Using just the conditions of life it finds, Satipatthana does not require complete *seclusion* or *monastic life*, though in some who undertake the practice, the desire and the need for these may grow. Occasional periods of seclusion, however, are helpful for initiating methodical and strict practice, and for stepping up the progress in it. Western society, too, should provide opportunities for such periodical seclusion in suitable environment."[16] He goes on to affirm that more advanced mindfulness is basically out of the reach of laypeople involved in normal lifestyles: "Such a detailed application of Mindfulness involves a considerable slowing-down of one's movements which can be maintained only in periods of strict practice, and not, or only rarely, during every-day life."[17]

Newer advocates of mindfulness, especially lay promoters who have never trained with Buddhist monks, rarely make such pronouncements. The balance of power to define proper practice in the mindfulness movement seems to shift further from formally trained lay teachers to authors who can make mindfulness appear accessible to the widest audiences, with the minimal expenditure of effort. Ordinary, non-teaching lay practitioners are further empowered in this process, with individual Americans who rarely or never darken the doors of formal mindfulness groups or retreat centers developing into the numerical majority and becoming the model for average practitioners. It is no longer necessary even to have a Buddhist or meditation instructor—with the proliferation of books, blogs, and articles on mindfulness, practice can be taken up without personal interaction with other practitioners. From ten-day or longer retreats, the growing edge of mindfulness has become bite-size portions that can be inserted into otherwise normal routines. New books appear to capitalize on such trends, such as *Meditation in a New York Minute: Super Calm for the Super Busy* (2006), *Mindfulness to Go: How to Meditate While You're on the Move* (2011), and *5-Minute Mindfulness: Simple Daily Shortcuts to Transform Your Life* (2011).[18]

Instead of an arduous, lifelong process attempted in a renunciatory, monastic religious context, the original context for mindfulness practice is obscured. Rather, mindfulness is promoted as providing instant benefits that can be gained after a single trial attempt at meditation practice. One of the most noteworthy evolutions in the language surrounding mindfulness is how the quotidian comes to be the measure of mindfulness's value. Authors appear to fear the possible foreign connotations of mindfulness and thus go to lengths to stress that mindfulness practice is normal, easy, and conducted in everyday life. This also appears to be an influence from the self-help genre, the form in which much of contemporary mindfulness discourse takes place (as opposed to religious instruction as a literary sub-genre). The keywords for mindfulness in America have become ordinary, simple, easy, gentle, and everyday. This is reflected in the titles of books, such as *It's Easier Than You Think: The Buddhist Way to Happiness* (1995), *Buddhism Plain and Simple: The Practice of Being Aware, Right Now, Every Day* (1999), *The Mindfulness Solution: Everyday Practices for Everyday Problems* (2010), and *Just One Thing: Developing a Buddha Brain One Simple Practice at a Time* (2011).[19] *Just One Thing* serves as a good example of the trend in mindfulness framing. It is divided into five sections: Be Good to Yourself; Enjoy Life; Build Strengths; Engage the World; and Be at Peace. Chapters include titles such as Fill the Hole in Your Heart; Love Your Inner Child; and Dream Big Dreams. In these sorts of books, mindfulness is not monastic, not renunciatory, not demanding, not complex. It is readily accessible by anyone, anywhere, in a spiritual idiom easily recognizable to every American, and barely distinguishable from any number of other self-help programs.

Removal of Buddhist Context

Throughout premodern Asian Buddhist history mindfulness instruction was always accompanied by teachings about proper behavior and morality. In fact, morality (*sila*) was held to be the necessary foundation for any sort of fruitful meditation practice. This is where Mahasi Sayadaw always began his instruction in vipassana: "Preparatory Stage: If you sincerely desire to develop contemplation and attain insight in this your present life, you must give up worldly thoughts and actions during training. This course of action is for the purification of conduct, the essential preliminary step toward proper development of contemplation. You must also observe the rules of discipline prescribed for laymen (or for monks, as the case may be), for they are important in gaining insight. For layfolk, these rules comprise the eight precepts that Buddhist devotees observe on holidays (uposatha) and during periods of meditation. An additional rule is not to speak with contempt, in jest, or malice to or about any of the Noble Ones who have attained states of Sanctity."[20] This "essential" adherence to morality is one reason why mindfulness was primarily a monastic endeavor: in most cases, only ordained members of the sangha who followed the hundreds of monastic rules and were relatively less involved in the chaotic, tempting world of everyday life could realistically hope to achieve the mental stability required for advanced meditation practice. Mindfulness in turn provided a powerful crutch to the practice of correct Buddhist morality, as it facilitated the observation of dangerous mental patterns, fostered awareness of one's actions and their impacts, and because of the simple fact that while quietly meditating one was by definition not off somewhere indulging in karmically unwise activities.

Monastic promoters of mindfulness continue to advocate Buddhist morality, as did many of the first generations of Westerners who returned from training in Asia (and we should note that most of these early lay teachers are still alive and continue to offer instruction). For instance, Joseph Goldstein's *The Experience of Insight* is a book of mindfulness instruction, based on actual talks he regularly gave while teaching Americans on retreat. His very first lecture delivered on the first evening of instruction states emphatically: "An indispensable beginning for meditation practice is following certain moral precepts. It is a way of maintaining the basic purity of body, speech, and mind. The five precepts that should be taken are: not killing, which means refraining from knowingly taking any life, not even swatting a mosquito or stepping on an ant; not stealing, which means not taking anything which is not given; refraining from sexual misconduct, which in the context of the retreat means observing celibacy; not lying or speaking falsely or harshly; and not taking intoxicants, which again in the context of the meditation course means not taking alcohol or drugs. Following these precepts will provide a strong base for the development of concentration, and will make the growth of insight possible."[21] These are not just basic moral ideas—these are specifically the five traditional Buddhist lay precepts. For Goldstein, and most other teachers of his generation, mindfulness could not be easily divorced from Buddhist morality.

But over time the explicit connection of mindfulness practice to Buddhist morality has become attenuated for significant portions of the subsequent movement. This is related in part to the absence of teachings on karma and rebirth, which undergird the Buddhist concepts of morality but are contested by many Westerners. Removing mindfulness's connection to explicit teachings on morality allows non-Buddhists to engage more directly in the practice, and puts the focus of attention squarely on awareness practices themselves, without the possible distraction of other elements of Buddhism. Mindfulness in many works comes to be presented in a basically amoral manner, denuded of context and thus available for application to simple tasks: to eat mindfully, have mindful sex, use mindfulness to deal with depression, or play the guitar in a mindful manner is simply to carry out such activities with greater attention. Frequently there is no implication that such behavior leads to good karma, better rebirth, social improvement, or has anything to do with ethics per se.

Downplaying or removing Buddhist moral teachings from the presentation of mindfulness is only one way in which mindfulness's Buddhist wellsprings are mystified. Often, authors directly challenge or minimize such connections. One of the oldest such practices is to insist that practitioners need not be Buddhist in order to engage in mindfulness or benefit from meditation. The exact manifestations of this attitude have changed over time. In the beginning, various mindfulness promoters affirmed that personal Buddhist adherence was not necessary, but they nonetheless expected that non-Buddhists would carry out mindfulness in a Buddhist context. In other words, the individual practitioner didn't have to believe in Buddhism, as Buddhist techniques would be effective through their practice, regardless of personal belief or non-belief—but the practitioner would still certainly be going through the motions of Buddhism, in a Buddhist setting, with Buddhist instructors. Marie Beuzeville Byles's *Journey into Burmese Silence* demonstrates this. "It goes without saying that I am convinced from my own experience that the practice of vipassana meditation, coupled with training in the other steps of the Buddha's Eightfold Path, provides a practical way for finding deliverance from suffering here and now. I am also convinced that this way to zest, calm, peace and happiness, is open to anyone who is prepared to undertake the training and pay the price demanded. Embracing Buddhism or any other religion is not, however, part of the price."[22] Byles expected Westeners to journey *into* Buddhism, and follow the eightfold path while practicing inside a Buddhist container for the purpose of mindfulness training, but felt they did not have to confess Buddhist beliefs within their own hearts. They could remain Christian, or agnostic, so long as they played the part of Buddhist. Without that role-playing, mindfulness simply wouldn't be effective.

The next stage along the scale is to paint mindfulness as generically Asian without making much explicit reference to Buddhism specifically as a tradition. Writers who use this approach speak of mindfulness as coming to us from indistinct Eastern societies, Asian traditions, or even just unnamed ancient cultures. Susan Albers, author of several books on mindful eating, provides a case in point. In *Eating Mindfully: How to End Mindless Eating and Enjoy a Balanced Relationship with Food* (2003), Albers's first chapter begins: "The four foundations of mindfulness are an important aspect of Buddha's teachings. As a young adult, Buddha discovered that mastering mindful eating was essential to his spiritual growth."[23] She goes on to describe this traditional list in detail, telling the reader that it was derived from the *Satipatthana Sutta*. But a few years later, she decided to target a more specific audience of university students, many of whom presumably had no particular interest in religion. Thus in *Mindful Eating 101: A Guide to Healthy Eating in College and Beyond* (2006), she modifies her approach, simply telling readers that "Ancient civilizations knew how important it is to have a clear and present mind."[24] Mindfulness's specifically Buddhist beginnings are hidden by this newer, fuzzier language. The Buddha quotes that open various sections of *Eating Mindfully* are absent from *Mindful Eating 101*.

Other authors try to bridge the gap between mindfulness practice and its perception among non-Buddhists by suggesting that mindfulness can be found in various religions, and therefore isn't essentially Buddhist. For example, in *Bounce: Living the Resilient Life* (2010), Robert Wicks begins his chapter "Solitude, Silence, and Mindfulness: Centering Yourself in a Driven World" by describing the range of places that one can find mindfulness: "Many of the world's religions and ancient philosophies extol the benefits of solitude and mindfulness."[25] He moves quickly into examples from various sources, including Catholic and Jewish writers. He asserts clearly that "Whether a person is without a proclaimed religion or is a Buddhist, Muslim, Jew, Christian, or Hindu, or has another religious or spiritual identity is not of primary concern. The point in speaking about silence and solitude, or mindfulness meditation, is that there is a benefit—especially for those of us who seek to be resilient."[26] All very good. But having framed mindfulness as multi-religious, he proceeds to quote only Buddhists—including Clark Strand, Andrew Harvey, Achaan

Chah, Pema Chodron, David Brazier, Jack Kornfield, Shunryu Suzuki, Andrew Weiss, and Bhante Henepola Gunaratana—for his actual discussion of how to perform mindfulness. It's clear to anyone paying attention that Buddhism is in fact his source for mindfulness instruction. Here we see the mystification of Buddhist mindfulness by gesturing first toward all sorts of non-Buddhist phenomena, so that readers presumably are distracted from the fact that what is actually being taught is Buddhism.

Likewise, the co-authors of *The Complete Idiot's Guide to Mindfulness* are upfront about their own personal training in Buddhist mindfulness, but they attempt to persuade their largely non-Buddhist readership that no one needs to believe in or practice Buddhism to do mindfulness. The inside cover flap reassures readers that "While mindfulness meditation draws on Buddhism, it isn't Buddhism."[27] On page 1 they state "You can practice mindfulness no matter your faith tradition. While it draws from Buddhist teachings, mindfulness techniques are separate and apart from religion."[28] On pages 16–21 they try to offer examples of mindfulness-like practices in Christianity, Judaism, Islam, and Hinduism. They then move on to an extended section on Buddhist mindfulness, but preface it with a special insert box that claims "You may have hesitated to explore mindfulness or anything that sounds Eastern. But mindfulness is not narcissistic, not a cult, not out of touch, not anti-Christian."[29] Finally, on the penultimate page of the book, the authors' anxiety over Buddhism's relationship to mindfulness breaks through in a noticeably defensive fashion:

> We started out this book telling you that you don't have to be a Buddhist to practice mindfulness. And then we've talked about Buddhism throughout the book! What's up with that?...People in some religious traditions would have you see this book and Buddhist teachings as a cult or as a turning away from God and Jesus. But this comes from a fundamental misunderstanding of the practices of mindfulness and meditation. You do not worship the Buddha when you practice mindfulness; you explore your inner landscape, which includes your mind and your soul. Your mind and your soul are gifts from God or Allah or Spirit—why wouldn't you want to explore them and open your heart to them as fully as you can?[30]

A yet further form of this tactic is to downplay the origins of mindfulness in any religious tradition at all. This is often the preferred method by those who seek to exert scientific, medical, or therapeutic authority over mindfulness practice, phenomena that are explored in depth in Chapter 3. A prime example is Daniel J. Seigel, co-director of the UCLA Mindful Awareness Research Center. He published two different books on mindfulness in 2010: *Mindsight: The New Science of Personal Transformation* and *The Mindful Therapist: A Clinician's Guide to Mindsight and Neural Integration*. In the first book, Seigel writes: "People sometimes hear the word *mindfulness* and think 'religion.' But the reality is that focusing our attention in this way is a biological process that promotes health—a form of brain hygiene—not religion. Various religions may encourage this health-promoting practice, but learning the skill of mindful awareness is simply a way of cultivating what we have defined as the integration of consciousness."[31] His spin is slightly different, and goes even further, in *The Mindful Therapist*: "We've seen that while mindfulness is practiced throughout the world, East and West, ancient and modern, it is a human skill that religions use—not itself a religious practice. While some educational programs appropriately shy away from bringing uninvited religion into a secular setting, it is in fact the case that research has now demonstrated that mindful awareness practices, such as mindfulness meditation, are actually ways of strengthening the healthy functioning of the body, the brain, the mind, and interpersonal relationships."[32] So mindfulness isn't just not a religion, it is something that doesn't originate in religion and that religions have no rights over—they just happen to use it. These sorts of tactics raise intriguing questions about the ultimate fate of Buddhism in a society devoted in many ways to secular and commercial values. Seigel is trained in vipassana meditation, and though he never frames them as Buddhist, his writings are peppered with keywords important to that Buddhist tradition, such as lovingkindness, compassion, and the concept that everything changes. There is no doubt that he is aware that mindfulness has come to us primarily from the Buddhist tradition. In that case, is his failure to admit that connection in *Mindsight* and other books a sort of cultural plagiarism? Or is it a skillful use of Buddhist means to bring relief of suffering to populations that would not otherwise partake in the benefits mindfulness practice can bestow?

Seigel brings us close to the ultimate form of mystification: simply leaving out all reference to Buddhism, religion, or spirituality altogether. Many examples of this approach can be found. Readers of *How to Be Happier Day by Day: A Year of Mindful Actions* (1994) by Alan Epstein would be excused for not realizing that some of the ideas they are reading about are related to Buddhist practice, since the author never once brings up the connection.[33] Actress Goldie Hawn's best-selling *10 Mindful Minutes: Giving Our*

Children—and Ourselves—the Social and Emotional Skills to Reduce Stress and Anxiety for Healthier, Happier Lives (2011) is a passionate plea for incorporating mindfulness into the public school system and other educational settings. She never once mentions religion.

It is easy to understand why some authors might wish to omit Buddhism from their teachings on mindfulness. Epstein is trying to sell a fairly generic self-help book, and limiting his audience to Buddhists and Buddhist sympathizers could reduce sales. Hawn is trying to insert a religiously derived meditation practice into the secular school system, which is already an intense battleground over the place of religion due to the governing policy of separation of church and state. The quote from Seigel's book given earlier illustrates that some people have balked at mindfulness in schools. Schoolteachers are not supposed to lead their students in prayer, and if leading them in Buddhist meditation raised flags, then Hawn's desire to help students with their study habits might fall victim to competing religious or anti-religious agendas.

This approach of hiding Buddhism's presence when bringing meditation into non-religious settings seems to be working for the moment, as there is not yet substantial resistance to mindfulness based on church–state issues. Such resistance may show signs of emerging, however, and interestingly it is sometimes former practitioners of mindfulness who refuse to allow mindfulness movement advocates to get away with promoting it as secular. For instance, Marcia Montenegro is the founder of Christian Answers for the New Age, an evangelical missionary organization. A former practitioner of Buddhism and other alternative religions, she converted to Christianity in 1990. In a January 2012 article posted to her website, Montenegro directly takes on Goldie Hawn and her MindUP™ program for misleading the public about mindfulness's connection to Buddhism:

> Although presented as spiritually neutral, the origins and goals of mindfulness belie that stance. Many are not aware that the true goal of Buddhism, *nirvana*, is not some kind of Buddhist heaven, but is actually the state one reaches when one has shed all attachments and illusions, thus freeing oneself from desire and rebirth. *Nirvana* means "to extinguish" and is the state of cessation of desire and illusion, and therefore of suffering. What is this state like? Buddhism offers no clear answer…Children are the most vulnerable and are totally unable to critique or assess such ideas; for that reason, they make the best targets. Parents need to monitor and mind carefully what is going on in their child's classroom. They need to ask questions about all activities.

Parents can talk to the teacher or principal and ask to opt their child out based on religious views. Even if the school denies that mindfulness is religious, the parent can state that it conflicts with his or her faith. There is much data online that would help make a parent's case that mindfulness is religious.[34]

Montenegro is not the only person to express concerns over mindfulness's Buddhist connections. According to the *Akron Beacon*, in April 2013 Warstler Elementary School stopped its mindfulness program for schoolchildren "after some parents and community members raised concerns the technique was linked too closely to Eastern religions like Buddhism."[35] The superintendent explained in an interview, "As we kept digging and researching, we found the roots to it. We have to be careful as a public school that we don't cross over church and state."[36] In this case, at least, caution won out over the claims from promoters that mindfulness is purely non-religious. In the growth of the mindfulness movement, Buddhist advocates contend that mindfulness is non-religious, while Christian opponents describe totally denatured meditation as nonetheless indelibly religious. The question must be asked: Is mindfulness, by the time it is being presented by people without Buddhist teaching credentials in a purely secular manner, in fact still Buddhist? Is it religious or not?

The answer appears to lie in the agenda of the particular commentator, with no easy resolution that can satisfy all. The simple truth is that terms like religion, spirituality, Buddhism, and secular are judgments of qualities and value, not inherent categories existing somehow prior to their application by individual observers. Their application always carries meaning, and they are deployed in different ways, for different reasons, at different times by different interested parties. For our purposes here, we should note the deliberate strategies that different mindfulness advocates employ to make Buddhism more appealing by removing its Buddhistness. These are indeed purposeful, calculated moves, as an editorial in *Shambhala Sun* makes clear. Part house organ for the Shambhala movement started by Chogyam Trungpa, part ecumenical Buddhist-cum-spirituality journal with a strong emphasis on meditation practices, *Shambhala Sun* is one of the primary Buddhist periodicals in the West. In March 2013, editor-in-chief Melvin McLeod explained how Jon Kabat-Zinn visited the magazine's editorial office seven years prior and inspired the editors to promote Buddhism in a secular manner, based on mindfulness. As McLeod discussed, "Mindfulness is not inherently religious. It is about expressing the best of who we are as human beings. It does not depend on any belief or philosophy… That day, Jon talked with us about the basic principles of Mindfulness-Based Stress Reduction (MBSR) and the broader mindfulness movement of which he is considered the founder. There were three, all beautifully conceived to remove barriers and make meditative practice as accepted, universal, and helpful as possible. Mindfulness was present as: secular (available to all, regardless of belief); evidence based (validated by personal experience and sound science); and beneficial to our lives right now (to our health, happiness, families, society, etc.)."[37]

The editors were impressed and embarked on what they called their Mindfulness Initiative. "We began extensive coverage of the mindfulness movement in the *Shambhala Sun*, spearheaded by senior writer Barry Boyce. [Consultation with others] resulted in the creation of a new nonprofit, the Foundation for a Mindful Society. Today, in partnership with the Hemera Foundation, the FMS is the publisher of Mindful.org and of the new bimonthly magazine, *Mindful*, whose first issue appears in February with Barry Boyce as editor-in-chief."[38] Thus the Buddhist magazine *Shambhala Sun* was transformed to make it a vehicle for mindfulness, and a new magazine *Mindful* was created to advance crypto-Buddhist mindfulness in society at large. Mindfulness could thereby be disseminated in two parallel modes: Buddhist for those who wanted such flavoring, and non-Buddhist for those who didn't. From the evidence of books such as Seigel's, Epstein's, and Hawn's, this newer form of mindfulness is already thriving.

The Whitening of Mindfulness

For foreign religious practices to be successfully appropriated by mainstream American society, they need to be rendered spiritual and personal to best fit into prevailing trends in religious orientation. Those that can undergo such a process most fully are likely to become widespread, while those that are resistant to such recontextualizations will remain relatively niche interests of the alternative few. Hinduism is appropriated as yoga, Islam as Sufi poetry, Daoism as tai-chi, Japanese folk healing as reiki, and Buddhism as mindfulness. Religiously derived practices must be framed so as to suggest the primacy of individual experience, rather than authoritarian structure. This is to say, the historic authority over these practices of Asians, Middle Easterners, and other groups coded as nonwhite in American society must be dissolved so that white Americans can claim authority over them, an authority that issues from the fact that these are now self-evidently universal, spiritual, or medical practices available to all comers, which new constituencies have a right to use, and to sell, as they wish. This necessitates a process of detachment from Asian and/or premodern belief systems and ethnic identities, traces of which we can see in the preceding sections. In other words, practices such as mindfulness must be rendered as "white," that is, deracialized, blank, pure, available, and superior to the ethnic or tradition-bound.[39] They can retain only the whiff of exoticness in order to add flavor to our lives.

Examples of this de-racialization (arguably, actually a re-racialization), spiritualization, and individualization can be found throughout the mindfulness movement. Steve Hagen's *Buddhism Plain and Simple* provides a particularly clear instance, but his rhetoric differs little from that of countless other books. In his introduction, he states his view on Buddhism: "When the Buddha was asked to sum up his teaching in a single word, he said, 'awareness'. This is a book about awareness. Not awareness of something in particular, but awareness itself—being awake, alert, in touch with what is actually happening. It's about examining and exploring the most basic questions of life. It's about relying on the immediate experience of this present moment. It's not about belief, doctrine, formula, or tradition. It's about freedom of mind."[40] Hagen removes all aspects of Buddhism that he dislikes by boiling the entire 2,500-year-old tradition down to a single word: awareness. With this axiom, he is now able to discard anything that he feels interferes with awareness. Buddhism, it turns out, isn't about all the messy stuff of belief and doctrine; it is about personal freedom, a quintessentially American value.

Hagen continues: "The Buddha learned to see directly into the nature of experience. As a result of his teaching and his life, a new religion arose and spread throughout the world. In the process, like all religions, Buddhism accumulated (and generated) a variety of beliefs, rituals, ceremonies, and practices. As it spread from country to country, it acquired a wide variety of cultural trappings: special clothes and hats, statues, incense, gongs, bells, whistles—even peculiar architectural forms, icons, and symbols. This book leaves all that behind. Rituals, ceremonies, prayers, and special outfits are inevitable, but they do not—they cannot—express the heart of what the Buddha taught. In fact, all too often, such things get in the way. They veil the simple wisdom of the Buddha's words, and distract us from it."[41] Here Hagen is essentially replicating the Protestant critique of Catholic "priestcraft," inherited from Western tradition and now transposed to a new religious situation. Echoing the titles of two classic works for the mindfulness movement—*The Heart of Buddhist Meditation* and *What the Buddha Taught*—he distinguishes between what matters (mindful awareness) and what opposes it (the practices of perhaps 99 percent of living Buddhists). The latter are mere cultural trappings.

Hagen continues: "This is a major problem, and not just for those of us raised in the West. It is not easy to know where Buddhism ends and Asian culture begins, or to distinguish the original and authentic teachings of the Buddha from what was added later by people with less acute insight."[42] Hagen implies here that his insight is superior to that of generations of Asian Buddhists and that with it he can mold Buddhism into what it was supposed to be. In doing so, he alters Buddhism into a form suited for non-Asian Americans coming to Buddhism as individual adults, an alteration that is allegedly a return to the proper, pre-corrupted form intended by the Buddha: "Buddhism is not about these beliefs and practices. The observations and insights of the Buddha are plain, practical, and eminently down-to-earth. They deal exclusively with *here* and *now*, not with theory, speculation, or belief in some far-off time or place. Because these teachings remain focused on this moment—even as you read this—they remain relevant and of profound value, to every culture and every person who investigates them seriously. It is to these uncluttered, original insights and observations that this book returns."[43] Being based solely in awareness, the Buddha's real teachings are available to every culture, such as America, and all persons, such as whites. Many Asian Buddhists would agree with Hagen, of course, that Buddhism is accessible for everyone—but perhaps not with the tinge of white ethnic chauvinism that pervades these quotes.

Here we find a replication of a common pattern in the white American encounter with Asian religious cultures. In her book *Virtual Orientalism: Asian Religions and American Popular Culture,* Jane Naomi Iwamura has argued that the most pernicious forms of this pattern amount to "a *modernized cultural patriarchy* in which Anglo-Americans reimagine themselves as protectors, innovators, and guardians of Asian religions and culture and wrest the authority to define these traditions from others."[44] In the case of the mindfulness movement, it may be objected that Asians and Asian Americans are also important advocates for mindfulness in America. This is so, and their contributions should not be overlooked or minimized. But although there are important Asian monks, such as Thich Nhat Hanh, and Asian American laypersons, such as Chade-Meng Tan, who have significant followings, the overwhelming whiteness of the mindfulness movement in the United States is a fact that needs to be observed, because it impacts how mindfulness is Americanized and what daily behaviors it is (and isn't) applied to.

Predominantly white Buddhist media do include some Asian meditation masters, in part to take advantage of their celebrity Buddhist cachet, but the vast majority of information about mindfulness is disseminated by white people, in media venues controlled by white people, for the primary consumption of white people. Mindfulness articles and books are primarily illustrated by pictures of smiling, happy white folks. One place to examine the racial dynamics of the dominant streams in the American mindfulness movement is the new publication *Mindful*, whose origins were discussed earlier in this chapter. Although *Mindful* launched as a regular periodical in 2013, it was preceded by a one-shot publication of the same name in January 2011 packaged along with that month's *Shambhala Sun*, apparently a trial run to gauge potential reader interest and work out the kinks in the production of a new magazine. The 2011 *Mindful* cover is graced by a smiling white woman of approximately early middle age, wearing casual clothing and sitting cross-legged in the grass (the next several issues likewise depict attractive, seated white people smiling into the camera). The inside cover has an advertisement for mindful investing, as a white hand carefully stacks pebbles. Page 1 has the table of contents, with its list of exclusively white writers. On page 3, editor-in-chief Barry Boyce's pleasant, mustachioed white face hovers over an editorial that introduces *Mindful* without ever once mentioning Buddhism or Asia. To the left of the editorial is the publication masthead, populated entirely by white people.

Not counting a paid advertisement from the Mind & Life Institute that includes small photographs of Tibetan monks, the first discernable people of color appear on page 7, in a stock photograph showing a multiracial classroom, offered as an accompaniment to a brief article on how mindfulness is being taught to help inner-city school teachers. Pages 34–35 of *Mindful* provide a spread of reader-submitted photographs with brief descriptions entitled "Look Who's Practicing Mindfulness and Awareness." Who is doing so? White people, mostly. Ten of the photographs show white people, with explanations of how mindfulness has helped each of them in very practical ways. A single photograph shows an interracial family, with an Asian father, a white mother, and two children. No other nonwhite people appear in this issue of *Mindful*. Pages 36–39 provide book reviews of various mindfulness works, all by white authors. The word "Buddhism" is completely absent from the magazine; "Buddhist" appears twice, in the subtitles of books advertised by Wisdom Publications on the back cover; "Zen" appears once, in a story told by a writer; and the

"Insight Meditation Society" is referenced a single time in an interview with Jon Kabat-Zinn. Otherwise Buddhism makes no overt appearance, although in fact *Mindful* is shot through with Buddhist material, such as a sidebar on page 19 that urges readers to use the Theravada-derived metta (lovingkindness) meditation, without actually identifying its source in Buddhism.

Mindful is hardly alone in this sort of phenomenon. A randomly selected issue of *Insight Journal* (Winter 2010) yields only white contributors, with the only nonwhite faces those of statues, drawings, or paintings of Buddhas and monks. A random catalog from *DharmaCrafts: The Catalog of Meditation Supplies* (Summer 2008) depicts only white models sitting, standing, and smiling among an array of Asian Buddha statues and expensive meditation cushions. Issues of *Tricycle, Shambhala Sun, Buddhadharma, Inquiring Mind*, and other important publications are always dominated by white authors and white faces. When nonwhites appear in such publications, they often fall within a narrow range of presentations that do not challenge the white majority of the mindfulness movement. For instance, there are occasional articles describing how black people *also* are getting into mindfulness—especially in prison and inner-city schools—thus proving how mindfulness is indeed for everyone. This is the situation in the first official issue of *Mindful* (April 2013): it features an article about mindfulness in Baltimore, where a trio of Latino and African American teachers is depicted bringing mindfulness to the tough urban jungle, as illustrated by pictures of multiracial (mostly African American) student classes doing yoga and listening to their teachers.[45] Nonwhites are otherwise absent from the magazine, except as local color in a few photographs of Asia accompanying a travel diary by Indian-British author Pico Iyer, and in occasional advertisements.[46] These publications also sometimes include interviews with black celebrities favored by white liberal intellectuals, such as bell hooks and Alice Walker. And they include interviews with or practice-oriented articles by Asian and Asian American meditation teachers, such as the Dalai Lama and Thich Nhat Hanh. Race itself is rarely tackled, and consciousness-raising articles, such as those in the Winter 2011 issue of *Buddhadharma*, though laudable, simultaneously help to cement white control over the image of mindfulness: with titles like "Why Is American Buddhism so White?" and "Yes, We're Buddhist Too!," people of color are very clearly positioned at the margins of the movement.[47]

Constructing a Lineage

One way to make mindfulness seem more American is to create histories that detail its long presence in the United States, and to assert that mindfulness isn't foreign at all. This can be seen in such works as *New World Mindfulness: From the Founding Fathers, Emerson, and Thoreau to Your Personal Practice* (2012), by Donald McCown and Marc Micozzi. They begin their first chapter by proclaiming, "There is nothing new about meditative and contemplative practice, and nothing exclusively Asian, Buddhist, or otherwise exotic…In a profound sense, mindfulness belongs to us."[48] The "us" is Americans specifically, and apparently white people in particular, because they are the Americans who receive sustained treatment in the book. The authors contextualize mindfulness as attention, allegedly a timeless force that is not a specific cultural product of Asian Buddhist societies. They then demonstrate how this timeless mindfulness was already present in such 19th century spiritual heroes as Ralph Waldo Emerson and Henry David Thoreau—not because they practiced mindfulness (they didn't), but because they were sensitive types who read Asian texts in translation and had a penchant for long, quiet sits contemplating life and nature. McCown and Micozzi rehearse a selective version of the bringing of Buddhism to America, focusing on white people and the individual Asian missionaries who taught them (the numerically larger Buddhism of Asian American communities is mentioned but not examined). They also spice this with observations about other awareness-type practices beyond Buddhism, and make the classic move of trying to draw parallels between Buddhist mindfulness and various contemplative prayer forms in Judaism, Christianity, and Islam.

One of the interesting aspects of this type of mystification is that it tries to have it both ways: thus mindfulness is simultaneously noncultural (it can be found anywhere and is not exclusively Asian) *and* it is a part of our own historic culture (i.e., it is American). Therefore when Americans engage in mindfulness practice, they are simply following long-established traditions that they have a full right to. This fully appropriates not only the practice of mindfulness but its history as well, domesticating it as a truly American religion. In some ways, this process mirrors that of the formation of Chan (Zen) Buddhism, which manufactured a (historically inaccurate) native Chinese lineage and imagined an Indian precedent that teleologically led to the Chinese sectarian school of Chan.[49] In so doing the Chan founders seized the authority over Buddhism for themselves, wrote their forms and groups into the history of Buddhism, and produced a compelling narrative that could be used for both external propaganda and internal group cohesion. Buddhism ceased to be Indian and became Chinese instead; or, it had been incidentally Indian, but now it was Chinese, and its Indian roots were important only insofar as India had nurtured the dharma until it could take fullest flower in China, as Chan. In similar fashion, Americans turn cultural touchstones such as Emerson, Thoreau, and William James into patriarchs of an imagined lineage of American mindfulness, making mindfulness nonthreatening and asserting their full rights to the tradition.

Mindfulness for People of Color

Despite the undeniable white dominance of representations of mindfulness in America, there are in fact significant numbers of people of color also involved in practicing meditation. Few will be surprised that mindfulness is a popular—though infrequently central or numerically dominant—practice in many Asian American Buddhist communities. But there are also many practitioners of African American, Latino, and/or Native American descent, as well as Asian Americans from historically non-Buddhist heritage (such as Filipino Americans), or from communities that have not offered lay mindfulness practice as part of their Buddhist activities. Many of these practitioners have little choice but to seek mindfulness instruction in majority- or virtually all-white environments. Another category of persons of color in America are Asian missionary monks, of course, though their situations tend to be somewhat different from those of people of color who first encounter mindfulness in the United States.

People of color from African American, Caribbean, Latino, Aboriginal, Asian American, mixed, and other backgrounds often share little in terms of heritage between these groups, and naturally within each group there is tremendous variety. But what they do all share is the experience of not being fully white in the mainstream American construction of racial identity. So though we do find many different individual approaches to mindfulness within the overall population of people of color, we can also discern some common patterns that emerge from similar experiences and social locations.

Some of the same tactics of appropriation and mystification as we find in the dominant discourse also appear in the writings of racial and ethnic minority mindfulness proponents. Many insist that one can find mindfulness-like practices in non-Asian cultures, for instance, or that mindfulness practice is not a barrier to those who also wish to subscribe to non-Buddhist religions.

The cultures and religions referred to in the case of people of color, however, are often not those of the Euro-American majority culture, but instead those of one's own minority heritage. For example, AfroCuban-American Zen priest Hilda Gutiérrez Baldoquín recalls her Cuban grandmother teaching her to pray for protection, peace, happiness, and well-being. "My grandmother was my first Dharma teacher," she asserts.[50] Similarly, Eduardo Duran combines Buddhism with his Native American heritage in his essay "Buddhism in the Land of the Redface," where he writes: "My years of daily meditation and mindfulness in the vipassana Buddhist tradition have been augmented by Aboriginal ceremonial practice. Through the integration of intense ceremonial practice and vipassana practice, I have discovered what our great great grandpa the Buddha taught: The Dharma was already here in the so-called West long before we had that name for it. The ceremonial practices of the many tribal groups that were here have, as a core quality, the ability to bring strong levels of concentration to the participants."[51] Because the dharma was already here in the form of Aboriginal awareness practices, practicing Asian-derived mindfulness is actually a way of remaining true to one's Native heritage, according to these interpretations.

The lineages conjured by people of color are often more personal than those of white mindfulness practitioners, based in one's own family or in-group heritage. Baldoquín traces her exposure to the dharma back through her own (non-Buddhist) grandmother; Duran emphasizes that mindfulness has been right here on his own native soil, and uses kinship tropes to knit the Buddha into his own family. This contrasts with the more abstract lineages based on cultural heroes such as that found in *New World Mindfulness*: the white authors do not profess themselves to be actually genetically related to the American founding fathers, Emerson, Thoreau, or the other figures they draw upon.

When distant cultural figures are referenced, they are likely to be ones that relate to the struggles of people of color, such as in Viveka Chen's essay, "Finding True Freedom." She states: "The revolutionary spirit of the Third Noble Truth is akin to the messages of civil rights leaders like Dr. Martin Luther King, Jr. who urge us to wake up and rise up from life-robbing oppression. The Buddha was a freedom fighter who launched a spiritual movement empowering people to end mental, physical, and spiritual enslavement."[52] As with white Americans, many people of color emphasize the notions of "liberation" and "freedom" in connection with mindfulness. In the minority accounts, there is the added attention to freedom from outside attack due to nonwhite status. As Chen asserts, "Even in oppressive conditions, freedom can be had by freeing the mind."[53] Baldoquín further amplifies this understanding: "Teachings of liberation heard clearly in a culture driven by ignorance, fear, anger, and hate is like the breaking of chains after centuries of subjugation. This is the gift the Buddha Shakyamuni gave us…It is our birthright to be free and it's our responsibility to wake up to that freedom."[54] As with some of the white commentators, the appropriations of mindfulness sometimes mix a little oddly (is mindfulness a gift or a birthright?), but the point is always unmistakable: people of color have a right to practice mindfulness, and, like white people, to apply it to the needs in their lives.

Those needs take on an extra dimension when racial and ethnic discrimination affect mindfulness practitioners. Charles Johnson explains how mindfulness offers a solution to negative aspects of the African American experience:

If we wish to understand the special meaning that the Buddhadharma has for blacks in America—and why in the 21st century it may be the next step in our spiritual evolution toward what Martin Luther King Jr. called the "beloved community"—we need look no farther than the teaching of mindfulness, which is the root and fruit of all Buddhist practice…It reveals the object as it is before it has been plastered over with conceptual paint, overlaid with interpretations. To practice mindfulness is thus a matter not so much of doing but of undoing: not thinking, not judging, not associating, not planning, not imagining, not wishing. For black Americans in the post–Civil Rights period, this systematic undoing of the cultural indoctrination, the "conceptual paint" we have received from a very decadent, violent, materialistic, and Eurocentric society, is crucial for our liberation, personally and as a people.[55]

So mindfulness is a cure for internalized oppression and can be used to help fulfill the dreams of King and other black ancestors who struggled to achieve a brighter day for their communities. African American Buddhist nun Sister Chan Chau Nghiem experienced such a healing while on retreat with Thich Nhat Hanh: "Up came a very deep, old hurt feeling of feeling rejected, discriminated against, unloved because of my skin color. It was very painful. But I had never embraced this pain with my mindfulness before. It had just been lying there, stuck in my consciousness. Now it could circulate freely, massaged by mindful breathing. I held my pain—this feeling that I had missed out on something important as a little girl—with tenderness and love and allowed the hot tears to flow down my cheeks…[I] released this heavy burden of ignorance, separation, and pain. In its place I felt a lightness, a deeper confidence in myself, in the practice of mindfulness and in a very real connectedness with my ancestors."[56]

But because people of color so often encounter mindfulness in white environments, further complications can arise. For some, these white-dominated practice groups feel uncomfortable, even threatening. In an article in *Inquiring Mind*, Charlie Johnson relates the story of a panic attack he had while on a month-long vipassana retreat where he was one of the only persons of color. After someone left him an anonymous note about the disturbance his snoring was causing, he experienced flashbacks of an attempted lynching he endured years earlier. Terrified that white retreatants might break in and attack him, he looked for ways to block his door. Eventually he went to the meditation hall, where he could throw chairs at any attackers. At first light he hastily got in his car and drove home.[57] Marlene Jones, an African American mindfulness teacher, explains that "In my own community experience I have felt marginalized, invisible, and conspicuous all at the same time...I ended up feeling the same sense of isolation and alienation that I experience in mainstream society."[58]

One way of dealing with such experiences has been the creation of people of color sanghas and retreats. These are groups/activities designated for people of color only, so that the fears, silencing, or simple feelings of cultural lack of fit occasioned by practicing mindfulness in white-dominated spaces will be removed. This stream within the mindfulness movement began to appear in the late 1990s, with Spirit Rock Meditation Center as one of the pioneering communities looking for ways to make mindfulness more accessible to people of color, create spaces where people of color felt comfortable to practice mindfulness, and promote leadership of people of color.

Are such developments further forms of mystification? In some ways, they do move Buddhism further away from its Asian predecessors, as these communities make sense only in a framework of American white supremacist culture. They repeat many of the same practices found in the mainstream white mindfulness movement: promotion of lay teachers, mindfulness in non-renunciatory settings, mindful awareness in ordinary life, creation of indigenous lineages, application to nontraditional foci and for nontraditional ends, and so on. So they do reinforce some of the same evolutions. At the same time, they are mainly a reaction to white society and/or mindfulness communities and seem less concerned about hiding the Asian roots of mindfulness practice. Indeed, for some, mindfulness's roots in nonwhite religion and culture are precisely what make it attractive and suitable for people of color. This puts a check on some of the strongest impulses toward mystification that occur in certain sections of the mindfulness movement.

Gender Implications of Mindfulness's Evolution

The mystification of mindfulness in America has mixed impact on racial minorities: when it removes Asian authority or overly whitens Buddhism, some people of color experience it as deleterious, but when it results in greater access to those who would be left out of Asian monastic mindfulness traditions, it presumably appears to be more beneficial. For women, meanwhile, the reduction or severing of mindfulness's Asian Buddhist roots has often been experienced as liberating.[59]

Asian Buddhist history has a mixed record in relationship to women, but overall it is no mischaracterization to say that Buddhism has produced, perpetuated, and promoted ideas and practices that relegated women to second-class status in Buddhist societies. Lack of interest in women's religious opportunities or leadership contributed to the extinction of the fully ordained nun's order in Theravada Buddhism, the lack of full ordination for women in Himalayan Vajrayana Buddhism, and the neglect of the women's order in East Asian Mahayana. Women monastics were always subject to rules not imposed on men, including the need to submit to the authority of monks. Quasi-ordained eight- and ten-precept nuns in Southeast Asia were typically treated as servants of the fully ordained monks, and until the modern era were rarely given instruction in mindfulness practice. The *Satipatthana Sutta* and the other main mindfulness sources of the Pali Canon are notably male: delivered by a male Buddha to male monastics and preserved through history primarily by the monks' order.

The alterations that loosen mindfulness's attachment to traditional Buddhism often make meditation practice more accessible to women and increase the potential for female authority over mindfulness. Like many of the changes that take place in the modern global mindfulness movement, the greater access for women began in Asia. The Asian experiences of women such as Marie Beuzeville Byles, Dipa Ma, Sharon Salzburg, Ruth Denison, and others point to this relative opening of the dharma. At the same time, like many of the aspects of the specifically Western and especially American sections of the mindfulness movement, these changes are greatly furthered and take on new aspects in the United States.

The redistribution of authority from monks to laypeople that accompanies the disentanglement of mindfulness from traditional Buddhist forms allows women to participate in much greater numbers and with more central roles. Because women normally cannot be ordained as full nuns in mainstream Theravada Buddhism (there are various small-scale nunhood revival efforts in contemporary Theravada, mostly ignored or condemned by the majority), removing monks as the proprietors of and role models for mindfulness automatically expands women's status. This also tends to undercut traditional views about the polluted or tempting nature of women's bodies, as such teachings were especially promulgated by monks in order to reinforce their commitment to monastic celibacy. Ignoring Buddhist cosmology or rendering it merely symbolic also raises the status of women, as longstanding teachings about birth in a woman's body as punishment for karmic misdeeds, the inability of women to become buddhas or be born in the highest heavens, and the many misogynist stories about women suffering in the hellish realms are also thereby removed. The reorientation from renunciatory, nirvanic motivations for practicing mindfulness toward everyday approaches embedded in normal life is also a boon for many women—disproportionately tied to managing family life, raising children, and maintaining homes, women have had significantly less ability to go on extended retreats, attend frequent meditation sessions, or travel to meet prominent mindfulness teachers. But when mindfulness comes to be promoted as part of normal life, with mindful cooking and dishwashing (as well as mindful work, given the common experience of contemporary women as both homemakers and breadwinners), it meets ordinary women where they are, and mindfulness becomes more innately relevant to their real lives.

It is no mistake that many of the mindfulness promoters quoted in this chapter are women. Today, women make up a very significant proportion of the teachers and authors spreading mindfulness in American culture, and quite likely represent an actual majority of the American practitioners of mindfulness. The new applications of mindfulness that have emerged are often designed to meet needs that contemporary women feel they have, and in some sub-segments of the mindfulness movement—such as mindful eating and mindful parenting—women are clearly the dominant voices. These phenomena are given greater attention in Chapter 5. The appropriation of mindfulness by the helping professions, and especially its deep penetration in therapy and counseling practices, have brought great numbers of women into contact with mindfulness and produced some of the most active female authorities on mindfulness. Chapter 3 details many examples of this phenomenon. The appropriation of mindfulness by the self-help genre—a form of writing widely written by and marketed to women—also gives a boost to the presence of women in American mindfulness. And the actions undertaken to make mindfulness more available to whites naturally make it more available to white *women*. It isn't a mistake that the covers of both the preliminary and first official issues of *Mindful* were illustrated by images of women, that much of the *Shambhala Sun* staff is female, or that *Tricycle* was founded by a woman. The process of deculturizing Buddhism to make it available to all naturally brings it closer to being gender neutral.

Conclusion

Obscuring how mindfulness operated in historic Buddhist practice, or even going so far as to hide mindfulness's origins and Buddhist connections makes it (allegedly) available to everyone, increasing the sellers who can appropriate it and the buyers who can consume it. There is a progressive process: first Buddhism is made palatable via mindfulness in order to sell Buddhism (a process on display in Chapter 1), then mindfulness is made palatable via eliminating Buddhism in order to sell mindfulness (something we can see in this chapter), then mindfulness is so appealing and denatured that it can be used to sell other products, such as financial services, vacations, clothing, computer software, etc. (a further process explored in Chapter 5).

Especially as represented in its most extreme forms of de-Buddhification and simplification, mindfulness is the arrival of meditation that is truly for the masses. It requires no gurus, no initiation, no foreign mantras, no years on a cushion, no silence, no devotion, no moral restraint, no belief, no physical flexibility, no wisdom, no patience, no submission, no money, no community, no costumes. In some cases, it doesn't even require meditation for more than a minute at a time. Yet as we will soon see, especially in Chapters 4 and 6, it promises everything: it can allegedly improve any conceivable activity and provide unlimited practical benefits. Perhaps it can even save the world.

We should not lose sight of the fact that there are still many teachers who continue to promote mindfulness as fully and irreducibly Buddhist, and many non-Buddhist meditators nonetheless know that they are involved in a form of Buddhist practice. Even those who seek to disaggregate mindfulness and Buddhism to some degree often also wish to retain some connection between them or at least feel the need to acknowledge their historic relationship. The mindfulness movement ecosystem is extremely diverse, with promoters of monasticism, religious Buddhism, personal spirituality, multiple religious belonging, secular meditation, mindful therapy, and more.

Yet there is an ever more diffuse chain of custody that characterizes the mindfulness movement in America, as described in Chapter 1. First the property of monks, it moved to also becoming the property of lay teachers trained in traditional methods. From there it moved to lay teachers trained in nontraditional settings, and then on into the hands of promoters primarily trained as doctors, therapists, counselors, dieticians, and so forth. Eventually it ends up in the hands of self-help authors, financial advisors, and all manner of non-Buddhist advocates of mindfulness. The result is a significant population of non-Buddhists teaching other non-Buddhists about Buddhist mindfulness, with many of them probably never aware that mindfulness has Buddhist connections. Is this the triumph of Buddhism in a non-Buddhist culture or its death knell? Most people in the mindfulness movement seem not to worry about such questions. For them, reducing suffering (a very Buddhist motivation) appears to be the primary concern, and if that is best accomplished by transferring mindfulness out of Buddhism, a great many find that to be an acceptable price.

3 MEDICALIZING MINDFULNESS: HOW IS MINDFULNESS MODIFIED TO FIT A SCIENTIFIC AND THERAPEUTIC CULTURE?

Medicalize: to give a medical character to; to involve medicine or medical workers in; to view or interpret in (esp. unnecessarily) medical terms

—*Oxford English Dictionary*[1]

Henepola Gunaratana turned twenty years old in 1947, and thus qualified for the higher ordination as a full Theravada monk. A few days after the ceremony, he was allowed to participate in a week-long chanting of paritta—verses taught by the Buddha to exorcise evil spirits. In Sri Lanka, as in much of Buddhist Asia, it was commonly believed that illness, famine, drought, and similar misfortunes were caused by spirit attack, and that monks had the power to drive off the spirits and bring about healing. Large ceremonies were one way for Buddhist monks to make a positive impact on their communities and provide practical benefits to the laypeople who supported them. To take part in the paritta ceremony was an honor, and Gunaratana went at it with gusto. For days he chanted at the top of his lungs, refusing to sleep.

Unfortunately, his youthful zeal had negative consequences. He drove himself so hard that the strain resulted in a mental breakdown. His mind became jumbled and he lost his memory, including the ability to read. He struggled with temper problems, difficulty sleeping, and other symptoms. He failed his school exams and became a burden on those around him. Month after month, the monks and villagers sought ways to cure him. Various medicines were applied topically and taken internally, but nothing seemed to work. The natural conclusion, clearly, was that Gunaratana was the victim of evil spirits. Exorcists were called in, but one after another they failed to heal him. Gunaratana's teacher made a talisman out of sections of the *Ratana Sutta*, one of the Pali Buddhist scriptures. This traditional Buddhist medical treatment should have worked, but still his memory refused to return.

With most of a year expended futilely, it appeared that all options had been exhausted. But out of the blue, a strange idea came to Gunaratana: "At this point of utter desperation, a very unusual thought occurred to me: Perhaps meditation would help. When my friends heard that plan, they burst out laughing. The practice of meditation was hardly a common thing to do in those days, even for a bhikkhu. 'Are you crazy?' one friend asked. 'Meditation is only for old people who can't do anything else anymore. You're still young, too young to meditate. Don't be foolish.'"[2] It was a truly bizarre idea. Like all monks, Gunaratana had learned about the four foundations of mindfulness as part of his training in Buddhist doctrine, but like most, he had never actually meditated. Buddhist monks were supposed to preach, chant, and perform blessings. Too much meditation was believed to cause mental illness. And anyway, the proper Buddhist methods for dealing with psychological issues, sickness, and other health impairments were exorcism and chanting, not mindfulness. The common contexualization of meditation was purification, not healing, as he later explained: "Meditation is intended to purify the mind. It cleanses the thought process of what can be called psychic irritants, things like greed, hatred, and jealousy, which keep you snarled up in emotional bondage."[3]

But Gunaratana had nothing to lose at that point. So he began to meditate in secret, when he thought no one was looking. Month after month, he practiced mindfulness. Over time, his memory improved. Finally, two years after his breakdown, he realized he was cured, and that in the process he had achieved peace of mind as well. Against all odds, the unimaginable had happened: mindfulness had actually helped restore him to mental health.

Gunaratana wasn't just ahead of the curve in 1947—he was completely over the cliff. To engage in mindfulness in order to heal oneself was literally the act of a madman. But he lived long enough to see this perception change in incredible ways. Today Bhante Henepola Gunaratana is one of the foremost Buddhist teachers of mindfulness in the United States, and mindfulness has been incorporated into countless hospitals, clinics, therapeutic practices, and other aspects of the medical and psychological professions.

This chapter continues the theme of mystification of Buddhist mindfulness from Chapter 2 and moves toward the discussion of mainstreaming via everyday benefits that forms the focus of Chapter 4. It does so by examining a very specific type of mystification and reapplication: the recontextualization of mindfulness as a psychological technique intended to provide physical and mental benefits, and therefore properly part of the purview of the medical and psychological establishments in the United States, especially as embodied in its most significant representation: Mindfulness-Based Stress Reduction (MBSR). In Chapter 2, I asserted that foreign religious practices can be successfully appropriated by American culture if they are spiritualized and privatized. Medicalization presents the other major avenue for penetration into American culture, as we also see with yoga, acupuncture, and so on. These two trends are in no way automatically opposed to each other. Being able to approach mindfulness as a technique of personal spirituality and also having the option of seeing it as a biological or psychological process related to health and science expands the possibilities for mindfulness in America, providing familiar access points to most of the population regardless of their individual religious or secular backgrounds. Medicalization specifically grants mindfulness access to many new sites otherwise off-limits for mere spirituality, such as hospitals, schools, and other places where secular culture tends to set the terms of acceptable discussion and practice.

Advocates for the medicalization of mindfulness believe that in Buddhist meditation they have found a powerful method for healing body and mind, a method that should not be confined to monks or even to the larger Buddhist community. The various strategies explored in this chapter are employed to hoist mindfulness out of a religious context and re-embed it specifically in a secular, scientific, Western biomedical framework. Once this is accomplished, mindfulness becomes available as a resource for any American doctor, therapist, or scientist who wishes to adapt it to his or her interests and needs.

Beginning originally with mindfulness applied to reduce stress and enhance relaxation, this process has resulted in an explosion of specifically mindfulness-based new forms of therapy, prescriptions of mindfulness for the treatment of an ever-growing list of physical ailments, and clinical tests to determine the extent and mechanism of mindfulness's power to aid in the treatment of illness. A whole industry of medical mindfulness has emerged, with conferences, speaking circuits, centers for the study and dissemination of mindfulness, a vast and growing book culture, newsletters, and practical implementation in a large number of venues. All of this takes place outside of formal Buddhism in the United States.

But that does not mean that Buddhism is uninvolved in the transfer of authority over mindfulness from religion to science, nor is it unaffected by the process. This encounter and exchange between Asian Buddhist practice and American medical practice is a two-way street. As this chapter also demonstrates, American Buddhists are pervasively influenced by the medicalization and especially psychologization of mindfulness. Major figures in the medicalized mindfulness movement are quoted by Buddhists in Buddhist settings, and mindfulness has come to be valued as much (if not more) for its ability to provide practical medical and psychological benefits to Buddhist practitioners as for its ability to convey them across to the other shore of nirvana. Sensing the opportunity to attract large numbers of new adherents, as well as genuinely desiring the benefits proposed by the meditating doctors and therapists, Buddhists have actively cooperated in the medicalization of their religion. At the same time, there are voices of dissent from within the tradition, suspicious of the changes demanded by such recontextualizations. Some fear that the transcendent element of Buddhism is in danger of being lost entirely, while others feel that mindfulness has been misunderstood on a basic level by its newest fans. Even medical mindfulness's greatest proponents occasionally show signs of surprise or chagrin at the degree to which their program has been carried out, or some of the secondary affects it has had on Buddhism in America.

Meditation and Medicine Prior to 1979

The universally acknowledged turning point for the mindfulness movement's relationship with science and medicine is 1979, when Jon Kabat-Zinn started the Stress Reduction and Relaxation Program at the University of Massachusetts Medical School. That watershed development is examined in depth in the text that follows. But first a look at how Americans were relating to meditation practice prior to that moment helps to put Kabat-Zinn's work into greater context, reveals the extent to which he was innovating, and demonstrates how much he was continuing preexisting trends.

Early research on meditation by doctors tended to be concerned with discerning what was occurring during the process of meditation, especially the higher states of ecstasy and mystical union described by religious virtuosos. It sought psychological explanations for understanding these uncanny phenomena, rather than considering what practical benefits might be gained by medicine from teaching meditation to ordinary people. A good example of this type of research is Arthur Deikman's 1963 article "Experimental Meditation" in *The Journal of Nervous and Mental Disease.*[4]

By the 1950s, Zen Buddhism had already attracted the notice of certain segments of the American populace, primarily members of the emergent (especially California-based) counterculture and some style-conscious culture mavens of the (especially New York City–based) elite. Some psychotherapists had also taken note, and in particular there were prominent encounters and exchanges between Westerners and the Japanese Zen scholar D. T. Suzuki.[5] But though Suzuki talked about meditation in some of his works, he did not present himself as a meditation teacher, and the Western psychotherapists appeared entranced primarily by the "Zen attitude" and some elements of Buddhist cosmology and view, rather than the specifics of Zen meditation practices.

The first Asian meditation technique to truly gain widespread attention in the United States was Transcendental Meditation (TM), which first appeared here in the late 1950s and gained prominence in the later 1960s. By the early 1970s TM was being subjected to a variety of psychology-based clinical tests seeking to determine the physiological and psychological effects of meditation, often conducted by TM movement-connected figures and published in non–peer-reviewed media. TM itself was enthusiastically promoted by the Maharishi Mahesh Yogi as scientific, not religious, in a process eventually followed—indeed, perfected—by the mindfulness movement.[6] Many of the current applications of mindfulness find their parallel in the American encounter of TM by the 1970s, such as attempts to bring TM into the school system, a scientific and psychological framing, and the use of clinical trials to claim empirical demonstration of the beneficial nature of meditation.

At the same time, mindfulness has gone well beyond TM in terms of successful integration into American culture, both within the medical establishment and society at large, and easily eclipses TM in terms of cultural impact today, which began to decline in 1976.[7] This greater current success of mindfulness compared to TM is likely due to at least two factors. First, access to TM was relatively restricted—though it was widely publicized, actual practice could proceed only after one paid a fairly high fee and received a secret mantra from a guru during a mandatory initiation ceremony in the form of a puja (worship ceremony). This kept the power over TM relatively centralized and reduced the capacity of TM to flow into new communities and venues for new applications. Second, despite the persistent scientific framing of TM, it had an inherently greater religious component compared to mindfulness. This manifested in a variety of ways: TM was controlled by gurus, whom followers were encouraged to view in a devotional fashion; TM involved meditation on Sanskrit mantras derived from the Hindu tantric traditions, with connections to Hindu deities or concepts; TM was integrally connected to ideas such as reincarnation and God-consciousness (which were—perhaps unconvincingly—touted as scientific truths); and the benefits associated with TM included supernatural powers such as levitation. This decreased TM's ability to penetrate into secular arenas and provoked criticism from both liberal and conservative Christians.[8] These trends contrast with mindfulness, which progressively decentered its forms of authority, and was more effectively stripped of devotional, supernatural, and overtly Asian elements. We cannot ignore the possible effect of race in the situation as well. The Maharishi was a brown-skinned Indian man with a big beard and long, somewhat unkempt hair worn forward of the shoulders, who typically appeared in yoga robes with Hindu prayer beads. As Jane Naomi Iwamura demonstrates, reaction to TM was often mediated by stereotypes of "Oriental monks" applied to the Maharishi, the iconic face of the movement.[9] Jon Kabat-Zinn, the face of MBSR, is a clean-shaven white American doctor with short hair and rimless glasses, who delivers his teachings in business attire.

It is informative to note the way in which TM did most successfully establish an enduring presence in Western biomedicine and psychology: via the Relaxation Response. Transcendental Meditation was one important influence on the work of Herbert Benson, whose best-selling 1975 book *The Relaxation Response* recommends using single-pointed concentration (not mindfulness-type open awareness) to achieve relaxed, altered states of consciousness that purportedly have wide-ranging health benefits.[10] But the Relaxation Response is not TM: it just takes the general idea of focusing on something (a word, sound, thought, just about *anything*) and uses that to induce a release of stress via a passive mental and physical state. It does not carry the same label, use the same terms, utilize the same specific techniques, draw on the same concepts, or employ the same structures of organization and authority as TM.

Many of the first important American practitioners of mindfulness in the 1970s appear to have had an interest in Buddhism's intersection with psychology. One example is Daniel Goleman. Today Goleman is internationally famous as the best-selling author of the book *Emotional Intelligence* (which promotes Jon Kabat-Zinn's MBSR work) and similar works.[11] He wrote his Harvard University PhD dissertation in psychology on meditation and stress reactivity. Goleman became involved in meditation as a student in Berkeley during the 1960s and went to India on scholarship to pursue meditation techniques for his doctoral work. A student of the Hindu guru Neemkaroli Baba, Goleman was drawn into the orbit of Asian and Western Buddhist practitioners in northern India.[12] There Goleman practiced mindfulness meditation alongside Joseph Goldstein, Ram Dass, and others. He was also influenced by encounters with such mindfulness proponents as S. N. Goenka, Anagarika Munindra, and Nyanaponika Thera.

At least in his early writings, Goleman's interest wavered in respect to practical benefits that might result from mindfulness meditation. His 1976 article in the *American Journal of Psychotherapy* is concerned mainly with investigating how classical Buddhism approaches the achievement of mental health. He describes meditation as the primary means for mental health in the Buddhist system, with particular attention given to the practice of mindfulness, which he characterizes as a means of reprogramming perception and cognition in order to produce a transformation of mind: "This method involves facing each mind-moment, each experience, each event, as though it were occurring for the first time, rather than allowing perception to become habituated or overridden by cognitive coding…The net effect of mindfulness is deconditioning of habitual response patterns. As mindfulness progressively matures into insight, there is a gradual transformation of consciousness whereby, in a series of step-functions, subsets of unhealthy factors are said to be eradicated from one's psychologic economy."[13] This culminates in the attainment of the level of an arahat, the iconic Theravada Buddhist sage, who enjoys a package of benefits that Goleman characterizes in the following manner:

> *Absence* of greed for sense objects; anxiety, resentments, or fears of any sort; dogmatisms such as the belief that this or that is "the Truth"; aversion to conditions such as loss, disgrace, pain, or blame; feelings of lust or anger; experiences of suffering, need for approval, pleasure or praise; desire for anything for oneself beyond essential and necessary items; past conditioning as a major determinant of present behavior; and

> *Prevalence* of impartiality toward others and equanimity in all circumstances; ongoing alertness and calm delight in any and all situations; strong feelings of compassion and loving kindness; quick and accurate perception; composure and skill in actions; openness to others and responsivity to their needs; immunity from conditioning.[14]

It is important to note that Goleman never raises the most distinctive—from the traditional Buddhist point of view—aspect of an arahat: he or she has cut off the process of karma and therefore is no longer subject to wandering in endless eons of rebirth, but instead shall pass away into final nirvanic bliss at the end of his or her current lifetime. Indeed, rebirth, past lives, and posthumous states never enter into his discussion. Goleman speculates, based on the earlier quoted list, that mindfulness may prove beneficial to Western psychotherapy, but is more interested in the psychological mechanics that may be at work than the details of how to actually deliver a mindfulness-based psychotherapeutic program of action.

In his 1977 book *The Varieties of The Meditative Experience*, on the other hand, he is vaguely disdainful of using meditation "to fulfill those everyday goals and live out worldly visions."[15] Rather, he emphasizes that "meditation has been for millennia the path for the person who seeks to go beyond the limiting goals of the everyday world."[16] His interest is in altered states achieved via meditation, and the transcendent nirvanic horizon toward which such practice points. To this end, he explores various religious forms of meditation, including at least brief consideration of everything from Jewish Kabbalah to Zen. But his greatest interest is, once again, in the mindfulness practice associated with Southeast Asian Theravada Buddhism. He frames the entire book with an extended discussion of the *Visuddhimagga* (a traditional Buddhist commentary), which he characterizes as "a map for inner space."[17] He uses this map to explore how closely other forms of meditation conform to the archetypal presentation of the *Visuddhimagga*. Experiences that arise on the way to nirvana and could be independently promoted as practical benefits of mindfulness practice—such as feelings of rapture, tranquility, energy, happiness, and clear perception—are treated as mere side effects that can dangerously sidetrack the meditator from the authentic goal of nirvana.[18] As might be expected from a work by a recently minted PhD in psychology, there is a persistent framing of the ancient source material in psychological terms. For example, he opens his discussion of the *Visuddhimagga* by stating that "The classical Buddhist *Abhidharma* is probably the broadest and most detailed traditional psychology of states of consciousness."[19]

Insight Meditation Society co-founder Jack Kornfield was also investigating the intersection of Western psychology and Buddhist mindfulness. In his 1977 PhD dissertation, "The Psychology of Mindfulness Meditation," he carried out research on participants in long-term mindfulness retreats conducted in the United States.[20] He introduced his form of Buddhist practice with the following characterization: "Theravada Buddhism, the living tradition of Southeast Asia and Ceylon, is a religion and a system of mental culture that stems from an early school of psychology, founded by Sakyamuni Buddha in the sixth century."[21] Kornfield is basically having it both ways: he acknowledges that Buddhism is a religion, but he also frames it as an ancient form of psychology, with the implication that the Buddha was a type of psychologist. This is the approach he has taken throughout his career: for example, more than thirty years later his 2008 book was titled *The Wise Heart: A Guide to the Universal Teachings of Buddhist Psychology*.[22]

In his dissertation research, Kornfield was concerned to discern the mental effects of both the retreat experience and intensive mindfulness meditation practice. His interview data capture a wide range of effects, including many things that are left out of contemporary research on and advocacy of mindfulness. For example, many of his interviewees reported negative effects of mindfulness practice, such as nightmares, anger, pain, mood swings, fear, paranoia, hatred, uncontrollable bodily movements, hallucinations, and psychological tension. Another class of effects erased from current scientific discussions of mindfulness is psychic phenomena. Significant numbers of mindfulness practitioners on retreat reported manifestations of telepathy, precognition, or out-of-body experiences. Kornfield also notes that some people appear unable to meditate and that some report no positive effects from mindfulness practice, phenomena that are also left out of most current discussions of mindfulness for the masses.

Various more positive effects that some participants reported also show up in Kornfield's research, including greater feelings of love, resolution of psychological tension, reduced eating, elimination of stress and anxiety, and greater concentration. But he is not principally concerned with such low-level negative or positive effects of meditation. He always relates the greatest results to classical Buddhism: mindfulness's most transforming consequences, he claims, are the product of seeing through the illusion of the ego-self and discerning the fact of impermanency in a ceaselessly changing world.[23] He discusses at length how various psychological theories might help make sense of what happens in the process of mindfulness, as well as discussing the ways that Buddhist psychology and practice can contribute to Western theory. Significantly, on his list of research he hoped to see conducted in the future we find the following: "Study of the use of mindfulness in working with chronic pain, using attention directed to the pain as a strategy in pain relief."[24] So Kornfield, at least, was already speculating on the possibility of mindfulness applied to pain reduction prior to Kabat-Zinn's creation of MBSR. At the same time, we must note that it was an idea for the future, not part of Kornfield's research, and there is no indication that Kornfield foresaw systematic training in clinical settings as a way to deal with pain.

Kornfield's dissertation is, of course, thoroughly psychological. It is also thoroughly Buddhist. He draws on ancient and modern Buddhist texts for his analyses, advocates morality as the foundation for meditation, discusses everything from karma to chakras, and ends his text with a Theravadin prayer for lovingkindess. Though Buddhism is framed as psychology, it is also overtly and indelibly religious in his presentation. Kornfield is not concerned to minimize mindfulness's religious nature or to distance it from Buddhism. In fact, at this time period Kornfield was explicit that he considered psychology a useful adjunct to Buddhism, but that Buddhism was superior to psychology. As he put it in a symposium held at Mount Baldy Zen Center in July 1978: "There has been such an interchange between spiritual practice and psychological growth and human potential movements that there is a prevalent notion, at least in the psychological world, that western psychology can actually get you to the same place as spiritual practice. I think this is really quite a dangerous assumption. From my observation of how psychological techniques work I see that although they can lead to some very useful growth and transformation, they do not develop the penetrating insight that helps one cut through the deeper layers of illusion and hallucinations about individual separateness. They also do not create the space for what we might call a mystical appreciation of the world. They are useful techniques but their limitations have to be explicitly stated or people can get caught in them as a dead-end."[25]

But in a 1979 article in the *Journal of Transpersonal Psychology*, much of the religious material from his dissertation is muted.[26] Largely a summation of the findings of his dissertation research, Kornfield's more public article in an academic journal lacks the reverent attitude toward Buddhism and omits most of the Buddhist framing. Some of this could be due to the much shorter nature of the article versus the dissertation, but the change toward a much drier and more detached tone is clearly an effect of the different venue. In his dissertation, read by a carefully chosen small pool of sympathetic insiders, Kornfield doesn't hide his Buddhism. In the academic journal Kornfield holds Buddhism at arm's length—certainly not denying it, but writing in a way that puts some distance between Kornfield the scientist and Kornfield the meditation teacher.

Skillful Means and the Genesis of MBSR

As we've just seen, interest in the encounter between psychology and mindfulness was already brewing in the later 1970s, and some saw Buddhism as a kind of psychological school. Importantly, Jon Kabat-Zinn was already traveling in the same circles as Daniel Goleman, Jack Kornfield, and similar thinkers. In fact, it is directly from the Buddhist mindfulness community that MBSR appeared. Jon Kabat-Zinn describes the origin of MBSR in a passage so remarkable it bears extensive quotation:

On a two-week *vipassanā* retreat at the Insight Meditation Society (IMS) in Barre, Massachusetts, in the Spring of 1979, while sitting in my room one afternoon about Day 10 of the retreat, I had a "vision" that lasted maybe 10 seconds... It was rich in detail and more like an instantaneous seeing of vivid, almost inevitable connections and their implications. It did not come as a reverie or a thought stream, but rather something quite different, which to this day I cannot fully explain and don't feel the need to. I saw in a flash not only a model that could be put in place, but also the long-term implications of what might happen if the basic idea was sound and could be implemented in one test environment—namely that it could spark new fields of scientific and clinical investigation and would spread to hospitals and medical centres and clinics across the country and around the world, and provide right livelihood for thousands of practitioners. Because it was so weird, I hardly ever mentioned this experience to others. But after that retreat, I did have a better sense of what my karmic assignment might be. It was so compelling that I decided to take it on wholeheartedly as best I could...[27]

In the midst of an extended mindfulness retreat at a Buddhist center, Kabat-Zinn has a decidedly non-rational visionary experience that resolves his decade-long search for a meaningful purpose in life. In other religious traditions, we would call this a divine revelation. But the calling is to be a profoundly secular prophet of sublimated Buddhist practice, as he explains: "It struck me in that fleeting moment that afternoon at the Insight Meditation Society that it would be worthy work to simply share the essence of meditation [...] with those who would never be able to hear it through words and forms that were being used at meditation centres... Why not try to make meditation so commonsensical that anyone would be drawn to it? Why not develop an American vocabulary that spoke to the heart of the matter, and didn't focus on the cultural aspects of the traditions out of which the dharma emerged...[because] they would likely cause unnecessary impediments for people who were basically dealing with suffering and seeking some kind of release from it."[28] As in Chapter 2, we see here the anxiety that Buddhism's foreignness prevents its message of liberation from being heard in American society. Many practitioners of Buddhist meditation fear that Americans are fundamentally unable to accept things that are unfamiliar. There also seem to be underlying unresolved tensions in such practitioners themselves, who feel benefitted by Buddhism but are uncomfortable with aspects of the tradition as they have received it. Allegations of xenophobia by others can also provide a convenient reason for removing parts of Buddhism that adapters themselves dislike.

The role of hospitals as the environment for this newly Americanized mindfulness was the central feature of Kabat-Zinn's vision: "What better place than a hospital to make the dharma available to people in ways that they might possibly understand it [...] since the entire raison d'etre of the dharma is to elucidate the nature of suffering and its root causes, as well as provide a practical path to liberation of suffering? All this to be undertaken, of course, without ever mentioning the word 'dharma.' "[29] To understand what Kabat-Zinn means here, it is crucial to examine how Kabat-Zinn construes the term dharma. A Sanskrit term, dharma (Pali = *dhamma*) carries different meanings in Buddhism, Hinduism, and Jainism. Even within Buddhism alone, a wide range of meanings are attached to this word, including the nature of liberated reality itself, teachings that correctly accord with that reality and lead to liberation, and the specific teachings of the Buddha (which accord with reality and result in nirvana). The word can be translated literally as "law," which for some implies that dharma is akin to the laws of nature, that is, universal, scientific, rational, non-theistic, natural, self-evident, discernible, embedded in and regulating the world.

This is the tact that Kabat-Zinn takes, using the idea of reality itself to pry dharma loose from Buddhism and make it available for recontextualization. As he states: "The word *Dharma* refers to both the teachings of the Buddha and also the way things are, the fundamental lawfulness of the universe. So although the Buddha articulated the Dharma, the Dharma itself can't be Buddhist any more that the law of gravity is English because of Newton or Italian because of Galileo. It is a universal lawfulness."[30] Because no one can own the dharma, not even Buddhists, it is therefore free for appropriation by anyone, so long as the person remains faithful to the universal truths it expresses. It is not really religious, since truth transcends religion. "What the Buddhists call the Dharma is an ancient force in this world, much like the Gospels, except that it has nothing to do in essence with religious conversion or with organized religion, for that matter, or even with Buddhism per se, if one wants to think of Buddhism as a religion at all."[31] This separation of dharma from Buddhism allegedly does no violence to the dharma; in fact, it frees it from the potentially stifling effect of being accidentally wed to premodern, non-Western ideas and traditions.

As to harm it might do to Buddhism, Kabat-Zinn's level of concern seems to fluctuate. At times he is relatively dismissive of Buddhism, even in the company of Buddhists. At the First Buddhism in America Conference, held in Boston in 1997, he told his audience: "I really don't care about Buddhism. It's an interesting religion but it's not what I most care about. What I value in

Buddhism is that it brought me to the Dharma."[32] By this time he had stopped calling himself a Buddhist—not because he disagreed with Buddhism, but because he found the label too restrictive when his real focus was the universal dharma.

However, his remarks about Buddhism have to be understood in the light of his feelings about the universality of Buddhism's essence—the dharma—and his long-standing personal involvement in Buddhist organizations and practices. Kabat-Zinn is no opponent of Buddhism, only of certain interpretations or restrictions that might arise from too narrow an understanding of Buddhism and its goals. From the beginning of MBSR he has frequently been upfront about its origins in Buddhism, even as he sought to supersede them in certain ways. He was troubled when a participant at the Mind and Life III Conference, held in 1990, criticized the secularization of Buddhism. As Kabat-Zinn recalled in a later interview: "He was basically saying that we were taking some half-baked, reduced version of Buddhism and putting it out there as the total thing. He argued that such occurrences contribute to the decline of religion by secularizing it so that its sacred power is lost. I thought to myself, If that were true, I would quit tomorrow."[33] Such consequences were not his intention: "The intention and approach behind MBSR were never meant to exploit, fragment, or decontextualize the dharma, but rather to *recontextualize* it within the frameworks of science, medicine (including psychiatry and psychology), and healthcare so that it would be maximally useful to people who could not hear it or enter into it through the more traditional dharma gates, whether they were doctors or medical patients, hospital administrators, or insurance companies."[34]

Kabat-Zinn hasn't quit, so clearly he decided that he was not contributing to the decline of religion. Yet such questions continue to haunt him: "Maybe we're watering down the true Dharma and trying to justify that to ourselves. I actually ask myself that every day, and I don't believe that's the case."[35] Kabat-Zinn answers his own question in the negative, especially when the issue is framed as faithfulness to "true Dharma," not Buddhism per se. But we have to note, the question persists, day after day. This may be one reason why he has gone out of his way to seek validation for his methods from Buddhist tradition and Buddhist authorities. His stories repeatedly reference the permission provided by the 14th Dalai Lama.[36] He even describes traveling to an old temple in Kyoto where he asked a Rinzai Zen master whether he was right to abandon terms such as Buddha and Zen; when the master affirmed Kabat-Zinn's approach, he "felt this incredible reassurance that all the stuff I'd been reading and practicing had been a kind of living manifestation."[37]

It is important for Kabat-Zinn to emphasize the scientific nature of dharma. As he describes it: "In some ways it is appropriate to characterize dharma as resembling scientific knowledge, ever growing, ever changing, yet with a core body of methods, observations, and natural laws distilled from thousands of years of inner exploration through highly disciplined self-observation and self-inquiry, a careful and precise recording and mapping of experiences encountered in investigating the nature of the mind, and direct empirical testing and confirming of the results…Mindfulness and dharma are best thought of as universal descriptions of the functioning of the human mind regarding the quality of one's attention in relationship to the experience of suffering and the potential for happiness. They apply equally wherever there are human minds, just as the laws of physics apply equally everywhere in our universe."[38] This sort of description makes Kabat-Zinn's project a simple continuation of Buddhist tradition itself, which is a scientific tradition of psychology that has always been doing the same work as Kabat-Zinn, but confined within a particular religion.

In Chapter 2, we saw that mindfulness movement authors often render traditional Buddhist cosmology into metaphorical or symbolic terms. Because he is concerned to medicalize mindfulness and make it appear scientific, Kabat-Zinn tends to argue that Buddhist tropes are simply empirical descriptions of basic realities in nature. For example, his definition of karma in *Wherever You Go, There You Are* frames it scientifically: "Karma means that this happens because that happened. B is connected in some way to A, every effect has an antecedent cause, and every cause an effect that is its measure and its consequence, at least at the non-quantum level. Overall, when we speak of a person's karma, it means the sum total of the person's direction in life, and the tenor of the things that occur around that person, caused by antecedent conditions, actions, thoughts, feelings, sense impressions, desires."[39] There are two important things to note here. First, Kabat-Zinn uses scientific language to explain karma, drawing on basic physics. Second, Kabat-Zinn omits virtually everything that Buddhism historically taught about karma. In this description it is not connected to morality and immorality; does not arise from actions committed in previous lifetimes; will not result in rebirth in nonhuman states; and is not part of an invisible merit economy that can be manipulated by prayers, chanting, merit donation, and other religious practices. Karma is approached in a completely naturalistic fashion, without a trace of aspects that might contradict current Western scientific understandings of reality.[40]

Not only is Buddhism already scientific, but the Buddha was also a sort of doctor: "From the point of view of its universality, it is helpful to recall that the Buddha himself was not a Buddhist. He was a healer and a revolutionary, albeit a quiet and inward one. He diagnosed our collective human dis-ease and prescribed a benevolent medicine for sanity and well-being."[41] This idea does not originate with Kabat-Zinn. Many commentators have drawn an analogy between the Buddha and doctors. This allows Kabat-Zinn to pick up such analogies and use them in a rather literal way to justify his approach: "The Four Noble Truths were articulated by the Buddha in a medical framework, beginning with a specific diagnosis, dukkha itself: then a clearly stated etiology, that the dis-ease or dukkha has a specific cause, namely craving: a salutary prognosis, namely the possibility of a cure of the dis-ease through what he called cessation: and fourth, a practical treatment plan for bringing liberation from suffering, termed *The Noble Eightfold Path*."[42] If the Buddha is a doctor, then his course of treatment belongs in a medical setting, and there should be no difficulty in making the transition.

Mindfulness was not just a tool of attention in the understanding of the Stress Reduction Clinic workers. As Kabat-Zinn details in the foreword to *Clinical Handbook of Mindfulness*, the word was intended to cover both the act of awareness and "as an umbrella term that subsumes all of the other elements of the Eightfold Noble Path, and indeed, of the dharma itself, at least in implicit form... The choice to have the word *mindfulness* [do] double-duty [...] was made as a potential skillful means to facilitate introducing what Nyanaponika Thera referred to as *the heart of Buddhist meditation* into the mainstream of medicine and more broadly, health care and the wide society in a wholly universal rather than Buddhist formulation and vocabulary. I felt that Nyanaponika Thera's inclusive and non-dual formulation offered both validation and permission to trust and act on my own direct experience of the meditation practice and the dharma teachings I had received over the course of my life."[43] Mindfulness is an English word, not a foreign Sanskrit, Pali, or other Asian term. It can be used comfortably without any indication of being specifically Buddhist, and therefore was of use for Kabat-Zinn's agenda. At the same time, he intended mindfulness to mean not only awareness and meditation but also be shorthand for the Buddhist tradition, so that Buddhism could be brought into non-Buddhist settings by simply substituting a different word that would not set off alarm bells. Arguably, then, when Kabat-Zinn speaks of Mindfulness-Based Stress Reduction he in fact *means* Buddhist-Based (or at least Dharma-Based) Stress Reduction, given this intended double definition of mindfulness.

One of the key concepts that Kabat-Zinn gestures to here is skillful means. This is a common term employed when explaining why he decided to take the dharma to the medical establishment, and do so in a way that minimized its Buddhist context: "mindfulness-based stress reduction (MBSR) was developed as one of a possible infinite number of skillful means for bringing the dharma into mainstream settings. It has never been about MBSR for its own sake."[44] Skillful means (Sanskrit = *upaya*) is an important concept in Buddhism, one that Americans often gesture toward in their adaptive processes. Essentially, it means adjusting the teaching of Buddhism to fit the capacities of the particular audience in any given situation. The idea is especially associated with the Mahayana branch of Buddhism (such as Zen), where it finds its most classic exposition in the Lotus Sutra. In the sutra, the Buddha proclaims that many of his previous teachings were just skillful or expedient means meant to entice ignorant people to begin practicing Buddhism. Now, however, he is prepared to reveal the truest, highest teachings of Buddhism, which seem to contradict the earlier ones because those were just partial or false ideas designed for people of lower capacities. Various parables illustrate this concept, such as a father who pretends to be dying so that his children will drink medicine to cure their poisons; a father who tells his children that he will give them various kinds of carts if they exit a burning house, but actually only intends to give them the best kind; and a caravan-leader who conjures an illusory city so that weary travelers can rest before pushing on with their journey to the real destination. The point of all of these stories is that the Buddha deceives his followers for their own good, but cannot be accused of mistreating them because he acts out of compassion and everyone is better off in the end. In vociferous attacks on non-Mahayana forms of earlier Buddhism, the authors of the Lotus Sutra allege that other Buddhists are misled by the mere expedient teachings the Buddha initially gave, whereas the Mahayana Buddhists are following the true teachings—teachings that appear to be contradictory because the earlier teachings were incorrect ideas ladled out to the inferior monks who couldn't handle the full truth yet.

Despite being associated with the Mahayana school, skillful means also appear in Theravada Buddhism as well. One example is the story of Kisa Gotami, a traditional narrative that has become one of the most popular tales in American Buddhism. Gotami's infant child dies and she is driven mad with grief. She carries the rotting corpse with her everywhere, refusing to acknowledge the baby's death. When she encounters the Buddha, she requests that he heal her son so that he will recover. Surprisingly, the Buddha agrees to do so. But he requires that she first bring him a mustard seed from a home that has never known death. Gotami eagerly rushes off to the village, but at house after house she learns that someone has previously died there. Finally it dawns on her that death comes to all. This shakes her from her madness, and leaving her child's body at the charnel ground she returns to the Buddha to become a nun. In the story the Buddha promises to magically heal the child, something he has no intention of doing (and perhaps is incapable of). But the false promise is actually intended to bring about the healing of the mother's disordered mind, so that she can proceed on to nirvana. Thus the Buddha acts rightly—this is not an instance of wrong speech, but a moment of compassion via the skillful use of situationally appropriate means. Buddhists were not unaware of the potential for abuse in these concepts, and traditionally these fine-tunings of the teaching to meet various circumstances were usually reserved for actual buddhas and advanced bodhisattvas, as only they are so wise, compassionate, and skilled that deception can be used appropriately to help others farther back on the path.

When Kabat-Zinn and other Americans draw on the concept of skillful means, they authorize themselves via the example of the Buddha to change aspects of the tradition to better suit the different environmental circumstances of Buddhism outside its premodern and Asian historical context. This can mean using English rather than an Asian language to transmit Buddhism, instituting democratic modes of decision making into Buddhist communities, charging for teachings normally provided for free, or any number of other innovations. Invocation of the doctrine of skillful means is nearly universal in American Buddhism. Most applications do not involve deception, though some degree of mystification is quite common. In the case of Kabat-Zinn's development of MBSR, skillful means authorizes not only wholesale changes in where, how, and for what ends Buddhism is taught, but it also sanctions the intentional muting of the connection between mindfulness and Buddhism, the better to serve the interests of the universal dharma.

This usage of skillful means rhetoric in fact leans toward an even more urgent interpretation: if people can best be freed from their suffering by being taught a Buddhist meditation technique never identified as such, then not only is that OK, but it is also what *should* be done. In Kabat-Zinn's rhetoric, MBSR actually becomes the proper next stage for Buddhism's development: "One might say that in order for Buddhism to be maximally effective as a dharma vehicle at this stage in the evolution of the planet, and for its sorely needed medicine to be maximally effective, it may have to give up being Buddhism in any formal religious sense, or at least, give up any attachment to it in name or form."[45] Buddhists should not be attached (attachment being the great bugaboo of Buddhism) to Buddhism, we are told—they should freely let Buddhism be subsumed into the medical industry, the better to achieve the Buddhist goal of ending suffering.

Mindfulness-Based Stress Reduction: Buddhism by Any Other Name

How is MBSR actually taught and practiced?[46] Variations on the practice have been worked out in different clinics across America, but it seems best to look first and foremost at that used by the Center for Mindfulness in Medicine, Health Care, and Society, which grew out of the original Stress Reduction Clinic. In examining the process of MBSR, we see both how it retains considerable aspects of its Buddhist parentage, as well as undergoes evolution in response to its new situation.

The classic MBSR course was originally a ten-week program, held once a week for two hours in the clinic. It was based primarily on extended vipassana meditation courses Kabat-Zinn had experienced at Insight Meditation Society. But instead of a ten-day intensive retreat, the course was delivered once a week over ten weeks so that ordinary people with busy lives could be involved. Participants were also assigned home practice for six days a week, consisting of forty-five minutes of daily meditation, guided by audio recordings. Other homework assignments included exercises such as noticing a pleasant event each day of the week; the following week they repeat, but now focusing on unpleasant events. In either case, they were simply to be present with the sensations, not moving toward or away from them mentally.

This model remains mostly intact today, though more commonly the course is delivered in eight weeks with 2.5-hour sessions (so the total amount of time is the same, but the course is completed 20 percent sooner). The weekly sessions typically enroll thirty to forty people, who sit together in a circle or lie on the floor depending on the exercise being practiced. Instructors guide participants in learning how to do basic mindfulness meditation. One method is the body scan. Participants begin by focusing their attention on their breathing, especially the rising and falling of the chest, similar to the method practiced in the Mahasi Sayadaw lineage of vipassana meditation. Next they move their attention to their left foot, connecting it to their awareness of the breath. On the out breath, they mentally release tension in the physical area under attention. They note any sensations, neither attaching to them nor pushing them away. This proceeds through the entire body, part by part, in a process that takes about forty-five minutes.

After working with the body scan, participants are taught sitting meditation. They follow the breath in and out with their mind, eventually expanding their awareness to encompass the whole body. If they discover areas of pain—physical or emotional—they can maintain their focus there. But they are not told to do anything about it. The process is simply one of noting and allowing things to be how they are. Further instructions direct participants to focus on an object other than the physical body, such as the flow of consciousness, feelings, or sounds. Sitting meditation ends with pure awareness focused on no specific object. MBSR also includes yoga stretching and postural forms, conducted with the same Buddhist-based mindfulness techniques.

Various other exercises occur during the training, such as a raisin-eating practice based on vipassana retreat techniques: participants eat one raisin at a time, slowly, experiencing each physical movement and taste sensation. One important emphasis that is imparted is that mindfulness is supposed to be taken into each person's daily life, not just confined to the moments of formal meditation. As Kabat-Zinn writes, "The heart of the practice in MBSR lies in what we call informal meditation practice, i.e. mindfulness in everyday life. The true meditation practice is when life itself becomes the practice."[47] Mindfulness is to be a way of life, so that one walks, washes dishes, showers, and so on in a mindful manner. In this way, MBSR is not about short-term management of illness, the model most common in biomedical institutions and that governs the average patient's interaction with hospitals and clinics. Rather than dealing with sickness, MBSR proponents stress that they are trying to promote healing through a fundamental shift in understanding. Kabat-Zinn makes an important distinction in his book *Full Catastrophe Living*: "*Healing*, as we are using the word here, does not mean 'curing,' although the two words are often used interchangeably. As we shall see in the next chapter, there are few if any outright *cures* for chronic diseases or for stress-related disorders. While it may not be possible for us to *cure* ourselves or to find someone who can, it is possible to *heal* ourselves. Healing implies the possibility for us to relate differently to illness, disability, even death as we learn to see with the eyes of wholeness. As we have seen, this comes from practicing such basic skills as going into and dwelling in states of deep psychological relaxation and seeing and transcending our fears and our boundaries of body and mind. In moments of stillness you come to realize that you are already whole, already complete in your being, even if your body has cancer or heart disease or AIDS or pain."[48]

We should recognize right away that this is essentially a Buddhist approach to the existential facts of pain. "When we use the term *healing* to describe the experiences of people in the stress clinic, what we mean above all is that they are undergoing a profound transformation of view. This transformation is brought about by the encounter with one's wholeness, catalyzed by meditation practice."[49] Transformation of view is the essence of the Buddhist program for liberation from suffering in the round of rebirths: one overcomes ignorance and wrong attitude about oneself and the world, and the consequent mental realignment results in nirvana. This is ordinarily accomplished through a complex of practices that include purifying the mind, perfecting morality, and so on—but in the modern Buddhist world many practitioners—especially in Western, white-dominated Buddhist groups—hold that meditation is the most important (sometimes, the only necessary) practice for achieving this transformative vision of reality that delivers wisdom, compassion, and cessation of suffering.

In week six an eight-hour silent meditation retreat is held, using rules very close to those for actual Buddhist retreats: maintain silence; don't make eye contact with each other; and do all activities with mindfulness, such as mindful walking and mindful eating, etc. Vows against immorality aren't taken, but practically speaking it is hard to commit wrong actions while sitting in silence.

MBSR instructors stress the nonjudgmental application of awareness in the practice of mindfulness, and this is also how discussion in the MBSR classroom is conducted. Together, the instructors and participants explore in intimate detail the experiences of mindfulness and their relation to real life, in a process that Kabat-Zinn claims is influenced by Zen "dharma combat" modes of exchange.[50] There are also at least two personalized interviews built into the process, one at the start and one at the conclusion of the course. These are modeled on Zen interviews, though without using that label.[51] Buddhist-derived concepts such as suffering and impermanence are discussed, though more seemingly "religious" ideas such as reincarnation and nirvana are omitted. Crypto-Buddhism appears in many other aspects of MBSR as well. The choice to focus on "stress" reduction was a strategic way to talk about dukkha, the central concept in Buddhism, which can be rendered into English as stress or suffering (and picks up many new associations in the process).[52] Tibetan Buddhist Kalachakra mandalas are the inspiration for a teaching device often employed in MBSR training, involving concentric expanding rings of responsibility for the organization of MBSR sessions.[53] The symbol for the Center for Mindfulness in Medicine, Health Care, and Society is a depiction of Indra's Net, a motif drawn from the *Avatamsaka Sutra* that represents the infinite interconnection and mutual support of all things in the universe. Weekly MBSR teachers' meeting at the Center are referred to as "collegial sangha."[54]

The bar for instructors of MBSR is set relatively high. As the *Principles and Standards* of the Center for Mindfulness explain, "The teacher of MBSR [...] him or herself needs to have a longstanding grounding in meditative practices and be a committed student of the dharma, as it is expressed both within the Buddhist meditation traditions and in more mainstream and universal contexts exemplified by MBSR. This has nothing to do with being or not being a Buddhist."[55] Teachers must have an ongoing personal meditation practice, complete various training courses, receive certification, and regularly go on seven- to ten-day meditation retreats (preferably actual vipassana-oriented Buddhist ones). Not surprisingly, a quite significant number of MBSR teachers appear to be Buddhist practitioners (based on their various writings and public lectures), though there are many who come from other traditions, such as Christianity, Judaism, Bahai, and no affiliation.

Practical Medical Results of MBSR

A key part of the medicalization of mindfulness is the assertion that it delivers beneficial health effects, and that these can be measured and demonstrated in a scientific manner. The logic behind such endeavors should be obvious. If mindfulness improves health, then it deserves to be adopted by the medical and psychological establishments; if the benefits can be empirically shown via responsibly conducted clinical experiments, then denying the usefulness of mindfulness becomes an obstruction of the scientific process: to object to mindfulness is to object to the goal of health care itself.

The practical benefit that Kabat-Zinn most often claims is reduction in the amount of pain that MBSR practitioners report, as well as increased ability to deal with the pain that does persist. He also frequently claims that MBSR positively affects practitioners' moods and reduces their stress and anxiety. Precisely how these work is not totally clear, but he provides a laundry list of possible mechanisms at work in MBSR:

> There are many ways that mindfulness might influence susceptibility to, or ability to recover from, disability and disease. These may include (1) decreased perception of pain severity; (2) increased ability to tolerate pain or disability; (3) reduced stress, anxiety, or depression; (4) diminished usage of, and thereby reduced adverse effects

from analgesic, anxiolytic, or antidepressant medication; (5) enhanced ability to reflect on choices regarding medical treatments (eg, decision to seek a second opinion); (6) improved adherence to medical treatments; (7) increased motivation for lifestyle changes involving diet, physical activity, smoking cessation, or other behaviors; (8) enriched interpersonal relationships and social connectedness; and (9) alterations in biological pathways affecting health, such as the autonomic nervous system, neuroendocrine function, and the immune system.[56]

The final item on this list partially points to the recent popularity of neuroscientific studies of mindfulness, which appear to suggest that mindfulness actually alters the functioning and physical structure of the brain itself.

Naturally, Kabat-Zinn and his colleagues set out at an early stage in MBSR history to measure and demonstrate the health effects of mindfulness practice. The first significant journal publication on the topic was an article titled "An Outpatient Program in Behavioral Medicine for Chronic Pain Patients Based on the Practice of Mindfulness Meditation: Theoretical Considerations and Preliminary Results," appearing in *General Hospital Psychiatry* in 1982.[57] Authored by Kabat-Zinn, it very briefly describes the Buddhist origins of mindfulness and contrasts the practice with TM and other concentration forms of meditation. "All meditation practices used in the SR&RP were taught independent of the religious and cultural beliefs associated with them in their countries and traditions of origin," Kabat-Zinn assures his readers.[58] He also describes how meditation can itself lead to pain, due to the long periods of sitting involved. "Although this specialized use of attention can be used for the purpose of coping with pain in meditation sessions, it did not develop historically for that purpose," he points out. The basic process of MBSR (SR&RP, at that time) is laid out, as well as the general theory of mindfulness-based stress reduction. Kabat-Zinn then provides tables and extensive discussion to prove that participants in his study reported highly significant reductions in chronic pain, negative moods, and ability to function normally despite what pain persisted.[59]

Kabat-Zinn went on to publish over a dozen similar studies in medical journals, including *Journal of Behavioral Medicine, American Journal of Psychiatry, Journal of Urology*, and *Journal of the American Academy of Dermatology*, describing mindfulness-based treatment for everything from breast cancer to psoriasis. And he encouraged others to carry out many more studies, while cultivating a pool of students, protégés, and colleagues who furthered his work. With publications on mindfulness in the *Journal of the American Medical Association*, it is clear that Kabat-Zinn's approach has been accepted by the mainstream: mindfulness is acknowledged as having health benefits and to be appropriate for use in clinical environments.[60] This is despite caveats that Kabat-Zinn himself raises: "The available research on mindfulness has major limitations, precluding any definitive assessment of effectiveness at this time. Published clinical studies frequently have small numbers of participants, lack an active control group, and include only subjective end points. Most of these studies do not adequately consider participant characteristics (making it difficult to generalize the effects to other groups), treatment methods (relating to reproducibility), study staff protocol adherence and participant skill acquisition (treatment fidelity), and relevant covariates (confounders and mediators)."[61]

The influence of MBSR can be seen diverging along two primary tracks, based on the particular experts who promote them and the specific conditions mindfulness is applied to. On the one hand, there are the biomedical applications, such as Mindfulness-Based Stress Reduction in hospitals and the various brain studies that have derived from MBSR research. This research travels further into fields such as sports medicine and biofeedback techniques. This is the track that Kabat-Zinn has most often emphasized himself. His original training is neither in medicine nor psychology per se, but in molecular biology. This inclined him more toward the biomedical approach, as did his location specifically within a hospital setting. The biomedical track is reflected in many of the journal publications that Kabat-Zinn himself and his direct associates have published. It also appears in books for more popular audiences, such as *Here for Now: Living Well with Cancer Through Mindfulness* (2005), *Reversing Chronic Pain: A 10-Point All-Natural Plan for Lasting Relief* (2007), *Stop Pain: Inflammation Relief for an Active Life* (2010), and *Living a Healthy Life with Chronic Conditions: Self-Management of Heart Disease, Arthritis, Diabetes, Depression, Asthma, Bronchitis, Emphysema, and Other Physical and Mental Health Conditions* (2012).[62] All of these titles draw on MBSR to promote healing of specific medical conditions.

The other track is the specifically psychotherapeutic. The influence of MBSR appears in four interrelated areas: (1) use of mindfulness techniques in general therapeutic practice; (2) development of specific mindfulness-based therapies; (3) application of mindfulness to specific mental conditions; and (4) general books on mindfulness by psychiatrists, psychologists, and counselors for the consumption of the mainstream audience interested in self-help, popular psychology, and/or alternative lifestyles. Of course, we should not draw too hard a distinction between biomedical and psychotherapeutic applications. Both are forms of medical treatment, and MBSR clearly straddles any alleged line between them, as it is a mental technique that uses focused attention on one's physical body to bring about changes in both mood and perception of physical ailment.

Mindfulness as a general technique to use in counseling and psychotherapy has become quite popular, based especially though not exclusively on the MBSR model. For example, in *Meditation for Therapists and Their Clients* (2009), C. Alexander Simpkins and Annellen Simpkins describe mindfulness and other techniques that can enhance the therapeutic process: "Meditation can assist the therapeutic process from the very first session... Therapists who meditate develop clear, insightful understanding that improves discernment. This skill may help them to perceive beyond the presenting difficulty to the real problem, so that correct treatment can then follow."[63]

Just as MBSR has found biomedical approbation as represented by its presence in top journals, so mindfulness's utility in psychotherapy has been recognized in publications issued by the American Psychological Association. One example is Lorne Lader's chapter "Mindfulness" in *Spiritually Oriented Interventions for Counseling and Psychotherapy* (2011). As he describes, "I recall talking with colleagues as recently as the 1990s about our hesitance to present mindfulness meditation to clients, worrying that they might perceive such a practice as too spiritual, or Eastern, or Buddhist. The huge number of research articles, well-written books, conference presentations, and workshops on the integration of mindfulness—and other types of meditation—with psychotherapy have really put such concerns to rest."[64] Nonetheless, Lader states that he doesn't bring up Buddhism unless a client asks about it.[65] He asserts that many benefits can come of using mindfulness in therapy. For clients these include a sense of calm, lowered stress, less anxiety, improved self-control, greater self-acceptance, better communication of thoughts and feelings to the therapist, and other benefits. He suggests that mindfulness is "particularly beneficial for therapists," in order to "cultivate openness, non-judgmental awareness, and impartial or evenly hovering attention that is so important to psychoanalytically oriented therapies."[66]

Shari Geller and Leslie Greenberg go further in *Therapeutic Presence: A Mindful Approach to Effective Therapy* (2012), also published by the American Psychological Association. They reconceive of the entire therapeutic process as one of mindfulness:

> *Therapeutic presence* is the state of having one's whole self in the encounter with a client by being completely in the moment on a

multiplicity of levels—physically, emotionally, cognitively, and spiritually. Therapeutic presence involves being in contact with one's integrated and healthy self, while being open and receptive to what is poignant in the moment and immersed in it, with a larger sense of spaciousness and expansion of awareness and perception. This grounded, immersed, spacious awareness occurs with the intention of being with and for the client, in service of his or her healing process. The inner receptive state involves a complete openness to the client's multidimensional internal world, including bodily and verbal expression, as well as openness to the therapist's own bodily experience of the moment in order to access the knowledge, professional skill, and wisdom embodied within. Being fully present then allows for an attuned responsiveness that is based on a kinesthetic and emotional sensing of the other's affect and experience as well as one's own intuition and skill and the relationship between them.[67]

What we see here is that the therapist has become so mindful that she is in complete synch with the client. These seemingly Buddha-like powers of mindfulness enable her to discern the inner reaches of the body and mind via total attention, greatly assisting the process of healing sought through therapy.

Specific new forms of therapy are being produced that are based on or influenced by MBSR. These include Dialectical Behavior Therapy (DBT), Acceptance and Commitment Therapy (ACT), and Mindfulness-based Cognitive Therapy (MBCT). DBT originally was created to help treat people with borderline personality disorder. As the name implies, it focuses on balancing opposing ideas, especially acceptance and change. Mindfulness is employed to control attention, regulate emotion, increase tolerance to distress, and develop a generally aware approach to life. Both MBSR's medicalized model and the teachings of Thich Nhat Hanh have been important in the development of DBT.[68] ACT is influenced by relational frame theory and focuses on overcoming avoidance of negative thoughts, feelings, and urges.[69] Mindfulness is used to help clients acknowledge those internal states that have been avoided, the better to work with them in a healthy manner rather than using substance abuse and other harmful behaviors.[70] MBCT grew directly out of MBSR but was developed by Zindel Segal (based in Canada) and Mark Williams and John Teasdale (both based in the United Kingdom).[71] Like MBSR, it is delivered to small groups over an eight-week period, and uses many of the same mindfulness exercises. It includes Theravada

Buddhist-derived lovingkindness meditation, and is primarily focused on managing depression.[72]

MBSR has also given birth to a whole host of therapies for specific application, including Mindfulness-Based Eating Awareness Therapy (MB-EAT), Mindfulness-Based Art Therapy (MBAT), Mindfulness-Based Relapse Prevention (MBRP), and Mindfulness-Based Relationship Enhancement (MBRE). The basic method is to take a preexisting form of therapy and restructure it around the practice of mindfulness, using awareness as the new emphasis for achieving healing results. The range of uses for which MBSR is put can be discerned with a look at some recent representative publications that incorporate mindfulness in treating specific conditions. These include:

Anxiety: *Calming Your Anxious Mind: How Mindfulness and Compassion Can Free You from Anxiety, Fear, and Panic* (2003); *The Mindful Way Through Anxiety: Break Free from Chronic Worry and Reclaim Your Life* (2011)

Asperger's syndrome: *Mind/Body Techniques for Asperger's Syndrome: The Way of the Pathfinder* (2008); *Asperger Syndrome and Anxiety: A Guide to Successful Stress Management* (2009)

Attention deficit/hyperactivity disorder: *AD/HD for Dummies* (2005)

Bipolar disorder: *The Bipolar Disorder Answer Book: Answers to More Than 275 of Your Most Pressing Questions* (2007)

Depression: *Anxiety and Depression Workbook for Dummies* (2006); *The Mindful Way Through Depression: Freeing Yourself from Chronic Unhappiness* (2007)

Emotional disorders: *Emotional Healing Through Mindfulness: Stories and Meditations for Women Seeking Wholeness* (2002); *The Mindful Path to Self-Compassion: Freeing Yourself from Destructive Thoughts and Emotions* (2009); *Mind and Emotions: A Universal Treatment for Emotional Disorders* (2011)

Grief: *Grieving Mindfully: A Compassionate and Spiritual Guide to Coping with Loss,* (2005)

Perfectionism: *Present Perfect: A Mindfulness Approach to Letting Go of Perfectionism and the Need for Control* (2010)

Posttraumatic stress disorder: *Acceptance and Commitment Therapy for the Treatment of Post-Traumatic Stress Disorder and Trauma-Related Problems: A Practitioner's Guide to Using Mindfulness and Acceptance Strategies* (2007); *Post-Traumatic Stress Disorder for Dummies* (2008)

Shyness: *The Mindful Path Through Shyness: How Mindfulness and Compassion Can Help Free You from Social Anxiety, Fear, and Avoidance* (2009); *True Belonging: Mindful Practices to Help You Overcome Loneliness, Connect with Others, and Cultivate Happiness* (2011)

Substance addiction: *Mindful Recovery: A Spiritual Path to Healing from Addiction* (2002); *Creative Recovery: A Complete Addiction Treatment Program that Uses Your Natural Creativity* (2008)

Worry: *The Mindful Path Through Worry and Rumination: Letting Go of Anxious and Depressive Thoughts* (2009); *The Mindfulness Code: Keys to Overcoming Stress, Anxiety, Fear, and Unhappiness* (2010)[73]

As this list—which is not close to exhaustive—indicates, many of the medicalized mindfulness books published in the past decade or so are directed toward a general reading audience, often with the intention of giving them tools derived from Buddhism-based psychology to use in their own lives, outside of any formal therapist–client relationship. They vary in how much they discuss Buddhism: some are quite explicit in their connection to Buddhism, while others never mention religion at all. The thing to take away from all this is how MBSR is impacting the medical and psychological professions, being applied to an ever-expanding list of ailments and conditions, and providing income and employment for a substantial pool of therapists, authors, editors, publishers, and others who benefit from medicalized mindfulness. Kabat-Zinn intended MBSR to provide right livelihood for thousands, by which he meant the ability to make money in ways that contributed to the health of others and society without violating one's moral principles. By all appearances, he is well on the way to achieving this goal.

Conclusion

In this chapter, we have explored how Buddhism has entered into medical practice in America via mindfulness. But there is another side to this story: medicalized mindfulness has in turn influenced the presentation and self-understanding of American Buddhist practitioners. As MBSR increases in popularity and clinical tests suggest verifiable effects of mindfulness practice, Buddhists adjust their approach to their religion to take on board these seemingly positive developments. The result is that Buddhism becomes ever more enmeshed in medical, psychological, and scientific frameworks, with correspondingly less stress on supernatural, transcendent, or nirvanic elements.

Jon Kabat-Zinn's work is widely cited in the American Buddhist world and is held in nearly universal esteem. In his work Buddhists see validation of their decision to engage in or hold to religious practices that are outside the Judeo-Christian mainstream. Rather than possible framings of Buddhists as backwards, foreign, irrational, or idol-worshipping, MBSR and related neuroscientific research on mindfulness allows Buddhists to present themselves as being cutting-edge, compassionate, scientific, and useful. Thus we find Kabat-Zinn referenced approvingly in works by the most important authors in the American Buddhist scene, including Thich Nhat Hanh, Jack Kornfield, Lama Surya Das, Tara Brach, Pema Chodron, and many others.[74] A good example of this phenomenon is Ilana Rabinowitz's edited collection, *Mountains Are Mountains and Rivers Are Rivers: Applying Eastern Teachings to Everyday Life* (1999).[75] It collects excerpts from many of the most prominent names in American Buddhism, including Shunryu Suzuki, Alan Watts, Charlotte Joko Beck, Robert Aitken, and Gary Snyder. But who particularly dominates the volume? It is Jon Kabat-Zinn, who has eight different contributions, the most of any author. Fellow medicalized mindfulness authors Daniel Goleman, Mark Epstein, Jerry Braza, and Ronna Kabatznick all have contributions as well, as do mindfulness teachers Sylvia Boorstein, Joseph Goldstein, Sharon Salzberg, Larry Rosenberg, Myla Kabat-Zinn, Thich Nhat Hanh, Jack Kornfield, and Henepola Gunaratana. The result is that what Buddhism seems to offer American society is primarily mindfulness, and what mindfulness appears to be is primarily a set of therapeutic techniques for managing stress and similar issues. More to the point: Buddhism appears simply to be mindfulness, and mindfulness is a scientifically verified, non-supernaturalistic method for healing. As we saw in Chapter 2, *Shambhala Sun* was transformed by a visit from Jon Kabat-Zinn, with his secular, medicalized mindfulness becoming a major framing device for how the magazine delivered Buddhism to its large audience, and a second publication, *Mindful*, emerging wherein Shambhala's Buddhist publishers actively promote a de-Buddhicized version of mindfulness. The medicalization of mindfulness has so convincingly influenced North American Buddhism that many Buddhists see non-Buddhist therapeutic mindfulness as basically identical to their own practice; by implication, traditional aspects of Buddhism that are not psychotherapeutic or scientific come to seem strange or even to be direct obstructions to "correct" understandings and practices of Buddhism.

Reconceptualizing mindfulness as a biomedical or psychological technique moves the expertise into the scientific realm and aligns it with secular, modernist ideals. It legitimates mindfulness through the gatekeeping authority of science and institutionalized medicine. This allows it to infiltrate spaces that are held as off-limits to many religious practices, such as hospitals and public schools. Mindfulness advocates who would raise an outcry against Bible-reading or prayer as insurance-deductible medical practices or in-classroom stress-management activities readily promote Buddhist-derived mindfulness as a modern miracle technique and see no issue with HMOs covering MBSR. Doctors, therapists, teachers, principals, Buddhists, atheists—all can nod in agreement when Jon Kabat-Zinn asserts that "far from being magical or mystical, meditation is actually quite down-to-earth and practical."[76]

The process of domesticating mindfulness involves altering the sources of authority over Buddhist practice: the books and articles that stress the physical and psychological benefits of mindfulness practice often urge readers to seek out professional counselors to help them with mindfulness, but don't recommend receiving advice from an ordained Buddhist teacher or attending a temple in order to further their practice. In the mindfulness movement Buddhist practice has been removed from the realm of religion and professionalized to become the property of psychologists, doctors, scientists, and diet counselors, to be engaged in by clients rather than believers, who are not expected to take refuge, read scriptures, believe in karma or rebirth, or to become Buddhist. Meditation can be taught just as easily by non-Buddhists as by Buddhists, and Buddhists have no special claim to mindfulness practice.

Thus today large numbers of people engage in mindfulness in completely secular settings, overseen by experts trusted for their medical qualifications, and presumably benefitting from Buddhist meditation practices without ever learning about Buddhism. A further pool of people read about mindfulness in books stored in the health and fitness sections of libraries and bookstores, and carry out MBSR-derived practices in the privacy of their homes, guided by authors whose training took place in clinical environments, not zendos or ashrams. The strategy of promoting Buddhism by not promoting it as Buddhism seems to have worked amazingly well, and especially the tactic of emphasizing the positive results that accrue from mindfulness practices. In Chapter 4 we explore the myriad specific benefits that mindfulness is being marshaled to deliver.

4 MAINSTREAMING MINDFULNESS: HOW IS MINDFULNESS ADAPTED TO MIDDLE-CLASS NEEDS?

Mainstream: to bring into the mainstream

—Oxford English Dictionary[1]

Dr. Valerie Davis Raskin knew that America's mothers were having a bad time in the bedroom. A mother herself and a psychiatrist specializing in treating women with reproduction-related issues, she was keenly aware that motherhood and healthy sexuality often seemed mutually exclusive in today's society. As she explained in *Great Sex for Moms: Ten Steps to Nurturing Passion While Raising Kids* (2002): "I hear women feeling guilty, certain their husbands got cheated in the karma lottery when they got stuck with them, instead of all those other women who climax at the mere thought of intercourse. I hear how love and romance fade into the background of carpools, laundry, and bake sales. I hear about how years of Doing It the same way gets old. I hear about kids who barge into the parental bedroom, and kids who drain all energy, sexual and otherwise."[2]

In many ways, the lack of fun sex was indicative of larger troubling patterns in the United States, which sent people casting about for tools to deal with modern pressures. "Many Americans—rushed, driven, pressured, hassled, and drained—have turned to Eastern philosophy and spirituality to help them find meaning," she pointed out. "We're frustrated by a cultural heritage that values the goal, not the journey. We literally focus so much of our attention on achieving particular outcomes that we are always in motion, never where we want to be."[3] This spilled over to sex life, of course.

Luckily, Raskin had ten solutions for bringing back the spark. Among the recommendations such as buying sex toys, watching (tasteful) porn, improving partner communication, and so on, was the perhaps less anticipated step six: "Cultivate Sexual Mindfulness."[4] To achieve the goal, focus on the journey via mindfulness during foreplay and intercourse, she counseled. "Mindful sex means paying attention, engaging, giving, and staying open. It means letting go of performance anxiety, distraction, history, and body self-hatred...The concept of mindful sex is very simple. The goal of mindfulness in the context of lovemaking is to transform doing or performing into being—experiencing."[5] As she emphasized, "The key step to becoming more mindful in the bedroom is staying present in the erotic moment."[6] The result, she promised, would be greater sexual intimacy.

One searches in vain for discussion of mindful sexual intercourse in the traditional sati-related Pali suttas. But that does not mean that elaborations such as Raskin's are utterly foreign in the history of Asian Buddhism. Rather than focusing on the specifics of how mindfulness has been used, we should focus on the tradition of adapting Buddhism to meet the needs of each new culture that Buddhism has encountered. Recall the discussion of genze riyaku—practical or this-worldly benefits—in the introduction: Ian Reader and George Tanabe have identified practical benefits as one of the primary orientations of Japanese Buddhism. It is the ability of Japanese Buddhism to provide such everyday benefits desired by average Japanese people that allowed Buddhism to become entrenched in Japan, and as society changes, the benefits desired change too: today Japanese temples do a brisk business in automobile blessings and lucky charms to prevent car accidents, benefits that obviously weren't sought before the 20th century. So too the adaptability displayed in the modern mindfulness movement is emblematic of how Buddhism as a fluid religious system has survived and influenced a wide range of nations and cultures. In other words, what at first seems like a development without precedent—the changes made in the process of Americanizing mindfulness—actually reflect significant patterns within Buddhism's Asian history.

It should not be surprising that as Buddhism moves into a markedly different cultural sphere—the modern, industrialized, and apparently profoundly stressed-out West—it is being reshaped yet again to fit the desires of a new host country. This chapter investigates the ways in which mindfulness is being marshaled to meet the demands of mainstream American society, especially people in the urban/suburban, middle-class, married with 2.5 kids population that politicians seem to mean when they refer to "the American people." Buddhism is mainstreamed by being adapted to make the lives of these harried hockey dads and soccer moms better, one mindfully eaten cookie at a time. By looking at mindful eating, mindful sex and relationships, mindful work, and mindful parenting, we can discern the needs that most mindfulness movement authors feel, and we can observe how Buddhism is adjusted to help deliver culturally specific practical benefits. It is by meeting the mainstream needs of new cultures like America that Buddhism survives and take roots, even as it is profoundly changed in the process.

Practical Benefits of Mindfulness in the Pali Canon

Mindfulness meditation techniques developed within early Indian Buddhism and are recorded in various classic Pali scriptures, as discussed in Chapter 1. As reported in these scriptures and their commentaries, these techniques were used primarily by monks and nuns, for the purposes of detaching from the mind, body, and world and developing penetrative insight that leads to the achievement of nirvana. Thus benefits sought from mindfulness were mainly other-worldly in orientation and confined to the monastic sangha. Additional results were also sometimes said to come from diligent mindfulness practice. For example, in the *Kayagatasari Sutta* (Mindfulness of the Body Sutta) the Buddha provides a long list of benefits that come from proper mindfulness: conquering discontent, delight, fear, and dread; the ability to bear cold, heat, hunger, thirst, insect bites, wind, sun, insults, and severe pain; attainment of the highest concentrative trance meditative states; supernatural powers of hearing and sight; recollection of thousands of past lives and many complete cycles of creation and destruction of the physical universe; mind reading; the ability to multiply one's body; invisibility; the ability to pass through walls, dive into the earth, and walk on water; supernatural flight; the ability to stretch one's arms to touch the moon and sun; bodily mastery that extends throughout the universe, all the way to the highest immaterial heavenly realms; and purified mind.[7] The majority of benefits received from practicing mindfulness, therefore, were magical powers, and the Buddha and his most advanced monks are depicted using such powers many times in the Buddhist scriptures. One can see how much of this list would appeal to monastics, who need to develop equanimity while practicing in unfavorable conditions, discern the spiritual needs of laypeople, and use supernormal powers to impress the unconverted with the truthfulness of the Buddha's teaching; many of these powers are also helpful on one's own arduous journey to nirvana, such as recollection of past lives, which provides insight into the workings of karma, suffering, impermanence, and no-self. The Buddha speaks of such mindfulness-based powers with approval, but ultimately such powers are framed as ancillary to the main goal of detachment and nirvana.

The magical nature of the historical Buddha is not widely favored in the Western mindfulness movement, and so it is not surprising that the *Kayagatasari Sutta* is not often translated into English, even though it follows directly after the popular *Anapanasati Sutta* and deals with a subject (mindfulness of the body) that receives major attention in American publications. Likewise, the magical benefits of mindfulness are rarely referenced by Western meditation teachers with experience of practice in Asia. In his early book *Living Buddhist Masters*, Jack Kornfield writes: "Although meditation masters are few in contrast to the hundreds of thousands of other Buddhist monks in Southeast Asia, they are still among the best-known and the most highly respected members of their society. They are revered for their qualities of mind, their purity and saintliness, and in many cases for their powers that they are believed to possess. In this book, I have made almost no mention of the powers developed through meditation. This is in keeping with the meditation tradition of Southeast Asia, where even the most powerful and highly developed teachers do not particularly talk about or bother with magic, mystical energies or powers. Infatuation with power and mystery tends to sidetrack the development of compassion and wisdom, and all of these masters are concerned with only one thing—the deepening of insight leading to the full liberation of all beings."[8] Kornfield acknowledges that powers are common among Asian meditators, and that this accounts for a significant portion of their popularity, but refuses to discuss them with his English-reading American audience. He attributes reticence to talk about them to Asian teachers as well, but we should note that such teachers do not need to discuss them: they live in cultures that already expect meditation teachers to manifest such powers, and thus the laity automatically seek out benefits from association with teachers and swap stories about the magical abilities of high-level monks. Southeast Asian societies support a tremendous industry of Buddhist amulets, lucky charms, empowered images, photographs of advanced monks, and other material items similar to those found in Japan and other Buddhist countries, and the best meditators are frequently also the best sources of obtaining practical benefits (as well as merit for use in future lives). Meanwhile, meditation instructors trained solely in the West and lay American mindfulness practitioners are often completely unaware that mindfulness is embedded in magical contexts in Asia.

Instead of talking about powers or quoting from scriptures that reference them, American commentators tend to draw primarily from three more favored suttas: the *Satipatthana Sutta, Mahasatipatthana Sutta*, and the *Anapanasati Sutta*. These scriptures also teach of the benefits of mindfulness, but in less directly supernatural form. In the *Satipatthana Sutta* and the nearly identical *Mahasatipatthana Sutta* the Buddha teaches his monks a variety of methods for maintaining awareness of the body and mind.[9] In the opening section of both scriptures, he describes the purpose of mindfulness practices: "Bhikkhus, this is the direct path for the purification of beings, for the surmounting of sorrow and lamentation, for the disappearance of pain and grief, for the attainment of the true way, for the realization of Nibbāna— namely, the four foundations of mindfulness."[10] These are the seven benefits most commonly associated with mindfulness. That they are the expected benefits from mindfulness is confirmed by the way both suttas return to them for their conclusions, ending with this identical seven-part formula. They thus form the frame within which mindfulness practice is understood.

How are these seven benefits traditionally understood? We can get a glimpse of monastic attitudes by looking at commentaries, such as that provided by the Burmese monk Sayādaw U Janakābhivaṃsa.[11] As he explains, purification means eliminating the mental defilements, such as greed, desire, lust, craving, attachment, love, hatred, anger, ill-will, aversion, delusion, wrong view, concept, skeptical doubt, sloth, sleepiness, restlessness, remorse, and moral shamelessness and fearlessness.[12] The next two benefits he characterizes thusly: "The Second Benefit of mindfulness is the overcoming of sorrow and worry. You will not be worried about failure, or be sorry about the death of your relatives, or about the loss of your work. You will not be sorry about anything if you practice this mindfulness meditation...The Third Benefit is that of overcoming lamentation. Although your parents, children or relatives die, you will not have any lamentation for them because you have fully realised that mental and physical processes constitute the so-called 'child' or the so-called 'parents'. In this way, lamentation can be overcome by mindfulness meditation."[13] Janakābhivaṃsa then recites a story from a premodern commentary on the *Mahasatipatthana Sutta* to demonstrate this point. The disappearance of pain and grief mean elimination of physical and mental suffering, such as pain, itchiness, stiffness, and numbness, as well as unhappiness and depression. Janakābhivaṃsa actually feels that pains should be retained to some degree rather than eliminated, calling them "good friends" for the meditator: "This numbness or any painful sensation is the key to the door of *nibbāna* [nirvana]. When you feel pain, you are lucky. Pain is the most valuable object of meditation because it attracts the 'noting mind' to stay with it for a very long time...Proceeding with the practice, you will be able to realise the common characteristics of impermanence, suffering and no-soul or no-self nature or mental and physical phenomena. Then that will lead you to the cessation of all kinds of sufferings. So you are lucky if you have pain."[14] As he points out, some meditators who eliminate too much pain become dissatisfied with themselves and tuck their legs in a fashion designed to cause agony, so that they can continue to use it in their mindfulness practice. The final benefits are attaining enlightenment and nirvana.

In the suttas and monastic commentaries such as Janakābhivaṃsa's, mindfulness is clearly associated with traditional transcendent monastic concerns (nirvana). But when translated into English and not given any particular commentarial framing, language such as eliminating "sorrow," "pain," and "grief"—which in Asian monastic context suggests severing interpersonal attachments and escaping from this suffering world into nirvana—is ambiguous enough that it can be re-read to suggest applications to improve and enhance ordinary lay life. For example, Jon Kabat-Zinn quotes this exact passage from the sutta, but he does not put it in a traditional monastic commentarial context of nirvanic striving—he reads it to be pointing toward the elimination of the ordinary sufferings arising from inattention so that one can lead a "more satisfying and authentic life."[15] It is precisely this sort of slippage that allows for creative new adaptations, such as we see in the diversity of ways meditation is used in the mindfulness movement. In the American context, this means that mindfulness—historically associated with the transcendent, renouncing side of Buddhism, as well as in a more minor way with attainment of monastically-desired superpowers—is assimilated instead to an alternate but equally venerable strand of Buddhist tradition: the quest for practical, worldly benefits by lay Buddhists.

Thich Nhat Hanh and Everyday Miracles

How do Americans come to associate mindfulness as a technique that can potentially provide practical benefits in a nearly endless number of situations? There are a number of contributing sources. We have already seen that the Mindfulness-Based Stress Reduction program created by Jon Kabat-Zinn was oriented around using Buddhist meditation to deliver concrete healing benefits in both biomedical and psychotherapeutic situations. Given the immense cultural power of the biomedical and therapeutic establishments, and the popularity of MBSR as a specific program, this influence naturally is one major source for practical benefits-oriented mindfulness. Mindfulness moves from being taught in clinical situations to being discussed in books for general consumption, and soon enough techniques for the management of severe pain and crippling psychological issues are applied to the ordinary aches, frustrations, and stresses of contemporary life. More generally, we can note that many Buddhist teachers have promoted the practical mental benefits of meditation, either as a way of attracting newcomers to formal Buddhism, or as a sufficient reason to engage in Buddhist meditation.

Another primary source for practical benefits in mindfulness is the teachings of Zen Buddhism. Zen in the American mode is taught with a heavy stress on personal meditation practice on the one hand, and on the quotidian as the source of insight and pleasure, on the other. This approach arguably reaches its apogee in the works of Thich Nhat Hanh, the most popular of all Zen figures in America and perhaps the person most associated with mindfulness by Americans. His breakthrough book *The Miracle of Mindfulness!*, announces his stress on mindfulness teaching, and highlights its sublime nature. But what exactly is that miracle? He explains: "I like to walk along on country paths, rice plants and wild grasses on both sides, putting each foot down on the earth in mindfulness, knowing that I walk on the wondrous earth. In such moments, existence is a miraculous and mysterious reality. People usually consider walking on water or in thin air a miracle. But I think the real miracle is not to walk either on water or in thin air, but to walk on earth. Every day we are engaged in a miracle which we don't even recognize: a blue sky, white clouds, green leaves, the black, curious eyes of a child—our own two eyes. All is a miracle."[16] This miracle passes unnoticed unless one practices mindfulness. Then every moment and everything in this world becomes miraculous, wondrous, with no need to resort to supernatural powers or traditional Buddhist deities. This is the constant refrain of Thich Nhat Hanh's teaching of mindfulness, announced again and again in titles such as *Present Moment, Wonderful Moment: Mindfulness Verses for Daily Living* (1990), *Peace Is Every Step: The Path of Mindfulness in Everyday Life* (1991), and *You Are Here: Discovering the Magic of the Present Moment* (2009).[17] While he himself is a celibate monk, his positive, world-affirming message has attracted a large number of people with little interest in full renunciation. In this he is similar to other teachers, especially lay leaders of the vipassana movement, many of whom have sought to deemphasize traditional elements of Theravada Buddhism in order to propagate a stripped-down, meditation-based practice that they see as more appealing to everyday Americans.

Passages like the one just quoted tap into a deep well of nature spirituality in American religion, an orientation especially appreciated by the alternative spirituality types often drawn to Buddhism.[18] But Thich Nhat Hanh's real success comes about because of his way of making transcendence immanent in every action, no matter how mundane. Another passage from *The Miracle of Mindfulness!* illustrates this well: "If while washing dishes, we think only of the cup of tea that awaits us, thus hurrying to get the dishes out of the way as if they were a nuisance, then we are not 'washing the dishes to wash the dishes.' What's more, we are not alive during the time we are washing the dishes. In fact we are completely incapable of realizing the miracle of life while standing at the sink. If we can't wash the dishes, the chances are we won't be able to drink our tea either. While drinking the cup of tea, we will only be thinking of other things, barely aware of the cup in our hands. Thus we are sucked away into the future— and we are incapable of actually living one minute of life."[19] Thich Nhat Hanh's method of constant mindfulness returns the practitioner to the present moment and current activity, using that activity to hone one's mindfulness. In the process, the activity itself is enjoyed to a degree absent in the mindless dishwasher. This is not a mindfulness of detachment but of appreciation. Boring or arduous tasks become vehicles for touching the miraculous nature of life.

Thich Nhat Hanh promises that benefits will be derived from meditation. The fourth chapter of *The Miracle of Mindfulness!* begins "Why should you meditate?" Hanh answers that meditation provides total rest. The chapter concludes with a thorough discussion of Hanh's perceived benefits of mindfulness: "Sitting in meditation is nourishment for your spirit and nourishment for your body, as well. Through sitting, our bodies obtain harmony, feel lighter, and are more at peace. The path from the observation of your mind to seeing into your own nature won't be too rough. Once you are able to quiet your mind, once your feelings and thoughts no longer disturb you, at that point your mind will begin to dwell in mind. Your mind will take hold of mind in a direct and wondrous way which no longer differentiates between subject and object. Drinking a cup of tea, the seeming distinction between the one who drinks and the tea being drunk evaporates. Drinking a cup of tea becomes a direct and wondrous experience in which the distinction between subject and object no longer exists."[20] Here, Thich Nhat Hanh is smudging the line between the transcendent and this-worldly. He is gesturing toward deep Mahayana teachings about the interconnectedness of all things and the emptiness of self-nature of every phenomenon, which are realizations connected to the attainment of Buddhahood. But he is not speaking explicitly of Buddhahood—he is talking of nourishment for the spirit and body, and promising that mindfulness will bring peacefulness, harmony, and a lessening of burdens.

In language that directly connects Asian Buddhist monastic meditation practices with the metaphysical strain of religion in America, Thich Nhat Hanh says: "When possessed by a sadness, an anxiety, a hatred, or a passion or whatever, the method of pure observation and recognition may seem difficult to practice. If so, turn to meditation on a fixed object, using your own state of mind as meditation's subject. Such meditation reveals and heals. The sadness or anxiety, hatred or passion, under the gaze of concentration and meditation reveals its own nature—a revelation that leads naturally to healing and emancipation."[21] Healing and emancipation: here we have the two goals of American metaphysical religion and Asian monastic Buddhism directed conjoined. Writing in 1976, Hanh's method of mindfulness synchs up perfectly with older orientations toward "mind cure" in American history, surely one of the important reasons for his tremendous success as a teacher and author. Sadness, anxiety, hatred, passion: mindfulness reveals and heals each of these emotions, resulting in emancipation. Hanh is *not* promising that mindfulness will make you a better eater, lover, worker, or parent—those elaborations would come later, sometimes by Hanh and sometimes by subsequent figures in the mindfulness movement—but he and similar authors are promoting mindfulness in a way that speaks to the sad, anxious parents and workers of America yearning for healing and contact with a natural miracle that doesn't require renunciation of pleasures or affirmation of the supernatural.

Mindful Eating and Embodiedness

Given widespread popularity, belief in mindfulness's practical benefits, and its ability to capture the attention of both influential middle-class Buddhists and the therapy and self-help industries, it comes as little surprise that mindfulness has been applied to virtually every problem or issue imaginable. Eating, however, is an especially good example to study—not only is it an activity that all Americans engage in daily, but it is also a source of considerable anxiety, desire, confusion, and stress in modern society, as evidenced by the multibillion dollar dieting industry and the constant popular culture obsession with celebrities and their physical appearance.

It must be admitted that Buddhism has always had a relationship with food. Monks' eating practices were minutely managed according to codes of discipline, but the teachings set forth in the new Western literature on mindful eating represent a radically new application of Buddhism (though it is usually presented as if it were traditional). Whereas the older Asian Buddhist teachings about food and the body emphasize renunciation and self-denial, these American authors utilize Buddhism to promise in helping the reader to "*enjoy* a balanced relationship with food" and promote "a healthy and *joyful* relationship with food."[22] Mindfulness, it is alleged by these books, will increase the pleasure of eating, help readers lose weight, conquer eating disorders, avoid multiple health problems, and use food as a vehicle for personal spiritual attainment. In the mindful eating movement, Buddhism goes from being self-denying (indeed, denying the existence of a self) to self-affirming. This is in line with current American thinking about selves. As Robert Wuthnow observes, "many people have come to the view that they can cultivate deeper spirituality only by gaining a better understanding of themselves. In this view, the self is territory rich in potential and simply waiting to be cultivated. From therapists to writers interested in addictions and from theologians to New Age devotees, the self has been reconceptualized to offer personal power and to serve as the key to spiritual wisdom. In the process, spirituality has often been redefined to focus on empowerment and inward discovery."[23]

Mindfulness-meditation books published before the rise of mindful eating as a full-fledged movement sometimes used eating-related examples in explaining Buddhist practice. For example, in *The Miracle of Mindfulness!* Thich Nhat Hanh uses the example of eating a tangerine slowly, with close attention slice by slice, as a way of learning how to develop one's powers of meditation.[24] In fact, this tangerine-meditation technique has been widely quoted by other authors as a way of introducing newcomers to simple meditation practices. However, in these earlier books food is merely used as an example of how to become mindful in general, whereas in the later books that this chapter focuses on, the arrow is reversed: mindfulness is specifically applied to food in order to gain the benefits derived from eating and drinking in a mindful manner. Instead of everyday activities being used as a skillful means by which to awaken transcendental Buddhist insight into no-self and impermanence, monastic techniques now are being used to transform everyday activities so that they provide greater happiness, health, and self-control to laypeople, many of whom do not consider themselves Buddhist.

In mindful eating we find mindfulness meditation being abstracted from its Buddhist context and marketed as a way of providing health, weight loss, happiness—and spiritual insight. Because Buddhism in America has been closely aligned with the Human Potential Movement, New Age, and other particular later 20th century and early 21st century phenomena, they impact the specific manifestations and trajectories that Buddhism shows as it is domesticated.

The demographics of who is writing these books and whom they seem to target also affects the process of domestication. As discussed earlier, these authors are mostly white, from non-Buddhist family backgrounds, with middle-class professional occupations, especially as counselors and psychologists. Their clients and target audience seem to share these traits: the texts always assume readers have ready access to food; can afford therapy; are able to eat out; and primarily experience personal, self-critical, middle-class suffering rather than social suffering caused by poverty, discrimination, or disability. Everyone in the stories these authors use as examples have cars, televisions, desk jobs, and so on, and are often depicted in the midst of travel for business or pleasure. For example, Pavel Somov in *Eating the Moment: 141 Mindful Practices to Overcome Overeating One Meal at a Time* (2008) poses a sort of koan: "If the backseat of your Ford Taurus is good enough to make love, why is it not good enough to make love to a $250 Fritz Knipschildt dark truffle?"[25] It is taken for granted that the reader will be able to afford a Ford Taurus and spend hundreds of dollars on a bon-bon.

Another notable aspect of the authors (and especially the audiences) is the gender dynamic. A sizable portion of mindful eating authors are female, and the great majority of the stories they tell about clients involve women. Despite protestations that "Mindless eating is not just a 'girl thing,'" it is clear that the mindful eating movement is directed mainly toward women, and it's not coincidental that the discernibly gendered persons on the covers of mindful eating books are female. [26] This comes about in part because women experience eating disorders in far greater disproportion compared to men, because women are especially well represented in the counseling professions, and because women are the main consumers of the weight loss and dieting industries. Many observers of American Buddhism have suggested that the role of women in adapting Buddhism is a particularly noteworthy phenomenon to pay attention to.[27] Here we see this insight borne out, as Buddhism is domesticated in a manner designed specifically to provide the sort of practical benefits that women seek, especially those of the middle class.

Reader and Tanabe, in their discussion of practical benefits in Japan, propose that Japanese religion is fundamentally world-affirming.[28] Thus even seemingly world-denying aspects, such as the major place of funerary rites and beliefs in heavenly posthumous Pure Lands, are connected to tangible benefits that are received in this lifetime. For example, rituals performed for spirits and ancestors are believed to bring the favor of these otherworldly beings, such that living petitioners and descendants are granted material and spiritual boons. Similarly, Pure Land Buddhist beliefs too are frequently this-worldly at root, for the assurance of future happiness provides an immediate sense of peace and allows believers to continue their daily business in the face of hardship.

Modern America too is a realm of world-affirming culture and religion. Though it is easy to over-caricature the instant gratification and materialistic orientations of Americans, they are undeniably a strong force in American culture. The country that brought the world the prosperity gospel can hardly be called world-denying. Mindful eating proponents are aware of this and play off this dynamic as both critics and supporters. For example, they tend to be harshly critical of ordinary American culture, especially as it relates to eating practices: "Patience is not easily understood in our culture. If anything, our lifestyle is greatly measured by speed. Think about it: We drive on expressways. We even check out our food in 'express lanes.' TV meals are ready in minutes, and some takeout pizza restaurants promise 'thirty-minute delivery to your door or your money back.'"[29] On the very first page of her book *Eating Mindfully* (2003), Dr. Susan Albers paints the situation in the bleakest possible terms: "Deciding what to eat is not an easy task. It's so tricky that in the United States eating concerns and weight obsessions have reached epidemic proportions, with serious health consequences for a large part of the population."[30] Zen priest and pediatrician Jan Bays is even more critical: "We have added protein, vitamins, fiber, artificial fat, and chemical sweeteners. This war on food has meant increased revenues for companies that create processed food, but it has not altered our expanding waistlines or brought us back to a wholesome way of eating[31]... The situation is clear. The developed countries are in the midst of a serious epidemic of disordered relationships to food and eating. We are in urgent need of a treatment that will work equally for children and their parents[32]... A generation is growing up also thinking that the various 'fruit flavors' of jelly beans and Kool-Aid are the true flavors of blueberries, grapes, apples, watermelon, and cherries. I wonder if there will come a time when real fruit will no longer satisfy and only the candy substitute will do?[33]... In this culture we seem to be very uncomfortable with the collection of sensations we call hunger or thirst. We keep a drink always at hand. We snack all day long[34]... Thus over a single generation we humans have developed a new form of suffering."[35] At first glance, the messages attached to some forms of mindfulness might seem to contradict the general affirmative cultural trend. But in fact these mindful eaters are not nearly as countercultural as they may appear. When certain aspects of

American consumerism, distractedness, and super-sized restaurant portions are criticized in these books, it is because excessive consumption—especially of low-quality foods—is seen to be unhealthy. This is not a critique of consumption per se, but of unbalanced consumption that to some interpreters seems to denote a type of addiction (that is to say, an attachment).

When we look at the goals of mindfulness-based self-help programs, we still find that they are oriented toward delivering this-worldly benefits. Cutting down on one's eating is a strategy for achieving happiness—the problem with overeating is not that it is consumeristic, but that it in fact fails to deliver happiness. Thus the apparent renunciation involved in mindful eating is actually a renunciation of misleading, ineffective methods for achieving benefits in favor of correct, useful methods informed by Buddhist wisdom and practice. Renunciation, in the American Buddhist world, is a world-affirming and self-fulfilling practice partially couched in the spiritual language of world-abnegation and self-denial. We can see this when we focus on some of the benefits alleged to be gained through mindful eating. For example, the process of eating and preparing to eat in a mindful way is said to produce delight: "As you become mindful of the many wonders in life, mundane tasks like fixing a bag lunch can be transformed into a cornucopia of delight. You are present enough to enjoy the graceful motion of each swipe of mustard on the bread and notice the colors of everything involved: brown bread, yellow mustard, green lettuce, purple onion, red tomato, and pale-white cheese. The variety of colors and motions is a lot more fun than wanting the dull task to be over."[36] As Ronna Kabatznick—for nine years the psychological consultant to Weight Watchers International—succinctly put it: "Mindfulness helps you fall in love with the ordinary."[37] Time and again, these authors stress that the act of eating can be pleasurable, not something to be detached from. "Mindful eating is a way to reawaken our pleasure in simply eating, simply drinking," Jan Bays states.[38] "What you could gain are a simple joy with food and an easy pleasure in eating that are your birthrights as a human being… When we learn to eat mindfully, our eating can be transformed from a source of suffering to a source of renewal, self-understanding, and delight."[39] A less renunciatory attitude could scarcely be imagined, especially when contrasted with the traditional monastic Buddhist view that life is a realm of inherent suffering that is to be shunned and escaped from. And this world-affirmation links Buddhist-derived mindfulness practices in America both within temples and meditation centers (that is, explicitly Buddhist spaces) and within the wider world of popular culture, psychology, and self-help movements that is shared by the mainstream non-Buddhist population.

Japanese religion distinguishes two categories to practical benefits: *yaku-yoke* (the prevention of danger) and *kaiun* (the receipt of good fortune). Both appear in the promotion of mindful eating by Americans. For example, a partial list of the dangers caused by lack of mindful eating appears in *Eating Mindfully*: 'Weakness, chronic tiredness, injuries that won't heal, cuts or bruises, inability to concentrate, headaches, palpitations, or fluttering, of the heart, stomach pain, gas, sore throat, vomiting blood, sensitive teeth, constipation, bloating, dehydration, dry skin, scar on fingers from inducing vomiting, aching muscles, easily broken bones, irregular periods, cramps, cold, lack of energy, fainting, dizzy, bowel movement problems."[40] The author of *Mindful Eating* adds: "Our struggles with food cause tremendous emotional distress, including guilt, shame, and depression. As a physician, I've also seen how our eating problems can lead to debilitating diseases and even to premature death."[41] Most authors of book-length mindful eating texts discuss obesity, poor self-esteem, hypertension, high cholesterol, cancer, and diabetes as further risks that mindful eating can ward off.

On the other hand, good fortune can also allegedly be received through mindfulness, as it provides physical attractiveness, self-confidence, pleasure in the act of eating, and enhanced self-control. These come about through the application of mindfulness to eating because it is a useful tool: "When you pay attention to what's true in the moment (as you shop, cook, eat, or dance) that focused awareness slows you down long enough to examine your old habits. If you *know* you're reaching for a chocolate chip cookie, that moment of mindfulness can break the automatic response to mindlessly put it in your mouth. This awareness helps cut through the compulsive habit of chasing desire after desire only to experience deeper and deeper levels of hunger."[42] Reducing such compulsions, one is able to replace them with healthy behaviors and reap their rewards. For example, "Another bonus of eating mindfully is that it improves self-esteem, while mindless eating, with the inevitable weight issues, significantly infringes upon self-confidence."[43] Indeed, for most of these authors self-esteem (sometimes couched as "self-acceptance and body acceptance"[44]) seems to be the key factor that must be improved to reach a better relationship with food. Donald Altman even proclaims that self-acceptance is what mindfulness is all about: "You can find compassion and acceptance for yourself in the moment—this is your strength and the essence of mindfulness."[45]

We should note that calls for acceptance of the body—and by extension one's total self—directly contradict scriptural mindfulness teachings. The *Satipatthana* and *Mahasatipatthana Suttas* have a lot to say about bodies, in fact, and it isn't very warm or fuzzy: "A monk reviews this same body up from the soles of the feet and down from the top of the hair, bounded by skin, as full of many kinds of impurity thus: 'In this body there are head-hairs, body-hairs, nails, teeth, skin, flesh, sinews, bones, bone-marrow, kidneys, heart, liver, diaphragm, spleen, lungs, large intestines, small intestines, contents of the stomach, feces, bile, phlegm, pus, blood, sweat, fat, tears, grease, spittle, snot, oil of the joints, and urine.' ... In this way he abides contemplating the body as a body internally, externally, and both internally and externally... And he abides independent, not clinging to anything in the world."[46] This traditional source for mindfulness practice advocates viewing the body as impure, full of guts and disgusting substances, and recommends detachment from—not love for and acceptance of—the body. Soon thereafter it goes into even more visceral detail, as the Buddha tells the reader to think of one's own body as a rotting, oozing corpse eaten by worms and disintegrating into its component parts. Mindful-eating authors never quote these passages. Thus we see that not only is mindfulness practice recontextualized, but foundational scriptures are selectively excerpted to create a new interpretation of Buddhism that can provide the sort of practical benefits Americans seek, while leaving out interpretations and benefits that are culturally undesirable.

Influenced by the medicalization of mindfulness and other forces of mystification, mindful eating is arguably as much about modern psychology as it is about Buddhism proper. Much of the mainstream Buddhist worldview is downplayed or simply left out of these books on mindful eating. For example, none of these authors suggests that eating problems might be the result of karma from previous lives—a traditional explanation for problems that many Asian lineages would include as likely explanations. Instead, readers are told that "mindless eating" results from psychological attitudes acquired during one's present lifetime. Even when Buddhism is referenced, it is often dramatically changed: "Buddhist theory identifies craving as the root of suffering. Emotional cravings can be more powerful, insatiable, and destructive than physical hunger. Your emotional desires aren't as clear-cut or predictable as your desire to eat. As you become more mindful, you will begin to realize exactly what your heart hungers for. Examples include cravings for companionship, love, power, and control. In contrast to food, these longings are not as easily fulfilled. Sometimes, people misinterpret their heart cravings, and try to feed their bodies when they actually need to take better care of their souls."[47] In this quote, clinical psychologist Susan Albers appears to gesture toward Buddhist understandings of suffering, as she highlights the role of desire in causing pain. Yet this description is almost exactly the opposite of traditional Buddhist advice: here the solution is to heal one's soul (Buddhism explicitly denies the existence of a soul) by giving it what it craves (rather than cultivating detachment and equanimity). Albers presents herself as a psychologist, not a Buddhist, but this approach is displayed by the overtly Buddhist authors as well, such as Zen priest Jan Bays: "Most unbalanced relationships with food are caused by being unaware of heart hunger. No food can ever satisfy this form of hunger. To satisfy it, we must learn how to nourish our hearts."[48] This demonstrates the selective adoption or dissemination of Buddhist aspects that these mindful eating proponents propose. They willingly appropriate Buddhist teachings about suffering and techniques such as mindfulness, but other core elements, such as no-self, impermanence, and nirvana are often left out. Or, if included, they are recontextualized in ways that appeal to the American mindset but are generally alien to historical Buddhism: "Change is good, natural, and inevitable,"[49] Albers asserts; Buddhism, meanwhile, has usually identified change as one of the primary sources of human suffering.

Of course, mindfulness itself is the practice that is being most altered. Proponents of mindful eating believe that it conveys practical benefits because by paying close attention to one's eating habits, the practitioner is able to recognize their unhealthy habits and pursue more balanced forms of consumption, and because awareness infuses the process of eating itself with fun. As Jan Bays states, "Mindfulness brings about change from within. A natural and organic process, it occurs in the manner and at the rate that fits us. It is the ultimate in natural healing."[50] All of these authors talk about the "healing" nature of mindfulness. Having mostly jettisoned the notions of karma, rebirth, and other realms in favor of more rationalistic and psychological modes in tune with Western science and skepticism, it is no surprise that science is frequently used to justify the claims around mindful eating: Jan Bays' assertion that "A large and growing body of scientific studies supports the claims about the surprisingly reliable healing abilities of mindfulness" is echoed throughout these books. [51]

Mindful Sex and Pleasurable Relations

As part of a celibate, renunciatory, home-leaving monastic Buddhist path, mindfulness in premodern Asian tradition was believed to be a powerful tool for managing or eliminating sexual desire and cultivating detachment from social relations—indeed, as we saw earlier in the commentary by Sayādaw U Janakābhivaṃsa, one of the traditional benefits of mindfulness practice is that it causes the meditator not to feel grief and lamentation when a family member dies.

But these are not benefits that the average lay American seeks. Instead, mindfulness is repurposed to enhance the pleasure of the sex act and produce greater intimacy between partners. Likewise, mindfulness is being advocated as a tool for strengthening spousal/dating relationships, producing greater accord, understanding, and bonding. Granted, sex has had a place in some Buddhist practices, such as tantra. But premodern Buddhist tantra used sexual techniques to reach spiritual goals such as nirvana, whereas the mindful sex movement uses spiritual techniques such as meditation to reach sexual goals. As Jeremy Adam Smith put it in the June 2013 issue of *Mindful*: "If mindfulness can make us happier, healthier, and more compassionate (that is, if the raft of current scientific research is to be believed), what can that same moment-to-moment awareness do for our sex lives?"[52] Typically the new American mindful sex goals are better orgasm and conquering of conditions such as erectile dysfunction, premature ejaculation, inhibition, and frigidity.

In the opening to this chapter, Dr. Valerie Raskin prescribed mindful sex for mothers seeking "great sex." That this application of mindfulness is intended for middle-class, heterosexual married couples is clearly apparent in the book. Raskin always addresses her comments to an imagined heterosexual woman, urging greater thankfulness for and understanding of one's husband (except "Appendix A: Sexual Advice for Dads," where she turns the tables and recommends sexual communication and mindful sex for husbands too).[53] Thus Raskin is speaking to a very mainstream, non-Buddhist audience, and urging mindfulness to meet their particular needs.

In the preceding section on mindful eating, traditional Pali scriptures on mindfulness were quoted to demonstrate early Buddhist attitudes toward the body. These non-affirming views on the body are in no way confined to the ancient Asian past. In his opening comments for new mindfulness practitioners, 20th century monk Mahasi Sayadaw always stressed the need to develop aversion to the body: "Reflect upon the repulsive nature of the body to assist you in diminishing the unwholesome attachment that so many people have for the body. Dwell upon some of its impurities, such as stomach, intestines, phlegm, pus, blood. Ponder these impurities so that the absurd fondness of the body may be eliminated."[54] Here systematic investigation of each part of the body results in revulsion.

But as it turns out, systematic investigation of each body part can also be used to heighten attraction. Raskin uses this technique: "Every single part of your body has erotic potential. Every bit of your skin contains nerves that can be aroused sexually. Certain body areas are intensely ener-vated, and we naturally gravitate toward those areas, such as the nipples, clitoris, and penis, especially when time is precious. Focused mindful touching reprograms and awakens forgotten areas. You literally uncover a world of erotic potential just by paying attention to different areas."[55] Raskin provides detailed instructions for how to heighten pleasure via mindfulness: "Start by distinguishing types of touch, including how his body feels to your fingertips and how his touches feel against your skin. Become conscious of the nuances of his touch: notice how his lips feel against your neck, how it differs when he strokes your skin lightly or firmly. Observe how sensations change geographically: What are you experienc-ing as he caresses your labia? And how does it change as he moved toward your clitoris? Find new tactile input: his heartbeat, the feeling of his boxers against his penis... When your mind wanders, pull your attention back to hearing his breathing, noticing murmurs, becoming aware of how your own breathing sounds at the moment."[56]

Turning your attention moment by moment to each part of your body and your partner's body does not result in repulsion, but in arousal and plea-sure, according to Raskin. Mindfulness, therefore, doesn't inherently pro-mote desire or revulsion: what matters is the framing that it receives prior to engaging in the activity itself. If one asserts that mindfulness should be used for detachment, it will be employed in that manner; if one asserts that mind-fulness should promote attachment, it will further that goal. The Buddhist tradition (and its secular mindfulness descendants) claim that mindfulness is about seeing things as they really are, without any screening of conditioning. As Bhante Henepola Gunaratana states in *Mindfulness in Plain English*: "The goal is awareness, an awareness so intense, concentrated, and finely tuned that you will be able to pierce the inner workings of reality itself."[57] But what one finds in mindful meditation, it turns out, is what one sought before beginning the practice, and the benefits that result (detachment/attachment, revulsion/orgasm) are determined by specific cultural and other factors.

An even greater advocate of mindfulness in sex is Nicole Daedone, founder of OneTaste, a movement based in centers across the country.[58] As their pro-motional materials state: "In a world of separation, OneTaste is about con-nection. We provide tools for intimacy in everyday life. Going to the root of experience, OneTaste integrates the principles of mindfulness with the prac-tice of sexuality: mindful sexuality. By nourishing and including this basic and essential part of life, we discover richer relationships, an embodied sense of self and the uncompromised feeling of wholeness."[59]

At the heart of OneTaste is Orgasmic Meditation (OM), a form of mindful clitoral stimulation that OneTaste devotees practice daily, either in a group setting at one of the OneTaste centers, or at home if they have taken OneTaste workshops. Daedone created Orgasmic Meditation based on Buddhist mindfulness techniques and widely touts the purported results of such practice.[60] As the OneTaste website states, "Practitioners experience benefits similar to other mindfulness practices such as sitting meditation, as well as the well-known health benefits associated with orgasm"[61]:

"Practitioners of OM have reported the following benefits:

- Increased Overall Vitality. It lights you up from the inside out.
- Increased Overall TurnON. When you're TurnedON, things flow.
- Increased Energy. There's a well of energy that lives inside of you.
- Increased libido. You'll want sex more.
- Increased sexual satisfaction. Your sex becomes what it was meant to be.
- Increased ability to feel and know desire. You'll be clear on what you want.
- Elongated sexual pleasure during intercourse. Yes, that "place" extends.
- Increased confidence with your body & in the bedroom.
- Gain skills of concentration & attention. Your life changes when your attention grows.
- Addresses chronic dissatisfaction. Yes, TurnON alters dissatisfaction.
- Reduces stress & irritability.
- Increased intimacy with your partner. OM creates more communication.
- You will communicate better, feel more connected, and have more overall TurnON for life."[62]

We can see here that mindfulness has been mainstreamed by providing the sex-positive benefits that Americans seek. But the list doesn't include just physical pleasures: OneTaste also seeks to use mindful sex to create better relationships. In fact, mindful relationships are a large and growing phenomenon within the mindfulness movement, represented by such publications as *How to Be an Adult in Relationships: The Five Keys to Mindful Loving* (2002), *Mindful Loving: 10 Practices for Creating Deeper Connections* (2003), *Love's Garden: A Guide to Mindful Relationships* (2008), *Five Good Minutes with the One You Love: 100 Mindful Practices to Deepen and Renew Your Love Every Day* (2008), and *Rewire Your Brain for Love: Creating Vibrant Relationships Using the Science of Mindfulness* (2012).[63] As the titles suggest, many believe that it is possible to use mindfulness to deepen love and create healthier relationships between couples.

The introduction to *The Mindful Couple: How Acceptance and Mindfulness Can Lead You to the Love You Want* (2009) lays out the basic philosophy of such books:

> The beauty and delight of human connection are timeless and universal. The connections felt between romantic partners are among the deepest bonds of love created on this earth. Strengthening these bonds is a fundamental value for many and brings meaning and purpose to their lives... Through the practice of awareness and acceptance of yourself and your partner, and the practice of living your values, you can create a union that is full of compassion, trust, deep understanding, and friendship. When you discover the power of being fully present in your relationship—and of mindfully watching your feelings, thoughts, imaginations, and memories—while also breathing life into what matters most to you, you will find freedom and a vast ability to extend yourself to your partner... [and] true intimacy, authenticity, sexual longevity, dynamism, and enduring connection.[64]

In the November 2008 issue of *Shambhala Sun,* mindfulness teacher and co-founder of Spirit Rock Meditation Center Sylvia Boorstein asserts, "The Buddha says that everything that is dear to us causes pain." In classic Buddhist understandings, this means that we should cultivate detachment, so that we do not suffer when impermanence inevitably results in suffering. But the desire for maintaining strong relationships leads Americans to re-understand basic Buddhist principles. Boorstein continues, "I didn't like that when I first read it at the beginning of my practice, but after a while I realized that it's simply an expression of the truth. It doesn't mean we shouldn't have relationships. It doesn't mean not to have things dear to you... This life is full of getting used to losses. The only adequate response is to love fully and realize we have a short life."[65]

For Americans, then, the proper response to impermanence is to drink as deeply as possible from the cup of life because it may be removed at any moment. Mindfulness assists in this action, because it binds us to what is going on, preventing us from missing time as it passes, and allowing us to appreciate what is actually happening instead of projecting onto our partner based on our desires, fears, or past hurts. As Dr. James Córdova writes in *The Marriage Checkup: A Scientific Program for Sustaining and Strengthening Marital Health* (2009):

Those who tend to reside naturally in a more mindful state of awareness are more likely to behave skillfully with their emotions due to the level and quality of attention that they are directing to their internal and external environment. Because of this greater capacity to be clearly aware of what really matters both in ourselves and in our partners, we become better able to know what we are feeling, to empathize with what our partner is feeling, and to communicate in an empathic and effective way. The quality of our marital health cannot help but benefit from this type of loving attention.[66]

So mindfulness can be applied to improve not only health of the body, but health of one's most important human relationships as well.

Mindful Parenting, Mindful Work, and the Death of Countercultural Buddhism

Mindfulness provides more benefits than a trim waistline, super sex, and deeper love. Mindfulness is also being applied to make happier, more effective workers, and is being marshaled as a method for improving one's parental skills. This is far cry from Buddhism's original big splash among beats, hippies, and other figures of the American counterculture. Plenty of such folks worked and parented, of course, but the zeitgeist of such movements was the search for alternatives to the staid nuclear family model with 9-to-5 dad and June Cleaver housewife. Many people joined Buddhist meditation groups because they wanted something different from life in suburbia, office jobs, conventional marriage, and parenting. As Jack Kerouac—channeling Zen poet Gary Snyder—proclaimed in his novel *The Dharma Bums*:

> ...see the whole thing is a world full of rucksack wanderers, Dharma Bums refusing to subscribe to the general demand that they consume production and therefore have to work for the privilege of consuming, all that crap they didn't really want anyway such as refrigerators, TV sets, cars, at least fancy new cars, certain hair oils and deodorants and general junk you finally always see a week later in the garbage anyway, all of them imprisoned in a system of work, produce, consume, work, produce, consume, I see a vision of a great rucksack revolution thousands or even millions of young Americans wandering around with rucksacks, going up to mountains to pray, making children laugh and

old men glad, making young girls happy and old girls happier, all of 'em Zen Lunatics who go about writing poems that happen to appear in their heads for no reason and also by being kind and also by strange unexpected acts keep giving visions of eternal freedom to everybody and to all living creatures…[67]

That future did not work out precisely how the beats envisioned it. As we'll see in Chapter 5, Buddhism has itself become a consumer item. Meanwhile, the "lunatics" stopped wandering, got married, and took up regular jobs to support their families. They therefore need practical benefits suited for such lifestyles, and mindfulness has been adapted to provide such to them in the form of mindful work and mindful parenting.

To some extent gender dualism applies here, so the mindfulness movement both replicates and subtly enforces common social wisdom. Many books on mindful work are written by (and often targeted at) men, especially when they seek to apply mindfulness to management principles and not just day-to-day cubicle stress. These include *Resonant Leadership: Renewing Yourself and Connecting with Others Through Mindfulness, Hope, and Compassion* (2005), *Acceptance and Mindfulness at Work* (2006), *The Mindful Leader: Awakening Your Natural Management Skills Through Mindfulness Meditation* (2008), and *Inner Productivity: A Mindful Path to Efficiency and Enjoyment in Your Work* (2009).[68] The lion's share of mindful parenting publications, meanwhile, pay particular attention to mothers, even when they are authored by men. A Google search for "mindful fathering" brings up 169 hits, mostly related to a specific program for welfare dads in Toronto. A search for "mindful mothering" provides 13,000 hits.[69] There is a Mindful Moms Network, many mindful mom blogs, works on mindful mothering—*Momfulness: Mothering with Mindfulness, Compassion, and Grace* (2007), *Momma Zen: Walking the Crooked Path of Motherhood* (2007), *Mindful Motherhood: Practical Tools for Staying Sane During Pregnancy and Your Child's First Year* (2009)—and books for every related stage, such as *The Mindful Way Through Pregnancy* (2012) and *Mindful Birthing* (2012).[70]

According to promoters, mindfulness in the workplace is supposed to reduce friction with co-workers, increase efficiency, reduce boredom, improve ethics in the office, and relieve work-related stress. Articles from *Forbes* suggest that you can "Meditate for More Profitable Decisions," while *Business2Community* alerts its readers to consider the links between "Mindfulness and Personal Branding Success."[71] This genre breaks into two distinctive parts. The first is works targeted at applying mindfulness to specific professions, such as lawyers (*The Six-Minute Solution: A Mindfulness Primer for Lawyers*, 2009), doctors (*The Mindful Medical Student*, 2009), teachers (*The Mindful Teacher*, 2009), and social workers (*Mindfulness and Social Work*, 2009).[72] These tend to cluster around two poles: highly stressful jobs and jobs in the helping professions (not that these are exclusive categories, of course). The former tend to emphasize mindfulness as a way to deal with the pressures of work, while the latter tend to focus more on mindfulness as a way to deliver one's services in a smoother, more compassionate and effective fashion—but both approaches tend to be mixed to some degree in every book.

The other side of the mindful work genre is books and articles targeting the general office worker. An example is *Five Good Minutes at Work: 100 Mindful Practices to Help You Relieve Stress and Bring Your Best to Work* (2007), co-authored by the founder of the Mindfulness-Based Stress Reduction Program at Duke University's Center for Integrative Medicine. As the authors rhetorically ask in their introduction, "Could your working life be more satisfying? Would you like to work more effectively? Would you like to function with more ease and less stress? Would you like to develop more enjoyable relationships with those you work with?...By practicing, in a friendly and curious way, the skills of mindful presence, clear intention, and wholehearted action, you open the possibility that exciting and enriching new experiences might arise in one of the most familiar places of your life—your work or professional world!"[73] They then provide 100 different short mindfulness exercises designed to deliver such benefits. For example:

> For many of us, there simply isn't enough time in the day to get all our work done. Despite your extraordinary efforts to multi-task, the in-box fills up, the voice messages multiply, and additional unforeseen tasks get added to your pile. You may feel overwhelmed, fatigued, and anxious about the impossibility of completing these pressing demands. The next few minutes are dedicated to returning your consciousness to the present moment, which starts with exactly where you are. This mindful meditation will help keep you on track. 1) Begin by centering yourself in the here and now. You may want to take a few breaths or roll your shoulders to loosen up any nagging tension. 2) Remind yourself that today is only one day. You are only one person. You have only so much time to get so much done. You may not catch up or complete everything in one day—and that's okay. 3) Take one last deep breath, and on the slow exhale say aloud, "I will accomplish a great deal today and tomorrow is a new day."[74]

The mindfulness here is a combination of (at this point, rather distant) sati meditation and generous doses of positive psychology.

Mindful parenting has two different geneses, one in the transition made by seeker-type Buddhists who began to fret over how children interfered with their personal practice, and the other in the MBSR-related quest to use Buddhism to provide practical benefits to all of society. This split is embodied in two seminal works, both published in the mid-1990s. In the first case, *Dharma Family Treasures: Sharing Buddhism with Children* came about because of changing patterns within American meditation-oriented Buddhism. Sandy Eastoak, the editor, explains the situation in her introduction: "This book began in 1985, when Michele Hill and Deborah Hopkinson realized that 'the issue of family involvement with lay Zen in America is perhaps the most important and controversial subject we would ever take up.' During their ten years experience in editing *Kahawai: A Journal of Women and Zen*, they had heard considerable rumblings from the impact of parenthood on women's practice. They sent out questionnaires to inquire about interest in a book on Zen practice for families. Over and over parents stressed their need to learn how other parents were adapting practice and basic concepts to the rhythms and readiness of their children."[75] Eastoak and the others she was in dialogue with resolved their tension between their individual meditation and demanding children by reorienting their practice: "Being present with our children and modeling stillness and simplicity is our real work."[76] In other words, bringing mindfulness into parenting was a way to continue working on mindfulness, while helping children learn mindful ways as well.

Myla and Jon Kabat-Zinn would certainly agree with this in their 1997 book *Everyday Blessings: The Inner Work of Mindful Parenting*, but their focus is slightly different—unlike Eastoak and her contributors, who were trying to figure out how to remain Buddhist while raising children, the Kabat-Zinn's were trying to convince harried parents that Buddhism had some practical benefits to offer them in their pursuit of a more blissful family life. "Mindful parenting means seeing if we can *remember* to bring this kind of attention and openness and wisdom to all our moments with our children. It is a true *practice*, its own inner discipline, its own form of meditation. And it carries with it profound benefits for both children and parents, to be discovered in the practice itself."[77] Many subsequent books designed to introduce non-Buddhist parents to mindfulness—such as *Mindful Parenting* (2005), *Parenting Without Fear* (2007), and *The Mindful Child* (2010)—elaborate on these sort of benefits.[78] Mindful parenting is alleged to allow openness to the ever-changing relationship between oneself and one's child, allowing the parent to respond in non-rigid ways to parenting challenges and nurturing more rounded, psychologically healthy offspring who perform better in an uncertain, changing, multicultural, and competitive world. And, not incidentally, mindful parenting is asserted to relieve parenting-related stress—although it is also often the child who is portrayed as the stressed out one, such as in *Parenting Your Anxious Child with Mindfulness and Acceptance* (2009) and *Parenting Your Stressed Child* (2011).[79]

In short, through mindful dieting, lovemaking, bonding, working, and parenting, Buddhism—which began to expand from Asian immigrant to new Euro-American Buddhist communities in the 1960s and 70s as an explicitly countercultural force—has evolved in nearly the opposite direction. Mindfulness is now a tool for managing mainstream middle-class concerns around self-image, health, relationships, work and children, reinforcing rather than challenging the status quo. Mindfulness has been adapted to the support of average American lifestyles, the quintessential form of mainstreaming.

The Dharma of Star Wars: Mindfulness in Pop Idiom

Another important part of mainstreaming Buddhism is to deliver it in an idiom that is shared by regular members of American society, so that it connects to familiar ideas and tropes and speaks in a language that is easily accessible to the average citizen. Translating Buddhist texts into English, speaking about healing, and using psychological terms all help to accomplish this. But a further step is to actually express Buddhist teachings using metaphors and examples overtly chosen in order to speak to the mainstream of society.

A prime example of such mainstreaming practices is *The Dharma of Star Wars* (2005) by Matthew Bortolin. His book is designed to introduce the teachings of Buddhism by using the Star Wars movies as a gateway whereby ordinary Americans could understand the dharma. Chapter 1 is "The Jedi Art of Mindfulness and Concentration" and begins with epigrammatic quotes (some of the opening lines of dialogue in the first of the prequel films) about being mindful of the present. Bortolin then asserts:

> The Star Wars epic begins, in this dialogue, with mindfulness and concentration. In Episode I: *The Phantom Menace*, Jedi Master Qui-Gon Jinn advises his Padawan, Obi-Wan Kenobi, on these practices while the two are aboard a Trade Federation Droid-Control Ship representing the Galactic Republic as ambassadors of peace. Obi-Wan gives

voice to his concern about and wariness of a far-off disturbance in the Force. Qui-Gon, sensing his apprentice is lost in the future and not grounded in the here and now, councils him to practice the Jedi art of mindfulness and concentration. Mindfulness and concentration are also the beginning and end of the practices handed down from Siddhartha that came to be known as Buddhism. These two practices are essential steps along the path of spiritual freedom and happiness; they are methods for cultivating understanding, which is necessary to love ourselves, others, and life; and they are vital elements for being in touch with the living Force, for living in the present.[80]

The traditional scriptures have little to say about Trade Federation Droid-Control Ships. But putting mindfulness into such a context allows it to connect with the tens of millions of Americans who have grown up with the Star Wars saga. Mindfulness is depicted as the essence of Buddhism, and a key power of Jedi knights, the lightsaber-wielding defenders of the galaxy. Thus practicing mindfulness will make you more like a Jedi, and living in the present moment a la Thich Nhat Hanh becomes a way of touching the mystical Force that surrounds and binds all things in the Star Wars universe. More than that: the Force actually *is* mindfulness. As Bortolin continues, "The Star Wars movies, food, running water, and life itself are just a few examples of the simple joy present right now. Living as Qui-Gon, remaining concentrated and mindful in the here and now, opens our eyes to these wonders, brings us happiness, and in itself relieves much of our daily suffering."[81] Happiness, relief of daily suffering, and Jedi powers: these are very much practical benefits, in a recognizable pop cultural idiom.

As Bortolin further points out, it was by letting go and being mindful of the present that Luke Skywalker was able to destroy the Death Star, and Skywalker was taught mindful breathing by Yoda during his training on the swamp planet Dagobah.[82] Botolin suggests that this has utility in our own lives. "Every day we accumulate stress and anxiety. This creates tension in the body and mind that can cause physical as well as psychological maladies. The practice of mindful breathing as a way of calming mind and body is a powerful remedy for illness. We don't need a doctor's prescription for the medicine of mindful breathing!"[83] The Star Wars movies become a way of teaching mindfulness, which becomes a way of acquiring practical benefits, such as healing.

The search for immediately understandable ways of explaining mindfulness to regular Americans is also the explicit purpose of *Wild Chickens and Petty Tyrants: 108 Metaphors for Mindfulness* (2009), by Dr. Arnie Kozak, a mindfulness-based psychotherapist. As he asserts, "Metaphors for mind and mindfulness can help to bring you closer to the ground of experience—the physical body that is also mind. From this perspective, mindfulness practice is a form of rational behavior that helps to reveal the embodied basis of mental life."[84] His metaphors typically draw on elements of everyday life or mainstream American culture, often with a connection to the benefits that can be drawn from mindfulness practice. So on page 23 mindfulness is a spam blocker for your mental email inbox, preventing you from becoming entangled in junk thoughts. Or on page 25 it is a mute button for your mental television, helping you keep your attention on your body and thus reduce suffering. On page 30 mindfulness is what prevents us from getting on the wrong subway, and by extension what keeps us from getting on the wrong mental train of thoughts. As with Bortolin, Kozak likes to draw on pop culture entertainment, but is more of a Trekkie. For example, he says that when Dr. McCoy saw through the disguise of the salt vampire in the Star Trek episode "The Man Trap," it showed how mindfulness practice helps us to perceive reality more clearly.[85] Later, we learn that mindfulness helps avoid conflicts, like when the Enterprise encountered some Klingons who thought they were still at war with the Federation.[86] Even the villainous Borg, he points out, knew that "Resistance is futile," and that means that it is better to inhabit the present moment with acceptance and mindfulness.[87] When the android Data on *Star Trek: The Next Generation* installed an emotion chip, he was able to experience negativity without becoming distressed, something we should emulate in our mindfulness practice.[88]

Some of the most quintessentially American of Kozak's metaphors are also the most patriotic. On page 60, the false ego is a foreign tyrant king trying to tax our minds without representation, something we must resist—otherwise "we are giving up representation in the congress of our own lives. The founders of the United States did not submit to such injustice and neither should you…Like the Founding Fathers, you too can challenge the despotic authority of your tyrannical self. This process does not require waging war or, if it is a war, it is one of acceptance, gentleness, and surrender—yielding to present-moment reality as it changes, moment-by-moment, breath-by-breath. Mindfulness practice helps us to identify the tyrannical credo and to recognize the tyrannical self as thoughts and opinions and not as ultimate truth."[89] Not all authors in the American mindfulness movement are so overt in their attempt to make mindfulness mainstream by applying familiar concepts and language. But in one way or another, most do try to mainstream mindfulness by drawing on shared cultural touchstones.

Conclusion

One possible irony of the mindfulness movement is that it emerged in part from movements that desired to reform Buddhism and get back to the original, authentic teachings of the historical Buddha. Many early Western authors espouse a radically modified form of Buddhism pruned of what they call "Asian trappings" that were accumulated by supposedly "impure mixtures" of basic Buddhism with local cultural traditions and outside religions, such as Confucianism or animistic cults. Such Buddhists believed they were getting back to the essence of "real" Buddhism, unencumbered by Asian cultural ideas of the divine right of kings or faith-healing, lucky charms, and love magic. In other words, they explicitly rejected the idea of cultural adaptation of Buddhism for practical benefits, which they depict as superstitious and anti-modern. The mindfulness movement follows in the shadow of these pioneers, often advancing similar ideas.

Yet, this newly pared-down Buddhism that supposedly returns to Indian roots is eminently prepared to be applied to the worldly cultural concerns of Americans, especially those in the middle-class, mainly white communities that have dominated the public conversation over what American Buddhism should be. This segment of the population has specific worldly concerns that arise out of its ethnic culture: they seek healthy relationships in the family, balanced living that doesn't harm the environment, management of stress from work, and individual fulfillment. Though these are hardly traditional concerns for mindfulness practice, Buddhist mindfulness is applied to assist in the achievement of all of these desires.

Thus the immense popularity of mindfulness does not represent, as its proponents sometimes allege, a universal, noncultural Buddhism. Instead, the application of mindfulness to so many aspects of American culture is in fact clearly yet another "practical benefits" approach to Buddhism, pursued in this case by American Buddhists and sympathizers. Though some believe they have done away with "attachment-based" utilizations of Buddhism, in fact their stripped-down approach makes aspects of Buddhism available for attachment to new culture-specific concerns such as overeating, wasteful consumption, parenting difficulties, and workplace stress—so available, in fact, that many of the people developing such applications are not Buddhist themselves. Repeating (in their own unique way) the ancient pattern of creative reinterpretation to meet local needs and anxieties, these prominent Buddhist teachers and their non-Buddhist counterparts are domesticating Buddhism for an American culture with different—but no less worldly or culturally determined—concerns than the Asian cultures from which they received Buddhism.

But surely the hallmark of contemporary American culture is the strength of market forces. Parenting, work, eating—all of these are phenomena profoundly impacted by large-scale commercial forces that shape the possibilities of every American life. These mainstreaming practices are largely reactions to concerns with economic connections of one sort or another, and the proliferation of the types of benefits provided by mindfulness is part of a process of marketing mindfulness as a commodity in the American lifestyle economy. Thus the next chapter looks further into the mainstreaming of mindfulness by considering how it is marketed, by whom, and for what purposes.

5 MARKETING MINDFULNESS: HOW IS MINDFULNESS TURNED INTO A COMMERCIAL PRODUCT?

Market: to place or establish (a product) on the market; esp. to seek to increase sales of (a product) by means of distribution and promotion strategies

—*Oxford English Dictionary*[1]

Mindfulness teacher Elias Amidon and twenty-five of his students spent the day doing contemplative nature walks and mindfully exploring the beautiful foothills of the Rocky Mountains. It was a natural place to engage in awareness of the wonders of the earth and our small place in the great ecosystem of life. Too natural, in fact. The next day Amidon decided to try something new, "to contrast the grounded wisdom achieved through walking mindfully in *non-human-made nature* with the lessons revealed through walking mindfully in that temple of *human-made nature*: the shopping mall."[2]

So, with some trepidation, he took his students to the mall. "One by one we passed in silence and alone into the well-lit climate-controlled space. We were to walk in a similar manner as we had during the contemplative nature walk: slowly and attentively…As I entered the mall I felt an astounding difference from any other time I had been there. By maintaining mindfulness, the environment became psychedelic in its intensity. A thousand simultaneous messages flooded in: colors, images, words, sounds, smells, movement, everything beckoning for attention: 'Buy me! Buy me!' I breathed calmly and witnessed this extraordinary onslaught."[3]

Amidon reflected on how this spot was once a prairie filled with buffalo and antelope, and on how the endless ocean of consumer products required untold environmental destruction to reach the mall. He wandered into a nature store, where pictures and plastic toys of wild animals created an artificial habitat replacing the real one that had existed here before. Nearby signs blared that more cell phone minutes would allow him to live beyond limits and spend his time on the things that most mattered. He recognized these ads as promulgating the "credo of the religion of consumerism" and began to despair of how so many are "addicted to the trinkets of commercial culture."[4] When he went to rejoin his students outside, they were visibly shaken by their mall mindfulness. " 'What do we love?' " he asked them. His own question haunted him, and he repeated it. " 'What do we love?' "[5]

One answer—suggested by the vast square miles of landscape given over to retail, the sprawling cyber-sea of online merchandise, the omnipresent advertisements delivered by every conceivable form of media, the annual Walmart stampedes on Black Friday, and the way that the latest electronic doohickey often gets more press than genocide, starvation, and war—is that Americans love to sell and buy things. The American dream, after all, is one of private property ownership and accumulating ever more consumer goods, often in a materialistic "arms race" to keep up with the neighbors in their pursuit of consumer happiness. The genius of late-modern American culture may reside in our ability to package and sell anything. The "religion of consumerism" provides us with new gods, who are either high-tech entrepreneurs inhabiting a Silicon Valley paradise of superhuman incomes (Bill Gates, Steve Jobs, Mark Zuckerberg) or carefully managed consumer products themselves (iPad, Batman, Justin Bieber). As Leigh Eric Schmidt reminds us, "inner quests, even for off-the-grid simplicity or spiritual enlightenment, never transcend the market."[6] If this is the basic reality of American culture, then what are the effects that occur when this market faith meets the practice of mindfulness?

In Chapter 4's emphasis on mainstreaming by providing practical benefits we saw one of the primary marketing strategies for selling mindfulness in general by stressing what great things it can do for the user. This chapter examines the economics of the mindfulness movement, especially as embodied in the many authors and public speakers jockeying to be the ones to satisfy the desires of Americans and in the range of products sold to enhance or support mindfulness (and the advertising campaigns to promote these products). Particular attention is paid to what marketing strategies are used to reach specific audiences, such as Buddhists, non-Buddhists, women, young people, and so forth. Whereas Buddhism has often been associated in the Western mind with mental technologies and other-worldliness, in the capitalistic milieu even abstract meditation practices become products and proliferate a range of supporting products in the American religious, health, and self-help marketplaces. Here we explore how mindfulness becomes a commodity and the implications of the marketing of mindfulness for practical benefits.

Mindful Products: Selling What You Can't Find

Like all good salespersons, mindfulness advocates have honed their pitches and offer promises of what their product will do (lead to happiness, health, better sex, etc.), scientific proof that it works (thus the importance of Jon Kabat-Zinn's work, which is cited countless times in the mindfulness literature), and exemplars of people just like you who've benefitted from trying mindfulness. Similar to the before and after photos of television infomercials for miraculous diets and bodybuilding contraptions, mindfulness pitchmen describe how they and their clients were once stressed out and unhappy, but now thanks to mindfulness they are blissed out and happy. You can be too, if you follow their simple plan. The website for the Center for Mindfulness in Medicine, Health Care, and Society, for example, includes testimonials from clients, paired with happy headshots: "The Stress Reduction Program at UMass Memorial Health Care became my life line—It literally saved my life. One can find peace and calm in the middle of chaos and confusion," claims one.[7] Christy Cassisa, creator of Mindful Clarity, was so inspired by her encounter with mindfulness that she changed her profession: "Discovering mindfulness meditation in 2010 saved my life and my sanity. I have taken a formal Mindfulness-Based Stress Reduction course through University of California, San Diego's Center for Mindfulness and I am committed to this practice for life."[8] She is now a professional mindfulness coach. The author of *From the Brig to the Boardroom* presents his story as a quasi-evangelical journey, told in the third person: "In January 2001, Matt Tenney attempted a 'shortcut' to success, arranging the unauthorized delivery of nearly $3 million in U.S. government money. Although he never attempted to acquire the funds, he spent more than five years confined to military brigs as a result of his actions. In 2002, he was introduced to mindfulness, which helped him transform the greatest failure of his life into his greatest success."[9]

With the various adaptations and permutations already explored in this book, mindfulness in America can be practiced on a complete spectrum from momentary indulgence (*One-Minute Mindfulness: 50 Simple Ways to Find Peace, Clarity, and New Possibilities in a Stressed-Out World*) to comprehensive plan (*Mindfulness: An Eight-Week Plan for Finding Peace in a Frantic World*).[10] It can be narrowly applied to a single preferred activity (*Mindful Dog Owner*) or extended all the way to a total saturation of life itself (*Living the Mindful Life*).[11] Mindfulness can potentially be practiced as religion (*The Heart of Buddhist Meditation*), science (*The Mindful Brain*), therapy (*Mindful Therapy*), hobby (*Mindful Knitting*), or sport (*Tennis Fitness for the Love of*

It: A Mindful Approach to Fitness for Injury-free Tennis).[12] With this infinite flexibility of momentariness or completeness, of ease or strenuousness, of preferred framework, and its proliferative employment to enhance virtually any activity that seems reasonable to the individual (*Mindful Horsemanship: Daily Inspirations for Better Communications with Your Horse*), mindfulness is the ultimate Buddhist product.[13]

Mindfulness is sold in any and every form of media available: books, articles, magazines, blogs, CDs, even film. It can be adapted to a wide range of genres, including fiction, memoir, self-help, science writing, travelogue, history, and spiritual manuals. Yet technically, mindfulness itself can never be commodified, because the act of awareness cannot be literally packaged, bottled, transmitted, weighed, or measured. It lies outside of the material dimension and therefore cannot be simply stored on a shelf or shipped through the mail. In a way, this situation recalls the famous mythical origin story of Zen in China: the aspiring student Huike waited in the snow outside the cave where Bodhidharma sat meditating, determined to gain access to the secrets of true dharma that the master possessed. But day after day he was repeatedly rebuffed, until finally he cut off his own arm and offered it to Bodhidharma in a demonstration of the depth of his intent. Bodhidharma then asked him what he wanted, and Huike pleaded, "Please pacify my mind!" Bodhidharma responded, "Very well. Hand over your mind so that I can pacify it for you." Huike stammered, "But I can't find any mind that I can give to you." Bodhidharma said, "There, I have pacified it for you." Huike achieved profound enlightenment.

The promoters of mindfulness in America face a similar dilemma: they know mindfulness is highly valuable and they know that they cannot actually sell the thing itself. Given this conundrum, peddlers of mindfulness must take two indirect approaches: they must either sell auxiliary products designed to introduce or augment mindfulness, or sell their expertise at teaching mindfulness and delivering the benefits of mindfulness.

Auxiliary products promise to help you become mindful or to enhance your meditation experience. For example, the Mindfulness Bell app (99¢) for the iPhone "rings a beautiful Tibetan Singing Bowl at a specified interval—or random intervals—throughout the day" so that you can pause and take a mindful breath in the midst of your other activities.[14] Actual bells for accompanying meditation practice are sold by many distributors in the United States, especially Buddhist organizations such as DharmaCrafts and Dharma Communications, both run by primarily white Buddhist organizations that participate in the mindfulness movement. DharmaCrafts' Bestsellers 2013 catalog offers bells ranging in price from $59 for a 3-inch diameter bell to $1499 for a 11 ¾-inch diameter "Japanese Hand Hammered Gong" (both come with a striker and cushion).[15] On the same page DharmaCrafts offers a $10 CD that consists of 70 minutes of silence, followed by three bell chimes to indicate that it is time to stop meditating. You may also choose a digital meditation timer ($99), an alarm clock and timer that draws a circle on its face and provides Japanese or Tibetan bell chimes.[16] The Fall 2012–Winter 2013 catalog for Dharma Communications' Monastery Store offers bells from $40 to $750, as well as Flattop Mountain Clappers: "The distinctive sound of these beautiful black walnut clappers will bring you to mindfulness as you mark periods of walking meditation and other elements of your practice."[17]

Even more popular are the tremendous variety of cushions for use during meditation. As DharmaCrafts points out, "Your meditation cushion is so much more than an ergonomic tool. Over time, it becomes your beloved companion."[18] The most esteemed cushion in American meditation circles is the zafu, a round pillow whose design was imported from Japan and is usually linked to formal Zen sitting meditation (zafu is Japanese for "sitting cushion"). These cushions are used in Mindfulness-Based Stress Reduction (MBSR) training, as DharmaCrafts alludes to: "In homes, meditation centers, hospitals, and schools across the country, thousands of people begin and end their day on a DharmaCrafts cushion."[19] DharmaCrafts sells them with a lifetime guarantee, in seven colors (from forest green to sand), with your choice of Classic ($59), Eco ($69), or Organic ($79).[20] They are typically paired with zabuton mats, also in Classic ($79), Eco ($89), and Organic ($138) styles.[21] If you prefer a kapok rather than a buckwheat hull zafu, they are available ($69).[22] And there are additional styles as well, such as the Stillness and Light Collection or Tibetan Splendor Meditation Cushions (all $69), which offer various patterns to match your other room décor.[23] Other support possibilities include the Pi Bench ($89), Omni Benches ($108), the Salubrion Seat™ ($79), and the Backjack ($57 regular, $67 XL).[24] The advertisements emphasize the hand-crafted quality of these products, the natural, often Asian materials, and the way they provide proper alignment for legs, spine, and other parts of the body. In the ads, various calm or smiling young white people in comfortable clothing sit on or manufacture the pillows and benches.

There is plenty of other paraphernalia on sale to augment your meditation. If you are cold while sitting mindfully for long periods of time, you may need a hand-woven wool prayer shawl ($89) or a hooded meditation cloak ($159).[25] You may want incense ($3.75–$108), in which case you'll need an incense burner ($19–$29) and a box ($124.95).[26] Perhaps you'll choose a CD of shakuhachi flute music ($16) to add the proper mood: the tracks "have been selected because of their ability to complement mindful activity, allowing the listener to feel the serenity that accompanies such mindfulness."[27] There is also a very wide array of jewelry, Buddha statues, and home décor. Of course, tucked among this stuff there are also books and CDs for teaching meditation, mostly by mindfulness authors such as Jack Kornfield (three selections, the most of any teacher), Jon Kabat-Zinn (two items), Thich Nhat Hanh (two items), Tara Brach (one item), and a set by Sharon Salzberg and Joseph Goldstein. Thus mindfulness provides the primary framework for the meditation supplies sold in the catalog.

The DharmaCrafts catalog is a mix of tradition and innovation. Some items are imported from various Asian cultures, while others are manufactured in the United States, using American materials and craft techniques, and influenced in subtle ways by American aesthetics. Many of the American-made products have ancestors in Asia, but that pedigree is sometimes little more than an echo. Other products are wholly inventions of the West, but conform to uses and styles that complement the pan-Asian feel of the total catalog. The various products are assembled into visual combinations that reflect no actual specific Buddhist society, but are designed to promote a series of practices: the practice of meditation, the practice of assembling a personal style based in concepts of individual spirituality and tasteful, high-quality, eco-friendly display, and the practice of buying products to support these other practices. This is mindful consumption and the consumption of mindfulness. With an extensive list of garden buddhas, benches, and decorations (some of them fairly large); shots of meditators posed in their own personal meditation, yoga, or altar rooms; and a variety of prints, flags, and wall hangings that seem to imply the possession of large amounts of wall space that need adornment, the DharmaCrafts catalog suggests a target audience of financially secure, suburban homeowners.

DharmaCrafts reflects an American conception of what a middle-class Asian Buddhist meditation catalog might look like, if one existed. On the other end of the mindfulness movement's marketing strategies is the online shop at OneTaste.us, the website for OneTaste, the female genitalia-oriented mindful sexuality organization described in Chapter 4. OneTaste too gestures toward Asian spirituality in its employment of mindfulness and yoga, but it much less overt in its connections to Buddhism, steering instead toward the fully Americanized, hip and of-the-moment current of the mindfulness movement. Promotional materials stress the innovation of OneTaste, not its traditional background—hardly surprising for a meditation community fundamentally built around mindful clitoral stimulation.

DharmaCrafts tries to support various Buddhist meditational groups, especially Zen, Tibetan, and Theravada-related approaches, as well as more generic mindfulness practitioners and those interested in alternative spirituality lifestyles. OneTaste has a more focused approach, because it is itself a specific quasi-spiritual group with a particular central practice—Orgasmic Meditation (aka OMing)—and therefore its products are designed to assist that practice. OMing follows a very specific procedure. The woman lies on a blanket on the floor, naked from the waist down, with her head on a pillow and her left leg on another pillow. The man sits on her right side on a zafu (referred to as a stroking cushion), and with his left index finger strokes the upper left quadrant of her clitoris for fifteen minutes, mindfully describing the changes in color and so on that he observes while she focuses her attention on the resulting sensations. The practitioner, therefore, will need a variety of support products. There is branded OneStroke Lube ($14.95) in regular and coconut, One Scrub All-Natural Salt ($15.97) to make sure you're clean, OM Warmers long socks ($28.97); the best deal is the OM Signature Kit, which includes a 100% organic cotton blanket, zafu, two linen-covered pillows, lube, and three hand towels ($184.97).[28] There are also books, personal training sessions, t-shirts, and videos for sale.

OneTaste is based in big urban locations (New York, Los Angeles, San Francisco, etc.), with a couple of offbeat funky places in the mix (Austin and Boulder). It is clearly pitched to a more urban, young, apartment-dwelling clientele than DharmaCrafts, who are interested in self-cultivation, personal indulgence, and fun, without the more overtly religious connections of the DharmaCrafts crowd. At the same time, it preaches a message of personal salvation and world redemption through the benefits provided by its special mindfulness techniques. As in any industry, mindfulness vendors adjust their pitch to the particular consumer audience they wish to reach.

A World of Mindful Experts

The second approach—selling mindfulness via asserting your expertise at teaching mindfulness—appears in the various forms of authority asserted in the teaching of mindfulness. The most classic form is expertise based on being a trained Buddhist monk, such as Thich Nhat Hanh or Bhante Henepola Gunaratana. Not far from this are the strategies of popular lay teachers who highlight their experience in Asia, founding of retreat centers, and/or years of training others in Buddhist meditation. These include Jack Kornfield, Joseph Goldstein, Sharon Salzberg, and many others. The back inside cover flap of *The Wise Heart* informs in typical fashion that "Jack Kornfield, Ph.D., is an internationally renowned meditation teacher and one of the leaders in introducing Buddhist practice and psychology to the West. After graduating in Asian studies from Dartmouth College, he joined the Peace Corps and later trained as a Buddhist monk in Thailand, Burma, and India. Kornfield is a cofounder of the Insight Meditation Society in Barre, Massachusetts, and of the Spirit Rock Center in northern California. A husband, father, and activist, he also holds a Ph.D. in clinical psychology."[29]

This description blends Buddhist bonafides with more professional qualifications. Often Americans assert mindfulness expertise based on their professions—this is especially apparent in the medicalized mindfulness discourse explored in Chapter 3. Endless numbers of books and articles are prominently advertised according to the string of university-bestowed letters tacked on to the end of the author's name, and their author bios often stress their experience in counseling, medicine, or laboratory settings. For example, potential readers are informed that they should buy and trust Saki Santorelli's *Heal Thy Self: Lessons on Mindfulness in Medicine* because of his extensive experience running the original MBSR program in his role as Jon Kabat-Zinn's most direct dharma heir.[30]

Other professional qualifications are called in as needed for application to various occupations and activities. Dinty Moore is an author and professor of creative writing, so he is qualified to pen *The Mindful Writer*.[31] The back cover of *Mindfulness Yoga* informs us that "Frank Jude Boccio is an interfaith minister and longtime student of Thich Nhat Hanh who integrates the practice and philosophies of yoga, Buddhism, and Ayurveda. His background includes a 700-hour training program under the guidance of the renowned Georg Feuerstein, and he is currently a senior student in Dharma Teacher Training under the guidance of Samu Sunim. Boccio is a certified yoga teacher/therapist through the Bateman Institute in New York City, and teaches yoga in Brooklyn and New Paltz, New York, as well as regularly leading Mindfulness Yoga sessions at Zen Mountain Monastery and other spiritual retreat centers."[32] Thus through a combination of name-dropping, religious authority, and professional experience we are assured that he is fully qualified as both Buddhist mindfulness instructor and as yoga teacher. To help increase the potential buyer's confidence, the top of the back cover carries a quote in huge font from Jon Kabat-Zinn ("It's about time somebody wrote this!"), and other blurbs come from famous yoga instructors, well-known book review publications, and senior mindfulness teachers. The mindful parenting books often mix authority based on psychological training with that gained by being a parent oneself; mindful recovery books mix the counseling expertise with insider knowledge based on being a recovered addict oneself. These tactics are especially important when promoting Buddhist-derived mindfulness in non-Buddhist religious works. Jonathan P. Slater's *Mindful Jewish Living* emphasizes his role as a rabbi; Brenda Shoshanna's *Jewish Dharma* stresses that she was raised in an Orthodox Jewish household; Mary Jo Meadow, Kevin Culligan, and Daniel Chowning's *Christian Insight Meditation* all highlight their affiliation with the Carmelites.[33]

Book sales are most robust when their promoters can combine many marketing strategies in a seamless and coherent full package. One of the top performers of 2012 was Chade-Meng Tan's *Search Inside Yourself: The Unexpected Path to Achieving Success, Happiness (and World Peace).*[34] The book's title immediately draws on Tan's expertise as a key employee at Google, one of the most prominent and respected companies of the new information economy—the title is even rendered in a font and color scheme reminiscent of the ubiquitous Google online search engine. The cover sports a recommendation by the executive chairman of Google, and promises forewords by best-selling medicalized mindfulness authors Daniel Goleman and Jon Kabat-Zinn. Back cover recommendations include His Holiness the Dalai Lama, thirty-ninth president of the United States Jimmy Carter, the sixth president of Singapore, the co-founder of Whole Foods, another best-selling author, and a tech entrepreneur. The title promises concrete practical benefits to be enjoyed right away in this life, as well as suggesting that the reader has a social conscience by buying the book. In nearly stereotypical fashion, the inside front cover flap offers a quote from Tan proclaiming that "For the benefits of meditation to become widely accessible to humanity, it cannot just be the domain of bald people in funny robes living in mountains, or small groups of New Age folks in San Francisco."[35] The content inside is breezy, self-deprecatingly funny, and even contains numerous cartoons as it teaches how to do "mindfulness without butt on cushion." It attributes Google's massive success in part to the mindfulness program for employees that Tan instituted at the company, and suggests that you can replicate this success in your own life through meditation. This is brilliantly marketed mindfulness, and sales figures reflected the various strategies at work.

This process has its basis in premodern Buddhism as well: Zen in China was nothing if not an attempt to seize power through asserting the unique qualifications of its teachers of its branded (Zen) new form of superior Buddhism. Classic texts such as the eighth-century *Platform Sutra of the Sixth Patriarch* claim to embody the true essence of Buddhism in profound teachings and meditation techniques transmitted mind-to-mind in a lineage descended in secret from the Buddha himself, only now being revealed to the public. As Philip Yampolsky points out, the *Platform Sutra* is one part propaganda for the author's (partially fictitious) lineage and one part fund-raising appeal to potential donors.[36] During Japan's long period of near iso-lation from the outside world, Soto Zen often promoted itself by asserting that meditation and precepts made its monks better at delivering practical benefits—such as exorcism and faith-healing—than other Buddhist sects.[37] Mindfulness movement promoters are more or less replicating these vener-able Buddhist patterns when they lay claim to the ability to provide culturally desired practical benefits due to their expertise, and seek money to support themselves and their teachings.

Tranquilistas, Mothers, and Crones: Marketing Gendered Mindful Lifestyles

Of course, we should not fully disassociate the two approaches of products designed to enhance meditation lifestyles and authors empowered to teach mindfulness due to their professional expertise. Often, what is being sold is mindfulness as a lifestyle product embodied in the iconic form of the expert self-help author, as in Kimberly Wilson's 2010 book *Tranquilista: Mastering the Art of Enlightened Work and Mindful Play*: "You may be wondering, 'What in the world is a tranquilista?' So glad you asked! A tranquilista is a woman who embraces her many sides: she is spiritual (she's a tranquility-seeker), creative (loves style), and entrepreneurial (calls her own shots). She hearts fashion and philanthropy. Parties and prayer. Entertaining and enlighten-ment. The golden rule and layers of vintage gold bangles. She is you and she is *moi*. She is full of aspirations and always seeking inspiration. Oh, and she sparkles. Literally."[38] So explains Wilson, who is a yoga teacher, Thich Nhat Hanh admirer, and successful author. Wilson is a tranquilista, and, as she points out to the reader, you want to be one too. A tranquilista is "mind-fully extravagant," a person who embraces "flair-filled must-haves such as shiny chandeliers, kitten heels, and little black dresses while also practicing yoga, meditating, caring for the environment, and be-ing a do-gooder."[39] Such modern divas go about "designing our lives as self-defined entrepreneurs who care about blending balance, bliss, and beauty…A tranquilista mixes spiritualty, creativity, and entrepreneurship in varied amounts to bake the perfect concoction that will help her attain her individual dreams and desires while making a positive impact."[40]

Tranquilista is an example of lifestyle commodification and expertise based on being a cool chick in the city. The reader identifies with the author and wishes to be like the author, who is popular, stylish, pretty, fit, happy, successful, in control, modern, urban, helpful, and feminine. A whole vision of contemporary femininity is conveyed in this book, one that uses mindfulness to achieve these gender goals and which uses mindfulness as a part of gender identity itself. It promises a satisfying balance of traditional American female concerns such as style and beauty combined with the feminist appeal to women as workers in the modern economy. A very particular demographic is being pitched to here, one that does not include most Americans. As Wilson's author bio points out, "She lives in a *petite* raspberry-colored flat in Washington, DC, with two fancy felines named after French impressionists, a supportive beau, and a black pug." For many young urban women, this is the new American dream. But we should note that this lifestyle, which is supposedly generated and maintained by the practices of mindfulness and yoga, is also deeply dependent on very particular choices and compromises. There is no home mortgage, only an apartment to look after; no children, only fashion-accessory pets; no husband, only a nice live-in guy; and the author lives in a place where public transportation is readily available to take her to the endless parade of tony restaurants, bookstores, concerts, and other diversions that fill her life as a tranquilista. Without a family to care for, conventional American female patterns of nurturance are available to be redirected inwards toward self-care and outward toward fulfilling social and environmental activism.

This sort of lifestyle marketing has a long history in American encounters with Asian religion, as Jane Naomi Iwamura points out: "Like Zen in the late 1950s, Americans approached Transcendental Meditation as *stylized religion* that signified a way of life, that is, an identity, more than something that transformed one's consciousness. One could sample this alternative perspective and subscribe to its outlook simply by wearing Indian attire and listening to the inspired sitar of Ravi Shankar. Inversely, by adopting this particular style of clothing and/or music, one demonstrated openness to such spiritual alternatives."[41] The mindfulness movement is entirely cognizant of the power of this sort of marketing. Witness the full-page advertisement for *Mindful* that appears on page 17 of the first official issue (and in various other spirituality and alternative-lifestyle publications). "It's who you are," the ad proclaims in huge letters at the top of the page.[42] "You want the best for your family and friends. You enjoy work that is meaningful and satisfying. You're dedicated to a more caring and sustainable society. You know the simple practice of being in the moment brings out the best in who you are. **You are mindful. And this is your magazine.**"[43] Placed directly above the smiling picture of a happy young white woman from the magazine's cover, the advertisement speaks directly in the second person to readers, telling them that they are already part of the mindfulness movement, and that their participation in this lifestyle is meaningful, caring, and self-nurturing. By being mindful you are living a positive lifestyle, and buying *Mindful* helps you support that lifestyle. In case anyone doesn't get the point, the ad continues: "Mindful is the groundbreaking new magazine dedicated to helping you live mindfully."[44] The advertisement is less thoroughly gendered than *Tranquilista*, though with its fashionably dressed female model and text about nurturing behaviors, at a minimum it is designed to appeal to female readers, if not exclusively.

Compared to *Tranquilista*, completely different gender identities are promulgated in books such as *Momfulness* by Denise Roy, which target an older, settled, married, more suburban audience with children (her other book is *My Monastery is a Minivan*), speaking to its desired mindful lifestyles. Here the advice is dispensed amidst houses with porch swings and backyards, while carpooling, doing laundry, and failing to live up to a seven-nights-in-a-row mindful sex commitment with one's husband. It is a less enticing vision than being a tranquilista, especially because it doesn't offer a plan for how to become something exciting, being instead a pragmatic (and hopefully comforting) battle strategy for using one's mothering skills to do triage on the already overwhelming situation.

Here the lifestyle is a world away from *Sex and the City*: motherhood is painted as difficult, tiring, body destroying, time-consuming, stressful, and messy. One of her mindfulness exercises involves locking yourself in the bathroom in order to "create a little zone of quiet."[45] Motherhood is challenging stuff: "As the mother of four children (and the foster mom of a fifth), I can attest to the fact that motherhood leaves stretch marks on us—in so many ways! I have been stretched physically, mentally, emotionally, spiritually. My limited notion of what constitutes a family has widened, and I have been pulled (sometimes kicking and screaming) into the present moment."[46] Yet,

Roy also suggests that it is profoundly rewarding—or can be, if approached mindfully. As she continues:

> Through great challenges and even greater love, my heart has grown to hold more than I ever thought possible. Motherhood continues to stretch me to this day, and I see no end in sight. It teaches lessons that many spiritual disciplines teach: the transforming effect of true presence, the importance of close attention, the need for deep compassion, the celebration of embodiment, the recognition of the sacred in all things, and the power of community. *Momfulness* is the word I use for this spiritual practice of conscious mothering. When we mother with mindfulness and compassion and a willingness to let this vocation awaken our hearts and transform our lives, we walk a spiritual path. We discover that care for our children and family is not a distraction from sacred practice but is the very essence of it."[47]

Women in Roy's book are not made up of kitten heels and bangles, but of laps, hugs, and "Mama Bear Instincts."[48] They find fulfillment through mothering, through transferring their responsibility solely from themselves and society in the abstract into nurturance for very specific small people with nightmares, stubborn opinions, developing breasts, and bowls of spaghetti upside-down on their heads. Roy is selling mindfulness wrapped in a gender identity that is possible only because of children, lifelong partners, and settled housing, and that conversely needs mindfulness in order to juggle all those things and appreciate them to the greatest possible depth. This is a gendered mindful lifestyle consumption as unobtainable for the tranquilistas as their lifestyle is for Roy, and thus they are marketed in different ways to capture the attention of different audiences.

A third gendered lifestyle is captured in *The Mindful Woman*. Sue Patton Thoelle readily admits to not being an expert on mindfulness, so it would seem that her main qualifications to write about the subject are that she is female and has a lot of life experience. Thoelle is a grandmother with an empty nest, who has gone through the motherhood stage and emerged to the other side in a life stage that mirrors that of the tranquilista in certain ways, yet is utterly different. She is still in the suburbs, divorced and remarried, still busy, but now has relative free space to devote to hobbies, exploring spirituality, and friends. Her anecdotes involve dealing with health issues, young people who tailgate her while she drives too slowly, and "croning" ceremonies wherein friends celebrate a woman's entrance into her later, wiser years. Her audience is older women who have spent decades putting others' needs ahead of their own, and who now find themselves with the time but not the know-how to try and cultivate a healthier lifestyle. Her solution: mindfulness, which she feels is particularly appropriate for women: "Even though the practice of mindfulness is deeply rooted in ancient, monastic traditions, I believe women are uniquely suited to its practice because we are naturally blessed with qualities such as sensitivity and diffuse awareness. *Diffuse awareness* is the ability to comfortably perceive and understand many things at once. *Sensitivity* is having feelings about what is seen, understood, and experienced. Women are multifocused, multifaceted, multitasking wonders. We are aware of and can pay attention to multiple things at once while also noting how we are feeling within the process. These are natural talents conducive to mindful living."[49] Because mindfulness is an especially female aspect, it is important to cultivate it in a manner that best suits a reader's innate feminine qualities: "Becoming mindful is an excellent avenue for self-care and self-realization. In order to get the most out of mindfulness, you need to practice it in ways that are harmonious with your basic nature—a woman's way. The practices contained in *The Mindful Woman* concentrate on feminine strengths, qualities, and energies."[50] Thoelle then provides a list of relevant feminine qualities, including emotionally grounded, intuitive, relational, compassionate, empowered, gentle, forgiving, receptive, and healing.[51] There is nothing here about being chic or sparkly, and though Thoelle counsels empowerment she is explicit that she means "soft power," which influences others while not forming a crusty, tough, unfeminine shell.[52]

Wilson, Roy, and Thoelle all use gender in very overt ways to market their books on mindfulness, but they adjust that marketing to reach different target audiences of women experiencing different stages of life. Each offers a particular vision of how mindfulness might enhance life and help build or manage an identity as a modern woman, so that mindfulness practice becomes an expression of one's femininity and provides practical benefits appropriate to one's particular situation. And though each author is also an accomplished career woman, they market their expertise at teaching mindfulness primarily through the vehicle of their own personal status as a woman in the same circumstances as their imagined readers.

Meanwhile, there are very few overtly male gendered depictions of mindfulness. One of the only ones is *Freeing the Angry Mind: How Men Can Use Mindfulness and Reason to Save Their Lives and Relationships,* by David Wexler and Peter Bankart.[53] Where female-oriented mindfulness books show a range of possible lifestyles and role models (as well as at times targeting gender-connected anxieties, such as eating habits and monogamous relationships), mindfulness offers little in the way of attractive, affirmative lifestyles designed specifically for men. *Freeing the Angry Mind* is crisis-intervention: get mindful or your male aggression will cost you your wife, family, and possibly your life. Though this does result in changes to one's lifestyle, it isn't depicted as exciting or affirmative of one's masculinity (indeed, poisonous masculinity is at the root of the problem that mindfulness is trying to solve in this book). It seems that one target audience as of yet untapped is men looking for mindful role models other than the monk, the male mindfulness instructor, or possibly the successful businessman.

It's a problem that some mindfulness authors have recognized. In his article "Five Ways to Make Mindfulness More Manly" (originally published in *Greater Good* and reprinted by *Mindful*), Kozo Hattori laments the lack of male involvement in mindfulness classes. This is especially troubling because "boys and men commit the vast majority of violent acts, from domestic violence to murder. Many struggle with expressing empathy and compassion."[54] Once again, when males receive particular attention from the mindfulness movement, they are pathologized. Hattori proposes five solutions to increase male involvement in mindfulness: (1) use pop culture to teach mindfulness to boys, (2) give boys role models of mindfulness and compassion, (3) start with boys in school, (4) meet men where they are (such as prisons, the military, and schools), and (5) make compassion training manlier. Hattori represents a call for a sort of "muscular mindfulness" similar in ways to the "muscular Christianity" popular in later 19th century and early 20th century America, and still found today in such movements as the Promisekeepers and Christian mixed martial arts competitions.

Branded Mindfulness

As the number of mindfulness books and promoters rises from the single digits to the dozens to hundreds, it becomes harder to stand out from the pack and capture a potential buyer's dollar. Different authors look for neglected arenas in which to apply mindfulness or novel approaches that may appeal to consumers. This drives the diversification of the mindfulness movement as it expands ever outward from food to sex to office work to parenting and so on, and establishes subgenres targeted to different potential customer audiences—some authors highlight mindful eating's

Buddhist spiritual connections, for instance, whereas others specifically downplay them in order to appeal to readers turned off by spiritual ideas. New audiences are targeted, such as college students in *Mindful Eating 101: A Guide to Healthy Eating in College and Beyond* and *Mindfulness for the Next Generation*.[55] As mindfulness seeps into ever more areas, Buddhism becomes increasingly Americanized and (not coincidentally) reaches and influences its largest possible audience.

The coining of terms like tranquilista and momfulness points to another important aspect of the selling of mindfulness in an open and increasingly crowded market for commercialized spirituality: the rise of branded and patented forms of mindfulness techniques. Finding ways to apply mindfulness to new niche concerns, asserting one's own *unique* personal expertise, claiming to have a new and improved method of mindfulness, or making one's methods exclusive and confined to a special pool of paying insiders are all strategies for dealing with this situation.

Real-World Mindfulness Training™ (RWMT) was created by Maya Frost, a mindfulness coach and practitioner of Buddhism for more than thirty years who found that many of her clients were attracted to mindfulness but repelled by meditation (that such a division could be conceptually coherent just goes to prove the power of previous efforts at mystifying and mainstreaming mindfulness, as discussed earlier). So she created RWMT as a response, with one central guiding principle: "instead of 'working' on mindfulness, start 'playing' with it instead!"[56] The idea was to make mindfulness fun, so that potential practitioners didn't find it to be a chore. As her website explains:

> Over the years, Real-World Mindfulness Training™ evolved as a way to blend practical teaching techniques, the latest neuroscience research on brain plasticity, and traditional contemplation practices. Maya stripped out the religious references, went easy on the science jargon, and wrapped it all up in a package that is very modern, fresh, and engaging.
> The basic ideas:
>
> 1) Mindfulness does not require meditation.
> 2) Paying attention is a powerful way to enhance creativity.
> 3) Fun is a huge motivator, and the more we enjoy playing with mindfulness, the more likely we are to develop it.
> 4) It's not difficult to be mindful—it's just difficult to *remember* to be mindful![57]

Here the trademarked form of mindfulness is contrasted with other approaches that are allegedly too Buddhist, scientific, or just plain hard.

Keeping mindfulness playful and pleasurable ensures it will continue to be used, even if—as Frost herself states—ideally meditation *should* be part of one's approach to mindfulness.[58]

Scott Rogers pursues a different audience with his creation of Jurisight®, "the mindfulness teaching method that uses legal terms and images to communicate fundamental mindfulness principles and exercises."[59] Designed specifically for lawyers and law students, Jurisight®, like Real-World Mindfulness, assumes its practitioners will not be initially interested in meditation: "*The Six-Minute Solution* offers lawyers a series of one-page passages from which to absorb mindfulness teachings that will lead to mindfulness insights without sitting on a cushion. The title is based on the six-minute interval used by most lawyers for billing clients—a reminder that even in this short period of time, it's possible to glean important mindfulness insights. For those interested in developing a meditative practice, six-minute long exercises are introduced."[60] The goals are to promote the happiness and well-being of those involved in the legal profession, to make them better at their jobs, and ultimately to transform the entire legal system "from one that creates unnecessary pain and suffering for its participants into one that fulfills its original mandate of contributing to a more peaceful society through a process of collaboration, wisdom, integrity, and professionalism."[61] Jurisight® is part of a package of mindfulness products that Rogers administers, including his Institute for Mindfulness Studies, various self-published books, lectures and workshops, and a collection of websites.[62] With his mission statement about transforming the legal profession, a common pattern appears: Jurisight® is a way for Rogers to make money and is intended to have a directly positive impact on society. For many people involved in marketing the mindfulness movement, these are not mutually incompatible goals.

In the sub-movements of mindfulness's American development, new branded forms are also necessary. Because MBSR is so huge a phenomenon, it becomes necessary to develop niche-specific forms of MBSR to market at new pools of clients. An example of this is Koru, a technique developed by Holly Rogers and Margaret Maytan and detailed in their book *Mindfulness for the Next Generation: Helping Emerging Adults Manage Stress and Lead Healthier Lives* (2012).[63] *Koru*, a Maori word that means looped or spiraled, developed from the work of Rogers and Maytan with university students. Both are employed at Duke University, whose Center for Mind-Body Medicine is one of the nation's most important promoters of MBSR. With a short, intriguing name (not unlike "Zen" in that way) that carries no immediate associations for the average North American, Koru is a way to deliver MBSR to a specific population of young adults away from home for the first time. The authors allege that "there is an excellent fit between the drive for identity development in emerging adults and the self-knowledge evoked by mindfulness practices."[64] They further claim that their plan is designed to take into account "the characteristic attitudes, perspectives, needs, and goals of typical university students."[65] More to the point, they feel that young people desperately need MBSR: "Students live in a high-tech world that involves constant multitasking and productivity. They write their papers while Facebooking, Twittering, and texting, with music blaring through their ear buds. Convincing them that less is more is a monumental task. That there is value in just sitting still and observing their breathing runs counter to their view of the world."[66] Much of Koru mirrors what one finds in standard MBSR: the raisin-eating exercise, the use of Jon Kabat-Zinn texts, the body scans, and so on. But the course is shortened to four weeks in order to accommodate the busy lives of students and is persistently framed in terms of how contemporary young people can best be impacted by MBSR.

Mindfulness even circles around to become branded once again as a special form of Buddhism. Thus we find the Mindfulness Based Zen Program™, promoted by Paul Harrison as "a modern mindfulness practice for today's lifestyles."[67] It seems that at this point, the connection between mindfulness and Buddhism has become attenuated enough that specific styles of mindfulness need to be created to recapture it.

Mindfulness in the Ranks

One of the more interesting forms of branded mindfulness is Mindfulness-Based Mind Fitness Training™ (MMFT). Developed by Elizabeth Stanley, a former U.S. Army officer who also trained as a Buddhist nun in Southeast Asia, MMFT is mindfulness for American soldiers. As one of the MMFT working documents states: "Today's complex, fluid, and unpredictable operational environment both demands more from the military in terms of mission requirements and exposes troops to more stressors and potential trauma than ever before. Mindfulness-based Mind Fitness Training (MMFT)® is a 20-hour course designed to improve performance and enhance resilience for individuals working in an extreme stress environment. MMFT blends (1) mindfulness skills training with (2) information and skills that promote stress resilience and (3) concrete applications for the operational environment. The result is a 'mental armor' which both increases warriors' operational effectiveness and enhances their capacity to bounce back from stressful experience."[68] In case the military lingo here is a bit too thick for the average reader, a little translation may be helpful. MMFT uses mindfulness techniques to make soldiers better at their combat, logistical, diplomatic, and other missions in the field, and helps them deal better with posttraumatic stress syndrome provoked by battle. PTSD is in fact a huge problem in the modern American military, with suicide (often associated with PTSD) outstripping battlefield casualties as a cause of death.[69]

MMFT draws directly (but obscurely) from Buddhist mindfulness, and more overtly from its medicalized MBSR form, as an article by Stanley and one of her main collaborators in *Joint Force Quarterly* makes clear: "These training techniques have existed for thousands of years, originating in Eastern spiritual traditions. In recent decades, they have been adapted for secular use, including in medical and mental health settings, corporations, prisons, and elementary schools. The most common and well-validated training program is mindfulness-based stress reduction (MBSR); more than 250 U.S. hospitals offer MBSR programs, and more than 50 research articles document its utility in many domains."[70] MMFT is similar to MBSR training, but some of its exercises are shortened, topics specific to military deployment are covered, there is a robust biofeedback component, and new content that highlights "parallels between physical and mental fitness for deployment readiness, and context created with real-world examples from the counterinsurgency environment" are added.[71] These include activities such as dropping MMFT participants into a mock Afghani village, complete with explosions and actors dressed as locals screaming at them.[72] If current clinical tests confirm early results that show MMFT's effectiveness, the U.S. Marines plan to train all new recruits in mindfulness (in 2010, the U.S. Marine Corps had 204,153 members).[73]

The use of terms like "mental armor" and "mind fitness" speak well to a military clientele, and the use of clinical trials and frequent reference to Kabat-Zinn's empirical research provide heft to MMFT, allowing its successful marketing to various arms of the U.S. military. These reflect the personal experience of Stanley, who is able to use her insider understanding of the military and the challenges it faces to effectively adapt MBSR into a form appealing to soldiers.

MMFT's application to PTSD is a natural extension of the Buddhist impulse to deal with suffering and the MBSR commitment to fighting stress specifically. But the program is also potentially controversial because of its application of Buddhist-derived meditation to warriors. By engaging in

Mindfulness-Based Mind Fitness Training™ a soldier is, among other things, better able to continue killing during a long and stressful combat scenario, and better equipped to deal with the stresses that arise from killing and being fired upon, so that he or she can be returned to the field quicker and/or better reintegrated into civilian society so as not to pose a hazard to him/herself or others. Use of Zen and related forms of Buddhism by the Japanese military during the Pacific War is a well-known, rather infamous case.[74] So even this sort of adaptation, while perhaps less mainstream than the use of mindfulness in hospitals and schools, is not without precedent in Buddhist history. And once detached from Buddhism, there seems to be no scenario to which mindfulness can be excluded.

Showing What Can't Be Seen

The marketing of mindfulness is complicated by the difficulty of its visual depiction. How do you sell something that can't be drawn or photographed? Few people want to watch extended video of people sitting still and meditating, and pictures of meditators are indistinguishable from people doing nothing at all, or perhaps sleeping. Mindful sex might be titillating, but how is the viewer supposed to tell it apart from regular porn? Watching someone eat mindfully probably just makes you hungry, rather than making you want to be mindful.

The only recourse is to be indirect. Ads have to imply values that are connected to mindfulness, such as peace, harmony, concentration, happiness, health, and so on. On the inside front cover of the one-shot issue of *Mindful* is an advertisement for Abacus, a Buddhist investment firm. A hand carefully balances six smooth, rounded rocks of different sizes and colors into a precarious tower. This image of stacked stones occurs with some regularity in mindfulness advertisements and seems to suggest great care and attention in its construction. Yet the image itself is not sufficient to sell the product. To clarify the ad's intent, some of the stones have words on them: "retirement, diversity, sustainability, stability." More to the point, a question hovers in the air over the fragile tower, querying, "Are you investing mindfully?" A sidebar carries a large font tagline meant to grab your attention—"Heal your money karma"—and goes on to explain that your life will be transformed by relying on the services of Brent Kessel and Spencer Sherman. Further information about the name of the service and how to contact them are naturally included.

The image cannot sufficiently sell the specific product (Abacus investment advice) nor can it sell the overall quality that Abacus wants you to associate with its product (mindfulness). Mindfulness and its various associated values such as harmony and health are difficult to depict directly, and so they almost always must be framed with words. The mindfulness movement therefore thrives on written text, even as it has exploded in popularity during a visually driven age in American popular culture. Thus the reliance by mindfulness movement books on text-heavy covers, especially subtitles, which can be so long as to recall book titles of the 18th century, and which often must do substantial come-hither work attracting the customer and explaining what is on offer. On a more basic level, text is required when one wishes to reveal to an outside audience the hidden internal processes of meditation—in the case of mindfulness, visual media are simply impotent to fully replicate the communicative power possessed by writing. This does not mean, of course, that visuals aren't used in the marketing of mindfulness. It's just that they become backgrounded, rather than foregrounded, providing less tangible senses of feeling, mood, and aesthetic rather than conveying significant amounts of direct information.

How are such moods evoked? Examining the covers of mindfulness books is one place to start. As Cat Yampbell notes in "Judging a Book by Its Cover":

> In the world of publishing, the paratext is not only equally significant, but many industry people argue that the cover is the foremost aspect of the book. Regardless of the quality of the literature, its cover often determines a book's success. D. F. McKenzie acknowledges the impossibility of divorcing "the substance of the text on the one hand from the physical form of its presentation on the other" and has defined "a *text* as a complex structure of meanings which embraces every detail of its formal and physical presentation in a specific historical context" (qtd. in Marotti xi). The paratext *is* the text. Literary merit becomes irrelevant if the book does not, or cannot, reach the reader. The cover of a book is often the reader's first interaction with it—the consumer's initial reading of the text. When a bookstore's shelves are filled with unknown books and authors, a book's cover must provide visual intrigue to entice a consumer.[75]

Cover art is a key factor in a book's success. Alan Powers explains the power of the cover: "The design of book covers helps to make a book something more than mere 'information,' something that, even though it may have many thousands of identical siblings, still demands a relationship, something that when given, defines the values of the giver and recipient.

The best book covers possess a form of hidden eroticism, connecting with some undefended part of the personality in order to say 'take me, I am yours.'"[76] Yampbell continues: "Publishers consider the entire design of a book, including the spine (which is often the book's sole introduction to a potential consumer), the size, shape, paper texture, font, and so forth. 'Grabability' is a key marketing concern. The book must visually leap off the shelf and 'grab.'"[77]

A review of the covers of 100 mindfulness books published between 2003 and 2012 reveals some of the common patterns of the "erotics" of the marketing of mindfulness.[78] Fifty-one covers use natural imagery, especially flowers, leaves, or sea/lakeshores. These floral images imply growth, nature, naturalness, organicness, simplicity, wholesomeness. One of the only to use an autumn leaf rather than a spring or summer one is *The Mindfulness Solution to Pain*. Water images evoke serenity, depth, purity. Despite a focus on the natural world, there are very few animals on display, except on books with actual animals in the title, and one of the more intriguing books of mindful lifestyle: *The Mindful Carnivore: A Vegetarian's Hunt for Sustenance*. And there is almost no depiction of modern technology at all: a cityscape for *Urban Mindfulness*, a "car" made out of flowers and leaves for *Mindfulness of the Go*, a women with a laptop for *Tranquilista*, and two wires crossed into a heart pattern for *Rewire Your Brain for Love* basically exhaust all of the invocations of technology. An image of stacked round rocks, similar to that referenced above of Abacus, appears on *Inner Productivity*.

Interestingly, seventy-five of the covers include no people whatsoever. People are apparently not very good images for selling mindfulness. The interpretation of what counts as a "person" for the remaining twenty-five covers is very liberal, including silhouettes, Buddha statues, drawings, body parts, and tiny figures almost lost in great natural landscapes. Many of these are just hands, often holding food for mindful eating or with thumb and index finger touching in an invocation of meditation postures. Of those persons whose race is discernible, seven are Asian (including three Buddha statues and a famous Asian monk), fourteen are white, and six are so abstract as to be undefinable.[79] There is only a single African American, part of a diverse set of women drawn on the cover of *Tranquilista*, which also includes the only visible Latino/a person, an Asian American, and a white woman (with the laptop). If we include all three Buddha statues and the famous monk, then there are seven books with clearly male figures or parts of figures (including one half of a pair on *The Mindful Couple*). There are fifteen books with clearly female figure or parts of figures (hands, etc.).

One of the most noticeable trends is the lack of Buddhist motifs. With a very liberal definition, seventeen covers could be said to have Asian imagery of some sort, including vaguely Zen sand or rock placement, quasi-mandala/ chakra images, a number of lotus flowers, and the aforementioned buddhas and monk. So Asian motifs are seriously outnumbered by both covers with natural imagery and covers with no images at all. Except in quite specific cases (*Why is Buddha Smiling?*, which features a smiling Buddha), Asian and particularly Buddhist tropes are rarely used to market mindfulness. Perhaps the most interesting thing to observe of all is that there are no full photographs or drawings whatsoever of people actually doing sitting meditation, and just a handful with bits of people that by their posture or hand positioning suggest that they could be meditating. Mindfulness does not mean meditation, or at least, meditation doesn't sell mindfulness.

If we recall the discussion of the whitening of mindfulness from Chapter 2, it seems apparent that similar racial dynamics play out on the book covers, though the general lack of human figures does mitigate this somewhat. African Americans are still almost absent from the depicted faces and bodies of mindfulness, but mindfulness in general doesn't have much of a human face at all. Perhaps this is connected to the mental nature of mindfulness. Because it is a technique that takes place within the mind, cover designers are often left with a small range of possible choices to work with, and authors and editors resort to long subtitles to convey what is between the covers of the book. Another common technique is to associate the book with a famous author. Not counting the five books that Jon Kabat-Zinn is an author or co-author of from our sample, we can observe that Kabat-Zinn's name is prominently featured as contributing a foreword on the front cover of ten books, and as recommending the book on the back cover of five more works. Other members of the celebrity mindfulness brigade whose names are referenced commonly on the front or back covers are Thich Nhat Hanh, the Dalai Lama, Jack Kornfield, and Daniel Goleman.

One of the greatest challenges, of course, is depicting mindfulness on film. YouTube and instructional videos from mindfulness teachers tend to show people talking about how to do mindfulness and what benefits should be expected. More ambitiously, in 2013 mindfulness instructor Paul Harrison released *The Mindfulness Movie*, a feature-length documentary about how mindfulness is influencing Western culture. Tellingly, of the thirty-five experts he interviewed, all but one (Thich Nhat Hanh) were white, and the majority were American. As with the periodicals and books discussed in this and other chapters, this stark racial disparity demonstrates who controls the apparatus of mindfulness in the West, which of course influences who gets to represent mindfulness, who feels comfortable practicing it, what race-specific applications are selected, and what social groups are (and are not) targeted as consumers. It is from these facts that the choices about marketing are made. As for *The Mindfulness Movie*, it appears that the movie is primarily made up of interviews with lots of so-called expert talking heads, that is, people sitting in a studio discussing the topic at hand: once again words, words, and more words are required to reveal the possible presence of experiential awareness, which evades easy visual depiction.[80]

Conclusion

The result of the successful adaptations described in early chapters is that mindfulness has become so mainstream that it is used as a generic appellation for anything good, spiritual, healthy, liberal, and so forth. It is traveling the same pathway that Zen did a generation earlier, where Zen ceased to mean a specific meditation practice or Buddhist tradition and instead became a universal term for aesthetic, artistic, meaningful, cool, and/or spiritual. And in the process of achieving mainstream generality, mindfulness becomes a label for supposedly enlightened consumption, which is at root a tool for getting people to spend money and consume products that they otherwise might not purchase.

There seems to be a particular attraction to the strategic use of mindfulness by companies selling food and beauty items. For example, the website for Earth Balance, an organic food company, uses mindfulness to hawk some of its products:

> Just outside Boulder, Colorado is where you'll find a company that's committed to quality on a whole new scale. That's us. We're Earth Balance®, and we can't wait to introduce you to our line of naturally irresistible buttery spreads, shortenings, nut butters, soymilk, soy nog, coconut spread and MindfulMayo™ Dressing and Sandwich Spreads. All of our products are 100% plant-based, vegan, non-GMO, lactose-free, gluten-free, egg-free, casein-free, have 0g of trans fat and, oh, did we mention they're absolutely delicious?...To put it simply: We use only natural ingredients. We're organic-minded. And we're whipping up the good stuff to share with everyone who follows a plant-based diet, suffers from food allergies, or just wants to lead a more health-conscious and earth-loving life.[81]

Nowhere is it spelled out precisely how this mayonnaise got to be mindful: Was it mindfully prepared, or are you supposed eat it slowly, with careful attention to each bite? It seems rather that mindful is meant to fit with an overall lifestyle of self-cultivation spirituality, concern for the earth, and alternative, vegetarian eating. The website's subpage titled "Wellness" features a drawing of a thin, comfortably dressed young woman in hipster glasses, levitating cross-legged while holding Earth Balance baked products.[82]

Mindful Mints goes considerably further. Mindfulness isn't just an alliterative name and a gesture toward healthy eating, as in MindfulMayo. Mindfulness is actively drawn upon to market the mints. The website lists the many possible benefits of eating its mints:

> Achieve a calm alert state of mind with Mindful Mints. It's meditation in a mint! Mindful Mints will destress your day by tapping into the power of L-Theanine, an amino acid found in green tea. L-Theanine naturally stimulates activity in the brain which has been shown to improve learning performance, concentration & awareness. Do you feel stressed? Reduces stress and nervous tension. Do you have trouble sleeping? Enriches quality of sleep. Is it hard to focus and concentrate? Helps to alleviate fogginess and hyper-activity. Want to feel more alert? Increases mental focus and alpha brain wave activity. Are you affected by caffeine? Reduces negative effects of caffeine. Looking to improve your mood naturally? Promotes relaxation without drowsiness. Is it safe? Safe and effective for both adults and children. Finding it hard to deal with the daily grind? Improves learning performance and concentration.[83]

Meditation in a mint: get all the alleged benefits of mindfulness, without doing any mindfulness practice. As the company claims, its core values are "Awareness + Compassion & Better health through mindful living."[84] Other products that also try to cash in on the cachet of mindfulness include Mindful Meals, Mindful Minerals, Mindful Beauty, and Mindful Software. Mindfulness allows us to feel good about our consumption. We can engage in the pleasure of shopping and self-indulgence while feeling that we are contributing to the healing of self and society. And we can enchant any activity—sex, shopping, eating, high-powered finance—by applying the magic of mindfulness. The label "mindful," when applied to seemingly unrelated consumer products can help to pry open a consumer's wallet by associating a product with a general sense of spirituality, health, intelligence, or civic-mindedness.

Perhaps mindfulness in pill-sized bites can solve our hungers and make us happy. Maybe when Amidon stood despairing in the mall, he should have looked for ways to sell products mindfully and to sell mindfulness as a product, and thus redeem through compassionate consumption the desire-driven society that disturbed him. Yet with all the effort expended to make mindfulness saleable, the troubling nature of mindfulness in the mall never totally evaporates, and thus in Chapter 6 we find Americans who wish to emphasize the more revolutionary, rather than satiating, potential of mindfulness. They are selling a product too, but a very particular one: a brand new, better society reformed through the power of mindfulness.

6 MORALIZING MINDFULNESS: HOW IS MINDFULNESS RELATED TO VALUES AND WORLDVIEWS?

Moralize: To make moral; to give a moral quality to or affect the moral quality of (actions, feelings, etc.)

—Oxford English Dictionary[1]

Long-time Google engineer, executive, and self-described "jolly good fellow" Chade-Meng Tan (usually just called Meng) hobnobbed with celebrities and politicians for years as one of Google's prominent in-house personalities. But he became a recognized celebrity in his own right after his 2012 book *Search Inside Yourself: The Unexpected Path to Achieving Success, Happiness (and World Peace)* rocketed onto the *New York Times* Best Seller list and stayed there, month after month after month. Like most books in the mindfulness movement genre, it promised practical, this-worldly benefits that anyone could access, and presumably every American wants. Page after page, he described the near-miraculous manner in which mindfulness delivers happiness, prosperity, and health, reinforced by forewords from his friends Jon Kabat-Zinn and Daniel Goleman, both best-selling mindfulness authors themselves. Filled with cartoons and jokes ranging from groan-inducing to genuinely amusing, *Search Inside Yourself* seemed to be the perfect embodiment of the mystifying, medicalizing, mainstreaming, and marketing trends explored in previous chapters. But although these aspects dominated most pages of the book, in a way these were just the mundane enticements that Meng used to attract skeptical readers—his real agenda was far larger than just ordinary self-help. This fine-tuned pop mindfulness confection had a very specific moral dimension as well, usually treated subtly but present at many points throughout the book. As Meng admitted near the end of the book, "*Search Inside Yourself* started with a simple dream, and that dream is world peace."[2]

A Buddhist since his student days, Meng's advocacy of mindfulness was tied to larger values and worldviews, not just desires for personal happiness and financial achievement. He believed that meditation was "the key active ingredient in the formula for world peace" and that realizing this fact constituted "an epiphany:" "I have found my life's goal. My life's goal is to make the benefits of meditation accessible to humanity...I am confident that the transformative power of contemplative practices is so compelling, anybody who understands it will find it irresistible."[3]

So how should he go about making mindfulness accessible worldwide? First, he would start with his workplace, where he enjoyed inside access to one of the world's most prominent and respected corporations. "The way to create the conditions for world peace," he realized, "is to create a mindfulness-based emotional intelligence curriculum, perfect it within Google, and then give it away as one of Google's gifts to the world."[4] As it turned out, the path to world peace lay not with large-scale economic change, social revolution, political solutions, or breakthrough scientific advancement. Instead, world peace required nothing more (or less) than creating a mindful world, one meditator at a time. "Like many others wiser than me, I believe world peace can and must be created from the inside out. If we can find a way for everybody to develop peace and happiness within themselves, their inner peace and happiness will naturally manifest into compassion. And if we can create a world where most people are happy, at peace, and compassionate, we can create the foundation for world peace. Fortunately, a methodology for doing that already exists and has already been practiced by various peoples for thousands of years. It is the art of using contemplative practices to develop the mind. Most of us know it as meditation."[5] He concluded by quoting Thich Nhat Hanh and imploring his readers to become bodhisattvas who save the world.[6]

Like other mindfulness movement authors, Meng genuinely wanted people to practice mindfulness in order to be happy. But personal happiness, though crucial and valuable in its own right, was not the final destination on the path of mindfulness. He believed that by being happy and mindful, people would become compassionate. Becoming compassionate and mindful, they would, he believed, naturally live and act in ways that automatically led to worldwide peace and harmony. So selling happiness via mindfulness ultimately supported a moral outlook that valued compassion and peace, promised a utopian future, and used religiously derived techniques and scientifically derived rhetoric to advance this vision of global salvation. Mindfulness, allegedly decoupled from religion and values in the process of being commodified for the wider American market, nonetheless often seems to carry evidence of an implicit (or, in many cases, explicit) value system that provides orientation in the world, a sense of transcendent purpose, a program of action, and a division of the world into insiders (the mindful) and outsiders (the mindless). This same program can be found in the works of Kabat-Zinn and Goleman, and virtually all the most prominent movers and shakers of the mindfulness movement.

This final chapter considers the ways in which mindfulness continues to operate in a religious or quasi-religious fashion, despite its advocates' frequent insistence that it is not (or, at least, need not be) connected to religion. As we've seen, religion and values are downplayed by mindfulness authors to garner larger audiences—but in many cases, the reason they want an audience in the first place is because they are convinced that mindfulness and other elements derived from Buddhism have a real ability to alleviate suffering (the goal of religious Buddhism); illuminate the truths of life (such as those of impermanence and interconnectedness); and bring about dramatic, even salvific improvement on the individual, national, and planetary levels. World peace turns out to be the ultimate practical benefit of mindfulness. And mindfulness can be used to provide an order to life that stabilizes, manages, labels, and assigns meaning to all possible activities and situations. Mindfulness is connected to a whole set of self-disciplinary and lifestyle practices that are given moral weight by their promoters. Even if we accept the protestations of many advocates that mindfulness is not a religion per se, it is nonetheless doing the work of religions.[7]

In the process of adapting mindfulness to meet the widest American market, and thus to create the greatest potential for peace, advocates have simultaneously worked out a type of American Buddhist civil religion. Civil religion is a longstanding trope in the field of American religious history, which has received many different interpretations over decades of scholarly discussion and dispute.[8] One way to approach the concept is to recognize the way that national symbols come to hold a sort of religious aura: the Constitution as divinely inspired scripture, the American flag as holy symbol, freedom as a sacred value, and so forth. Often this has been connected with a sort of generic monotheism on the one hand, and a visionary ideal of America as unique, anointed, or predestined nation of special cosmic importance, the major player in the next or final chapter of the divine storybook of the world's history, tasked with great responsibilities as savior and warned of terrible consequences should the country falter in its heavenly appointed role, on the other.

Another approach to civil religion considers religiously based descriptions of what a good society would look like, how to achieve it, and who would be included (and excluded) in such a society. Through the examination of mindfulness, we find that American Buddhists and fellow travelers have produced a vision of their own, with particular understandings of the United States and its mission and potential; the qualities Americans should possess; the practices they must cultivate; and the proper interaction of mindfulness with politics, education, law enforcement, the military, the legal and prison systems, economics and consumerism, and the medical establishment. The total transformation of all of these aspects of society through the adoption of mindfulness is indeed a vision of the good society—the "Mindful Society," as a regular column in *Shambhala Sun* puts it, or *A Mindful Nation*, the title of U.S. Congressman Tim Ryan's best-selling book. According to Jon Kabat-Zinn's foreword to *A Mindful Nation*, mindfulness is the way for America to fulfill its greatest national destiny: "Mindfulness can literally change our brains, improve our capacity for perspective taking and decision making, and enhance our emotional intelligence and our ability to act with clarity and wisdom, alone and in concert with others. It could also catalyze a renewed and authentic civility in public discourse. It proffers, in small but not insignificant ways, the possibility for our nation to wholeheartedly and authentically embody its deepest democratic principles and longings."[9] In passages like this and others offered in this chapter, we see a type of American Buddhist civil religion at work. Let us examine what the mindfulness movement imagines as the problems and solutions facing contemporary Americans.

American Buddhist Jeremiads: What's Wrong with America?

Religions are complex cultural products, providing everything from social control to recipes for matzah ball soup. It can be dangerous to reduce religions to any single dimension, but even if religions are many things, one thing that seems undeniable is that they are proposed solutions.[10] Religions imagine problems—such as sin, attachment, pollution, spirit attack—and provide programs of action that deal with the problems, resulting in desired benefits, be they this-worldly or transcendent. Often, and especially in the West, the problems that concern the religiously minded are individual in nature and linked to improper personal behavior and thought, which are determined according to religiously mandated systems of morality.

One of the primary concerns that mindfulness authors voice is the idea of disconnection. Throughout the various applications of mindfulness, there is the sense of alienation from oneself and one's surroundings. Modern Americans, apparently, are estranged from their minds, bodies, surroundings, and each other. They are parenting mindlessly, eating mindlessly, working mindlessly, and generally living in a detached, distracted manner. Leigh Eric Schmidt has pointed out that this feeling drove the emergence of mysticism in America: "Modern mysticism was always formed as much out of lacking and loss as it was out of epiphanic assurance. For many, it emerged out of an empty space of longing for 'a heightened, intensified way of life' and represented a troubled quest for a unifying and integrative experience in an increasingly fragmented world of divided selves and lost souls."[11] This earlier quest was a search for union with a God who seemed ever more distant in the industrializing, urbanizing, diversifying, increasingly rootless post-Darwinian world. If anything, the trend has intensified in the current age and is amplified not only by the changes in society and technology but also by the decreased centrality of God and Christianity in 21st century American culture. The result is a feeling not only that God or spiritual values are absent, but that we too are no longer even present. According to pediatrician and *Mindful Eating* author Jan Chozen Bays, "When we aren't present, it makes us feel vaguely but persistently dissatisfied. This sense of dissatisfaction, of a gap between us and everything and everyone else, leads to unhappiness."[12] Jon Kabat-Zinn is sure that this characterizes our common condition in America: "We are out of touch with our feelings and perceptions, with our impulses and our emotions, with our thoughts, with what we are saying, and even with our bodies. This is mostly due to being perpetually preoccupied, lost in our minds, absorbed in our thoughts, obsessed with the past or the future, consumed with our plans and our desires, diverted by our need to be entertained, driven by our expectations, fears, or cravings of the moment, however unconscious or habitual all this may be. And therefore, we are amazingly out of touch in some way or other with the present moment, the moment that is actually presenting itself to us now."[13] Out of touch, we spiral downward in a cycle of disaffection, compelled into an "incessant drive to fill up your time, to get somewhere else, or obtain what you feel you are lacking so you can feel satisfied and happy. In our loneliness and isolation, there is a deep longing, a yearning, usually unconscious or ignored, to belong, to be connected to a larger whole, to not be anonymous, to be seen and known."[14] For most mindfulness advocates, this process is actually a double-whammy, because not only are we cut off from our experiences, but also our very thought processes heap further torture upon ourselves. As Ronald Seigel points out: "We live most of our lives this way—lost in thought, more often thinking about life than experiencing it.

But missing out on the moment-to-moment richness of life isn't our biggest problem. Unfortunately, our thoughts frequently make us unhappy. We're all susceptible to a kind of *thinking disease*. In our attempt to ensure we'll feel good, we think of all the possible developments that might make us feel bad. While sometimes this is helpful, just as often it generates needless suffering, since every negative anticipatory thought is associated with a bit of tension or painful feeling."[15] The problem here is worry about the future. Another problem is negative thinking about the present. From the point of view of Susan Smalley and Diana Winston in *Fully Present: The Science, Art, and Practice of Mindfulness*, "One of the most disturbing aspects of contemporary U.S. culture is the degree to which self-hatred runs rampant. Nearly everyone I encounter expresses some amount of personal dissatisfaction and harbors a ruthless critic within who compares them to others and judges everyone they meet. I even once read an interview with Meryl Streep in which she confessed to believing she couldn't act. Unfortunately, most people have been conditioned by cultural norms, family, media, and a host of other influences to feel inadequate and unworthy."[16]

The human problem, it seems, is that we are unhappy, and our unhappiness stems from being disconnected from the world, each other, and ourselves, which is ultimately due to failure to live in the present moment—and then we ladle on top of this a generous portion of unhelpful, fearful, and often self-critical thoughts. In the mindfulness movement, all of this mindlessness leads to ill-health, stress, broken relationships, poor parenting, bad work performance, sexual dysfunction, and myriad other sources of unhappiness. Primarily, we are the source of our own problems—if we acted in wiser, more aware ways, we would avoid causing trouble for ourselves; our own failures at mindfulness cause or contribute to our unhappiness.

Religions also often posit not only a problem that exists for or within individual human beings—frequently, they also have a larger social or cosmic vision that suggests that there is an ideal way for the world to operate, yet it is not currently operating in that fashion. For example, in Christianity there has been not only a human fall from grace but also an expulsion from the garden, so that humankind wanders the face of the earth, struggling to eke out a living, quarrelling with each other, and violating God's commandments. Since the time of the British Puritan colonies, American religious history has rung with jeremiads, strongly worded sermons that claim the community and nation are off-track, and that failure to get right with God will result in imminent destruction. This venerable tradition continues to be a favored pastime in the present, for example in Pat Robertson's claims on *The 700 Club* that the

September 11th terrorist attacks were caused by God taking away his divine protection of the nation, due to rampant American materialism, pornography, secularism, occultism, abortion, and the removal of Christianity from the schools and courts.[17] It continues in the American mindfulness movement as well, where failure to be mindful results in behavior that threatens not only the individual but also the nation and indeed the entire world.

One place we encounter this is in *A Mindful Nation*. As narrated in the book, Congressman Tim Ryan was a fierce patriot and a dedicated statesman, but as he reflected on the state of the nation, that didn't prevent him from believing that there was an awful lot that was wrong with America: "The pain of war. Economic insecurity. The frustrations of being sick or taking care of sick relatives in a broken health-care system. The challenge of teaching children to pay attention and be kind to themselves and others as they swim in a world of distraction and aggression... [characterized by] lack of opportunity, divisiveness, daunting environmental and energy challenges."[18] Given all this, he mused, "Is it any wonder that the courageous spirit of America, and faith in our cherished values of self-reliance and stick-to-itiveness, have flagged?"[19] He thought back on his late grandfather, a man strong enough that he could afford to be gentle, kind, and compassionate. The contrast with modern America pained Ryan:

> I see in my grandfather an example for our country. Consider where bravado and ego-based posturing has put us over the past ten years. It has cost us too many lives, as well as a lot of money. America has always been strongest when we have been tough but gentle. Gentleness is not a sign of weakness; it's a sign of strength. We all know from the playground that the one who is acting the toughest is really the most insecure. America is at its best when we are confident. I am sorry to say that we have lost our footing. We are running around now, in different directions, looking over our shoulder, scared and unsure. We don't know what to do or when to do it. If we could just slow down a bit, perhaps we'd see the answer.[20]

Here Ryan, a Democrat, is looking back primarily over the years of George W. Bush's presidency and insinuating that American aggression in the Muslim world after September 11, 2001—and the sort of belligerent American attitude often connected with it—has led the country down the wrong path. Others see America as a culture of aggression, especially in the political realm, which has allegedly become completely toxic and nonfunctional. This is the view of David Rome and Hope Martin, who ask "Are You Listening?" in an exasperated tone in their essays for the anthology *The Mindfulness Revolution*. As they survey recent political trends, this is what they find:

> With cries of "Armageddon!" and "Baby killer!" the great U.S. health care debate in 2010 reached its tortured climax. The debate was adversarial, angry, hateful, even violent—a long-running case study in dysfunctional communication. Politicians on both sides were trapped in scripts that required them to assert fixed political positions and ignore or attack what the other side was saying, rarely sharing their true thoughts and feelings. Cable television pundits leapt into the fray like gladiators, interrupting and out-shouting each other with fierce abandon. The health care imbroglio may be an extreme example, but it reflects a larger pathology in our culture, one that is driven by combativeness on the one hand and disingenuousness on the other. If we are to survive the twenty-first century, we must become better communicators, speaking and listening honestly and compassionately across diversity and difference. Unsatisfying communication is rampant in our society: between spouses; between parents and children; among neighbors and coworkers; in civic and political life; and between nations, religions, and ethnicities.[21]

For Congressman Ryan, America was acting like a schoolyard bully, strutting around puffed up with stupid aggression in order to mask all the insecurities and problems lurking inside, while for Rome and Martin American society seemed a seething cauldron of anger and dysfunction. For Jan Chozen Bays, leader of Great Vow Zen Monastery, America was closer to a ravenous spirit from Buddhist mythology:

> Caught by desire. It's true of everyone, but somehow, it seems especially true of Americans... We have learned to stay in constant motion, chasing after desires, only vaguely aware of the chronic feeling of dissatisfaction and emptiness underneath. This treadmill of unending desire creates a nation of hungry ghosts. In Buddhist art, hungry ghosts are depicted with the huge swollen bellies of chronic malnutrition, but with necks so thin they cannot swallow one grain of rice without choking. It is the realm of unending craving. Hungry ghosts are not phantoms born of superstitious beliefs of medieval people. They are alive and starving here in America, which we often brag about as being

"the most affluent society in the world." We think we have the "goods" but actually, we don't. We don't have good public education, or good health care for all our citizens. We don't provide good pay for people who teach our children. We don't have good public transportation so people can get to their jobs, doctors, and schools. We don't even have good food. We are poor in the essentials and rich in the nonessentials. We have second snowmobiles, third cars, a freezer full of Haagen-Dazs and a TV in every room, including the bathrooms of our McMansions. But we don't have happiness.[22]

Desire, rather than insecurity or perhaps xenophobia, is the boogeyman for Bays. The result is a nation overloaded with second-rate institutions and more junk than anyone needs.

For many commentators in the mindfulness movement, America suffers from the rapid pace of modern life, often in connection with the instant and frivolous culture of electronic media, and the extremely fast (and, mostly, deleterious) changes in society being wrought by the online revolution. Susan Smalley and Diana Winston allege that "Modern society tends to condition us to be anything but mindful:" "The dominant American culture validates virtually mindless productivity, busyness, speed, and efficiency. The last thing we want to do is just be present. We want to do, to succeed, to produce…But this is life in America in the twenty-first century and, to an increasing degree, around the world. We are so focused on doing that we have forgotten all about being, and the toll this takes on our physical, mental, and emotional health is significant."[23] Jon Kabat-Zinn was even more sour on this development. In *Coming to Our Senses: Healing Ourselves and the World Through Mindfulness* he characterized America as "A.D.D. Nation," claiming "the entire society suffers from attention deficit disorder—big time—and from its most prevalent variant, attention deficit *hyperactivity* disorder. And it is getting worse by the day:"[24]

It is now harder to pay attention to any one thing and there is more to pay attention to. We are easily diverted and more easily distracted. We are continuously bombarded with information, appeals, deadlines, communications. Things come at us fast and furious, relentlessly. And almost all of it is man-made; it has thought behind it, and more often than not, an appeal to either our greed or our fears. These assaults on our nervous system continually stimulate and foster desire and agitation rather than contentedness and calmness. They foster reaction rather than communication, discord rather than accord or concord, acquisitiveness rather than feeling whole and complete as we are. And above all, if we are not careful, they rob us of time, of our moments. We are continually being squeezed or projected into the future as our present moments are assaulted and consumed in the fires of endless urgency. The relentless acceleration of our way of life over the past few generations has made focusing in on anything at all something of a lost art. That loss has been compounded by the digital revolution, which— think back just a few short years—rapidly found its way into our every-day lives in the form of home computers, fax machines, beepers, cell phones, cell phones with cameras, palm devices for personal organization, laptops, 24/7 high-speed connectivity, the Internet and its World Wide Web, and of course, e-mail, all now increasingly wireless, not that long ago an unthinkable dream, the stuff of science fiction.[25]

In this presentation, the things that many of us like to think of as conveniences and necessities of modern life are rendered as nightmares, a ceaseless flood of maddening technology by which we are "assaulted" and "consumed." The situation is dire. Kabat-Zinn has maintained that he is optimistic that mindfulness will eventually save us from ourselves, but he has also repeatedly cautioned about what may lie in store for us: "The fate of our species may hang in the balance, not in some far-off future, but perhaps in the next few generations, much sooner than we might imagine."[26] He, like many involved in the mindful parenting and mindful teaching movements, was especially concerned about the impact of modern society on children's development.

Finally, there are the environmentalist concerns commonly raised in the mindfulness movement. Stephanie Kaza, in *Mindfully Green*, succinctly encapsulates the widespread view that America, if not the world, could face imminent environmental collapse: "With all our best efforts, it will still be impossible to eliminate all the harm being done to the world. The scale of environmental suffering is too widespread and too deeply entrenched. Many of today's predicaments were set in motion long before our time. Many situations are simply out of our control. While we can do our best to reduce the harm associated with our own actions, we are limited in how much we can reduce the extensive harm caused by others...Today we look around the world and there is no shortage of environmental suffering. Strip-mining for coal now destroys whole mountains in West Virginia, filling valley streams with sludge and people's homes with toxic waste...In the middle of the Pacific Ocean a floating waste dump the size of Texas collects billions of pieces of plastic debris—false 'food' that attracts animals from up and down the food chain."[27] Such views are echoed by many other mindfulness advocates. Even mindfulness advocates like Thich Nhat Hanh—normally not a particularly alarmist writer— express grim worries about the future:

> We are like sleepwalkers, not knowing what we are doing or where we are headed. Whether we can wake up or not depends on whether we can walk mindfully on our Mother Earth. The future of all life, including our own, depends on our mindful steps. We have to hear the bells of mindfulness that are sounding across our planet. We have to start learning how to live in a way so that a future will be possible for our children and grandchildren. I have sat with the Buddha for a long time and consulted him about the issue of global warming, and the teaching of the Buddha is very clear. If we continue to live as we have been living, consuming without a thought to the future, destroying our forests and emitting dangerous amounts of carbon dioxide, then devastating climate change is inevitable. Much of our ecosystem will be destroyed. Sea levels will rise and coastal cities will be inundated, forcing hundreds of millions of refugees from their homes, creating wars and outbreaks of infectious disease.[28]

Buddha, it turns out, is an environmentalist. Hanh here is speaking prophetically, as a variety of other prominent mindfulness authors do, trying to wake us up (thus his reference to mindfulness bells, which shake us out of our auto-pilot stupor) to the extreme challenges that we face. Mindlessness and greed have brought us to the brink of destruction, and everything we hold dear is imperiled. Kaza and Hanh are by no means unusual in their cries for environmental mindfulness. In fact, one can easily find all of the above dynamics operating in many mindfulness books. Humans as a species, and especially Americans, are apparently aggressive, stressed out, greed-ridden, fractious, distracted, and wasteful. America is rushing toward destruction and pulling the whole planet down with us.

Mindfulness, Human Nature, and Values

But the doom-crying voice is not the only mindfulness movement perspective on human nature. In fact, the sturm und drang can be partially blamed on the fact that mindfulness is usually associated with a very lofty opinion of human nature, and of individual human beings—and thus when we fail to live up to that nearly divine potential, the frustration is all the greater.

Religions typically posit a theology of human nature, or at least of human capacity and worth. In the case of the mindfulness movement, human nature is unambiguously good. As a *Shambhala Sun* editorial put it, one of the magazine's basic principles is *"Mindful Living*. All people share the same basic nature of awareness, wisdom, and goodness. That is our human birthright. People of all spiritual paths, or none at all, increasingly want to live in a mindful, loving way, and they see that meditative traditions like Buddhism can help them do it."[29] This notion of birthright appears throughout the mindfulness literature and is a particular favorite phrase of Jon Kabat-Zinn, and therefore of the legions inspired by his Mindfulness-Based Stress Reduction (MBSR) program. As he explains, "These inner resources are our birthright. They are available to us across our entire life span because they are not in any way separate from us. It is in our very nature as a species to learn and grow and heal and move toward greater wisdom in our ways of seeing and in our actions, and toward greater compassion toward ourselves and others...Mindfulness is the final common pathway of what makes us human, our capacity for awareness and for self-knowing."[30] Spiritual teacher Joseph Naft agrees: "To be truly human is to be mindful. The direct awareness of primary perceptions is one of the primary wonders of being human, enriching our life beyond measure...Mindfulness is the authentic state for a human being: a relaxed, open awareness of our inner and outer perceptions in the moment."[31] This connection between mindfulness and authenticity appears frequently in mindfulness literature. Kabat-Zinn states it succinctly: "Ultimately, mindfulness can become an effortless, seamless element of our life, a way for our very being to express itself authentically, with integrity."[32]

Religions are primary sources of values for human culture. In the case of the mindfulness movement, we find that one of the highest values is the sacredness of happiness. Human beings are supposed to be happy—as Meng puts it, "Happiness is the default state of mind"—and we go off-track when we fail to be happy.[33] Failure to be happy results in suffering, stress, pain, and disease, which are the principle targets of the mindfulness movement. As Ryan explains, "Happiness is found by deeply experiencing the exact moment we are in. Happiness is being totally alive."[34] Suffering unhappily, by this logic, is equal to being sick, perhaps even dead. It is no coincidence that suffering is also the primary concern of traditional Buddhism, which seeks to eliminate suffering as its basic raison d'être. Despite the assertions from many mindfulness advocates that it is not Buddhism and that mindfulness's connections to Buddhism are circumstantial or unimportant, mindfulness is used specifically to attack suffering—deeply coded as negative—and bring about happiness, as in Buddhism. The difference is that the horizon of happiness has been reduced from future lives or attainment of nirvana to the present life and more mundane conceptualizations of happiness.

A further value widely associated with mindfulness is compassion, as well as its translation into altruistic action. As Ryan noted, "I wrote *A Mindful Nation* to promote the values of slowing down, taking care of ourselves, being kind, and helping each other. It seems to me that if we embrace these values individually, it will benefit us collectively. And our country will be a little bit better off as a result."[35] As he saw it, "We need to raise our children in a nation that teaches them to be mindful, that teaches them about the importance of kindness and being connected to their fellow human beings and the environment that sustains them. A nation that teaches them to appreciate their basic human goodness and see that goodness in others."[36] For many this too seems to be almost an inherent human quality, as with mindfulness. The authors of *Fully Present* see lovingkindness as innate: "It is valuable to see that you already have feelings of loving-kindness and to appreciate yourself for your innate capacity to love and experience compassion."[37] As Jeff Brantley puts it in his "Mindfulness FAQ:" "It is useful to call upon some other qualities we have within us. These qualities are kindness, compassion, and equanimity. It is important to realize that we are not imagining these qualities or inventing them. Rather, they are already within us, important elements of our deepest nature as human beings."[38]

This emphasis on compassion is found in a great many mindfulness books. Sometimes, it is marketed strategically as a tool for increasing one's own happiness: act nice to others and your life will be happier. But often the connection is more explicitly linked to ideals that genuinely value others. Many feel that mindfulness is an inherently compassionate activity. This has two sides. First, because mindfulness means just nonjudgmentally accepting whatever happens in your experiencing of the present moment, this is a form of extending compassion to one's experiences and self. As Smalley and Winston note, "The attitude you cultivate in mindfulness practice—one of acceptance and openness—feels similar to loving-kindness. In mindful acceptance, a quality of kindness is present; you are kind to yourself and to your experience of the moment."[39] Second, bare awareness of the present leads to insight into one's inescapable interconnection with all others, as well as equivalency of others' suffering with our own, both of which engender compassionate feelings toward other people, living things, and the world.

This valuing of compassion by the mindfulness movement often moves beyond simple mindfulness exercises to attempt to actively cultivate such feelings. A prime example of this is the popularity of metta (lovingkindness) meditations in mindfulness works. Like sati meditation, these techniques are derived originally from traditional Buddhist monastic practices. In the practice of lovingkindess meditation, one cultivates an ever-widening circle of loving feelings toward others. This form of Buddhist meditation is common in many MBSR programs and appears in dozens of mindfulness books. Smalley and Winston provide a good example:

> Bring to mind someone who makes you feel happy the moment you think of them—a relative, a close friend, someone with whom you don't have too complicated a relationship...While imagining your loved one in front of you, begin to wish this person well: *May you be safe and protected from danger. May you be happy and peaceful. May you be healthy and strong. May you have ease and well-being...* As you say these words, have a sense of letting this loving-kindness come from you and begin to touch your loved one...Let yourself bring to mind one person or a group of people whom you wish to send loving-kindness...Let this loving-kindness expand, spreading out and touching anyone you want to touch right now. Let it go in all directions, toward people you know, toward people you don't know, toward people you have difficulty with, toward people you love. Imagine expansive and pervasive loving-kindness, touching and changing every person and every animal...*So may everyone everywhere be happy and peaceful and at ease. May we all experience great joy.* [40]

MBSR and other mindfulness practitioners who encounter these teachings are not simply taught value-neutral awareness techniques—they are coached to cultivate profoundly universal feelings of compassion and love for all people and every living thing. This perspective on life is not only value laden but is also promoted as both improving the world and as key to one's own health and happiness.

Compassion typically extends into a valuing of peacefulness, pacifism, and nonviolence. Given the movement's Buddhist roots, the strong orientation toward healing in the mindfulness movement, and the involvement of large numbers of health care workers, this set of mindfulness-connected values is hardly surprising. As Jon Kabat-Zinn puts it, "The foundation for mindfulness practice, for all meditative inquiry and exploration, lies in ethics and morality, and above all, the motivation of non-harming."[41] Mindfulness advocates who simply focus on personal benefits such as success at work or sports wouldn't necessarily agree, but the many for whom mindfulness is part of a more comprehensive approach to life would typically concur.

Mindfulness rhetoric turns on the idea of freedom, of liberation from one's problems, whether they are practical (job loss, back pain) or internal (self-loathing, substance addiction). Mindfulness is part of the diffuse spirituality movement in the West and is often marketed as a friendly, easy, personal practice that has no rules or commandants. But we should recognize that self-control and discipline are also cardinal values for the mindfulness movement. As Thich Nhat Hanh puts it: "When we sit down peacefully, breathing and smiling, with awareness, we are our true selves, we have sovereignty over ourselves. When we open ourselves up to a TV program, we let ourselves be invaded by the program."[42] For those who actually comprehensively put into practice a full regimen of mindful activities, mindfulness programs are about establishing control over important aspects of one's life, reflecting an anxiety about powerlessness in a complex and fast-paced society where personal success is less than guaranteed. It seems likely that control over eating and other mundane tasks is asserted when control over one's job, family, and other aspects of life are impossible: anxieties are sublimated and transferred into a realm (such as eating) that *is* self-manageable.

Thus mindfulness authors frequently assert the need for strict personal discipline in one's approach to mindfulness. In her book *Eating Mindfully*, Susan Albers claims that "the key to changing the way you eat is not to develop discipline over your fork, but to master control of your mind... becoming aware is the first step of being in control... Mindful eating requires you to consciously say to yourself, 'I choose to change my eating, and I will work through any difficulties,' every time you sit down to eat a meal."[43] This search for discipline becomes totalistic in many of these books. Jan Chozen Bays demands "never, under any circumstances, eat in front of the TV, computer screen, while driving, or on the phone" and recommends discipline not only of the mind and body but of the physical environment itself:

> Find ways to turn a space in your environment into a place that fosters mindful eating. In that place, remove any clutter that could distract you while you eat. Objects like phones or clocks that pull you away from a mindful state should be moved elsewhere. Put your place setting so that it faces away from the kitchen (or refrigerator). Bring food to the table before you eat, so you won't have to get up. Or, create a

new space. Tailor it to be a calm, peaceful environment that brings you a mindful state. If you wish, burn incense or change the lighting. Add a pretty tablecloth and fresh flowers. Play soothing music. Hang up a sign in your danger area that says, 'Eat Mindfully' to realert you to your mindful stance.[44]

This emphasis on strict self-discipline is partially a trace of the monastic origins of these practices—seemingly, rigorously applied mindfulness during eating and other daily activities develops into a sort of lay, fully secularized neo-monasticism in the American context.

Above all, mindfulness movement writers value the present moment. In *Coming to Our Senses* Jon Kabat-Zinn says: "The power of the present moment is inconceivable, just as inconceivable for us as the huge energy of the vacuum or the tininess of un-unfurled dimensions deep inside our atoms or nested within the fabric of space itself. In the case of the present moment, there is no way to believe in it, and no need to. One need only experience it and see for oneself how it might add back a dimension to living that accords us other degrees of freedom, whole new realms and ways to inhabit our lives and our world for the briefest moments we are here, that sum so quickly to what we call a lifetime, and that are so easily missed."[45] In mindfulness movement writings the present moment becomes both savior and heaven: the vehicle for salvation and salvation itself. As Thich Nhat Hanh asserts in *You Are Here: Discovering the Magic of the Present Moment*: "The only moment in which you can be truly alive is the present moment. The present moment is the destination, the point to arrive at."[46] The mindfulness movement seeks to remedy existential suffering by re-inhabiting the present moment, the present body, the present mind, and the present environment. In strengthening one's connection to these immediate phenomena, it is believed that one can be continuously refreshed, revitalized, and made whole. In other words, a sort of rupture between the self and the mind, body, and world is being allegedly healed in the act of mindfulness.

Mindfulness: Meaning and Conversion Narratives

Because mindfulness is often packaged along with a set of values, it can become a powerful source for finding meaning in one's life. Many feel that mindfulness should ideally become a lens through which all of life is experienced.

They say things like "You can use mindfulness as a way to approach anything you do in the world, in the way you work, relate to people, or deal with painful issues in your life," and "When we use mindful eyes, everything is beautiful and everyone walks in beauty."[47] Ronald Siegel declares "Once we develop a bit of concentration, the whole world beings to feel more alive, more interconnected. Plants, animals, and even other people are experienced as part of a vibrant, interactive whole. If we have a theistic perspective, mindfulness helps us connect directly with God or the Divine. Everything becomes numinous, infused with the spirit of life."[48] Mindfulness, in other words, is not only a tool for gaining happiness—which, remember, is given positive, indeed quasi-sacred value by mindfulness advocates—for some of its most ardent advocates, mindfulness is also a complete way of viewing the world itself.

It is no surprise, therefore, that many mindfulness movement authors present their own conversion narratives to the way of mindfulness. Like traditional religious conversion narratives, these often appear in the wake of trauma, deep soul-searching, or hitting bottom in some profound manner. A good example is actress and mindful education advocate Goldie Hawn, as she explained in *10 Mindful Minutes*. Like many Americans, she could vividly recall the moment on September 11, 2001 when the phone rang and someone told her to turn on the television to see the real-time terrorist destruction of the World Trade Center towers. "Like relatives at a deathbed, we gathered in front of the TV—watching, waiting, and weeping. With each new image and every slow-motion replay, we mourned the passing of life as we had known it. This was real. This was a game changer. The world would never be the same after this. The events of 9/11 would polarize people of every country, religion, color, and creed. Reactions would ripple back and forth across oceans, creating a tidal wave of suspicion and fear. I saw the future unfolding before me, and it frightened me."[49]

This event was so huge, so terrifying, so disturbing, that it called out for some sort of reaction, something that would give positive meaning to the trauma and restore a sense of goodness in the world:

> I went to my knitting basket and found some old threads of red, white, and blue. Knitting has always been a form of meditation for me, and so I began to knit the American flag. As I sat there, tears falling onto my stitches, I came to a profound and deeply emotional decision. I felt compelled to do something, no matter how insignificant, that would be more meaningful and lasting than the joining of a few fragments of wool. My kind of patriotism doesn't have to do with being red or being

blue; it doesn't even have a label. It has to do with loving my country and its great potential and respecting our powers of resilience. No matter how small a gesture, I believe that we can all do something to make this world a better place. If I could help just one little girl or boy move beyond those images that will haunt us all, that would be a gift.

The result was the creation of MindUP™, a program designed to deliver mindfulness skills to schoolchildren throughout America. Hawn became a tireless advocate of inserting mindfulness into the school system, which she pursued by funding studies that demonstrate the benefits of mindfulness, speaking and writing on the topic, and working with educators and politicians to get schools to adopt the MindUP™ program. Thus, like many zealous new converts to religious traditions, Hawn was inspired by her newfound love of mindfulness to become an evangelist, proselytizing the gospel of mindfulness in order to save an imperiled world. She hoped to convert her fellow Americans—if not the whole world—to her chosen path, and in doing so set aright the world that was so traumatically blown askew when the Twin Towers crumbled and America became deeply polarized. In doing so, she not only acted out religious scripts but also expressed her patriotic civil religious devotion to the United States.

Tim Ryan's narrative follows the classic pattern of personal revelation, followed by assiduous evangelization. He described his experience of a "Power of Mindfulness" retreat in upstate New York led by Jon Kabat-Zinn in November 2008, just after Barack Obama's election as president: "Snow was falling on my face as I walked—silently and slowly—beneath still-colorful trees. Leaves crackled under my weight as my foot hit the ground. I heard water moving over rocks in the small stream just a few feet to my left. My body relaxed, my brow unfurled. Something just happened, but I wasn't doing anything. I just let it be. The landscape looked crisper; my breath in the cold air entranced me. It felt as if a cloud had lifted from my eyes. I had no desire to be elsewhere—no thoughts about a better place. There was nothing to achieve or anything to prove to anyone else. I didn't have to defend a political position and I felt no need to prove my self-worth through running for office. I didn't need to be liked. I didn't crave affirmation. I was... OK. I literally just *was*."[50] This stillness, couched in vaguely Buddhist enlightenment terms, was impactful to Ryan, who described it as pleasurable and blissful. Over the course of the retreat he sank further into this feeling, and it changed the way he perceived himself and the world: "The deeper the silence became, the deeper I realized the inanity, even the insanity, of putting so much effort into fictional story lines rather than listening to and noticing what's happening in and around me at any given moment...I couldn't believe I'd spent so much time and energy trying to uphold a story I created in my own head...Watching this crazy story line from a distance, I decompressed. The pain, the hurt, the judgments dropped away. And then I was in a state of disbelief that I had missed so much of my life. But now I could breathe. The pressure evaporated."[51] His view transformed by a source of peace, wisdom, relief, and forgiveness that he hadn't previously imagined, Ryan immediately decided to dedicate his life to spreading the word about mindfulness:

> The mindfulness retreat at the foot of the Catskills rocked my world. And now I felt that I wanted to share what I had experienced with my family and friends. I wanted to teach it to my two-year-old nephew, my brother, to my mom. "Everybody get off the roller coaster, I've found the answer," I wanted to scream...At that moment, I decided I would advocate in Congress and on the Appropriations Committee for integrating mindfulness into key aspects of our society. Since the committee I was sitting on funds health care, research, and education, I could use my position to help mindfulness become an element in various government programs. I had tried to use my life and talents to relieve people's suffering through social and economic justice. But I realized at that retreat in the Catskills that if I truly wanted to relieve people's suffering and make modest attempts to improve the social and economic situation of our country, there was more I could do. As I saw it, there would be no better way to help people than to dedicate my work to integrating mindfulness into health care, education, and society at large...I resolved that my life would no longer be driven by doing one thing after another or getting ahead or getting a new title. It would be guided more by seeing the wonder that unfolds in daily life and the millions of miracles that happen moment to moment.[52]

Since this experience, Ryan has written a book on mindfulness, given innumerable interviews, advocated for mindfulness in Ohio schools, and helped in numerous other ways to bring positive attention to the mindfulness movement. Part Paul, part Constantine, he has used his personal conviction and his position within the U.S. government to further the movement in ways beyond the capacity of most Americans. But his essential story—personal transformation, the desire to share with others, and the search for a better America—is repeated in the lives of many mindfulness teachers and practitioners.

The Dawning of a New Civilization: Mindful Society, Mindful World

So what is the civil religious vision for a good society as envisioned by mindfulness movement enthusiasts? For most, mindfulness itself is revolutionary (a good red meat American word): "A quiet revolution is happening in America. It's not a revolution fueled by anger lurking on the fringes of our democracy. It's a peaceful revolution, being led by ordinary citizens," Congressman Ryan asserted.[53] "At the core of this revolution is mindfulness."[54] This revolution will help bring about a change in America that is both transformative and yet simultaneously a return to quintessential American principles, because this mindfulness will help us embody our most sacred ideals as Americans: "We don't need a new set of values. I really believe we can reinvigorate our traditional, commonly held American values—such as self-reliance, perseverance, pragmatism, and taking care of each other—by adding a little more mindfulness to our lives."[55] Listening to Jon Kabat-Zinn during retreat, Ryan had an insight. "I started to see mindfulness as very much in line with the values of America. Our founding fathers acted from the heart when they transformed our world by stating that 'all men are created equal,' 'endowed by their Creator with certain unalienable rights' such as life, liberty, and happiness."[56] The results of the mindfulness revolution will be substantial: "The mindfulness movement is not quite as dramatic as the moon shot or the civil rights movement, but I believe in the long run it can have just as great an impact."[57]

As with Ryan, for many commentators the obvious solution to the problems facing us as individuals and as citizens is mindfulness deployed on a sufficiently large scale, so that it guides all aspects of our society, either because each individual is mindful or because mindfulness is somehow actively built into our institutions. A mindful society will either automatically be good, or it will at least establish a solid foundation for discerning what is good and necessary, and be able to effectively carry out programs of action that result in maximum success. Furthermore, American history and values have themselves been potentially leading to a mindful society all along. As Kabat-Zinn observes:

> In a society founded on democratic principles and a love of freedom, sooner or later meditative practices, what are sometimes called

consciousness disciplines, are bound to come to the fore as is happening now, as the climate for personal and collective independence and inquiry is nourished and blossoms. Democracy encourages and nurtures pluralism and a diversity of views. It encourages making use of our freedoms, inwardly as well as outwardly in the pursuit of happiness. We are naturally drawn to understand ourselves in deeper and deeper ways as individuals, as a society, as a species. It is part of the ongoing evolutionary process on this planet...[58]

Mindfulness is here written into the teleological evolution of the human race itself, destined to flower in democratic, freedom-loving societies such as America. So America leads to mindfulness, and mindfulness in turn will save America.

What would such a mindful society or world look like, according to members of the mindfulness movement? For Ryan, it would be effective, compassionate, happy, and harmonious:

> The evidence I've seen tells me that as we bring mindfulness into health care, we will find a tool that helps us to take care of ourselves better, to see the roots of many of our problems. An increase in self-care not only makes us feel better, but it also costs our system less, allowing us to focus more of our resources on illnesses beyond our control. When we bring mindfulness into education, we help our students increase attention, decrease their stress, and work more creatively with their social emotions. And teachers find they pay better attention to the real needs of all their students and foster a better classroom attention. When we bring mindfulness into the military, we help to enhance the greatest resource we have to ensure our own security and defense, something more powerful than any high-tech weaponry: well-functioning, high-performing *human beings* who have refined situational awareness. When we bring mindfulness into our approaches to energy, the environment, and the economy, we can find ways to live more simply while discovering a kind of prosperity that doesn't abuse our planet. When the caregivers and social workers bring mindfulness into the street, you would be surprised by how they can help the most traumatized people find courage and heart—and how the practice can help the caregivers themselves prevent the burnout that plagues their professions.[59]

All of these mindful applications will result in a truly mindful nation, which is a strong, compassionate society. As Susan Smalley and Diana

Winston state, "A more mindful society is ultimately a kinder society."[60] Ryan agrees: "My goal is that America will be a kinder, more compassionate nation, because I know deep down in my heart that we are a kinder, more compassionate country than is evident today. Reviving our compassionate spirit will allow us to listen carefully to each other, find points of agreement, and recapture the unity of purpose that made America great. A mindful nation is about recognizing that we are all connected: we are in this together... We know that when we join together, work together, and care about each other, our freedom actually increases. Real independence emerges when we know how to support each other. The Declaration of Independence was a communal act."[61]

According to Roman Catholic nun and mindfulness promoter Elizabeth Thoman, what is needed is "re-imagining the American dream."[62] As she explains, the American dream is one of ever-expanding consumerism, inculcated in us by a dangerous mediascape that sells us the idea that we must always be buying, always acquiring. The American dream is now unsustainable and must be changed. Instead, we need to move "toward a materially renewable lifestyle that would fulfill the physical, spiritual, and emotional needs of all— not just some—of the world's people, while allowing them to live in peace and freedom. Under such a system communication's most important aim would be to bring people together."[63] For Thoman, the key begins with altering our relationship to the media, so that we can redirect it into healthy pathways, rather than being a victim of corporations' desire to pick our pockets. "A positive alternative is needed. What I have called media awareness—the recognition of the media's role in shaping our lives and molding our deepest thoughts and feelings—is an important step. The steps I have outlined above provide simple but effective tools for beginning to work through this process. Although they seem basic, they have their roots in the profound state of being that Buddhism calls mindfulness: being aware, carefully examining, asking questions, and being conscious."[64] Thoman's prescriptions are echoed in many mindfulness publications.

Mindful Politics

Mindfulness programs for achieving the good society support liberal values (racial tolerance, gay rights, feminism, environmentalism) but are usually far from radical in their understanding of social change itself. For example, as we saw in the opening selections from *Search Within Yourself*, they usually advocate social change through cultivation of personal morality, one meditator at a time. The basic theory here is that personal, social, and environmental problems are (at least partially) caused by a lack of mindfulness. On a certain level this implies that one's sufferings are the result of poor life choices, but the harsher possible versions of this view are significantly mitigated by the general understanding that one's choices are themselves influenced by an aggressively anti-mindful culture, designed to generate desire through advertising and infected by historic prejudices from an earlier era. As each individual becomes convinced of mindfulness's power, they will begin to practice mindfulness as they see fit. This will lead to more compassion and flexibility in society, and as mindfulness practitioners approach a critical mass of the population, this will automatically result in kinder, more progressive lawmaking and enforcement, and corporations will voluntarily begin to produce healthier, more holistic products to be consumed by an enlightened, ever-improving consumer culture. Because mindfulness allows people to see things as they really are, without blinders or conditioning, they will naturally gravitate—individually, yet en masse—toward liberal American values and politics, because these are just self-evidently correct, based on reality and not on prejudice, one's social environment, or delusion.

The tendency to link mindfulness and liberal values is so pervasive that when someone objects, it tends not to compute with others in the mindfulness movement. Consider the following exchange that played out in the letters column of *Shambhala Sun*. The May 2012 issue carried a letter from Jen Evans, a woman in San Francisco, critiquing the liberal bias of the magazine: "I think you have a great magazine and I love the articles on practice and mindfulness, but it's difficult to swallow other articles, whose authors assume the readership is liberal or 'progressive.' Can someone not be both Buddhist and conservative? Is that not allowed? Why do you assume that your readership will simply follow along the liberal way of thinking about more government handouts and spreading the wealth around? I think it's wrong to wait for some entity to save you. Where is the self-reliance and resourcefulness in that? Please consider the groupthink you are displaying."[65] This writer had her finger on a real phenomenon. *Shambhala Sun, Buddhadharma, Tricycle, Inquiring Mind, Mindful*—the most widely circulated magazines that regularly promote mindfulness—rarely if ever include feature articles supporting politically conservative points of view, despite occasional calls from editors for submissions with more diverse political perspectives. No conservative viewpoints appear in major collections on the topic, such as *Mindful Politics: A Buddhist Guide to Making the World a Better Place* (2006) or *The Mindfulness Revolution: Leading Psychologists, Scientists, Artists, and Meditation Teachers on the Power of Mindfulness in Daily Life* (2011).[66] The constant stream of politically tinged books from Thich Nhat Hanh— such as *Creating True Peace: Ending Violence in Yourself, Your Family, Your Community, and the World* (2003), *Keeping the Peace: Mindfulness and Public Service* (2005), *One Buddha Is Not Enough: A Story of Collective Awakening* (2010), and *Good Citizens: Creating Enlightened Society* (2012)—all support liberal attitudes.[67]

Nonetheless, other readers were baffled by the allegations of liberal slant in *Shambhala Sun*. In the September 2012 issue Malcolm Clark, another reader from California, professed to be startled at such an accusation: "As a subscriber who has read every issue from cover to cover (sometimes twice) for years, I am hard pressed to recall anything that overtly intends to 'follow along the liberal way of thinking about government handouts and spreading the wealth around.' "[68] One wonders how this reader overlooked, for example, "The Meaning of Barack Obama" article in the November 2008 issue, delivered shortly before the presidential election, which essentially endorsed the Democratic candidate—and was partially reprinted for good measure the following year in the July 2009 issues as part of its "For 30 years the Best of American Buddhism" retrospective.[69] Or for that matter, the September 2006 "Mindful Politics" issue, which showcased only authors shopping various degrees of liberal attitudes and solutions. The liberal preference can hardly be said to be subtle in passages such as the following, from that issue:

Here in America, a plutocracy with a broken moral compass, a cook's tour of our dilemmas reveals that our ship of state has run aground on the problems of immigration; poverty; the lack of universal health care; the complex issue of a planet-altering global warming; political corruption such as influence peddling by lobbyists like Jack Abramoff; the aftermath of Hurricane Katrina; racism; the startling decline of literacy (only 31 percent of college graduates can read a complex book and extrapolate from it); the loss of not only civility and courtesy but also safety in so many of our public spaces; the failure of 1,750 schools to meet No Child Left Behind standards for math and reading (all fifty states received an *F* from the federal government on demonstrating their teachers had a bachelor's degree, a state license, and proven competency in every subject they teach); a burgeoning prison industry; the failure to address the plight of young black males who are increasingly alienated from society in violent, drug-ridden neighborhoods; the outsourcing of jobs; growing economic electronic surveillance and accumulation of private information on citizens; a president (and congress) with the lowest approval ratings since Richard Nixon; and the saddling of future generations with a staggering national debt.[70]

This is a laundry list of mid-George W. Bush–era liberal grievances, roiling with barely concealed anger and angst. And while particularly exhaustive, it is in no way out of line with the usual range of concerns and attitudes expressed in the primary mindfulness forums.

Clark, in responding to Evans's letter, was so convinced that mindfulness and Buddhist practice lead to liberal values that he forecast a coming change in the original writer's views: "I do know conservatives who embrace Buddhist principles, but my consistent observation is that they shift their political outlook toward the center in the process. Is this because 'reality has a well-known liberal bias'? I believe Ms. Evans has much joy to look forward to as she begins to see herself in everyone she encounters, inspiring the compassionate generosity that is the cornerstone of all lasting spiritual orientations, regardless of political leaning."[71] The nod to other political leanings is disingenuous, as the previous paragraph states that fundamental Buddhist values lead to a communalistic view that punctures the ideas of self-reliance that Evans suggests. From the standpoint of most mindfulness authors, no, you really can't be both Buddhist and conservative, because mindfulness of interconnection confirms liberal points of view.

As might be expected from a politics that emerges primarily from white middle-class America—or in the case of Thich Nhat Hanh and similar figures, has especially been embraced by white, middle-class Americans—mindful civil religion does not call for mandatory participation in mindful activities, radical changes to the economic structure, aggressive or combative political struggle, or class warfare. Rather, for many it is apparent that mindful capitalism will be sufficient, as will mindful politics, mindful consumption, mindful work, and so on. As Kabat-Zinn asserts:

How we choose from moment to moment to live and act influences the world in small ways that may be disproportionately beneficial, especially if the motivation our choices come out of is wholesome, i.e., healthy, and the actions themselves wise and compassionate. In this way, the healing of the body politic can evolve without rigid control or direction, through the independent and interdependent agency and efforts of many different people and institutions, with many different and rich perspectives, aims, and interests, and with a common and potentially unifying interest as well, that of the greater well-being of the world…We are sitting atop a unique moment in history unfolding, a major tipping point. This time we are in provides singular opportunities that can be seized and made use of with every breath. There is only one way to do that. It is to embody, in our lives as they are unfolding here and now, our deepest values and our understanding of what is important—and share it with each other, trusting that such embodied actions, on even the smallest of scales, will entrain the world over time into greater wisdom and health and sanity.[72]

The way to heal the world is to be vigilantly mindful in every moment of our own lives, which will lead to good life choices, and hope that this will rub off on others in the long run.

Most mindfulness authors expect change to come about slowly, peacefully, through the established political system. They also rarely call for wholesale shifts to a totally new form of economic organization. A mindful America will still be a consumerist, capitalist nation—it'll just be a kinder, more ecologically aware one. As Daniel Goleman tries to persuade readers in his essay "A Mindful Consumer Can Help Change the World:" "Mindful shopping is a potentially important practice, a socially engaged act that could collectively help us save the world from its greatest threat: us. It seems likely that if we practice mindfulness, we will become more in tune with our world ecologically. We will get more in touch with our actual needs and will be driven less by our desires."[73] So being mindful will save us because we will buy less. Furthermore, we will make more intelligent choices, so the products we buy will be more eco-friendly. This allows the market itself to become our savior:

To the extent that more people shop mindfully, it will have a telling impact on the market. Market share will shift toward the more ecologically virtuous products. Brand managers will pay attention, creating a virtuous cycle whereby our choices based on sound, transparent information influence the market. It will pay for companies to innovate, to change their practices, to go after our dollar by upgrading the ecological impacts of what they're trying to sell us. Finally, our mindful shopping habits could shift the debate within the corporate world about sustainability, which is stalled right now. Most voices for corporate social responsibility say that companies should pay attention to ecological impacts because it's the morally and ethically correct thing to do. The counterargument is that the first duty of corporations is to their investors. But if doing good also becomes what is most economically advantageous, that debate will be over. They will make better choices because we've made the better choice.[74]

This is not a call for comprehensive wealth redistribution. Most mindfulness authors pin their hopes on a mindful capitalism as sufficient to bring about the kinder, wiser society they envision.

It should be stated that for some mindfulness authors, there is an implicit further step to this process. It isn't simply that everyone will become mindful and therefore save the world through mindful consumption and mindful voting—because mindfulness promotes compassion, it is expected that mindfulness will lead many into actual social justice, environmental conservation, and political activism. So mindfulness is not just about sitting down quietly: there is an expectation that the meditator will eventually stand up energized to get to work on improving the world. When this happens, not only will mindfulness guide wise choices of voting, lobbying, protesting, helping, and consuming, but will also assist the worker in fighting burnout, political cynicism, and hopelessness in the face of setbacks and the scale of complex problems facing the world.

Conclusion

No matter how much effort is expended to remove the religious nature of mindfulness, it still continues to have the capacity to operate in a religious manner. We might call this a secular religion, one devoid of the supernatural and the afterlife yet operating as a deep well of values, life orientation, and utopian vision. This secular mindful religion can be married to a specific religious tradition such as Buddhism (as in the case of Chade-Meng Tan) or Christianity (as in the case of Tim Ryan, a devout Roman Catholic), and it can also operate on its own as a free-standing system.

The total mindfulness movement in America is a broad spectrum. For every practitioner hoping mindfulness will bring about peace on earth, you can easily find another whose mindfulness practice doesn't value anything higher than making money through increased attention at work or losing weight through more conscious eating habits. Those who do attach morals to or derive values from their mindfulness practice are often people with a connection to a religious tradition, especially Buddhism. They are people like

Thich Nhat Hanh (a monk), Joseph Goldstein (trained as a monk in Asia), Jon Kabat-Zinn (trained by Buddhist missionaries in America), Jan Bays (a Zen priest), or Barry Boyce (employed by a Buddhist organization). Though they may mystify the religious origins of mindfulness in order to market it to a non-religious (or, at least, non-Buddhist) crowd, they are in fact motivated by Buddhist concerns to reduce suffering, spread compassion, and help society. Or, in the case of Catholics such as Tim Ryan, the social concerns reflected in how they contextualize mindfulness reveal perennial patterns related to longstanding progressive American Catholic concerns with workers, families, education, and economic justice.

The mindfulness movement can thus be said to have two ideal types, or at least two ideal types of expression: those that pursue or market mindfulness primarily for specific personal benefit, and those that pursue or market mindfulness out of commitment to a larger social vision (but one that emphasizes self-healing as the essential first step to larger healing of the body politic). From the point of view of the benefits-only crowd, socially concerned mindfulness teachers such as Jon Kabat-Zinn and Thich Nhat Hanh are still excellent instructors from whom one can learn a great deal. And from the point of view of the socially engaged mindfulness faction, even relatively self-oriented pursuers of mindfulness will be of benefit to society as they naturally reduce their level of stress, become more aware of their connections with others, and perhaps back their way into greater alignment with liberal political views, progressive values, and a more ecological outlook.

POSTSCRIPT

MAKING SENSE OF MINDFULNESS

Mindfulness, as we have seen, is a highly complicated movement. To penetrate American society, mindfulness is transformed along mainstream and medical lines to meet native sensibilities and needs, and by successfully doing so, it transforms American spirituality and institutions in their turn. Buddhist mindfulness at times goes underground as its origins and original purposes are mystified, dropping the title "Buddhism" while still retaining many of its characteristics and often some degree of moral orientation, so that it can be adopted by non-Buddhists and inserted into non-religious environments. Successfully marketed to an ever-expanding audience, it is reaping profits for authors, publishers, researchers, pundits, and Mindfulness-Based Stress Reduction (MBSR) trainers, and, many assert, driving down medical costs, improving the American workplace, and increasing the mental and physical health of the nation.

The most important aspect of the mindfulness movement is its orientation toward practical benefits, an orientation we find present in Buddhist meditation groups, MBSR seminars, and the self-help aisle of the nearest bookstore. The role of practical benefits has not been sufficiently studied in American Buddhism. Often the concept has been reserved for application to Soka Gakkai, one of the largest explicitly Buddhist movements in America, which promotes its chanting practices as a method for achieving worldly benefits such as job success, love, overcoming addiction, and achieving material gains, such as a new car or housing. There is a tendency to deride Soka Gakkai in meditation-oriented Buddhist groups (and some scholarship), as "chanting for dollars." Yet when we examine the mindfulness movement, we can see that many people are essentially "sitting for dollars"—for isn't that what mindful work amounts to? Likewise, the miraculous stories Soka Gakkai practitioners tell about medical conditions that improved after assiduous mantra practice cease to seem unusual when paired with the countless health-related ends to which mindfulness meditation is continually put. American Buddhists of various stripes—chanters and meditators, monks, and medical doctors—are heavily involved in the pursuit of personal needs and wishes via their practices. Thus meditating and chanting converts are part of a common phenomenon of adopting and adapting Buddhism in America based on practical benefits and this-worldly concerns.

The Mindful Transformation of American Buddhism

One of the most interesting aspects of the mindfulness movement is how totalizing it begins to become. Reformers from the Theravada tradition, Thich Nhat Hanh, and Jon Kabat-Zinn's work together form the major influences on the mindfulness movement, such that time and again the books on mindfulness that populate chain bookstores make reference to Theravada mindfulness teachings, quote Thich Nhat Hanh, and refer positively to Kabat-Zinn's work for validation of their claims. Along with a more diffuse background of other famous Buddhist teachers who occasionally included mindfulness practice in their teachings, these sources have helped to define Buddhism for many Americans as inherently based on mindfulness meditation—a shift not only from historic Buddhist tradition but also from most of American Buddhist history. Especially in the groups influenced by these teachers, which tend toward a majority white, middle-class lay demographic, mindfulness has come to be a near universal practice that binds different traditions together in what some have argued is an emergent general American Buddhism.[1]

The omnipresence of the mindfulness movement and its redefinition of mindfulness as the core of Buddhism exert profound pressure on American Buddhist lineages to come to understand Buddhism through the lens of mindfulness. Bhante Henepola Gunaratana's book *Mindfulness in Plain English* leads naturally to new books such as *The Four Foundations of Mindfulness in Plain English* and *Beyond Mindfulness in Plain English;* his autobiography must, of course, be titled *Journey to Mindfulness;* mindfulness comes to subsume all of Buddhism, so that his book on the Noble Eightfold Path is titled *Eight Mindful Steps to Happiness: Walking the Buddha's Path*, and mindfulness breaks free of its spot as step seven to become the defining characteristic of every aspect of Buddhism.[2] Gunaratana's very success has transformed him into "that mindfulness monk," and in every book he writes he must conform to his Dharmic type-casting. So too Thich Nhat Hanh's scores of books all revolve around the theme of mindfulness, and eventually mindfulness becomes a total-izing hermeneutic for him as well, such that he later rebrands the traditional lay precepts (which earlier in his career he called the Five Wonderful Precepts) into the Five Mindfulness Trainings, and the fourteen precepts of the Order of Interbeing as the Fourteen Mindfulness Trainings.[3]

Mindfulness, having emerged from Buddhism and proven astoundingly successful, returns to become the complete framework for Buddhism (rather than the other way around), so that new titles such as *Why Is the Buddha Smiling? Mindfulness as a Means of Bringing Calm and Insight into Your Life* (2003) represent the entire Buddhist history from its beginning as a mindful-ness technique for making life happier and less stressful. Thich Nhat Hanh even goes so far at times as to define mindfulness as more or less the defining quality of Buddhism: "Buddhism is made of mindfulness, concentration, and insight. If you have these things, you are a Buddhist. If you don't, you aren't a Buddhist. When you look at a person and see that she is mindful, she is compassionate, she is understanding, and she has insight, then you know that she is a Buddhist. But even if she's a nun and she does not have these energies and qualities, she has only the appearance of a Buddhist, not the content of a Buddhist."[4] So an insightful, mindful Baptist is a Buddhist, while the masses in Southeast Asia devoted to achieving practical benefits through support of the monastic sangha and adherence to moral precepts are not Buddhist.

Given this development, groups that historically have been uninvolved in silent meditation, such as the Buddhist Churches of America, come to allow space for meditation in their temples; lineages that have stressed devo-tional transformation, such as Tibetan guru worship, find themselves offering classes on mindful stress relief; and traditions that have offered a rounded array of Buddhist practices, such as Thai-American temples, begin to creep toward focusing on one technique to the relative neglect of others. Zen ceases to be promoted as a way to access the mystical Big Mind and becomes instead a process for connecting with the quotidian self. Theravada and Mahayana Buddhists read each other's works and adopt each other's perspectives and techniques, which are then studied scientifically by biomedical and psycho-therapeutic clinicians, whose findings and attitudes are reincorporated into their thinking by American Buddhist communities, and so on, in a pattern that endlessly repeats and reinforces itself. Thus non-Buddhists who encoun-ter mindfulness-based stress reduction in a secular setting are nonetheless exposed to ideas and techniques derived from Buddhism, and Americans who read about Buddhism or attend Buddhist meditation centers are continually exposed to scientific and therapeutic ideas about practice designed to minimize their religious nature. The result is that the gap between the secular world and Buddhism becomes extremely thin, with mutual influence whose precise nature as secular, religious, and/or Buddhist becomes extremely difficult to determine.

Mindfulness in American Religious History

There are three interrelated approaches from the discipline of American religious history that I think are most important for figuring out where the mindfulness movement fits into American society. These are metaphysical religion, spirituality, and liberal religion. These are not fully discrete streams in American history: liberal religion more or less birthed spirituality as it has come to be known by Americans today, and metaphysical Christianity (as well as non-Christian movements) can often be classified productively as part of or at least related to the liberal stream of American religion.

Catherine Albanese, in her award-winning *A Republic of Mind and Spirit*, asserts that metaphysical religion "is at least as important as evangelicalism in fathoming the shape and scope of American religious history and in identifying what makes it distinctive."[5] This major—yet often overlooked—form of American religion has four characteristics that Albanese distinguishes: (1) a focus on the mind and its powers; (2) concern with correspondence between different interrelated spheres of existence, such as inner and outer or macrocosm and microcosm; (3) a preference for concepts and metaphors of movement and energy; and (4) a therapeutic orientation that conceives of salvation in terms of healing. One of the primary manifestations of metaphysical religion in America has been the movement known as New Thought. New Thought is a complex phenomenon well-deserving of attention in its own right; for our purposes here, let us concentrate on historian of the movement John S. Haller, Jr.'s observation that its common denominator is "the proposition that illness resulted from erroneous belief."[6]

It should be obvious that these ideas from American religious history relate to the mindfulness movement's present. Failure to operate in a proper mental fashion is the basic "sin" from the point of view of mindfulness advocates. When we believe that happiness or stress management will result from the distracting devices and dangerous compensating methods (sex, food, alcohol, work) that surround us, the result is ill-health in our bodies, relationships, social institutions, and environment. What is needed according to this way of thinking is to get in tune with the infinitude of the present moment, aligning our consciousness with the pure, nonjudgmental flow of experience itself.

One of the pioneering studies related to this book is Wakoh Shannon Hickey's 2008 dissertation "Mind Cure, Meditation, and Medicine: Hidden Histories of Mental Healing in the United States."[7] Although it is concerned only with MBSR, not the wider mindfulness movement in toto, and much of the research is focused on the history of Protestant-derived Mind Cure and similar movements, Hickey's dissertation was an important first attempt to consider the role of a mindfulness phenomenon from the perspective of American religious history. As she demonstrates, using the powers of the mind to effect healing has been a perennial concern of American religion, and movements from Christian Science to Transcendental Meditation did important work laying the foundation upon which MBSR (and, I would argue, the later 20th century mindfulness movement as a whole) would build. As Hickey points out, MBSR fits rather seamlessly with Catherine Albanese's criteria (though she's slightly less certain that concepts of energy apply) and can in fact be understood as a "species" of metaphysical religion. I appreciate this perspective and feel that there is ample evidence that the mindfulness movement as a whole can be considered part of the metaphysical strain in American religion, even when manifested in its most apparently secular or medical forms. The powers of the mind and focus on healing are clear, and we also find concern for the correspondence of worlds, such as in this quote from Jon Kabat-Zinn: "Resting in awareness in any moment involves giving ourselves over to all our senses, in touch with inner and outer landscapes as one seamless whole, and thus in touch with all of life unfolding in its fullness in any moment and in every place we might possibly find ourselves, inwardly and outwardly."[8] I would like to bolster Hickey's argument, as I feel that when considering the mindfulness movement as a whole (not just MBSR), ideas about energy too are clearly present. A quote from Thich Nhat Hanh should suffice: "The energy of mindfulness is the energy of the Buddha, and it can be produced by anybody. Buddha is the ability to be mindful. Every time you take a step or breathe mindfully, you generate the energy of the Buddha. This protects and heals you."[9]

In this book I have emphasized the Buddhist background aspects of mindfulness. But we should pause when we see something that is allegedly Asian synching up so perfectly with an American religious tradition already present. Does this mean that mindfulness isn't really Buddhist after all, that it is more properly understood as metaphysical religion? I don't believe these are mutually exclusive categories or forms of analysis. Rather, the mindfulness movement is an expression of both Buddhism and of American metaphysical religion: it is an American Buddhist metaphysical religion. It is not only the adaptations chronicled here that made it possible for mindfulness to find a home in America. Mindfulness also benefits from its assimilation into already present trends in American religion, such as metaphysical traditions and the rise of spirituality. These preexisting phenomena influence what elements of Buddhism are chosen to be appropriated, and without them Buddhism might be so thoroughly foreign as not to be capable of finding a place here.

When very broadly defined, we can see that meditation in some form has existed in the United States for a considerable length of time and has been an important part of the phenomenon known as spirituality. Leigh Eric Schmidt's book *Restless Souls* charts the rise of spirituality in America, which began with 19th century religious liberals such as Unitarians and Transcendentalists and came eventually to characterize one of the main modern modes in which Americans relate to religion. As Schmidt shows, American interest in meditation began as a way to tap into cosmic or Divine (i.e., belonging to the Christian God in some sense) power. It then developed into a way of quieting the mind so that the hassled modern self could be reconstituted. Through all this, meditation was most often imagined as a form of retreat, a temporary hermitage taken out of the day.

The genius of mindfulness is that it takes this trajectory all the way to the end-point: now meditation takes place while doing activities: you don't focus on objects of religious desire (such as God, Christ, Buddha) or self-help mantras, but on the actual activity you're doing right now. The goal is no longer detachment but thorough inhabitation of the moment, the better to enliven the activity and spiritualize it. The distance between the spiritual and the everyday, between the religious act and the mundane, has been completely collapsed and erased. This seems to relate to sociologist Robert Wuthnow's observations in *After Heaven: Spirituality in America Since the 1950s.* Wuthnow asserts that an earlier period of dwelling-oriented religion has given way to a new pattern of seekership. Yet he also noted the continued presence of a hunger for dwelling, for emplacement in the chaos and complexity of end-of-the-20th-century society. Thomas Tweed tried to capture some of these elements when he produced his theory of religion in *Crossing and Dwelling.* For Tweed, based on his late-20th century fieldwork in Miami and further reflections, religion can be defined in the following manner: "Religions are confluences of organic-cultural flows that intensify joy and confront suffering by drawing on human and suprahuman forces to make homes and cross boundaries."[10] Through mindfulness practitioners seek to dwell in the present moment, yet they also emphasize that mindfulness is profoundly portable: in speaking of mindfulness of the breath—the most basic form of mindfulness—they often stress that one's breath is the one thing you take with you always, everywhere, and therefore it makes mindfulness available every minute of the day, in every situation. Mindfulness is thus a way to attempt dwelling and crossing at the same time, to combine perpetual seekership in the eternal now with home-making in the mind, body, and world. And we can certainly note that mindfulness is used by Americans to intensify joy and confront suffering.

A third lens through which to consider the mindfulness movement is liberal religion. When so many mindfulness advocates labor to establish lineages descended from Ralph Waldo Emerson and Henry David Thoreau, this should be a natural frame of interpretation for examining the mindfulness movement. As with other religious liberals, mindfulness movement authors champion adapting religion to suit changed cultural and historical circumstances, take nonliteral interpretations of scriptures and traditional elements of religion, allow for multiple valid viewpoints in religious matters, insist on the primacy of individual experience and conscience, assert the harmony of religion and science (and accept the findings of the latter as a primary source of knowledge), and take a positive view of basic human nature. Matt Hedstrom has noted (following a line of argumentation earlier laid out by Christian Smith) in *The Rise of Liberal Religion* that American religious liberal institutions lost ground over the course of the 20th century at the same time that liberal religious sentiments became indelibly embedded in American culture as a whole.[11] Hedstrom chronicles how in an ironic twist this came about largely because religious leaders' drive for significance brought about their ultimate superfluity: tantalized by the chance to redeem America and American souls via extra-church arenas such as social activism, literary culture, and psychology, they successfully liberalized America culture and thereby diminished their own necessity.

A similar process seems to be at work in the mindfulness movement. As liberal Buddhists work ever harder to diminish the role of traditional Buddhism in mindfulness, Buddhism not only loses control over mindfulness but potentially comes to be extraneous, lacking any meaningful role in mindfulness and failing to shape the further trajectories that mindfulness takes in American culture. A further insight that can be taken from Hedstrom's work is his division of 20th century religious liberals into laissez-faire liberals and ethical liberals. The former seek only practical, material benefits from religion, typically through orientations and practices derived from New Thought and psychology. Ethical liberals, on the other hand, not only included the psychological orientation but also combined it with social activism, critique of American society, and in some cases pacifism. If we transplant these terms, we can recognize two broad, sometimes overlapping streams in the mindfulness movement. There are laissez-faire mindfulness practitioners who pursue their own practical benefit via meditation, and there are ethical mindfulness practitioners for whom mindfulness provides an alternative to mainstream American society, a foundation on which to build a healthier and more compassionate America, and tools for bringing about that liberal vision. It is practitioners in the second category who teach mindfulness in places like prisons and schools, and who advocate incorporating mindfulness into American institutions in a systematic fashion.

All Things to All People

Mindfulness allows people to participate in Buddhism along a very wide spectrum of degrees of engagement, and it authorizes new developments as well. One can be a traditionalist, a secular Buddhist, a spiritual person, a non-religious practitioner, and so on. It provides a base for hipster urban Buddhism/post-Buddhism such as the Interdependence Project, for Jewish and Christian revitalization efforts, and is value-added to postural yoga. One can religionize mindfulness by saying it is connecting to your original nature, spiritual energy, true reality, the sacralized present moment, etc., or one can secularize it by saying that mindfulness is about calm, physical health, and great orgasms.

Mindfulness originates in Asian Buddhist monasticism but can become entirely American, secular, and everyday—these processes do not just happen, however. They are choices, employing power and the cultural tools available to their users, always made because some sort of benefit is believed to flow from such choices. Ultimately, mindfulness does not need to be religious OR spiritual OR therapeutic OR secular. It can operate in any of these modes, in more than one of these modes at the same time, and the same person can move from one mode to another with ease. Mindfulness and the movement it has spawned can draw on multiple, seemingly contradicting, modes of authority as each situation and user demands: it is by turns religious, spiritual, therapeutic, or secular as necessary. Thus the mindfulness movement can gesture to ancient tradition as evidence of authenticity, to scientific proof as evidence of reliability, to external authority (lineage, text, teacher, experimental results) for strength, and internal/personal experience and intuition for support.

In this, it demonstrates the central Buddhist insight that all things are empty of self-nature, including every single element of Buddhism and the tradition as a whole. Being empty of self-nature, mindfulness can be used to achieve nirvana and to cleave more tightly to this suffering world, to focus on the loathsomeness of bodies and to dwell on their attractiveness, to destroy attachment and to mend broken relationships, to promote religion and to confirm scientific worldviews, to foster white dominance and to empower people of color, to achieve magical powers and to disenchant the world, to see through the traps of hypercommercialism and to make a buck, to promote revolution and to make everyone happy in their cubicles, to bring new people to Buddhism and to justify breaking free of Buddhism, to reveal the truth of no-self and to heighten one's sense of identity, to reinforce tradition, and to produce radical innovation.

Moving Forward

Mindful America is a first foray into a largely understudied phenomenon. As such, there are many potentially useful approaches that were regrettably left aside due to space considerations or because we do not yet have a sufficient mass of data on the movement to carry out certain forms of analysis. There is a need for many future research projects that help us to chart and understand this explosively growing movement. I close this initial examination by taking a moment to point out some possible research avenues that ambitious graduate students and curious scholars may find fruitful.

First, there are many players in this movement (and in this book), but none have been explored in particular depth. We need sustained studies of specific mindfulness advocates, especially those who are most influential, most representative, or who are pushing the boundaries of mindfulness in America. The two most needed biographies, I believe, are for very different sorts of mindfulness promoters: Thich Nhat Hanh and Jon Kabat-Zinn. Both have vast published bodies of work; have conducted countless seminars, retreats, and appearances; have legions of disciples; and oversee large multinational organizations. Yet the Vietnamese monk and the Jewish-American scientist are quite different in their backgrounds and frames for mindfulness. We need studies of these and other figures that consider where they came from, how they got involved in mindfulness, how their teaching has changed over the decades, and what specific inputs they have made to the mindfulness movement.

Second, we need sophisticated ethnographic work on various aspects of the mindfulness movement. Budding anthropologists should consider MBSR classes, Google's Search Inside Yourself and similar corporate programs, and Buddhist mindfulness groups as subjects for long-term qualitative investigation, perhaps in a comparative mode. Another group that cries out for deeper exploration is OneTaste, whose promiscuous puncturing of categories related to religion, spirituality, the secular, health, medicine, sexual liberation, and commercialism promises a rich site for the theorization of cultural phenomena in the 21st century.

Third, we need studies of the legal and political ramifications of the mindfulness movement, especially its push into public aspects of society such as the schools and military. Important issues of law, religion, and freedom are raised by the mindfulness movement, and scholars with expertise in legal studies, political science, education, and related fields will have much to say about these developments in concert with their colleagues in religious studies, sociology, anthropology, and cultural studies.

Fourth, we need to examine in greater detail how mindfulness is used and altered by non-Buddhists, especially those who claim or participate in some other religious tradition. There are mindful Christians, mindful Jews, and more in modern America, and their experiences need to be cataloged and analyzed. We also need to study those who resist the mindfulness movement, whether due to Christian commitments or other reasons.

Fifth, we need studies that focus on the international elements of mindfulness. This book looks solely at the United States, but many aspects of the mindfulness movement are shared in other places. We must consider the global phenomenon of mindfulness as well as its local manifestations, examining the flows and blockages between various societies. How is mindfulness adapted to Canada, or Germany, or Israel? Hopefully researchers with expertise in these areas will carry out their own projects and enlighten us on mindfulness phenomena around the world.

Sixth, further consideration of the economics of the mindfulness movement is necessary. Few scholars have applied an economic lens to the study of Buddhism in America, whether in relation to meditation or other topics. Much more work can be done that takes into account the production, marketing, and consumption of Buddhist practices, objects, and personalities.

Finally, the specific themes advanced in this book can all be taken up, extended, contested, and refined by future research. Do all six processes I described occur in every manifestation of the mindfulness movement, or are some aspects of the movement operating in a different manner that drops some of these processes or adds additional ones? If there are differences, why do they come about? What about the perspectives of Buddhists who attempt to resist these processes—how and why do they do so? Can all of Buddhism in America be understood through the lens of practical benefits, or are there other movements that fail to fit into this mode of analysis? With these and other studies, we can look forward to a more comprehensive, nuanced understanding of mindfulness's place and impact in America.

NOTES

INTRODUCTION

1. Bev Bennett. "How to Lose a Pound a Week Without Feeling Like You're on a Diet." *Spirit of Women* (Spring 2013): 27.

2. *The New York Times* Best Sellers. Retrieved from http://www.nytimes.com/best-sellers-books (Accessed May 17, 2013); Daphne Oz. *Relish: An Adventure in Food, Style, and Everyday Fun*. New York: HarperCollins, 2013; Tana Amen. *The Omni Diet: The Revolutionary 70% PLANT + 30% PROTEIN Program to Lose Weight, Reverse Disease, Fight Inflammation, and Change Your Life Forever*. New York: St. Martin's Press, 2013; Brene Brown. *Daring Greatly: How the Courage to be Vulnerable Transforms the Way We Live, Love, Parent, and Lead*. New York: Gotham, 2012; David Sheff. *Clean: Overcoming Addiction and Ending America's Greatest Tragedy*. Chicago: Houghton Mifflin Harcourt, 2013.

3. UCLA Mindful Awareness Research Center. Retrieved from http://marc.ucla.edu/body.cfm?id=85 (Accessed May 10, 2013).

4. Inward Bound Mindfulness Education. [advertisement] *Mindful*, 1.2 (June 2013): 13.

5. Wisdom 2.0 Business. [advertisement]. *Mindful*, 1.2 (June 2013): 20.

6. Magnolia Grove Monastery. Retrieved from http://magnoliagrovemonastery.org/index.php?option=com_content&view=article&id=145:dom&catid=34:dom&Itemid=89 (Accessed May 10, 2013).

7. National Center for Complementary and Alternative Medicine. Retrieved from http://nccam.nih.gov/health/meditation/overview.htm (Accessed October 10, 2012); Julie Carr Smyth. "'Mindfulness' Grows in Popularity—and Profits." Associated Press, June 11, 2012. Retrieved from http://bigstory.ap.org/article/mindfulness-grows-popularity-and-profits (Accessed October 10, 2012).

8. Mindfulness Research Guide. Retrieved from http://www.mindfulexperience.org/resources/MRG_pubs_2010.pdf (Accessed October 10, 2012); The Center for Mindfulness in Medicine, Health Care, and Society. Retrieved from http://

w3.umassmed.edu/MBSR/public/searchmember.aspx (Accessed October 10, 2012). Only articles in English were surveyed, and this does not include publications in nonacademic venues.

9. Google. Retrieved from http://adwords.google.com (Accessed October 10, 2012).

10. Carrie Gann. "Brain Imaging Illuminates Neuro Basis of Meditation." ABC News, November 22, 2011. Retrieved from http://abcnews.go.com/Health/meditation-brain-rewire-study/story?id=15001280#.UZfJsMqHShm (Accessed May 18, 2013); Robert Wright. "Mindful Eating and Fast-Food Buddhism." *The Atlantic*, February 10, 2012. Retrieved from http://www.theatlantic.com/health/archive/2012/02/mindful-eating-and-fast-food-buddhism/252896/ (Accessed February 11, 2012); Sean Alfano. "Getting Into Our Minds." *CBS Sunday Morning*, April 9, 2006. Retrieved from http://www.cbsnews.com/8301-3445_162-1483025/getting-into-our-minds/ (Accessed May 18, 2013); Val Willingham. "Mindfulness Training Busts Stress." CNN, June 1, 1009. Retrieved from http://www.cnn.com/2009/HEALTH/06/01/mindfulness.training.stress/ (Accessed May 18, 2013); "The Surprising Way to Feel Happier." *Cosmopolitan*. Retrieved from http://www.cosmopolitan.com/advice/tips/The-surprising-way-to-feel-happier (Accessed October 1, 2012); Louisa Kamps. "Just Hit Refresh." *Elle*, December 22, 2009. Retrieved from http://www.elle.com/life-love/sex-relationships/just-hit-refresh-38941 7?click=main_sr (Accessed May 18, 2013); Laurie Tarkin. "Improve Job Satisfaction with Mindfulness." FOX News, January 24, 2013. Retrieved from http://www.foxnews.com/health/2013/01/23/improve-job-satisfaction-with-mindfulness/ (Accessed May 18, 2013); Denise Foley. "Conquer Your Food Cravings." *Good Housekeeping*. Retrieved from http://www.goodhousekeeping.com/health/diet-plans/conquer-food-cravings-4 (Accessed October 1, 2012); Arianna Huffington. "Mindfulness, Meditation, Wellness and Their Connection to Corporate America's Bottom Line." *Huffington Post*, March 18, 2013. Retrieved from http://www.huffingtonpost.com/arianna-huffington/corporate-wellness_b_2903222.html (Accessed March 23, 2013); Tula Karras. "10 Tips for Mindful Living." *Ladies' Home Journal*. Retrieved from http://www.lhj.com/health/stress/relaxation-techniques/10-tips-for-mindful-living/ (Accessed October 1, 2012); Leslie Bennetts. "Can You Think Yourself Thin?" *Marie Claire*, July 20, 2011. Retrieved from http://www.marieclaire.com/health-fitness/news/meditation-diet (Accessed October 1, 2012); *The Dylan Ratigan Show*. "The Buddhist Practice that Could Fix Congress. MSNBC, April 9, 2012. Retrieved from http://www.msnbc.msn.com/id/31510813/#46997405 (Accessed May 19, 2013); Lisa Napoli. "Buddhist Meditation: A Management Skill?" *Morning Edition*, September 13, 2012. Retrieved from http://www.npr.org/2012/09/13/161050141/buddhist-meditation-a-management-skill (Accessed May 19, 2013); James Atlas. "Buddhists' Delight." *The New York Times*,

June 17, 2012: SR4; "Oprah Talks to Thich Nhat Hanh." *O: The Oprah Magazine*, March 2010. Retrieved from http://www.oprah.com/spirit/Oprah-Talks-to-Thich-Nhat-Hanh (Accessed May 19, 2013); Laura Riley. "Take a Mindful Walk." *Parents*. Retrieved from http://www.parents.com/pregnancy/week-by-week/15/mindful-walk/ (Accessed May 19, 2013); Cary Barbor. "The Science of Meditation." *Psychology Today*, May 1, 2001. Retrieved from http://www.psychologytoday.com/articles/200105/the-science-meditation (Accessed May 19, 2013); Leo Babauta. "10 Steps to Mindfulness." *Readers Digest*. Retrieved from http://www.rd.com/slideshows/10-steps-to-mindfulness/ (Accessed May 19, 2013); "Zen Lessons." *Redbook*. Retrieved from http://www.redbookmag.com/health-wellness/advice/zen-lessons-yl-2 (Accessed May 19, 2013); Paula Derrow. "Stop Emotional Eating." *Self*. Retrieved from http://www.self.com/takecareofyou/emotional-eating-slideshow#slide=1 (Accessed May 19, 2013); John Cloud. "Losing Focus? Studies Say Mindfulness Can Help." *Time*, August 6, 2010. Retrieved from http://www.time.com/time/health/article/0,8599,2008914,00.html (Accessed May 19, 2013); Mandy Oaklander. "Mindfulness Meditation Linked to Improved Brainpower: 3 Ways to Get Smarter and Boost Your Happiness While You're At It." *Prevention*, March 2013. Retrieved from http://www.prevention.com/mind-body/emotional-health/mindfulness-meditation-linked-improved-brainpower (Accessed May 19, 2013); Beth Gardiner. "Business Skills and Buddhist Mindfulness." *Wall Street Journal*, April 3, 2012. Retrieved from http://online.wsj.com/article/SB10001424052702303816504577305820565167202.html (Accessed August 17, 2012); "Mindfulness-Based Stress Reduction—Topic Overview." WebMD, May 23, 2011. Retrieved from http://www.webmd.com/balance/tc/mindfulness-based-stress-reduction-topic-overview (Accessed May 19, 2013); Gretchin Rubin. "May's Challenge: Be Mindful." *Woman's Day*. Retrieved from http://www.womansday.com/life/mays-challenge-be-mindful-105804 (Accessed May 19, 2013).

11. "Mindfulness Goes Corporate." *Mindful*, 1.1 (April 2013): 58.

12. Barry Boyce. "Creating a Mindful Society." In *The Mindfulness Revolution: Leading Psychologists, Scientists, Artists, and Meditation Teachers on the Power of Mindfulness in Daily Life*, edited by Barry Boyce and the Editors of *Shambhala Sun*. Boston: Shambhala, 2011: 252–264.

13. Charles Orzech, trans. "The Scripture on Perfect Wisdom for Humane Kings Who Wish to Protect Their States." In *Chinese Religions in Practice*. Donald S. Lopez, Jr., ed. Princeton: Princeton University Press, 1996: 372–380.

14. Ian Reader and George J. Tanabe, Jr. *Practically Religious: Worldly Benefits and the Common Religion of Japan*. Honolulu: University of Hawaii Press, 1998: 2.

15. Lynn P. Eldershaw. "Shambhala International: The Golden Sun of the Great East." In *Wild Geese: Buddhism in Canada*, John S. Harding, Victor Sōgen Hori,

and Alexander Soucy, eds. Montreal and Kingston: McGill-Queens University Press, 2010: 236–267.

16. Ryan Bongseok Joo. "Countercurrents from the West: 'Blue-Eyed' Zen Masters, Vipassanā Meditation, and Buddhist Psychotherapy in Contemporary Korea." *Journal of the American Academy of Religion*, 79.3 (September 2011): 614–638.

17. Jeff Wilson. *Mourning the Unborn Dead: A Buddhist Ritual Comes to America*. New York: Oxford University Press, 2009.

18. Jeff Wilson. *Dixie Dharma: Inside a Buddhist Temple in the American South*. Chapel Hill, NC: University of North Carolina Press, 2012.

19. Wakoh Shannon Hickey. "Mind Cure, Meditation, and Medicine: Hidden Histories of Mental Healing in the United States." PhD dissertation, Duke University, Durham, NC, 2008; Wendy Cadge. *Heartwood: The First Generation of Theravada Buddhism in America*. Chicago: University of Chicago Press, 2004; Gil Fronsdal. "Insight Meditation in the United States: Life, Liberty, and the Pursuit of Happiness." In *The Faces of Buddhism in America*, Charles S. Prebish and Kenneth K. Tanaka, eds. Berkeley: University of California Press, 1998: 163–180; David L. McMahan. *The Making of Buddhist Modernism*. New York: Oxford University Press, 2008; Anne Harrington. *The Cure Within: A History of Mind-Body Medicine*. New York: W.W. Norton, 2008. This list does not exhaust the good, but very preliminary, work done to this point on mindfulness.

CHAPTER I

1. "Mediate" In *The Compact Edition of the Oxford English Dictionary*. Oxford: Oxford University Press, 1971: 1758.

2. Kiera Van Gelder. "My Practice Without Meds." *Buddhadharma: The Practitioner's Quarterly*, 10.3 (Spring 2012): 62. Describing *Buddhadharma* as American could be—like my description of *Shambhala Sun* in the introduction—slightly controversial. *Buddhadharma*'s editorial offices are in Halifax and its editor-in-chief is Canadian. But a look at the magazine's full masthead reveals a superabundance of Americans, and the magazine, like *Shambhala Sun*, explicitly targets an American audience.

3. Gretchin Rubin. *The Happiness Project, Or, Why I Spent a Year Trying to Sing in the Morning, Clean My Closets, Fight Right, Read Aristotle, and Generally Have More Fun*. New York: Harper, 2009: 3.

4. Rubin, 2009: 237.

5. Van Gelder subsequently became a Buddhist—my point is that both women were not Buddhist when they initially encountered mindfulness, and their encounters were not with Buddhism per se as a full religious tradition, but with mindfulness practice removed from Buddhism.

6. Thomas A Tweed. *The American Encounter with Buddhism, 1844–1912: Victorian Culture and the Limits of Dissent.* Chapel Hill: University of North Carolina Press, 2000: xxxi.

7. Smṛti. I have chosen not to use diacritical marks in the main text; if a term is not already commonly Anglicized, then I will provide the proper Asian spelling in the footnotes the first time it appears.

8. See, for example, the translations by Thanissaro Bhikkhu at Access to Insight (www.accesstoinsight.org), the Teachings of the Buddha series from Wisdom Publications (such as Maurice Walshe. *The Long Discources of the Buddha: A Translation of the Dīgha Nikāya.* Boston: Wisdom Publications, 1995 and Bhikkhu Nāṇamoli and Bhikkhu Bodhi. *The Middle Length Discources of the Buddha: A New Translation of the Majjhima Nikāya.* Boston: Wisdom Publications, 1995), and Nyanaponika Thera and Bhikkhu Bodhi. *Numerical Discources of the Buddha: An Anthology of Suttas from the Aṅguttara Nikāya.* Lanham, MD: Rowman and Littlefield, 1999.

9. Satipaṭṭhāna Sutta; Mahāsatipaṭṭhāna Sutta; Ānāpānasati Sutta.

10. Sammā-sati.

11. R. Spence Hardy. *A Manual of Buddhism in Its Modern Development.* London: Partridge and Oakley, 1853: 412, 498.

12. Captain T. Rogers. *Buddhaghosha's Parables, Translated from the Burmese, With an Introduction, Containing Buddha's Dhammapada, or "Path of Virtue," Translated from Pâli by F. Max Müller.* London: Trübner and Co., 1870: cxxxix–cxl.

13. Henry Alabaster. *The Wheel of the Law. Buddhism, Illustrated from Siamese Sources.* London: Trübner and Company, 1871: 200.

14. Henry S. Olcott. *A Buddhist Catechism According to the Canon of the Southern School.* London: Trübner and Company, 1881: 10. In later editions issued after Olcott's death, the wording was eventually changed to "Right Remembrance and Self-Discipline."

15. Henry Clarke Warren. *Buddhism in Translations.* Cambridge, MA: Harvard University Press, 1896: 353.

16. Paul Carus. *The Dharma, or the Religion of Enlightenment: An Exposition of Buddhism.* Chicago: Open Court Publishing, 1907: 25.

17. T. W. Rhys Davids. *Lectures on the Origins and Growth of Religion as Illustrated by Some Points in the History of Indian Buddhism.* London: Williams and Norgate, 1881: 65, 180.

18. T. W. Rhys Davids. *Buddhism: Being a Sketch of the Life and Teachings of Gautama, the Buddha.* London: Society for Promoting Christian Knowledge, 1886: 108, 172.

19. T. W. Rhys Davids. *The Questions of King Milinda [The Sacred Books of the East, volume XXXV].* London: Oxford University, 1890: 58.

20. Albert J. Edmunds. *Hymns of Faith (Dhammapada), being an ancient anthology preserved in the short collection of the sacred scriptures of the Buddhists.* Chicago: Open Court Publishing Company, 1902: 70–71.

21. T. W. Rhys Davids and C. A. F. Rhys Davids. *Dialogues of the Buddha, Part II.* London: Luzac and Company, 1910: 327.

22. Lord Chalmers. *Further Dialogues of the Buddha, Translated from the Pali of the Majjhima Nikāya* (Vol. I). London: Humphrey Milford, Oxford University Press, 1926: 41; Lord Chalmers. *Further Dialogues of the Buddha, Translated from the Pali of the Majjhima Nikāya* (Vol. II). London: Humphrey Milford, Oxford University Press, 1927: 199; I. B. Horner. *The Collection of the Middle Length Sayings (Majjhima-Nikāya), Vol. I: The First Fifty Discourses (Mūlapaṇṇāsa).* London: Luzac and Company, 1954: 70; I. B. Horner *The Collection of the Middle Length Sayings (Majjhima-Nikāya),* Vol. III: *The Final Fifty Discourses (Uparipaṇṇāsa).* London: Luzac and Company, 1959: 121.

23. Apramāda.

24. Max Müller, in his 1870 translation of the *Dhammapada,* used "recollection" to render the term appamada. Thus in his rendition the first two lines of the second chapter of the *Dhammapada* become "Reflection is the path of immortality, thoughtlessness the path of death. Those who reflect do not die, those who are thoughtless are as if dead already." In Müller's discussion of the verse, he states that appamada "expresses literally the absence of that giddiness of thoughtlessness which characterizes the state of mind of worldly people…I have translated it by 'recollection,' sometimes by 'earnestness.'" In Albert J. Edmunds's 1902 translation of the *Dhammapada* he rendered appamada as "earnestness." Rogers, 1870: lxiii; Edmunds 1902: 6.

25. Vipassanā; vipaśyanā.

26. Śamatha.

27. Joseph Goldstein. *The Experience of Insight: A Natural Unfolding.* Santa Cruz: Unity Press, 1976: 4.

28. Goldstein, 1976: 4.

29. Bhikkhu Ñāṇamoli and Bhikkhu Bodhi, trans. *The Middle Length Discourses of the Buddha: A New Translation of the Majjhima Nikāya.* Boston: Wisdom Publications, 1995: 145.

30. Jhāna; dhyāna.

31. Patrick A. Pranke. "Vipassanā." In *Encyclopedia of Buddhism,* Vol. II, Robert E. Buswell, ed. New York: Thomson Gale, 2004: 889–890.

32. David L. McMahan. "Meditation, Modern Movements." In *Encyclopedia of Buddhism,* Damien Keown and Charles S. Prebish, eds. London and New York: Routledge, 2007: 502–505.

33. Mahasi Sayadaw. *Practical Insight Meditation: Basic and Progressive Stages.* Kandy, Sri Lanka: Buddhist Publication Society, 1976: iii.

34. Readers interested in the modern Asian roots of mindfulness practices are urged to acquire Erik Braun's *The Birth of Insight: Meditation, Modern Buddhism, and the Burmese Monk Ledi Sayadaw* (Chicago: University Chicago Press, 2013). Released in late 2013 as *Mindful America* was undergoing final editing, it debuted too late for Braun's research to be incorporated into this book. The present chapter is most concerned with revealing the channels of mediation that bring mindfulness to the American public, rather than with the details of the history per se. Braun's work provides an important investigation of the Burmese history in full detail, with attention to both precolonial and colonial forces that contributed to the rise of mindfulness in Burma and, ultimately, the rest of the world.

35. Soma Thera. *The Way of Mindfulness: The Satipatthana Sutta and Commentary* (4th edition). Kandy: Buddhist Publication Society, 1975: 3 (first edition is Kandy: Sagganubodha Samiti, Nandana, Asgiriya, 1941).

36. Soma Thera, 1975: 2.

37. Nyanaponika Thera. *Satipatthana, The Heart of Buddhist Meditation: A Handbook of Mental Training Based on the Buddha's Way of Mindfulness.* Sri Lanka: Colombo: The Word of the Buddha Publishing, 1953. The original editions of this book present a bewildering mess. Some of the material originated in German publications beginning in 1950; the English versions—apparently expanded—are listed as published first in 1953, but Nyanaponika claims the first editions were 1954 and 1956. I rely on the 1965 paperback reprint from Samuel Weiser, which became the standard version accessible to most Americans, which is itself a new issue from the 1962 edition published by Rider and Co. (Nyanaponika Thera. *The Heart of Buddhist Meditation*. New York: Samuel Weiser, 1965).

38. Nyanaponika Thera, 1965: 7.

39. Nyanaponika Thera, 1965: 7.

40. Walpola Rahula. *What the Buddha Taught*. Bedford, UK: Gordon Fraser Gallery, 1959: 67.

41. Rahula, 1959: 69.

42. Rahula, 1959: 70–71.

43. Rahula, 1959: 71.

44. Rahula, 1959: 72.

45. Anonymous, "Mindfulness." *The Golden Lotus*, April–May, 1958: 53. Although unsigned, the article is presumably penned by A. L. Roger, the editor.

46. Christmas Humphreys. *An Invitation to the Buddhist Way of Life for Western Readers*. New York: Schocken Books, 1969: 97. This quote comes from a reprint of an article originally published in the *Middle Way*, 40.3 (1965). A bhikkhu is a Theravada Buddhist monk.

47. Donald K. Swearer. *Secrets of the Lotus: Studies in Buddhist Meditation.* New York: Macmillan Company, 1971: 4–10.

48. Shunryu Suzuki. *Zen Mind, Beginner's Mind.* New York: Weatherhill, 1970: 113–115. The word mindfulness is actually barely even used in these few pages, and indicates simply a concentrated mind during activity.

49. E. H. Shattock. *An Experiment in Mindfulness.* London: Rider, 1958.

50. Marie Beuzeville Byles. *Journey Into Burmese Silence.* London: George Allen and Unwin, 1962.

51. John E. Coleman. *The Quiet Mind.* New York: Harper and Row, 1971.

52. Rick Fields. *How the Swans Came to the Lake: A Narrative History of Buddhism in America* (3rd edition). Boston: Shambhala, 1992: 316–323.

53. Fronsdal, 1998: 168.

54. Jack Kornfield. "This Fantastic, Unfolding Experiment." *Buddhadharma: The Practitioner's Quarterly*, 5.4 (Summer 2007): 39.

55. Steve Silberman. "Wise Heart." *Shambhala Sun*, 19.2 (November 2010): 50.

56. Thich Nhat Hanh. *The Miracle of Mindfulness! A Manual on Meditation.* Boston: Beacon Press, 1976.

57. Parallax Press. Retrieved from http://www.parallax.org/cgi-bin/shopper.cgi?search=action&category=BOOK&keywords=hanh (Accessed December 23, 2012).

58. Sangha Directory. Retrieved from http://www.iamhome.org/directory/index.cgi (Accessed December 23, 2012).

59. Jon Kabat-Zinn. *Full Catastrophe Living: Using the Wisdom of Your Body and Mind to Face Stress, Pain, and Illness.* New York: Delacorte Press, 1990 (Fifteenth Anniversary Edition, New York: Delta, 2005: xxi).

60. Kabat-Zinn, 2005 (1990): 2.

61. Chogyam Trungpa, ed. *Garuda IV: Foundations of Mindfulness.* Boulder: Vajradhatu, 1976.

62. Trungpa, 1976: 15.

63. Thich Nhat Hanh. *Being Peace.* Berkeley: Parallax Press, 1987; Thich Nhat Hanh. *The Sun My Heart: From Mindfulness to Insight Contemplation.* Berkeley: Parallax Press, 1988; Thich Nhat Hanh and Annabel Laity. *The Sutra on the Full Awareness of Breathing: With Commentary by Thich Nhat Hanh.* Berkeley: Parallax Press, 1988.

64. Jon Kabat-Zinn, Leslie Lipworth, and Robert Burney. "The Clinical Use of Mindfulness Medicine for the Self-Regulation of Chronic Pain." *Journal of Behavioral Medicine*, 8.2 (1985): 163–190.

65. Joan Borysenko. *Minding the Body, Mending the Mind.* New York: Bantam Books, 1988.

66. Thich Nhat Hanh. "Opening the Door…And Letting the Ladies In." *Tricycle: The Buddhist Review*, 1.1 (Fall 1992): 26–29; Sylvia Boorstein. "Body as Body." *Tricycle: The Buddhist Review*, 1.2 (Winter 1991): 28–29; Thich Nhat Hanh. "Commentary." *Tricycle: The Buddhist Review*, 1.3 (Spring 1992): 26–27;

Janet Howey. "Mindful to the Quarter-inch." *Tricycle: The Buddhist Review*, 2.1 (Fall 1992): 74–75.

67. Sogyal Rinpoche. *The Tibetan Book of Living and Dying*. San Francisco: HarperSanFrancisco, 1992.

68. Jon Kabat-Zinn. *Wherever You Go, There You Are: Mindfulness Meditation in Everyday Life*. New York: Hyperion, 1994.

69. "About Us." Duke Integrative Medicine. Retrieved from http://www.dukeintegrativemedicine.org/about-us/our-history. (Accessed January 24, 2013).

70. Phil Jackson and Hugh Delehanty. *Sacred Hoops: Spiritual Lessons of a Hardwood Warrior*. New York: Hyperion, 1995: 5–6.

71. As early as the 1984 US. Olympic Men's Rowing team, Jon Kabat-Zinn and his associates in Mindfulness-Based Stress Reduction had been working with athletes to use mindfulness to improve their performance. But it wasn't until the popularity of Michael Jordan and all things Bulls in the 1990s that the wider public really began to take notice of mindful sports. George Mumford, an associate of Kabat-Zinn, was part of the training of the 1990s Bulls. See Jon Kabat-Zinn. "Indra's Net at Work: The Mainstreaming of Dharma Practice in Society." In *The Psychology of Awakening: Buddhism, Science, and Our Day-to-Day Lives*, Gay Watson, Stephen Batchelor, and Guy Claxton, eds. Boston: Weisser Books, 2000: 247–248.

72. Thomas Bein and Beverly Bien. *Mindful Recovery: A Spiritual Path to Healing from Addiction*. New York: John Wiley & Sons, 2002; Sameet M. Kumar. *Grieving Mindfully: A Compassionate and Spiritual Guide to Coping with Loss*. Oakland: New Harbinger Publications, 2005; Mark Williams, John Teasdale, Zindal Segal, and Jon Kabat-Zinn. *The Mindful Way Through Depression: Freeing Yourself from Chronic Unhappiness*. New York: Guilford Press, 2007; Steve Flowers. *The Mindful Path Through Shyness: How Mindfulness and Compassion Can Help Free You From Social Anxiety, Fear, and Avoidance*. Oakland: New Harbinger Publications, 2009.

73. Susan Albers. *Eating Mindfully: How to End Mindless Eating and Enjoy a Balanced Relationship with Food*. Oakland: New Harbinger Publications, 2003; Henry Grayson. *Mindful Loving: 10 Practices for Creating Deep Connections*. New York: Gotham Books, 2003; Denise Roy. *Momfulness: Mothering with Mindfulness, Compassion, and Grace*. San Francisco: John Wiley and Sons, 2007; Elizabeth MacDonald and Dennis Shirley. *The Mindful Teacher*. New York: Teachers College Press, 2009; Christopher R. Edgar. *Inner Productivity: A Mindful Path to Efficiency and Enjoyment in Your Work*. Christopher R. Edgar, 2009.

74. Tara Jon Manning. *Mindful Knitting: Inviting Contemplative Practice to the Craft*. Boston: Tuttle Publishing, 2004.

75. Valerie Davis Raskin. *Great Sex for Moms: Ten Steps to Nurturing Passion While Raising Kids*. New York: Simon and Schuster, 2002; Frank Gardner and Zella

Moore. *Clinical Sport Psychology*. Champaign, IL: Human Kinetics, 2006; Gerald J. Musante. *The Structure House Weight Loss Plan: Achieve Your Ideal Weight Through a New Relationship with Food*. New York: Simon and Schuster, 2007; James V. Cordova. *The Marriage Checkup: A Scientific Program for Sustaining and Strengthening Marital Health*. Lanham, MD: Rowman and Littlefield, 2009.

76. Scott L. Rogers. *Mindfulness for Law Students: Using the Power of Mindful Awareness to Achieve Balance and Success in Law School*. Scott L. Rogers, 2009; Real World Mindfulness. Retrieved from http://www.real-worldmindfulness.com/ (Accessed June 14, 2012); Elizabeth A. Stanley and John M. Schaldach. "Mindfulness-based Mind Fitness Training (MMFT)." Mind Fitness Training Institute, 2011. Retrieved from http://www.mind-fitness-training.org/MMFTOverviewNarrative.pdf (Accessed June 14, 2012).

77. Anne Ihnen and Carolyn Flynn. *The Complete Idiot's Guide to Mindfulness*. New York: Alpha Books, 2008.

CHAPTER 2

1. "Mystify." *The Compact Edition of the Oxford English Dictionary*. Oxford: Oxford University Press, 1971: 1889.
2. Andrew Weiss. *Beginning Mindfulness: Learning the Way of Awareness, a Ten-Week Course*. Novato, CA: New World Press, 2004: xvi.
3. Weiss, 2004: xvi.
4. Weiss, 2004: xvi.
5. John Corrigan and Lynn S. Neal, eds. *Religious Intolerance in America: A Documentary History*. Chapel Hill, NC: University of North Carolina Press, 2010.
6. William Alexander. *Cool Water: Alcoholism, Mindfulness, and Ordinary Recovery*. Boston: Shambhala, 1997: 17.
7. Susan Albers. *Eat, Drink, and Be Merry: How to End Your Struggle with Mindless Eating and Start Savoring Food with Intention and Joy*. Oakland, CA: New Harbinger, 2008: 115.
8. Judy Lief. "The Middle Way of Stress." *Shambhala Sun*, 21.1 (September 2012): 45.
9. Lief, 2012: 46–47.
10. Lief, 2012: 89.
11. Ronna Kabatznick. *The Zen of Eating: Ancient Answers to Modern Weight Problems*. New York: Perigee, 1998: 85.
12. Kabatznick, 1998: 86.
13. Coleman, 1971: 102–103.
14. I mean generation in terms of stages in a lineage, not in terms of chronological age of the participants. Often the second-generation individuals who trained entirely in the United States were the same age as their returned lay teachers.

15. Janet Taylor. *Buddhism for Non-Buddhists: A Practical Guide to Ease Suffering and Be Happy*. [Kindle edition]. Kansas City, MI: Janet Taylor, 2012: 1–2.
16. Nyanaponika Thera, 1965: 82–83. Italics in original.
17. Nyanaponika Thera, 1965: 93.
18. Mark Thornton. *Meditation in a New York Minute: Super Calm for the Super Busy*. Boulder, CO: Sounds True, 2006; David Harp. *Mindfulness to Go: How to Meditate While You're on the Move*. Oakland, CA: New Harbinger, 2011; David B. Dillard-Wright, Heidi E. Spear, and Paula Munier. *5-Minute Mindfulness: Simple Daily Shortcuts to Transform Your Life*. Avon, MA: Adams Media, 2011.
19. Sylvia Boorstein. *It's Easier Than You Think: The Buddhist Way to Happiness*. San Francisco: HarperSanFrancisco, 1995; Steve Hagen. *Buddhism Plain and Simple: The Practice of Being Aware, Right Now, Every Day*. New York: Broadway Books, 1999; Ronald D. Siegel. *The Mindfulness Solution: Everyday Practices for Everyday Problems*. New York: Guilford Press, 2010; Rick Hanson. *Just One Thing: Developing a Buddha Brain One Simple Practice at a Time*. Oakland, CA: New Harbinger, 2011.
20. Mahasi, 1976: 1.
21. Goldstein, 1976: 1–2.
22. Byles, 1962: 9–10.
23. Albers, 2003: 7.
24. Susan Albers. *Mindful Eating 101: A Guide to Healthy Eating in College and Beyond*. New York: Routledge, 2006: 10.
25. Robert J. Wicks. *Bounce: Living the Resilient Life*. New York: Oxford University Press, 2010: 129.
26. Wicks, 2010: 135.
27. Ihnen and Flynn, 2008.
28. Ihnen and Flynn, 2008: 13.
29. Ihnen and Flynn, 2008: 23.
30. Ihnen and Flynn, 2008: 263.
31. Daniel J. Seigel. *Mindsight: The New Science of Personal Transformation*. New York: Bantam Books, 2010: 83.
32. Daniel J. Seigel. *The Mindful Therapist: A Clinician's Guide to Mindsight and Neural Integration*. New York: W.W. Norton, 2010: 239.
33. Alan Epstein. *How to Be Happier Day by Day: A Year of Mindful Actions*. New York: Penguin Books, 1994.
34. Marcia Montenegro. "Mindfulness Goes to Kindergarten." Christian Answers for the New Age. Retrieved from http://www.christiananswersforthenewage. org/Articles_MindfulnessForChildren.html (Accessed January 31, 2013).
35. Stephanie Warsmith. "Plain Township School Stops 'Mindfulness' Program after Some in Community Raise Concerns." *Akron Beacon*, April 15, 2013. Retrieved from http://www.ohio.com/news/plain-township-school-st

ops-mindfulness-program-after-some-in-community-raise-concerns-1.389761 (Accessed May 17, 2013).

36. Warsmith, 2013.

37. Melvin McLeod. "A Magazine for Everyone." *Shambhala Sun*, 21.4 (March 2013): 11.

38. McLeod 2013: 11.

39. I do not mean that white people actually lack race—my point is that in predominant American society white is coded with an essentially neutral value: it is the natural default state of human beings, from which those with particular race (African Americans, Asian Americans, etc.) are perceived as deviations.

40. Hagen 1999: 3.

41. Hagen 1999: 3.

42. Hagen 1999: 3–4.

43. Hagen 1999: 4.

44. Jane Naomi Iwamura. *Virtual Orientalism: Asian Religion and American Popular Culture*. New York: Oxford University Press, 2011: 21.

45. Carsten Knox. "Raising Baltimore One Child at a Time." *Mindful*, 1.1 (April 2013): 42–51.

46. Pico Iyer. "Still on the Road." *Mindful*, 1.1 (April 2013): 60–63.

47. Charles Johnson. "Why Is American Buddhism so White?" *Buddhadharma*, 11.2 (Winter 2012); Jan Willis. "Yes, We're Buddhists Too!" *Buddhadharma*, 11.2 (Winter 2012).

48. Donald McCown and Marc S. Micozzi. *New World Mindfulness: From the Founding Fathers, Emerson, and Thoreau to Your Personal Practice*. Rochester, VT: Healing Arts Press, 2012: 2–3.

49. John R. McRae. *Seeing Through Zen: Encounter, Transformation, and Genealogy in Chinese Chan Buddhism*. Berkeley: University of California Press, 2003; Alan Cole. *Fathering Your Father: The Zen of Fabrication in Tang Buddhism*. Berkeley: University of California Press, 2009.

50. Hilda Gutiérrez Baldoquín. "Introduction." In *Dharma, Color, and Culture: New Voices in Western Buddhism*. Hilda Gutiérrez Baldoquín, ed. Berkeley, CA: Parallax Press, 2004: 15.

51. Eduardo Duran. "Buddhism in the Land of the Redface." In *Dharma, Color, and Culture: New Voices in Western Buddhism*. Hilda Gutiérrez Baldoquín, ed. Berkeley, CA: Parallax Press, 2004: 47.

52. Viveka Chen. "Finding True Freedom." In *Dharma, Color, and Culture: New Voices in Western Buddhism*. Hilda Gutiérrez Baldoquín, ed. Berkeley, CA: Parallax Press, 2004: 111.

53. Chen, 2004: 111.

54. Baldoquín, 2004: 19, 21.

55. Charles Johnson. "Mindfulness and the Beloved Community." East Bay Meditation Center. Retrieved from http://www.eastbaymeditation.org/media/

docs/3604_TWSummer03MindfulnessAndTheBelovedCommunity.pdf (Accessed February 1, 2013). Originally published in *Turning Wheel: The Journal of Socially Engaged Buddhism* (Summer 2003).

56. Sister Chan Chau Nghiem. "Coming Home." In *Dharma, Color, and Culture: New Voices in Western Buddhism*. Hilda Gutiérrez Baldoquín, ed. Berkeley, CA: Parallax Press, 2004: 118–119.

57. Charlie Johnson. "Looking at Fear: Memory of a Near Lynching." *Inquiring Mind: A Semiannual Journal of the Vipassana Community*, 10, no. 1 (Spring 2003): 16–17.

58. Marlene Jones. "Moving Toward an End to Suffering." In *Dharma, Color, and Culture: New Voices in Western Buddhism*. Hilda Gutiérrez Baldoquín, ed. Berkeley, CA: Parallax Press, 2004: 43.

59. Obviously, women and people of color are not mutually exclusive categories. I am simply framing the issues in these ways in order to tease out the particular dynamics that occur due to race vs. those that occur due to gender specifically.

CHAPTER 3

1. "Medicalize." Oxford English Dictionary Online. Retrieved from http://www.oed.com (Accessed February 2, 2013).

2. Bhante Henepola Gunaratana. *Journey into Mindfulness: The Autobiography of Bhante G*. Boston: Wisdom Publications, 2003: 96.

3. Gunaratana, 1991: 8.

4. Arthur J. Deikman. "Experimental Meditation." *The Journal of Nervous and Mental Disease*, 136.4 (April 1963): 329–343.

5. D. T. Suzuki, Erich Fromm, and Richard De Martino. *Zen Buddhism & Psychoanalysis*. New York: Harper Colophon Books, 1960.

6. Mahesh had studied physics at university and named his TM teaching training course "Science of Creative Intelligence.

7. Lola Williamson. *Transcendent in America: Hindu-Inspired Meditation Movements as New Religion*. New York: New York University Press, 2010: 94.

8. George E. La More, Jr. "The Secular Selling of a Religion." *Christian Century*, 92.10 (1975): 1133–1137; John Allan. *TM: A Cosmic Confidence Trick*. Leicester, England: Inter-Varsity Press, 1980.

9. Iwamura, 2011.

10. Herbert Benson, with Miriam Z. Kipper. *The Relaxation Response*. New York: Avon Books, 1975. Benson also drew on early research on yoga and Zen Buddhism, as well as Christian versions of meditation or mystical experience, though TM remains by far the primary influence on the Relaxation Response.

11. Daniel Goleman. *Emotional Intelligence: Why It Can Matter More Than IQ*. New York: Bantam Books, 1995: 182–183.

12. Daniel Goleman. *The Varieties of the Meditative Experience*. New York: Halsted Press, 1976: xiv–xxi.

13. Daniel Goleman. "Meditation and Consciousness: An Asian Approach to Mental Health." *American Journal of Psychotherapy*, 30.1 (1976): 46.

14. Goleman, "Meditation and Consciousness," 1976: 46.

15. Goleman, *Varieties,* 1976: xxiii.

16. Goleman, *Varieties,* 1976: xxiii.

17. Goleman, *Varieties,* 1976: xxiii.

18. Goleman, *Varieties,* 1976: 27–28.

19. Goleman, *Varieties,* 1976: xxiii.

20. It is interesting to note that Daniel Goleman, by then employed at *Psychology Today*, was one of the readers for Kornfield's dissertation committee.

21. Jack Murray Kornfield. The Psychology of Mindfulness Meditation. Ph.D. dissertation. Humanistic Psychology Institute, 1977: 9.

22. Jack Kornfield. *The Wise Heart: A Guide to the Universal Teachings of Buddhist Psychology*. New York: Bantam Books, 2008.

23. Kornfield, 1977: 151–152; 171.

24. Kornfield, 1977: 183.

25. Jack Kornfield, Ram Dass, and Mokusen Miyuki. "Psychological Adjustment Is Not Liberation." *Zero: Contemporary Buddhist Life and Thought*, 2 (1979): 76.

26. Jack Kornfield. "Intensive Insight Meditation: A Phenomenological Study." *Journal of Transpersonal Psychology*, 11.1: 41–58.

27. Jon Kabat-Zinn. "Some Reflections on the Origins of MBSR, Skillful Means, and the Trouble with Maps." *Contemporary Buddhism*, 12.1 (May 2011): 287.

28. Kabat-Zinn, 2011: 287–288.

29. Kabat-Zinn, *Contemporary Buddhism*, 2011: 288. My apologies for the many edits in these extended quotes, especially those in parentheses to indicate cutting within sentences: Kabat-Zinn adopts a run-on, almost stream of consciousness style for his writing in this article, perhaps as a way of better bringing to mind memories of events over three decades in the past. It works moderately well in the original article, but would excessively bog down the discussion here.

30. Jon Kabat-Zinn. "Why Mindfulness Matters." In *The Mindfulness Revolution: Leading Psychologists, Scientists, Artists, and Meditation Teachers on the Power of Mindfulness in Daily Life*, Barry Boyce, ed. Boston: Shambhala, 2011: 57. This is the same sense that Kornfield means when he refers to the "universal teachings of Buddhist psychology" in the 2008 book title mentioned earlier in the chapter. Importantly, in these interpretations dharma as a universal law corresponds to not only the laws of nature but to the inner workings of the human mind as well.

31. Jon Kabat-Zinn. *Coming to Our Senses: Healing Ourselves and the World Through Mindfulness*. New York: Hyperion, 2005: 136.

32. Jon Kabat-Zinn. "Toward the Mainstreaming of American Dharma Practice." In *Buddhism in America: Proceedings of the First Buddhism in American Conference*, Al Rappaport and Brian Hotchkiss, eds. Boston: Charles E. Tuttle, 1998: 515.

33. Barbara Gates and Wes Nisker. "Bringing Mindfulness into Mainstream America: An Interview with Jon Kabat-Zinn." In *The Best of Inquiring Mind: 25 Years of Dharma, Drama, and Uncommon Insight*, Barbara Gates and Wes Nisker, eds. Boston: Wisdom Publications, 2008: 39.

34. Kabat-Zinn, *Contemporary Buddhism*, 2011: 288.

35. Gates and Nisker, 2008: 37.

36. Gates and Nisker, 2008: 39–40; Kabat-Zinn 2011: 57.

37. Kabat-Zinn, *The Mindfulness Revolution*, 2008: 523–524.

38. Kabat-Zinn, 2005: 136–137.

39. Kabat-Zinn, 1994: 220.

40. Kabat-Zinn's exact descriptions of key Buddhist terms sometimes change depending on the perceived audience for his work, as well as his career stage. For example, in the quote just offered, from 1994, he does not talk about morality. *Wherever You Go, There You Are* was marketed as "Health/Psychology," according to the book's back cover. In his 2005 *Coming to Our Senses*, marketed as "Self-Help/Spirituality," he does connect karma to ethics (though not with previous and future lives). With an audience more willing to discuss karma in the context of moral behavior, and with the increased confidence of a further decade of mainstream success, Kabat-Zinn seems willing to let certain traditional aspects of Buddhism more overtly back into the conversation.

41. Kabat-Zinn, 2005: 137.

42. Kabat-Zinn, *Contemporary Buddhism*, 2011: xxviii.

43. Jon Kabat-Zinn. "Foreword." In *Clinical Handbook of Mindfulness*, Fabrizio Didonna, ed. New York: Springer, 2008: xxviii–xxix.

44. Kabat-Zinn, *Contemporary Buddhism*, 2011: 281.

45. Jon Kabat-Zinn. "Dharma." in *In the Face of Fear: Buddhist Wisdom for Challenging Times*, ed. by Barry Boyce. Boston: Shambhala, 2009: 11.

46. The following is based on descriptions provided in the published literature by figures associated with the MBSR movement, especially extended explanations by Jon Kabat-Zinn at the Mind and Life III Conference and the First Buddhism in America Conference, and in *Full Catastrophe Living*.

47. Kabat-Zinn, 2000: 240.

48. Kabat-Zinn, 1990: 173.

49. Kabat-Zinn, 1990: 168.

50. Kabat-Zinn, *Contemporary Buddhism*, 2011: 289.

51. Kabat-Zinn, 1998: 487.

52. Kabat-Zinn, 2000: 228–229.

53. Kabat-Zinn, 2000: 238.

54. Saki Santorelli. *Heal Thy Self: Lessons on Mindfulness in Medicine*. New York: Bell Tower, 1999.

55. "Training Teachers to Deliver Mindfulness-Based Stress Reduction: Principles and Standards." Center for Mindfulness in Medicine, Health Care, and Society. Retrieved from http://www.umassmed.edu/cfm/trainingteachers/index.aspx (Accessed February 10, 2013).

56. David S. Ludwig and Jon Kabat-Zinn. "Mindfulness in Medicine." *Journal of the American Medical Association*, 300.11 (Sept 17, 2008): 1351.

57. Jon Kabat-Zinn. "An Outpatient Program in Behavioral Medicine for Chronic Pain Patients Based on the Practice of Mindfulness Meditation: Theoretical Considerations and Preliminary Results." *General Hospital Psychiatry*, 4.1 (1982): 33–47.

58. Kabat-Zinn, 1982: 33.

59. I will spare the reader from quoting the medical results of these articles in the main text. A typical selection, from page 39 of Kabat-Zinn's 1982 article: "In cycle II, the PRI decreased from a mean of 17.5 premeditation training to a mean of 7.9 postmeditation training for the 10 individuals for whom both pre and post questionnaires were obtained. This represents a 51% reduction and is highly significant in the matched (pre and post) t-test (P <.OOl, *Iff* = 9, two-tailed). In cycle II, the PRI decreased from a mean of 17.5 premeditation training to a mean of 7.9 postmeditation training for the 10 individuals for whom both pre and post questionnaires were obtained. This represents a 51% reduction and is highly significant in the matched (pre and post) t-test (P <.OOl, *Iff* = 9, two-tailed)."

60. Ludwig and Kabat-Zinn, 2008.

61. Ludwig and Kabat-Zinn, 2008: 1352.

62. Elana Rosenbaum. *Here for Now: Living Well with Cancer Through Mindfulness*. Hardwick, MA: Satya House Publications, 2005; Maggie Philips. *Reversing Chronic Pain: A 10-Point All-Natural Plan for Lasting Relief*. Berkeley, CA: North Atlantic Books, 2007; Vijay Vad. *Stop Pain: Inflammation Relief for an Active Life*. Carlsbad, CA: Hay House, 2010; Kate Loring, Halstead Holman, David Sobel, Diana Laurent, Virginia González, and Marian Minor. *Living a Healthy Life with Chronic Conditions: Self-Management of Heart Disease, Arthritis, Diabetes, Depression, Asthma, Bronchitis, Emphysema, and Other Physical and Mental Health Conditions* (4th ed.). Boulder, CO: Bull Publishing, 2012. These examples are a tiny portion of the books that draw on MBSR or MBSR research.

63. C. Alexander Simpkins and Annellen M. Simpkins. *Meditation for Therapists and Their Clients*. New York: W.W. Norton, 2009: 3.

64. Lorne Lader. "Mindfulness." In *Spiritually Oriented Interventions for Counseling and Psychotherapy*. Jamie D. Aten, Mark R. McMinn, and Everett L. Worthington, Jr., eds. Washington, DC: American Psychological Association, 2011: 229.

65. Lader, 2011: 238.

66. Lader, 2011: 234.

67. Shari M. Geller and Leslie S. Greenberg. *Therapeutic Presence: A Mindful Approach to Effective Treatment*. Washington, DC: American Psychological Association, 2012: 7.

68. Ruth A. Baer and Jennifer Krietemeyer. "Overview of Mindfulness- and Acceptance-Based Treatment Approaches." In *Mindfulness-Based Treatment Approaches: Clinician's Guide to Evidence Base and Applications*, Ruth A. Baer, ed. Burlington, MA: Academic Press, 2006: 23.

69. Shauna L. Shapiro and Linda E. Carlson. *The Art and Science of Mindfulness: Integrating Mindfulness into Psychology and the Helping Professions*. Washington, DC: American Psychological Association, 2009: 56.

70. Baer and Krietemeyer, 2006: 23–24.

71. Zindel V. Segal, J. Mark G. Williams, and John D. Teasdale. *Mindfulness-Based Cognitive Therapy for Depression: A New Approach to Preventing Relapse*. New York: Guilford Press, 2002.

72. Shapiro and Carlson, 2006: 51–52.

73. Jeffrey Brantley. *Calming Your Anxious Mind: How Mindfulness and Compassion Can Free You from Anxiety, Fear, and Panic*. Oakland, CA: New Harbinger, 2003; Susan M. Orsillo and Lizabeth Roemer. *The Mindful Way Through Anxiety: Break Free from Chronic Worry and Reclaim Your Life*. New York: Guilford Press, 2011; Ron Rubio. *Mind/Body Techniques for Asperger's Syndrome: The Way of the Pathfinder*. London: Jessica Kingsley Publishers, 2008; Nick Dubin. *Asperger Syndrome and Anxiety: A Guide to Successful Stress Management*. London: Jessica Kingsley, 2009; Jeff Strong and Michael O. Flanagan. *AD/HD for Dummies*. Hoboken, NJ: John Wiley & Sons, 2005; Charles H. Elliot and Laura L. Smith. *Anxiety and Depression Workbook for Dummies*. Hoboken, NJ: John Wiley & Sons, 2006; Charles Atkins. *The Bipolar Disorder Answer Book: Answers to More Than 275 of Your Most Pressing Questions*. Naperville, IL: Sourcebooks, 2007; Williams, Teasdale, Segal, and Kabat-Zinn, 2007; Barbara Miller Fishman. *Emotional Healing Through Mindfulness: Stories and Meditations for Women Seeking Wholeness*. Rochester, VT: Inner Traditions, 2002; Christopher K. Germer. *The Mindful Path to Self-Compassion: Freeing Yourself from Destructive Thoughts and Emotions*. New York: Guilford Press, 2009; Matthew McKay, Patrick Fanning, and Patricia Zurita Ona. *Mind and Emotions: A Universal Treatment for Emotional Disorders*. Oakland, CA: New Harbinger, 2011; Kumar, 2005; Pavel Somov. *Present Perfect: A Mindfulness Approach to Letting Go of Perfectionism and the Need for Control*. Oakland, CA: New Harbinger, 2010; Robyn D. Walser and Darrah Westrup. *Acceptance and Commitment Therapy for the Treatment of Post-Traumatic Stress Disorder and Trauma-Related Problems: A Practitioner's Guide to Using Mindfulness and Acceptance Strategies*. Oakland, CA: New Harbinger Press, 2007; Mark Goulston. *Post-Traumatic Stress Disorder for*

Dummies. Hoboken, NJ: John Wiley & Sons, 2008; Flowers, 2009; Jeffrey Brantley and Wendy Millstine. *True Belonging: Mindful Practices to Help You Overcome Loneliness, Connect With Others, and Cultivate Happiness.* Oakland, CA: New Harbinger, 2011; Bien and Bien, 2002; Eric Maisel and Susan Raeburn. *Creative Recovery: A Complete Addiction Treatment Program that Uses Your Natural Creativity.* Boston: Shambhala, 2008; Sameet M. Kumar. *The Mindful Path Through Worry and Rumination: Letting Go of Anxious and Depressive Thoughts.* Oakland, CA: New Harbinger, 2009; Donald Altman. *The Mindfulness Code: Keys to Overcoming Stress, Anxiety, Fear, and Unhappiness.* Novato, CA: New World Library, 2010.

74. Thich Nhat Hanh. *The Energy of Prayer: How to Deepen Your Spiritual Practice.* Berkeley, CA: Parallax Press, 2006; Kornfield, 2008; Lama Surya Das. *Awakening the Buddha Within: Eight Steps to Enlightenment, Tibetan Wisdom for the Western World.* New York: Broadway Books, 1997; Tara Brach. *Radical Acceptance: Embracing Your Life with the Heart of a Buddha.* New York: Bantam, 2003; Pema Chodron. *Start Where You Are: A Guide to Compassionate Living.* Boston: Shambhala, 1994.

75. Ilana Rabinowitz, ed. *Mountain Are Mountains and Rivers Are Rivers: Applying Eastern Teachings to Everyday Life.* New York: Hyperion, 1999.

76. James M. Rippe and William Southmayd, with Arthur Pappas, Nancy Clark, and Jon Kabat-Zinn. *The Sports Performance Factors.* New York: Perigee Books, 1986: 132.

CHAPTER 4

1. "Mainstream." Oxford Dictionaries. Retrieved from http://oxforddictionaries.com/definition/english/mainstream. (Accessed January 26, 2013).

2. Raskin, 2002: 9.

3. Raskin, 2002: 136.

4. Raskin, 2002: 136.

5. Raskin, 2002: 137.

6. Raskin, 2002: 136.

7. Kāyagatāsari Sutta. Nāṇamoli and Bodhi, 1995: 957.

8. Jack Kornfield. *Living Buddhist Masters.* Santa Cruz, CA: Unity Press, 1977: 25.

9. The *Mahasatipatthana Sutta* differs from the *Satipatthana Sutta* only in having a more extended subsection on the Four Noble Truths.

10. Nāṇamoli and Bodhi, 1995: 145. Identical language appears in the *Mahasatipatthana Sutta.* See Maurice Walsh, trans. *The Long Discourses of the Buddha: A Translation of the Dīgha Nikāya.* Boston: Wisdom Publications, 1995: 335.

11. I choose Janakābhivaṃsa's commentary because it is clearly expressed and representative of mainstream Asian monastic attitudes. A great many similar examples could have been chosen. For a more concise version, for example, see the discussion by a disciple of Sunlun Sayadaw in Kornfield 1977 (p. 115) that closely adheres to Janakābhivaṃsa's approach.

12. Sayādaw U Janakābhivaṃsa. *Vipassanā Meditation: Lectures on Insight Meditation.* Taiwan: Corporate Body of the Buddha Educational Foundation, 1997 [1985]: 52–54.

13. Janakābhivaṃsa, 1997: 54–56.

14. Janakābhivaṃsa, 1997: 60–61.

15. Kabat-Zinn, 2005: 128.

16. Hanh, 1976: 12.

17. Thich Nhat Hanh. *Present Moment, Wonderful Moment: Mindfulness Verses for Daily Living.* Berkeley, CA: Parallax Press, 1990; Thich Nhat Hanh. *Peace Is Every Step: The Path of Mindfulness in Everyday Life.* New York: Bantam, 1991; Thich Nhat Hanh. *You Are Here: Discovering the Magic of the Present Moment.* Boston: Shambhala Publications, 2009.

18. Catherine L. Albanese. *Nature Religion in America: From the Algonkian Indians to the New Age.* Chicago: University of Chicago Press, 1990; Bron Taylor. *Deep Green Religion: Nature Spirituality and the Planetary Future.* Berkeley: University of California Press, 2009.

19. Hanh, 1976: 4–5.

20. Hanh, 1976: 42.

21. Hanh, 1976: 61.

22. Albers, 2003; Jan Chozen Bays. *Mindful Eating: A Guide to Rediscovering a Healthy and Joyful Relationship with Food.* Boston: Shambhala, 2009.

23. Robert Wuthnow. *After Heaven: Spirituality in America Since the 1950s.* Berkeley: University of California Press, 1998: 152.

24. Hanh, 1976: 5–6.

25. Pavel G. Somov. *Eating the Moment: 141 Mindful Practices to Overcome Overeating One Meal at a Time.* Oakland, CA: New Harbinger, 2008: 124.

26. Albers, 2003: 68.

27. Charles S. Prebish. *Luminous Passage: The Practice and Study of Buddhism in America.* Berkeley: University of California Press, 1999: 75–79.

28. Reader and Tanabe 1998: 15.

29. Donald Altman. *Meal by Meal: 365 Daily Meditations for Finding Balance Through Mindful Eating.* Novato, CA: New World Library, 2004: (unpaginated: entry for March 11).

30. Albers, 2003: 1.

31. Bays, 2009: xviii.

32. Bays, 2009: xix.

33. Bays, 2009: 31.

34. Bays, 2009: 143.
35. Bays, 2009: 145.
36. Kabatznick, 1998: 32.
37. Kabatznick, 1998: 78.
38. Bays, 2009: 2.
39. Bays, 2009: 5.
40. Albers, 2003: 80–81.
41. Bays, 2009: xvii.
42. Kabatznick, 1998: 77.
43. Albers, 2006: 8.
44. Albers, 2008: 2.
45. Altman, 2004: (unpaginated: entry for November 24).
46. Nanamoli and Bodhi, 1995: 147.
47. Albers, 2003: 115.
48. Bays, 2009: 58 (italics in original).
49. Albers, 2003: 62.
50. Bays, 2009: 1.
51. Bays, 2009: 3.
52. Jeremy Adam Smith. "What's Sex Got to Do with It?" *Mindful*, 1.2 (June 2013): 56.
53. Raskin, 2002: 225.
54. Mahasi, 1976: 2.
55. Raskin, 2002: 144–145.
56. Raskin, 2002: 144–145.
57. Henepola Gunaratana. *Mindfulness in Plain English*. Boston: Wisdom Publications, 1991: 12.
58. OneTaste is also the title of the food department of *Mindful* magazine. The use of the term by *Mindful* came after the creation of the OneTaste mindful sex movement. They are not directly related in any way, and should not be confused with one another.
59. OneTaste. Retrieved from http://www.onetaste.us (Accessed March 18, 2009).
60. Patricia Leigh Brown and Carol Pogash. "The Pleasure Principle." *The New York Times*, March 15, 2009: ST8.
61. OneTaste. Retrieved from http://onetaste.us/ (Accessed October 17, 2013).
62. OneTaste. Retrieved from http://www.onetaste.us/welcome.php (Accessed February 21, 2013).
63. David Richo. *How to Be an Adult in Relationships: The Five Keys to Mindful Loving*. Boston: Shambhala, 2002; Henry Grayson. *Mindful Loving: 10 Practices for Creating Deeper Connections*. New York: Gotham Books, 2003; Peggy Rowe Ward and Larry Ward. *Love's Garden: A Guide to Mindful Relationships*. Berkeley, CA: Parallax Press, 2008; Jeffrey Brantley and Wendy Millstine. *Five Good Minutes with the One You Love: 100 Mindful Practices to Deepen and Renew Your Love Every Day*. Oakland, CA: New Harbinger, 2008; Marsha Lucas. *Rewire Your*

Brain for Love: Creating Vibrant Relationships Using the Science of Mindfulness. Carlsbad, CA: Hay House, 2012.

64. Robyn D. Walser and Darrah Westrup. *The Mindful Couple: How Acceptance and Mindfulness Can Lead You to the Love You Want.* Oakland, CA: New Harbinger: 2009: 1–2.

65. Sylvia Boorstein. "We Are All Wayfarers." *Shambhala Sun,* 17.2 (November 2008): 45.

66. Córdova, 2009: 84.

67. Jack Kerouac. *The Dharma Bums.* New York: Penguin Books, 1976 [1958]: 97–98.

68. Richard E. Boyatzis and Annie McKee. *Resonant Leadership: Renewing Yourself and Connecting with Others Through Mindfulness, Hope, and Compassion.* Boston: Harvard Business Review Press, 2005; Steven C. Hayes, Frank W. Bond, and Dermony Barnes-Holmes. *Acceptance and Mindfulness at Work: Applying Acceptance and Commitment Therapy and Relational Frame Theory to Organizational Behavior Management.* New York: Routledge, 2006; Michael Carroll. *The Mindful Leader: Awakening Your Natural Management Skills Through Mindfulness Meditation.* Boston: Trumpter, 2008; Edgar, 2009.

69. Google. Retrieved from http://www.google.com (Accessed February 21, 2012).

70. Roy, 2007; Karen Maezen Miller. *Momma Zen: Walking the Crooked Path of Motherhood.* Boston: Trumpeter, 2007; Cassandra Vieten. *Mindful Motherhood: Practical Tools for Staying Sane During Pregnancy and Your Child's First Year.* Oakland, CA: New Harbinger, 2009; Susan Piver. *The Mindful Way Through Pregnancy: Meditation, Yoga, and Journaling for Expectant Mothers.* Boston: Shambhala, 2012; Nancy Bardacke. *Mindful Birthing: Training the Mind, Body, and Heart for Childbirth and Beyond.* New York: HarperOne, 2012.

71. Zoe Kinias. "Meditate for More Profitable Decisions." *Forbes.* Retrieved from http://www.forbes.com/sites/insead/2013/09/25/meditate-for-m ore-profitable-decisions/ (Accessed September 25, 2013); Roger C. Parker "Mindfulness and Personal Branding Success." *Business2Community.* Retrieved from http://www.business2community.com/branding/ mindfulness-personal-branding-success-0635193 (Accessed October 3, 2013).

72. Scott L. Rogers. *The Six-Minute Solution: A Mindfulness Primer for Lawyers.* Mindful Living Press, 2009; Jeremy Spiegel. *The Mindful Medical Student: A Psychiatrist's Guide to Staying Where You Are While Becoming Who You Want to Be.* Hanover, NH: Dartmouth College Press, 2009; MacDonald and Shirley, 2009; Stephen F. Hick. *Mindfulness and Social Work.* Chicago: Lyceum, 2009.

73. Jeffrey Brantley and Wendy Millstine. *Five Good Minutes at Work: 100 Mindful Practices to Help You Relieve Stress and Bring Your Best to Work.* Oakland, CA: New Harbinger, 2007: 2–3.

74. Brantley and Millstine, 2007: 52–53.

75. Sandy Eastoak, ed. *Dharma Family Treasures: Sharing Buddhism with Children.* Berkeley, CA: North Atlantic Books, 1994: xiii.

76. Eastoak, 1994: xvi.

77. Myla and Jon Kabat-Zinn. *Everyday Blessings: The Inner Work of Mindful Parenting.* New York: Hyperion, 1997: 25.

78. Scott Rogers. *Mindful Parenting: Meditations, Verses, and Visualizations for a More Joyful Life.* Mindful Living Press, 2005; Paul J. Donahue. *Parenting Without Fear: Letting Go of Worry and Focusing on What Really Matters.* New York: St. Martin's Griffin, 2007; Susan Kaiser Greenland. *The Mindful Child: How to Help Your Kid Manage Stress and Become Happier, Kinder, and More Compassionate.* New York: Free Press, 2010.

79. Christopher McCurry. *Parenting Your Anxious Child with Mindfulness and Acceptance: A Powerful New Approach to Overcoming Fear, Panic, and Worry Using Acceptance and Commitment Therapy.* Oakland, CA: New Harbinger, 2009; Michelle L. Bailey. *Parenting Your Stressed Child: 10 Mindfulness-Based Stress Reduction Practices to Help Your Child Manage Stress and Build Essential Life Skills.* Oakland, CA: New Harbinger, 2011.

80. Matthew Bortolin. *The Dharma of Star Wars.* Boston: Wisdom Publications, 2005: 4.

81. Bortolin, 2005: 5.

82. George Lucas was of course drawing on Buddhism and other religions and cultures when he crafted his Star Wars universe. As an example, we may note that Dagoba is a Sri Lankan word for a stupa, the basic type of Buddhist reliquary monument.

83. Bortolin, 2005: 12.

84. Arnie Kozak. *Wild Chickens and Petty Tyrants: 108 Metaphors for Mindfulness.* Boston: Wisdom Publications, 2009: 7.

85. Kozak, 2009: 68–69.

86. Kozak, 2009: 101–103.

87. Kozak, 2009: 112.

88. Kozak, 2009: 120–121.

89. Kozak, 2009: 60–61.

CHAPTER 5

1. "Market." Oxford English Dictionary Online. Retrieved from http://www.oed.com (Accessed February 2, 2013).

2. Elias Amidon. "Mall Mindfulness." In *Dhama Rain: Sources of Buddhist Environmentalism*, Stephanie Kaza and Kenneth Kraft, eds. Boston: Shambhala, 2000: 332.

3. Amidon, 2000: 333.

4. Amidon, 2000: 334.

5. Amidon, 2000: 334.

6. Leigh Eric Schmidt. *Restless Souls: The Making of American Spirituality*. New York: HarperCollins, 2005: 20.

7. Center for Mindfulness in Medicine, Health Care, and Society. Retrieved from http://www.umassmed.edu/Content.aspx?id=41268 (Accessed May 17, 2013).

8. Mindful Clarity. Retrieved from http://www.mindfulclarity.com/About-Us.html (Accessed May 17, 2013).

9. Matt Tenney. *From the Brig to the Boardroom: Why Mindfulness Is the Ultimate Shortcut to Success*. Createspace, 2012.

10. Donald Altman. *One-Minute Mindfulness: 50 Simple Ways to Find Peace, Clarity, and New Possibilities in a Stressed-Out World*. Novato, CA: New World, 2011; Mark Williams, Danny Pennman, and Jon Kabat-Zinn. *Mindfulness: An Eight-Week Plan for Finding Peace in a Frantic World*. Emmaus, PA: Rodale, 2011.

11. Lori Stephens. *The Mindful Dog Owner: What Your Dog Is Teaching You About Living Enlightenment*. Verbatim, 2012; Charles T. Tart. *Living the Mindful Life*. Boston: Shambhala, 1994.

12. Nyanaponika, 1953; Daniel J. Siegel. *The Mindful Brain: Reflection and Attunement in the Cultivation of Well-Being*. New York: W.W. Norton, 2007; Thomas Bien. *Mindful Therapy: A Guide for Therapists and Helping Professionals*. Boston: Wisdom, 2006; Manning, 2004; Suzanna McGee. *Tennis Fitness for the Love of It: A Mindful Approach to Fitness for Injury-free Tennis*. Zuzi Publishing, 2010.

13. Cheryl Kimball. *Mindful Horsemanship: Daily Inspirations for Better Communications with Your Horse*. Middleton, NH: Carriage House, 2002.

14. Mindfulness Bell. Retrieved from https://itunes.apple.com/us/app/mindfulness-bell/id380816407?mt=8 (Accessed February 22, 2013).

15. DharmaCrafts Bestsellers 2013. Laurence, MA: DharmaCrafts, 10–11.

16. DharmaCrafts, 2013: 56.

17. The Monastery Store Fall 2012–Winter 2013. Mt. Tremper, NY: Dharma Communications, 2012.

18. DharmaCrafts, 2013: 20.

19. DharmaCrafts, 2013: 20.

20. DharmaCrafts, 2013: 18–21.

21. DharmaCrafts, 2013: 18–21.

22. DharmaCrafts, 2013: 21.

23. DharmaCrafts, 2013: 16–17.

24. DharmaCrafts, 2013: 5, 22–23, 48.

25. DharmaCrafts, 2013: 4, 15.

26. DharmaCrafts, 2013: 11, 38–41.

27. DharmaCrafts, 2013: 52.

28. OneTaste. Retrieved from http://www.onetaste.us/supplies.php (Accessed May 18, 2013).

29. Kornfield, 2008.

30. Santorelli, 2000.

31. Moore, 2012.

32. Frank Jude Boccio. *Mindfulness Yoga: The Awakened Union of Breath, Body, and Mind.* Boston: Wisdom, 2004.

33. Jonathan P. Slater. *Mindful Jewish Living: Compassionate Practice.* New York: Aviv Press, 2004; Brenda Shoshanna. *Jewish Dharma: A Guide to the Practice of Judaism and Zen.* New York: Da Capo Press, 2008; Mary Jo Meadow, Kevin Culligan, and Daniel Chowing. *Christian Insight Meditation: Following in the Footsteps of John of the Cross.* Boston: Wisdom, 2007.

34. Chade-Meng Tan. *Search Inside Yourself: The Unexpected Path to Achieving Success, Happiness (and World Peace).* New York: HarperOne, 2012.

35. The reproduced flap quote is taken from page 233 of the book.

36. Philip B. Yampolsky. *The Platform Sutra of the Sixth Patriarch.* New York: Columbia University Press, 1967.

37. Duncan Ryūken Williams. *The Other Side of Zen: A Social History of Sōtō Zen Buddhism in Tokugawa Japan.* Princeton, NJ: Princeton University Press, 2005.

38. Kimberly Wilson. *Tranquilista: Mastering the Art of Enlightened Work and Mindful Play.* Novato, CA: New World Library, 2010: xi.

39. Wilson, 2010: xi.

40. Wilson, 2010: xi–xii.

41. Iwamura, 2011: 93.

42. *Mindful*, 1.1 (April 2013): 17.

43. *Mindful*, 1.1 (April 2013): 17.

44. *Mindful*, 1.1 (April 2013): 17.

45. Roy, 2007.

46. Roy, 2007: x.

47. Roy, 2007: x.

48. Roy, 2007: 118.

49. Sue Patton Thoelle. *The Mindful Woman: Gentle Practices for Restoring Calm, Finding Balance, and Opening Your Heart.* Oakland, CA: New Harbinger, 2008: 21.

50. Thoelle, 2008: 23.

51. Thoelle, 2008: 24–25.

52. Thoelle, 2008: 145–146.

53. C. Peter Bankart and David B. Wexler. *Freeing the Angry Mind: How Men Can Use Mindfulness and Reason to Save Their Lives and Relationships.* Oakland, CA: New Harbinger Publications, 2006.

54. Kozo Hattori. "Five Ways to Make Mindfulness More Manly." *Mindful.* Retrieved from http://www.mindful.org/the-mindful-society/five-ways-to-make-mindfulness-more-manly (Accessed July 3, 2013).

55. Albers, 2006.

56. Real-World Mindfulness Training. Retrieved from http://www. real-worldmindfulness.com/index.htm (Accessed February 23, 2013).

57. About Real-World Mindfulness Training. Retrieved from http://www. real-worldmindfulness.com/aboutRWM.htm (Accessed February 23, 2013).

58. Maya Frost. *Real-World Mindfulness™: 101 Eyes-Wide-Open Ways to Boost Awareness and Creativity*. Maya Talisman Frost, 2008: 78.

59. Rogers, 2009.

60. Rogers, 2009: 1.

61. Rogers, 2009: 113.

62. As of February 2013, these included www.mindfulliving.net, www.themindfullawyer.com, www.themindfulparent.org, www. themindfullawstudent.com, www.themindfuldetox.com, www. themindfuldoctor.com, www.themindfulphysician.com, www.themindfuljudge. com, www.themindfullawprofessor.com, www.themindfullawschool.com, www. sobemindful.com, www.themindfultherapist.com, and www.themindfulmuscle. com.

63. Rogers and Maytan, 2012.

64. Rogers and Maytan, 2012: xv.

65. Rogers and Maytan, 2012: xv.

66. Rogers and Maytan, 2012: 8.

67. Where's My Zen. Retrieved from http://wheresmyzen.com/program (Accessed February 23, 2013).

68. Stanley and Schaldach, 2011: 2.

69. Ed Pilkington. "US Military Struggling to Stop Suicide Epidemic Among War Veterans." *The Guardian*, February 1, 2013. Retrieved from http://www.guardian. co.uk/world/2013/feb/01/us-military-suicide-epidemic-veteran (Accessed February 23, 2013).

70. Elizabeth A. Stanley and Amishi P. Jha. "Mind Fitness: Improving Operational Effectiveness and Building Warrior Resilience." *Joint Forces Quarterly*, issue 55 (2009): 147.

71. Elizabeth A. Stanley, John M. Schadach, Anastasia Kiyonaga, and Amishi P. Jha. "Mindfulness-based Mind Fitness Training: A Case Study of a High-Stress Predeployment Military Cohort." *Cognitive and Behavioral Practice*, 18.4 (2011): 571.

72. Ryan Carpenter. "Researchers Study Marines' Mind Fitness." 11th Marine Expeditionary Unit, July 18, 2011. Retrieved from http://www.11thmeu. marines.mil/News/NewsArticleDisplay/tabid/2683/Article/22079/ researchers-study-marines-mind-fitness.aspx (Accessed February 23, 2013); Julie Watson. "Marines Studying Mindfulness-Based Training." Associated Press, January 19, 2013. Retrieved from http://bigstory.ap.org/article/ marines-studying-mindfulness-based-training (Accessed February 23, 2013).

73. Watson, 2013; U.S. Marine Corps. Retrieved from http://www.marines.com/history-heritage/timeline (Accessed February 23, 2013).

74. Brian Victoria. *Zen at War*. New York: Weatherhill, 1998.

75. Cat Yampbell. "Judging a Book by Its Cover: Publishing Trends in Young Adult Literature." *The Lion and the Unicorn*, 29.3 (September 2005): 348–349.

76. Quoted in Yampbell, 2005: 349.

77. Yampbell, 2005: 349.

78. Albers, 2003, 2006, 2008; Laura Aldafer. *Mindful Monkey, Happy Panda*. Boston: Wisdom, 2011; Altman, 2004, 2010; Ruth A. Baer, ed. *Mindfulness-Based Treatment Approaches: Clinician's Guide to Evidence Base and Applications*. Burlington, MA: Elsevier, 2006; Bailey, 2011; Bardacke, 2012; Bays, 2009; Jan Chozen Bays. *How to Train a Wild Elephant: Simple Daily Mindfulness Practice for Living Life More Fully and Joyfully*. Boston: Shambhala, 2011; Gina M. Biegel. *The Stress Reduction Workbook for Teens: Mindfulness Skills to Help You Deal with Stress*. Oakland, CA: New Harbinger, 2009; Bien, 2006; Boccio, 2004; C.A. Bowers. *Mindful Conservatism: Rethinking the Ideological and Educational Basis of an Ecologically Sustainable Future*. Lanham, MD: Rowman and Littlefield, 2003; Barry Boyce and the editors of *Shambhala Sun*. *The Mindfulness Revolution: Leading Psychologists, Scientists, Artists, and Meditation Teachers on the Power of Mindfulness in Daily Life*. Boston: Shambhala, 2011; Brantley, 2003; Brantley and Millstine, 2007, 2008; Jeffrey Brantley and Wendy Millstine. *Five Good Minutes in Your Body: 100 Mindful Practices to Help You Accept Yourself and Feel at Home in Your Body*. Oakland, CA: New Harbinger, 2009; Brantley and Millstine, 2011; Angela Buttimer and Dennis Buttimer. *Calm: Choosing to Live Mindfully*. Self, 2011; Carroll, 2008; Tom Catton. *The Mindful Addict: A Memoir of the Awakening of a Spirit*. Las Vegas: Central Recovery Press, 2010; Tovar Ceruli. *The Mindful Carnivore: A Vegetarian's Hunt for Sustenance*. New York: Pegasus Books, 2012; Dillard-Wright, Spear, and Munier, 2012; Donahue, 2007; Edgar, 2009; Richard Fields. *Awakening to Mindfulness: 10 Steps for Positive Change*. Deerfield Beach, FL: Health Communications, 2008; Richard Fields. *A Year of Living Mindfully: 52 Quotes and Weekly Mindfulness Practices*. Tucson, AZ: FACES Conferences, 2012; Barbara Fine. *Just Being with the Mindful Breath: The Workbook*. Barbara Fine, 2011; Flowers, 2009; Steve Flowers and Bob Stahl. *Living with Your Heart Wide Open: How Mindfulness and Compassion Can Free You From Unworthiness, Inadequacy, and Shame*. Oakland, CA: New Harbinger, 2011; Terry Fralich. *Cultivating Lasting Happiness: A 7-Step Guide to Mindfulness (2nd ed.)*. Eau Claire, WI: PESI, 2007; Jackie Gardner-Nix. *The Mindfulness Solution to Pain: Step-by-Step Techniques for Chronic Pain Management*. Oakland, CA: New Harbinger, 2009; Diane R. Gehart. *Mindfulness and Acceptance in Couple and Family Therapy*. New York, Springer: 2012; Germer, 2009; Elisha Goldstein. *Mindfulness Meditations for the Anxious Traveler: Quick Exercises to Calm Your Mind*. New York: Atria Books, 2012; Grayson, 2003;

Greenland, 2010; David Gordon. *Mindful Dreaming: A Practical Guide for Emotional Healing Through Transformative Mythic Journeys*. Franklin Lakes, NJ: New Page Books: 2007; Gunaratana, 2003; Thich Nhat Hanh and Lilian Cheung. *Savor: Mindful Eating, Mindful Life*. New York: HarperCollins, 2010; Harp, 2011; Hawn, 2011; Hayes, Boyd, Barnes-Holmes, and Austin, 2006; James D. Herbert and Evan M. Forman. *Acceptance and Mindfulness in Cognitive Behavior Therapy: Understanding and Applying the New Therapies*. New York: John Wiley & Sons, 2011; Steven F. Hick and Thomas Bien. *Mindfulness and the Therapeutic Relationship*. New York: Guilford Press, 2008; Anna Hill. *The Mindful Heart*. Bloomington, IN: Balboa Press, 2012; Ihnen and Flynn, 2008; Kabat-Zinn, 2005; Jon Kabat-Zinn. *Letting Everything Become Your Teacher: 100 Lessons in Mindfulness*. New York: Delta, 2009; Jon Kabat-Zinn. *Mindfulness for Beginners: Reclaiming the Present Moment—And Your Life*. Boulder, CO: Sounds True, 2012; Jonathan S. Kaplan. *Urban Mindfulness: Cultivating Peace, Presence, and Purpose in the Midst of It All*. Oakland, CA: New Harbinger, 2010; Stephanie Kaza. *Mindfully Green: A Personal and Spiritual Guide to Whole Earth Thinking*. Boston: Shambhala, 2008; Kozak, 2009; Kumar, 2005; Kumar, 2009; Sasha T. Loring. *Eating with Fierce Kindness: A Mindful and Compassionate Guide to Losing Weight*. Oakland, CA: New Harbinger, 2010; Lucas, 2012; Macdonald and Shirley, 2009; Mark Magill. *Why Is the Buddha Smiling? Mindfulness as a Means of Bringing Calm and Insight to Your Life*. Gloucester, MA: Fair Winds Press, 2003; Manning, 2004; Lucia McBee. *Mindfulness-Based Elder Care: A CAM Model for Frail Elders and Their Caregivers*. New York: Springer, 2008; McCown and Micozzi, 2012; McCurry, 2009; Andrea Miller and the Editors of the *Shambhala Sun*. *Right Here with You: Bringing Mindful Awareness into Our Relationships*. Boston: Shambhala, 2011; Moore, 2012; Rogers and Maytan, 2012; Rachel Neumann. *Not Quite Nirvana: A Skeptic's Journey to Mindfulness*. Berkeley: Parallax Press, 2012; Orsillo and Roemer, 2011; Rogers, 2005, 2009a, 2009b; Elena Rosenbaum. *Being Well (Even When You're Sick): Mindfulness Practice for People with Cancer and Other Serious Illnesses*. Boston: Shambhala, 2012; Rosenbaum, 2005; Roy, 2007; Tim Ryan. *A Mindful Nation: How a Simple Practice Can Help Us Reduce Stress, Improve Performance, and Recapture the American Spirit*. Carlsbad, CA: Hay House, 2012; Deborah Schoeberlein. *Mindful Teaching and Teaching Mindfulness: A Guide for Anyone Who Teaches Anything*. Boston: Wisdom, 2009; Shapiro and Carlson, 2009; Siegel, 2010; Siegel, 2010; Douglas K. Silsbee. *The Mindful Coach: Seven Roles for Helping People Grow*. Marshall, NC: Ivy River Press, 2004; C. Alexander Simpkins and Annellen M. Simpkins. *Meditation for Therapists and Their Clients*. New York: W.W. Norton, 2009; Slater, 2004; Susan L. Smalley and Diana Winston. *Fully Present: The Science, Art, and Practice of Mindfulness*. Philadelphia: Da Capo, 2010; Jonathan C. Smith. *Relaxation, Meditation, and Mindfulness: Personal-Training Manual*. Jonathan C. Smith, 2005; Somov, 2008, 2010; Spiegel, 2009; Tan,

2012; Tenney, 2012; Thoelle, 2008; Vieten, 2009; Walser and Westrup, 2007, 2009; Ward and Ward, 2008; Karen Kissel Wegela. *What Really Helps: Using Mindfulness and Compassionate Presence to Help, Support, and Encourage Others.* Boston: Shambhala, 2011; Williams, Teasdale, Segal, and Kabat-Zinn, 2007; Wilson, 2010.

79. Twenty-five books carry cover images with people or parts of people, but some covers have more than one person, thus the numbers listed in this sentence do not add to twenty-five.

80. *Mindful* launched MindfulTV in late 2013, unfortunately too late for analysis in this volume.

81. Earth Balance Natural. Retrieved from http://www.earthbalancenatural.com/about-us/history (Accessed February 25, 2013).

82. Earth Balance Natural. Retrieved from http://www.earthbalancenatural.com/wellness/ (Accessed February 25, 2013).

83. Mindful Mints. Retrieved from http://www.mindfulmints.com/home.html (Accessed February 25, 2013).

84. Mindful Mints. Retrieved from http://www.mindfulmints.com/aboutUs.html (Accessed February 25, 2013).

CHAPTER 6

1. "Moralize." Oxford English Dictionary Online. Retrieved from http://www.oed. com (Accessed February 2, 2013).

2. Tan, 2012: 229.

3. Tan, 2012: 230–231.

4. Tan, 2012: 235.

5. Tan, 2012: 230.

6. Tan, 2012: 241.

7. I draw especially on the work of David Chidester in this approach. See David Chidester. *Authentic Fakes: Religion and American Popular Culture.* Berkeley: University of California Press, 2005.

8. For a cogent recent summation of the discussion, see the introduction to Arthur Remillard. *Southern Civil Religions: Imaging the Good Society in the Post-Reconstruction Era.* Athens, GA: University of Georgia Press, 2011.

9. Ryan, 2012: xi.

10. I do not suggest here that the problems imagined by religions really exist (or, for that matter, that they don't really exist), nor do I suggest that the solutions religions offer actually solve such problems. And the reader should not infer that I consider religions to be benevolent or nurturing owing to their offering of solutions. Religious solutions include loving thy neighbor, exterminating the Jews, burning witches, and many others. I am merely noting a common pattern of religious problem solving. This idea is hardly original to me; it has had a long

life in the discipline of religious studies. For one recent example of approaching religions as solutions to imagined problems, see Stephen Prothero. *God Is Not One: The Eight Rival Religions that Run the World—and Why Their Differences Matter*. New York: HarperOne, 2010.

11. Schmidt, 2005: 58.

12. Jan Chozen Bays. "What Is Mindfulness?" in *The Mindfulness Revolution: Leading Psychologists, Scientists, Artists, and Meditation Teachers on the Power of Mindfulness in Daily Life*, edited by Barry Boyce and the editors of *Shambhala Sun*. Boston: Shambhala, 2011: 4.

13. Kabat-Zinn, 2005: 118.

14. Kabat-Zinn, 2005: 144.

15. Seigel, 2010: 11–12.

16. Smalley and Winston, 2010: 138.

17. Bruce Lincoln. *Holy Terrors: Thinking About Religion After September 11*. Chicago: University of Chicago Press, 2003: 104.

18. Ryan, 2012: xviii–xix.

19. Ryan, 2012: xix.

20. Ryan, 2012: 160–161.

21. David Rome and Hope Martin. "Are You Listening?" in *The Mindfulness Revolution: Leading Psychologists, Scientists, Artists, and Meditation Teachers on the Power of Mindfulness in Daily Life*, edited by Barry Boyce and the editors of *Shambhala Sun*. Boston: Shambhala, 2011: 211.

22. Jan Chozen Bays. "Krispy Kreme Mind." *Shambhala Sun*, 9.3 (Spring 2011): 33–34.

23. Susan Smalley and Diana Winston. "Is Mindfulness for You?" in *The Mindfulness Revolution: Leading Psychologists, Scientists, Artists, and Meditation Teachers on the Power of Mindfulness in Daily Life*, edited by Barry Boyce and the editors of *Shambhala Sun*. Boston: Shambhala, 2011: 17.

24. Kabat-Zinn, 2005: 143.

25. Kabat-Zinn, 2005: 146–147.

26. Kabat-Zinn, 2005: 530.

27. Kaza, 2008: 15–16.

28. Thich Nhat Hanh. *The World We Have: A Buddhist Approach to Peace and Ecology*. Berkeley, CA: Parallax Press, 2008: 1–2.

29. Melvin McLeod. "For 30 Years the Best of Buddhism in America," *Shambhala Sun*, 17.3: (January 2009): 9.

30. Kabat-Zinn, 2005: 8–11.

31. Joseph Naft. "Mindfulness." Inner Horizons. Retrieved from http://www.innerfrontier.org/Practices/Mindfulness.htm (Accessed May 6, 2013).

32. Kabat-Zinn, 2012: 14.

33. Tan, 2012: 32.

34. Ryan, 2012: 14.

35. Ryan, 2012: xviii.
36. Ryan, 2012: 172.
37. Smalley and Winston, 2010: 140.
38. Jeff Brantley. "Mindfulness FAQ." in *The Mindfulness Revolution: Leading Psychologists, Scientists, Artists, and Meditation Teachers on the Power of Mindfulness in Daily Life*, edited by Barry Boyce and the editors of *Shambhala Sun*. Boston: Shambhala, 2011: 41.
39. Smalley and Winston, 2010: 138.
40. Smalley and Winston, 2010: 146–147.
41. Kabat-Zinn, 2012: 102.
42. Hanh, 1987: 7.
43. Albers, 2003: 3, 16, 45.
44. Bays, 2009: 126–127.
45. Kabat-Zinn, 2005: 605.
46. Hanh, 2009: 35.
47. Albers, 2003: 18; Bays 2009: 24.
48. Ronald D. Siegel. "From Me to Us." in *The Mindfulness Revolution: Leading Psychologists, Scientists, Artists, and Meditation Teachers on the Power of Mindfulness in Daily Life*, edited by Barry Boyce and the editors of *Shambhala Sun*. Boston: Shambhala, 2011: 207.
49. Hawn, 2011: xx–xxi.
50. Ryan, 2012: 25–26.
51. Ryan, 2012: 30, 33.
52. Ryan, 2012: 33–35.
53. Ryan, 2012: xvii.
54. Ryan, 2012: xvii.
55. Ryan, 2012: xviii.
56. Ryan, 2012: 31.
57. Ryan, 2012: xxi.
58. Kabat-Zinn, 2012: 553.
59. Ryan, 2012: 20–21.
60. Smalley and Winston, 2010: 222.
61. Ryan, 2012: 166–167.
62. Elizabeth Thoman. "Re-imagining the American Dream." In *Mindfulness in the Marketplace: Compassionate Responses to Consumerism*. Allan Hunt Badiner, ed. Berkeley: Parallax Press, 2002: 119.
63. Thoman, 2002: 123.
64. Thoman, 2002: 124.
65. Jen Evans. "A Conservative View." [Letter to the editor]. *Shambhala Sun*, 20.5 (May 2012): 15.
66. Melvin McLeod, ed. *Mindful Politics: A Buddhist Guide to Making the World a Better Place*. Boston: Wisdom, 2006; Boyce, 2011.

67. Thich Nhat Hanh. *Creating True Peace: Ending Violence in Yourself, Your Family, Your Community, and the World*. New York: Simon and Schuster, 2003; Thich Nhat Hanh. *Keeping the Peace: Mindfulness and Public Service*. Berkeley, CA: Parallax Press, 2005; Thich Nhat Hanh. *One Buddha Is Not Enough: A Story of Collective Awakening*. Berkeley, CA: Parallax Press, 2010; Thich Nhat Hanh. *Good Citizens: Creating Enlightened Society*. Berkeley, CA: Parallax Press, 2012.

68. Malcolm Clark. "Diverse Diversities" [Letter to the editor]. *Shambhala Sun*, 21.1 (September 2012): 13.

69. Charles R. Johnson. "The Meaning of Barack Obama." *Shambhala Sun*, 17.2: 19–22; Charles R. Johnson. "The Meaning of Barack Obama." *Shambhala Sun*, 17.6 (July 2009): 67–68.

70. Charles Johnson. "Dharma for a Dangerous Time." *Shambhala Sun*, 15.1: 44 (September 2006): 40–47.

71. Clark, 2013: 14.

72. Kabat-Zinn, 2005: 511–512.

73. Daniel Goleman. "A Mindful Consumer Can Help Change the World." In *The Mindfulness Revolution: Leading Psychologists, Scientists, Artists, and Meditation Teachers on the Power of Mindfulness in Daily Life*, edited by Barry Boyce and the editors of *Shambhala Sun*. Boston: Shambhala, 2011: 242.

74. Goleman, 2011: 246–247.

POSTSCRIPT

1. Joseph Goldstein. *One Dharma: The Emerging Western Buddhism*. San Francisco: HarperSanFrancisco, 2002: 5.

2. Gunaratana, 1991; Bhante Henepola Gunaratana. *The Four Foundations of Mindfulness in Plain English*. Boston: Wisdom, 2012; Bhante Henepola Gunaratana. *Beyond Mindfulness in Plain English*. Boston: Wisdom, 2009; Gunaratana, 2003; Bhante Henepola Gunaratana. *Eight Mindful Steps to Happiness: Walking the Buddha's Path*. Boston: Wisdom, 2001.

3. Thich Nhat Hanh. *For a Future to Be Possible: Commentaries on the Five Wonderful Precepts*. Berkeley, CA: Parallax Press, 1993; Plum Village. Retrieved from http://www.plumvillage.org/mindfulness-trainings/3-the-five-mindfulness-trainings.html (Accessed May 17, 2013); Olive Branch Sangha. Retrieved from http://here-and-now.org/wwwArticles/14precepts.html (Accessed May 17, 2013).

4. Andrea Miller. "Be Beautiful, Be Yourself: Andrea Miller's Exclusive Interview with Thich Nhat Hanh." *Shambhala Sun*, 20.3 (January 2012): 50.

5. Catherine Albanese. *A Republic of Mind and Spirit: A Cultural History of American Metaphysical Religion*. New Haven, CT: Yale University Press, 2007: 4.

6. John S. Haller, Jr. *The History of New Thought: From Mind Cure to Positive Thinking and the Prosperity Gospel*. West Chester, PA: Swedenborg Foundation Press, 2012: 4.

7. Hickey, 2008: 165–168.
8. Kabat-Zinn, 2005: 6.
9. Hanh, 2009: 42.
10. Thomas A. Tweed. *Crossing and Dwelling: A Theory of Religion*. Cambridge, MA: Harvard University Press, 2006: 54.
11. Matthew S. Hedstrom. *The Rise of Liberal Religion: Book Culture and American Spirituality in the Twentieth Century*. New York: Oxford University Press, 2013.

REFERENCES

Robert Aitken. *Taking the Path of Zen*. San Francisco: North Point Press, 1982.

Henry Alabaster. *The Wheel of the Law. Buddhism, Illustrated from Siamese Sources*. London: Trübner and Company, 1871.

Catherine L. Albanese. *Nature Religion in America: From the Algonkian Indians to the New Age*. Chicago: University of Chicago Press, 1990.

Catherine Albanese. *A Republic of Mind and Spirit: A Cultural History of American Metaphysical Religion*. New Haven, CT: Yale University Press, 2007.

Susan Albers. *Eat, Drink, and Be Merry: How to End Your Struggle with Mindless Eating and Start Savoring Food with Intention and Joy*. Oakland, CA: New Harbinger, 2008.

Susan Albers. *Eating Mindfully: How to End Mindless Eating and Enjoy a Balanced Relationship with Food*. Oakland: New Harbinger Publications, 2003.

Susan Albers. *Mindful Eating 101: A Guide to Healthy Eating in College and Beyond*. New York: Routledge, 2006.

Laura Aldafer. *Mindful Monkey, Happy Panda*. Boston: Wisdom, 2011.

William Alexander. *Cool Water: Alcoholism, Mindfulness, and Ordinary Recovery*. Boston: Shambhala, 1997.

Sean Alfano. "Getting Into Our Minds." CBS Sunday Morning, April 9, 2006. Retrieved from http://www.cbsnews.com/8301-3445_162-1483025/getting-into-our-minds/ (Accessed May 18, 2013).

John Allan. *TM: A Cosmic Confidence Trick*. Leicester, England: Inter-Varsity Press, 1980.

Gloria Taraniya Ambrosia and Andrew Olendzki. "The Fourth Foundation of Mindfulness." *Insight Journal* (Fall 2002): 13–17.

Tana Amen. *The Omni Diet: The Revolutionary 70% PLANT + 30% PROTEIN Program to Lose Weight, Reverse Disease, Fight Inflammation, and Change Your Life Forever*. New York: St. Martin's Press, 2013.

Elias Amidon. "Mall Mindfulness." In *Dhama Rain: Sources of Buddhist Environmentalism*, Stephanie Kaza and Kenneth Kraft, eds. Boston: Shambhala, 2000: 332–334.

Jamie D. Aten, Mark R. McMinn, and Everett L. Worthington, Jr., eds. *Spiritually Oriented Interventions for Counseling and Psychotherapy*. Washington, DC: American Psychological Association, 2011.

Charles Atkins. *The Bipolar Disorder Answer Book: Answers to More Than 275 of Your Most Pressing Questions*. Naperville, IL: Sourcebooks, 2007.

James Atlas. "Buddhists' Delight." *New York Times*, June 17, 2012: SR4.

Donald Altman. *Art of the Inner Meal: The Power of Mindful Practices to Heal Our Food Cravings*. Moon Lake Media, 2002.

Donald Altman. *Meal by Meal: 365 Daily Meditations for Finding Balance Through Mindful Eating*. Novato, CA: New World Library, 2004.

Donald Altman. *The Mindfulness Code: Keys to Overcoming Stress, Anxiety, Fear, and Unhappiness*. Novato, CA: New World Library, 2010.

Donald Altman. *One-Minute Mindfulness: 50 Simple Ways to Find Peace, Clarity, and New Possibilities in a Stressed-Out World*. Novato, CA: New World, 2011.

Jack Austin. *Zen-Brain Reflections: Reviewing Recent Developments in Meditation and States of Consciousness*. Cambridge, MA: MIT Press, 2006.

Leo Babauta. "10 Steps to Mindfulness." *Readers Digest*. Retrieved from http://www.rd.com/slideshows/10-steps-to-mindfulness (Accessed May 19, 2013).

Allan Hunt Badiner. *Mindfulness in the Marketplace: Compassionate Responses to Consumerism*. Berkeley, CA: Parallax Press, 2002.

Ruth A. Baer, ed. *Assessing Mindfulness and Acceptance Processes in Clients: Illuminating the Theory and Practice of Change*. Oakland, CA: New Harbinger, 2010.

Ruth A. Baer, ed. *Mindfulness-Based Treatment Approaches: Clinician's Guide to Evidence Base and Applications*. Burlington, MA: Elsevier, 2006.

Ruth A. Baer and Jennifer Krietemeyer. "Overview of Mindfulness- and Acceptance-Based Treatment Approaches." In *Mindfulness-Based Treatment Approaches: Clinician's Guide to Evidence Base and Applications*, Ruth A. Baer, ed. Burlington, MA: Academic Press, 2006: 3–27.

Michelle L. Bailey. *Parenting Your Stressed Child: 10 Mindfulness-Based Stress Reduction Practices to Help Your Child Manage Stress and Build Essential Life Skills*. Oakland, CA: New Harbinger, 2011.

Michael Baime. "This is Your Brain on Mindfulness." *Shambhala Sun*, 19.6 (July 2011): 44–48, 84–85.

Hilda Gutiérrez Baldoquín. "Introduction." In *Dharma, Color, and Culture: New Voices in Western Buddhism*. Hilda Gutiérrez Baldoquín, ed. Berkeley, CA: Parallax Press, 2004: 15–22.

C. Peter Bankart and David B. Wexler. *Freeing the Angry Mind: How Men Can Use Mindfulness and Reason to Save Their Lives and Relationships*. Novato, CA: New Harbinger Publications, 2006.

Cary Barbor. "The Science of Meditation." *Psychology Today*, May 1, 2001. Retrieved from http://www.psychologytoday.com/articles/200105/the-science-meditation (Accessed May 19, 2013).

Nancy Bardacke. *Mindful Birthing: Training the Mind, Body, and Heart for Childbirth and Beyond*. New York: HarperOne, 2012.

Susan Bauer-Wu. *Leaves Falling Gently: Living Fully With Serious and Life-Limiting Illness Through Mindfulness, Compassion, and Connectedness*. Oakland, CA: New Harbinger, 2011.

Jan Chozen Bays. *How to Train a Wild Elephant: Simple Daily Mindfulness Practice for Living Life More Fully and Joyfully*. Boston: Shambhala, 2011.

Jan Chozen Bays. "Krispy Kreme Mind." *Shambhala Sun*, 9.3 (Spring 2011).

Jan Chozen Bays. *Mindful Eating: A Guide to Rediscovering a Healthy and Joyful Relationship with Food*. Boston: Shambhala, 2009.

Jan Chozen Bays. "What Is Mindfulness?" In *The Mindfulness Revolution: Leading Psychologists, Scientists, Artists, and Meditation Teachers on the Power of Mindfulness in Daily Life*, edited by Barry Boyce and the editors of *Shambhala Sun*. Boston: Shambhala, 2011: 3–6.

Bev Bennett. "How to Lose a Pound a Week Without Feeling Like You're on a Diet." *Spirit of Women* (Spring 2013): 26–27.

Leslie Bennetts. "Can You Think Yourself Thin?" *Marie Claire*, July 20, 2011. Retrieved from http://www.marieclaire.com/health-fitness/news/meditation-diet (Accessed October 1, 2012).

Herbert Benson, with Miriam Z. Kipper. *The Relaxation Response*. New York: Avon Books, 1975.

Gina Biegel. "Sea Change." *Shambhala Sun*, 19.6 (July 2011): 50–53.

Gina M. Biegel. *The Stress Reduction Workbook for Teens: Mindfulness Skills to Help You Deal with Stress*. Oakland, CA: New Harbinger, 2009.

Thomas Bien. *Mindful Therapy: A Guide for Therapists and Helping Professionals*. Boston: Wisdom, 2006.

Thomas Bien and Beverly Bien. *Mindful Recovery: A Spiritual Path to Healing from Addiction*. New York: John Wiley & Sons, 2002.

Frank Jude Boccio. *Mindfulness Yoga: The Awakened Union of Breath, Body, and Mind*. Boston: Wisdom, 2004.

Sylvia Boorstein. "Body as Body." *Tricycle: The Buddhist Review*, 1.2 (Winter 1991): 28–29.

Sylvia Boorstein. *It's Easier Than You Think: The Buddhist Way to Happiness*. San Francisco: HarperSanFrancisco, 1995.

Sylvia Boorstein. "We Are All Wayfarers." *Shambhala Sun*, 17.2 (November 2008).

Matthew Bortolin. *The Dharma of Star Wars*. Boston: Wisdom Publications, 2005.

Joan Borysenko. *Minding the Body, Mending the Mind*. New York: Bantam Books, 1988.

Luk Bouckaert and Laszlo Zsolnai, eds. *The Palgrave Handbook of Spirituality and Business*. New York: Palgrave Macmillan, 2011.

C.A. Bowers. *Mindful Conservatism: Rethinking the Ideological and Educational Basis of an Ecologically Sustainable Future*. Lanham, MD: Rowman and Littlefield, 2003.

Richard E. Boyatzis and Annie McKee. *Resonant Leadership: Renewing Yourself and Connecting with Others Through Mindfulness, Hope, and Compassion.* Boston: Harvard Business Review Press, 2005.

Barry Boyce. "Books to Keep in Mind." *Shambhala Sun*, 18.4 (March 2010): 75–76.

Barry Boyce. "Building Harmony." *Shambhala Sun*, 20.1 (September 2011): 73–75.

Barry Boyce. "Business Not as Usual." *Shambhala Sun*, 19.2 (November 2010): 75–76.

Barry Boyce. "The Contemplative Curriculum." *Shambhala Sun*, 17.6 (July 2009): 79–83.

Barry Boyce. "Creating a Mindful Society." In *The Mindfulness Revolution: Leading Psychologists, Scientists, Artists, and Meditation Teachers on the Power of Mindfulness in Daily Life*, edited by Barry Boyce and the Editors of *Shambhala Sun*. Boston: Shambhala, 2011: 252–264.

Barry Boyce. "The Healing Power of Mindfulness." *Shambhala Sun*, 19.3 (January 2011): 42–50.

Barry Boyce. "The Kindest Thing You Can Do." *Shambhala Sun*, 20.6 (July 2012): 73–75.

Barry Boyce. "The Law of Mindfulness." *Shambhala Sun*, 18.5 (May 2010): 77–81.

Barry Boyce. "Learning the Ropes." *Shambhala Sun*, 19.5 (May 2011): 75–77.

Barry Boyce. "Making Peace in America's Cities." *Shambhala Sun*, 19.5 (May 2011): 32–41.

Barry Boyce. "The Man Who Prescribes the Medicine of the Moment." *Shambhala Sun*, 13.3 (May 2005): 28–34, 72–75.

Barry Boyce. "Meeting of the Mindful." *Shambhala Sun*, 20.3 (January 2012): 73–74.

Barry Boyce. "Overcoming Shyness; Mindful Divorce." *Shambhala Sun*, 18.3 (January 2010): 79–80.

Barry Boyce. "A Real Education." *Shambhala Sun*, 20.5 (May 2012): 75–77.

Barry Boyce. "The Secret Success of MBSR." *Shambhala Sun*, 18.6 (July 2010): 71–72.

Barry Boyce. "Showtime!" *Shambhala Sun*, 19.1 (September 2010): 71–72.

Barry Boyce. "Taking the Measure of Mind." *Shambhala Sun*, 20.4 (March 2012): 42–49, 81–82.

Barry Boyce. "Why We're Taking Mindfulness to Heart." *Shambhala Sun*, 18.4 (March 2010): 11.

Barry Boyce. "Wisdom 2.0: The Digital World Connects." *Shambhala Sun*, 19.6 (July 2011): 38–43, 89–90.

Barry Boyce and the editors of *Shambhala Sun*. *The Mindfulness Revolution: Leading Psychologists, Scientists, Artists, and Meditation Teachers on the Power of Mindfulness in Daily Life*. Boston: Shambhala, 2011.

Tara Brach. *Radical Acceptance: Embracing Your Life with the Heart of a Buddha.* New York: Bantam, 2003.

Jeffrey Brantley. *Calming Your Anxious Mind: How Mindfulness and Compassion Can Free You from Anxiety, Fear, and Panic.* Oakland, CA: New Harbinger, 2003.

Jeff Brantley. "Mindfulness FAQ." In *The Mindfulness Revolution: Leading Psychologists, Scientists, Artists, and Meditation Teachers on the Power of Mindfulness in Daily Life*, edited by Barry Boyce and the editors of *Shambhala Sun*. Boston: Shambhala, 2011: 38–45.

Jeffrey Brantley and Wendy Millstine. *Five Good Minutes at Work: 100 Mindful Practices to Help You Relieve Stress and Bring Your Best to Work*. Oakland, CA: New Harbinger, 2007.

Jeffrey Brantley and Wendy Millstine. *Five Good Minutes with the One You Love: 100 Mindful Practices to Deepen and Renew Your Love Every Day*. Oakland, CA: New Harbinger, 2008.

Jeffrey Brantley and Wendy Millstine. *Five Good Minutes in Your Body: 100 Mindful Practices to Help You Accept Yourself and Feel at Home in Your Body*. Oakland, CA: New Harbinger, 2009.

Jeffrey Brantley and Wendy Millstine. *True Belonging: Mindful Practices to Help You Overcome Loneliness, Connect With Others, and Cultivate Happiness*. Oakland, CA: New Harbinger, 2011.

Brene Brown. *Daring Greatly: How the Courage to be Vulnerable Transforms the Way We Live, Love, Parent, and Lead*. New York: Gotham, 2012

Patricia Leigh Brown and Carol Pogash. "The Pleasure Principle." *New York Times*, March 15, 2009: ST8.

Mark A. Burch. *Stepping Lightly: Simplicity for People and the Planet*. Gabriola Island, Canada: New Society, 2000.

Angela Buttimer and Dennis Buttimer. Calm: Choosing to Live Mindfully. *Self*, 2011.

Marie Beuzeville Byles. *Journey Into Burmese Silence*. London: George Allen and Unwin, 1962.

Wendy Cadge. *Heartwood: The First Generation of Theravada Buddhism in America*. Chicago: University of Chicago Press, 2004.

Wendy Cadge. "Reflections on Habits, Buddhism in America, and Religious Individualism." *Sociology of Religion*, 68.2 (2007): 201–205.

Linda Campbell and Bruce Campbell. *Mindful Learning: 101 Proven Strategies for Student and Teacher Success*. Thousand Oaks, CA: Corwin Press, 2009.

Ryan Carpenter. "Researchers Study Marines' Mind Fitness." 11th Marine Expeditionary Unit, July 18, 2011. Retrieved from http://www.11thmeu.marines.mil/News/NewsArticleDisplay/tabid/2683/Article/22079/researchers-study-marines-mind-fitness.aspx (Accessed February 23, 2013).

Michael Carroll. *The Mindful Leader: Awakening Your Natural Management Skills Through Mindfulness Meditation*. Boston: Trumpter, 2008.

Paul Carus. *The Dharma, or the Religion of Enlightenment: An Exposition of Buddhism*. Chicago: Open Court Publishing, 1907.

Tom Catton. *The Mindful Addict: A Memoir of the Awakening of a Spirit*. Las Vegas: Central Recovery Press, 2010.

The Center for Mindfulness in Medicine, Health Care, and Society. Retrieved from http://w3.umassmed.edu/MBSR/public/searchmember.aspx (Accessed October 10, 2012).

Tovar Ceruli. *The Mindful Carnivore: A Vegetarian's Hunt for Sustenance*. New York: Pegasus Books, 2012.

Lord Chalmers. *Further Dialogues of the Buddha, Translated from the Pali of the Majjhima Nikāya* (Vol. I). London: Humphrey Milford, Oxford University Press, 1926.

Lord Chalmers. *Further Dialogues of the Buddha, Translated from the Pali of the Majjhima Nikāya*. (Vol. 2) London: Humphrey Milford, Oxford University Press, 1927.

Viveka Chen. "Finding True Freedom." In *Dharma, Color, and Culture: New Voices in Western Buddhism*. Hilda Gutiérrez Baldoquín, ed. Berkeley, CA: Parallax Press, 2004: 111–116.

Pema Chodron. *Start Where You Are: A Guide to Compassionate Living*. Boston: Shambhala, 1994.

Thubten Chodron. "The Right Kind of Mindfulness." *Shambhala Sun*, 15.1 (September 2006): 25–28.

Richard Cimino and Don Lattin. *Shopping for Faith: American Religion in the New Millennium*. San Francisco: Jossey-Bass, 1998.

Malcolm Clark. "Diverse Diversities" [Letter to the editor]. *Shambhala Sun*, 21.1 (September 2012).

John Cloud. "Losing Focus? Studies Say Mindfulness Can Help." *Time*, August 6, 2010. Retrieved from http://www.time.com/time/health/article/0,8599,2008914,00.html (Accessed May 19, 2013).

Alan Cole. *Fathering Your Father: The Zen of Fabrication in Tang Buddhism*. Berkeley: University of California Press, 2009.

John E. Coleman. *The Quiet Mind*. New York: Harper and Row, 1971.

The Compact Edition of the Oxford English Dictionary. Oxford: Oxford University Press, 1971.

Paul Conrad. "On the Road." *Tricycle: The Buddhist Review*, 12.2 (Winter 2002): 69–71.

James V. Córdova. *The Marriage Checkup: A Scientific Program for Sustaining and Strengthening Marital Health*. Lanham, MD: Rowman and Littlefield, 2009. .

John Corrigan and Lynn S. Neal, eds. *Religious Intolerance in America: A Documentary History*. Chapel Hill, NC: University of North Carolina, 2010.

"The Surprising Way to Feel Happier." *Cosmopolitan*. Retrieved from http://www.cosmopolitan.com/advice/tips/The-surprising-way-to-feel-happier (Accessed October 1, 2012).

Rebecca Crane. *Mindfulness-Based Cognitive Therapy*. London: Routledge, 2009.

Lama Surya Das. *Awakening the Buddha Within: Eight Steps to Enlightenment, Tibetan Wisdom for the Western World*. New York: Broadway Books, 1997.

Arthur J. Deikman. "Experimental Meditation." *The Journal of Nervous and Mental Disease*, 136.4 (April 1963): 329–343.

Paula Derrow. "Stop Emotional Eating." *Self*. Retrieved from http://www.self.com/takecareofyou/emotional-eating-slideshow#slide=1 (Accessed May 19, 2013).

DharmaCrafts Holiday 2003. Laurence, MA: DharmaCrafts.

DharmaCrafts Holiday 2004. Laurence, MA: DharmaCrafts.

DharmaCrafts Holiday 2005. Laurence, MA: DharmaCrafts.

DharmaCrafts Spring 2007. Laurence, MA: DharmaCrafts.

DharmaCrafts Summer 2008. Laurence, MA: DharmaCrafts.

DharmaCrafts Bestsellers 2013. Laurence, MA: DharmaCrafts.

Fabrizio Didonna, ed. *Clinical Handbook of Mindfulness*. New York: Springer, 2009.

David B. Dillard-Wright, Heidi E. Spear, and Paula Munier. *5-Minute Mindfulness: Simple Daily Shortcuts to Transform Your Life*. Avon, MA: Adams Media, 2011.

Kathleen H. Dockett, G. Rita Dudley-Grant, and C. Peter Bankart, eds. *Psychology and Buddhism: From Individual to Global Community*. New York: Kluwer Academic, 2003.

Paul J. Donahue. *Parenting Without Fear: Letting Go of Worry and Focusing on What Really Matters*. New York: St. Martin's Griffin, 2007.

Dorothy C. Donath. *Buddhism for the West*. New York: McGraw-Hill, 1971.

Nick Dubin. *Asperger Syndrome and Anxiety: A Guide to Successful Stress Management*. London: Jessica Kingsley Publishers, 2009.

Duke Integrative Medicine. Retrieved from http://www.dukeintegrativemedicine.org (Accessed January 24, 2013).

Earth Balance Natural. Retrieved from http://www.earthbalancenatural.com (Accessed February 25, 2013).

Eduardo Duran. "Buddhism in the Land of the Redface." In *Dharma, Color, and Culture: New Voices in Western Buddhism*, Hilda Gutiérrez Baldoquín, ed. Berkeley, CA: Parallax Press, 2004: 47–50.

The Dylan Ratigan Show. "The Buddhist Practice that Could Fix Congress." MSNBC, April 9, 2012. Retrieved from http://www.msnbc.msn.com/id/31510813/#46997405 (Accessed May 19, 2013).

Sandy Eastoak, ed. *Dharma Family Treasures: Sharing Buddhism with Children*. Berkeley, CA: North Atlantic Books, 1994.

Christopher R. Edgar. *Inner Productivity: A Mindful Path to Efficiency and Enjoyment in Your Work*. Christopher R. Edgar, 2009.

Albert J. Edmunds. *Hymns of Faith (Dhammapada), being an ancient anthology preserved in the short collection of the sacred scriptures of the Buddhists*. Chicago: Open Court Publishing Company, 1902.

Lynn P. Eldershaw. "Shambhala International: The Golden Sun of the Great East." In *Wild Geese: Buddhism in Canada*, John S. Harding, Victor Sōgen Hori, and Alexander Soucy, eds.. Montreal and Kingston: McGill-Queens University Press, 2010: 236–267.

Charles H. Elliot and Laura L. Smith. *Anxiety and Depression Workbook for Dummies*. Hoboken, NJ: John Wiley & Sons, 2006.

Alan Epstein. *How to Be Happier Day by Day: A Year of Mindful Actions*. New York: Penguin Books, 1994.

Mark Eptstein. *Psychotherapy Without the Self: A Buddhist Perspective*. New Haven, CT: Yale University Press, 2007.

Jen Evans. "A Conservative View." [Letter to the editor]. *Shambhala Sun*, 20.5 (May 2012).

Richard Fields. *Awakening to Mindfulness: 10 Steps for Positive Change*. Deerfield Beach, FL: Health Communications, 2008.

Richard Fields. *A Year of Living Mindfully: 52 Quotes and Weekly Mindfulness Practices*. Tucson, AZ: FACES Conferences, 2012.

Rick Fields. *How the Swans Came to the Lake: A Narrative History of Buddhism in America* (3rd ed.). Boston: Shambhala, 1992.

Barbara Fine. *Just Being with the Mindful Breath: The Workbook*. Barbara Fine, 2011.

Barbara Miller Fishman. *Emotional Healing Through Mindfulness: Stories and Meditations for Women Seeking Wholeness*. Rochester, VT: Inner Traditions, 2002.

Paul R. Fleischman. *Karma and Chaos: New and Collected Essays on Vipassana Meditation*. Seattle: Vipassana Research Publications, 1999.

Steve Flowers. *The Mindful Path Through Shyness: How Mindfulness and Compassion Can Help Free You From Social Anxiety, Fear, and Avoidance*. Oakland: New Harbinger Publications, 2009.

Steve Flowers and Bob Stahl. *Living with Your Heart Wide Open: How Mindfulness and Compassion Can Free You From Unworthiness, Inadequacy, and Shame*. Oakland, CA: New Harbinger, 2011.

Denise Foley. "Conquer Your Food Cravings." *Good Housekeeping*. Retrieved from http://www.goodhousekeeping.com/health/diet-plans/conquer-food-cravings-4 (Accessed October 1, 2012).

James Ishmael Ford. "I Want to Be…Peaceful." *Shambhala Sun*, 20.6 (July 2012): 32–35, 91.

Terry Fralich. *Cultivating Lasting Happiness: A 7-Step Guide to Mindfulness*. 2nd ed. Eau Claire, WI: PESI, 2007.

Laura Fraser. "The Joy of Mindful Cooking: Practicing Awareness in the Kitchen." *Tricycle: The Buddhist Review*, 19.1 (Fall 2009): 62–67, 115–116.

Gil Fronsdal. "Insight Meditation in the United States: Life, Liberty, and the Pursuit of Happiness." In *The Faces of Buddhism in America*, Charles S. Prebish and Kenneth K. Tanaka, eds. Berkeley: University of California Press, 1998: 163–180.

Maya Frost. *Real-World Mindfulness™: 101 Eyes-Wide-Open Ways to Boost Awareness and Creativity*. Maya Talisman Frost.

Carrie Gann. "Brain Imaging Illuminates Neuro Basis of Meditation." ABC News, November 22, 2011. Retrieved from http://abcnews.go.com/Health/meditation-brain-rewire-study/story?id=15001280#.UZfJsMqHShm (Accessed May 18, 2013).

Beth Gardiner. "Business Skills and Buddhist Mindfulness." *Wall Street Journal*, April 3, 2012. Retrieved from http://online.wsj.com/article/SB10001424052702303816504577305820565167202.html (Accessed August 17, 2012).

Frank Gardner and Zella Moore. *Clinical Sport Psychology*. Champaign, IL: Human Kinetics, 2006.

Jackie Gardner-Nix. *The Mindfulness Solution to Pain: Step-by-Step Techniques for Chronic Pain Management*. Oakland, CA: New Harbinger, 2009.

Barbara Gates and Wes Nisker. "Bringing Mindfulness into Mainstream America: An Interview with Jon Kabat-Zinn." In *The Best of Inquiring Mind: 25 Years of Dharma, Drama, and Uncommon Insight*, Barbara Gates and Wes Nisker, eds. Boston: Wisdom Publications, 2008: 34–42.

Diane R. Gehart. *Mindfulness and Acceptance in Couple and Family Therapy*. New York: Springer, 2012.

Shari M. Geller and Leslie S. Greenberg. *Therapeutic Presence: A Mindful Approach to Effective Treatment*. Washington, DC: American Psychological Association, 2012.

Christopher K. Germer. *The Mindful Path to Self-Compassion: Freeing Yourself from Destructive Thoughts and Emotions*. New York: Guilford Press, 2009.

Christopher K. Germer, Ronald D. Siegel, and Paul R. Fulton. *Mindfulness and Psychotherapy*. New York: Guilford Press, 2005.

Christopher K. Germer and Ronald D. Siegel, eds. *Wisdom and Compassion in Psychotherapy: Deeping Mindfulness in Clinical Practice*. New York: Guilford Press, 2012.

Carolyn Rose Gimian, ed. *The Essential Chogyam Trungpa*. Boston: Shambhala, 1999.

Elisha Goldstein. *Mindfulness Meditations for the Anxious Traveler: Quick Exercises to Calm Your Mind*. New York: Atria Books, 2012.

Joseph Goldstein. *The Experience of Insight: A Natural Unfolding*. Santa Cruz: Unity Press, 1976.

Joseph Goldstein. "Forty Years in the Dhamma." *Insight Journal*, 31 (Winter 2009): 4–10.

Joseph Goldstein. *Insight Meditation: The Practice of Freedom*. Boston: Shambhala, 1994.

Joseph Goldstein. *One Dharma: The Emerging Western Buddhism*. San Francisco: HarperSanFrancisco, 2002.

Daniel Goleman. *Emotional Intelligence: Why It Can Matter More Than IQ*. New York: Bantam Books, 1995.

Daniel Goleman, ed. *Healing Emotions: Conversations with the Dalai Lama on Mindfulness, Emotions, and Health*. Boston: Shambhala, 1997.

Daniel Goleman. "Meditation and Consciousness: An Asian Approach to Mental Health." *American Journal of Psychotherapy*, 30.1 (1976).

Daniel Goleman. "A Mindful Consumer Can Help Change the World." In *The Mindfulness Revolution: Leading Psychologists, Scientists, Artists, and Meditation Teachers on the Power of Mindfulness in Daily Life*, edited by Barry Boyce and the editors of *Shambhala Sun*. Boston: Shambhala, 2011: 242–247.

Daniel Goleman. *The Varieties of the Meditative Experience*. New York: Halsted Press, 1976.

David Gordon. *Mindful Dreaming: A Practical Guide for Emotional Healing Through Transformative Mythic Journeys*. Franklin Lakes, NJ: New Page Books: 2007.

Mark Goulston. *Post-Traumatic Stress Disorder for Dummies*. Hoboken, NJ: John Wiley & Sons, 2008.

Henry Grayson. *Mindful Loving: 10 Practices for Creating Deeper Connections*. New York: Gotham Books, 2003.

Susan Kaiser Greenland. *The Mindful Child: How to Help Your Kid Manage Stress and Become Happier, Kinder, and More Compassionate*. New York: Free Press, 2010.

Susan Kaiser Greenland. "Mindfulness for Children." *Insight Journal*, 33 (Winter 2010): 25–29.

Kevin Griffin. *One Breath at a Time: Buddhism and the Twelve Steps*. New York: St. Martin's Griffin, 2004.

Bhante Henepola Gunaratana. *Beyond Mindfulness in Plain English*. Boston: Wisdom, 2009.

Bhante Henepola Gunaratana. *Eight Mindful Steps to Happiness: Walking the Buddha's Path*. Boston: Wisdom, 2001.

Bhante Henepola Gunaratana. *The Four Foundations of Mindfulness in Plain English*. Boston: Wisdom, 2012.

Bhante Henepola Gunaratana. *Journey to Mindfulness: The Autobiography of Bhante G.* Boston: Wisdom Publications, 2003.

Bhante Henepola Gunaratana. *Mindfulness in Plain English*. Boston: Wisdom Publications, 1991.

V. F. Gunaratna. "The Satipatthana Sutta and Its Application to Modern Life." *The Wheel*, issue 60 (1963).

Henry Grayson. *Mindful Loving: 10 Practices for Creating Deep Connections*. New York: Gotham Books, 2003.

Steve Hagen. *Buddhism Plain and Simple: The Practice of Being Aware, Right Now, Every Day*. New York: Broadway Books, 1999.

John S. Haller, Jr. *The History of New Thought: From Mind Cure to Positive Thinking and the Prosperity Gospel*. West Chester, PA: Swedenborg Foundation Press, 2012.

Thich Nhat Hanh. *Being Peace*. Berkeley, CA: Parallax Press, 1987.

Thich Nhat Hanh. *The Blooming of a Lotus: Guided Meditation Exercises for Healing and Transformation*. Boston: Beacon Press, 1993.

Thich Nhat Hanh. *Buddha Mind, Buddha Body: Walking Toward Enlightenment*. Berkeley, CA: Parallax Press, 2007.

Thich Nhat Hanh. "Commentary." *Tricycle: The Buddhist Review*, 1.3 (Spring 1992): 26–27.

Thich Nhat Hanh. *Creating True Peace: Ending Violence in Yourself, Your Family, Your Community, and the World*. New York: Simon and Schuster, 2003.

Thich Nhat Hanh. *Cultivating the Mind of Love: The Practice of Looking Deeply in the Mahayana Buddhist Tradition*. Berkeley, CA: Parallax Press, 1996.

Thich Nhat Hanh. *The Diamond That Cuts Through Illusion: Commentaries on the Prajnaparamita Diamond Sutra*. Berkeley, CA: Parallax Press, 1992.

Thich Nhat Hanh. *The Energy of Prayer: How to Deepen Your Spiritual Practice*. Berkeley, CA: Parallax Press, 2006.

Thich Nhat Hanh. *Finding Our True Home: Living in the Pure Land Here and Now.* Berkeley, CA: Parallax Press, 2003.

Thich Nhat Hanh. *For a Future to Be Possible: Commentaries on the Five Wonderful Precepts.* Berkeley, CA: Parallax Press, 1993.

Thich Nhat Hanh. *Fragrant Palm Leaves: Journals 1962-1966.* Berkeley, CA: Parallax Press, 1998.

Thich Nhat Hanh. *Going Home: Jesus and Buddha as Brothers.* New York: Riverhead, 1999.

Thich Nhat Hanh. *Good Citizens: Creating Enlightened Society.* Berkeley, CA: Parallax Press, 2012.

Thich Nhat Hanh. *A Guide to Walking Meditation.* Nyack, NY: Fellowship Books, 1985.

Thich Nhat Hanh. "Happiness in Every Breath." *Buddhadharma: The Practitioner's Quarterly*, 9.3 (Spring 2011): 35–38.

Thich Nhat Hanh. *The Heart of the Buddha's Teaching: Transforming Suffering into Peace, Joy, and Liberation.* New York: Broadway Books, 1999.

Thich Nhat Hanh. *The Heart of Understanding: Commentaries on the Prajnaparamita Heart Sutra.* Berkeley, CA: Parallax Press, 1988.

Thich Nhat Hanh. *Interbeing: Fourteen Guidelines for Engaged Buddhism.* Berkeley, CA: Parallax Press, 1993.

Thich Nhat Hanh. *A Joyful Path: Community Transformation and Peace.* Berkeley, CA: Parallax Press, 1994.

Thich Nhat Hanh. *Keeping the Peace: Mindfulness and Public Service.* Berkeley, CA: Parallax Press, 2005.

Thich Nhat Hanh. "Mindfulness is a Source of Happiness." *Shambhala Sun*, 18.4 (March 2010): 34–37, 73.

Thich Nhat Hanh. *The Miracle of Mindfulness! A Manual on Meditation.* Boston: Beacon Press, 1976.

Thich Nhat Hanh. *Nothing to Do, Nowhere to Go: Waking Up to Who You Are.* Berkeley, CA: Parallax Press, 2007.

Thich Nhat Hanh. *Old Path, White Clouds: Walking in the Footsteps of the Buddha.* Berkeley, CA: Parallax Press, 1991.

Thich Nhat Hanh. *One Buddha Is Not Enough: A Story of Collective Awakening.* Berkeley, CA: Parallax Press, 2010.

Thich Nhat Hanh. "Opening the Door…And Letting the Ladies In." *Tricycle: The Buddhist Review*, 1.1 (Fall 1992): 26–29.

Thich Nhat Hanh. *Peace Begins Here: Palestinians and Israelis Listening to Each Other.* Berkeley, CA: Parallax Press, 2004.

Thich Nhat Hanh. *Peace Is Every Step: The Path of Mindfulness in Everyday Life.* New York: Bantam, 1991.

Thich Nhat Hanh. *Present Moment, Wonderful Moment: Mindfulness Verses for Daily Living.* Berkeley, CA: Parallax Press, 1990.

Thich Nhat Hanh. *The Sun My Heart: From Mindfulness to Insight Contemplation.* Berkeley, CA: Parallax Press, 1988.

Thich Nhat Hanh. *Transformation and Healing: Sutra on the Four Establishments of Mindfulness*. Berkeley, CA: Parallax Press, 2006.

Thich Nhat Hanh. *Work: How to Find Joy and Meaning in Each Hour of the Day*. Berkeley, CA: Parallax Press, 2012.

Thich Nhat Hanh. *The World We Have: A Buddhist Approach to Peace and Ecology*. Berkeley, CA: Parallax Press, 2008.

Thich Nhat Hanh. *You Are Here: Discovering the Magic of the Present Moment*. Boston: Shambhala Publications, 2009.

Thich Nhat Hanh. *Zen Keys: A Guide to Zen Practice*. New York: Doubleday, 1995.

Thich Nhat Hanh and Annabel Laity. *The Sutra on the Full Awareness of Breathing: With Commentary by Thich Nhat Hanh*. Berkeley, CA: Parallax Press, 1988.

Thich Nhat Hanh and Lilian Cheung. *Savor: Mindful Eating, Mindful Life*. New York: HarperCollins, 2010.

Rick Hanson. *Just One Thing: Developing a Buddha Brain One Simple Practice at a Time*. Oakland, CA: New Harbinger, 2011.

R. Spence Hardy. *A Manual of Buddhism in Its Modern Development*. London: Partridge and Oakley, 1853.

David Harp. *Mindfulness to Go: How to Meditate While You're on the Move*. Oakland, CA: New Harbinger, 2011.

Anne Harrington. *The Cure Within: A History of Mind-Body Medicine*. New York: W.W. Norton, 2008.

Steven C. Hayes, Frank W. Bond, and Dermony Barnes-Holmes. *Acceptance and Mindfulness at Work: Applying Acceptance and Commitment Therapy and Relational Frame Theory to Organizational Behavior Management*. New York: Routledge, 2006.

Steven C. Hayes, Kirk D. Strosahl, and Kelly G. Wilson. *Acceptance and Commitment Therapy: The Process and Practice of Mindful Change*. New York: Guilford Press, 2012.

Matthew S. Hedstrom. *The Rise of Liberal Religion: Book Culture and American Spirituality in the Twentieth Century*. New York: Oxford University Press, 2013.

James D. Herbert and Evan M. Forman. *Acceptance and Mindfulness in Cognitive Behavior Therapy: Understanding and Applying the New Therapies*. Hoboken, NJ: John Wiley & Sons, 2011.

Steven F. Hick. *Mindfulness and Social Work*. Chicago: Lyceum, 2009.

Steven F. Hick and Thomas Bien. *Mindfulness and the Therapeutic Relationship*. New York: Guilford Press, 2008.

Wakoh Shannon Hickey. "Mind Cure, Meditation, and Medicine: Hidden Histories of Mental Healing in the United States." PhD dissertation. Duke University, Durham, NC, 2008.

Anna Hill. *The Mindful Heart*. Bloomington, IN: Balboa Press, 2012.

I. B. Horner. *The Collection of the Middle Length Sayings (Majjhima-Nikāya)*, Vol. I: *The First Fifty Discourses (Mūlapaṇṇāsa)*. London: Luzac and Company, 1954.

I. B. Horner. *The Collection of the Middle Length Sayings (Majjhima-Nikāya)*, Vol. III: *The Final Fifty Discourses (Uparipaṇṇāsa)*. London: Luzac and Company, 1959.

I. B. Horner. *Milinda's Questions,* Vol. I. London: Luzac and Company, 1963.

Janet Howey. "Mindful to the Quarter-inch." *Tricycle: The Buddhist Review,* 2.1 (Fall 1992): 75–75.

Arianna Huffington. "Mindfulness, Meditation, Wellness and Their Connection to Corporate America's Bottom Line." *Huffington Post,* March 18, 2013. Retrieved from http://www.huffingtonpost.com/arianna-huffington/corporate-wellness_b_2903222.html (Accessed March 23, 2013).

Christmas Humphreys. *An Invitation to the Buddhist Way of Life for Western Readers.* New York: Schocken Books, 1969.

Anne Ihnen and Carolyn Flynn. *The Complete Idiot's Guide to Mindfulness.* New York: Alpha Books, 2008.

The Interdependence Project. Retrieved from http://theidproject.org (Accessed October 1, 2013).

Jane Naomi Iwamura. *Virtual Orientalism: Asian Religion and American Popular Culture.* New York: Oxford University Press, 2011.

Pico Iyer. "Still on the Road." *Mindful,* 1.1 (April 2013): 60–63.

Phil Jackson and Hugh Delehanty. *Sacred Hoops: Spiritual Lessons of a Hardwood Warrior.* New York: Hyperion, 1995.

Sayādaw U Janakābhivaṃsa. *Vipassanā Meditation: Lectures on Insight Meditation.* Taiwan: Corporate Body of the Buddha Educational Foundation, 1997 [1985].

Charlie Johnson. "Looking at Fear: Memory of a Near Lynching." *Inquiring Mind: A Semiannual Journal of the Vipassana Community,* 10.1 (Spring 2003): 16–17.

Charles Johnson. "Dharma for a Dangerous Time." *Shambhala Sun,* 15.1: 44 (September 2006): 40–47.

Charles R. Johnson. "The Meaning of Barack Obama." *Shambhala Sun,* 17.2: 19–22.

Charles R. Johnson. "The Meaning of Barack Obama." *Shambhala Sun,* 17.6 (July 2009): 67–68.

Charles Johnson. "Mindfulness and the Beloved Community." East Bay Meditation Center. Retrieved from http://www.eastbaymeditation.org/media/docs/3604_TWSummer03MindfulnessAndTheBelovedCommunity.pdf (Accessed February 1, 2013).

Charles Johnson. "Why Is American Buddhism so White?" *Buddhadharma,* 11.2 (Winter 2011): 46–55.

Marlene Jones. "Moving Toward an End to Suffering." In *Dharma, Color, and Culture: New Voices in Western Buddhism,* Hilda Gutiérrez Baldoquín, ed. Berkeley, CA: Parallax Press, 2004: 43–45.

Jon Kabat-Zinn. *Coming to Our Senses: Healing Ourselves and the World Through Mindfulness.* New York: Hyperion, 2005.

Jon Kabat-Zinn. "Dharma." In *In the Face of Fear: Buddhist Wisdom for Challenging Times,* Barry Boyce, ed. Boston: Shambhala, 2009: 8–12.

Jon Kabat-Zinn. "Foreword." In *Clinical Handbook of Mindfulness,* Fabrizio Didonna, ed. New York: Springer, 2008.

Jon Kabat-Zinn. *Full Catastrophe Living: Using the Wisdom of Your Body and Mind to Face Stress, Pain, and Illness.* New York: Delacorte Press, 1990.

Jon Kabat-Zinn. "Indra's Net at Work: The Mainstreaming of Dharma Practice in Society." In *The Psychology of Awakening: Buddhism, Science, and Our Day-to-Day Lives,* Gay Watson, Stephen Batchelor, and Guy Claxton, eds. Boston: Weisser Books, 2000: 225–249.

Jon Kabat-Zinn. *Letting Everything Become Your Teacher: 100 Lessons in Mindfulness.* New York: Delta, 2009.

Jon Kabat-Zinn. "Meeting Pain with Awareness." *Shambhala Sun,* 15.6 (July 2007): 64–67, 114.

Jon Kabat-Zinn. *Mindfulness for Beginners: Reclaiming the Present Moment—And Your Life.* Boulder, CO: Sounds True, 2012.

Jon Kabat-Zinn. "An Outpatient Program in Behavioral Medicine for Chronic Pain Patients Based on the Practice of Mindfulness Meditation: Theoretical Considerations and Preliminary Results." *General Hospital Psychiatry,* 4.1 (1982): 33–47.

Jon Kabat-Zinn. "Some Reflections on the Origins of MBSR, Skillful Means, and the Trouble with Maps." *Contemporary Buddhism,* 12.1 (May 2011): 281–306.

Jon Kabat-Zinn. "Toward the Mainstreaming of American Dharma Practice." In *Buddhism in America: Proceedings of the First Buddhism in American Conference,* Al Rappaport and Brian Hotchkiss, eds. Boston: Charles E. Tuttle, 1998: 478–528.

Jon Kabat-Zinn. *Wherever You Go, There You Are: Mindfulness Meditation in Everyday Life.* New York: Hyperion, 1994.

Jon Kabat-Zinn. "Why Mindfulness Matters." In *The Mindfulness Revolution: Leading Psychologists, Scientists, Artists, and Meditation Teachers on the Power of Mindfulness in Daily Life,* Barry Boyce, ed. Boston: Shambhala, 2011: 57–62.

Jon Kabat-Zinn, Leslie Lipworth, and Robert Burney. "The Clinical Use of Mindfulness Medicine for the Self-Regulation of Chronic Pain." *Journal of Behavioral Medicine,* 8.2 (1985): 163–190.

Myla and Jon Kabat-Zinn. *Everyday Blessings: The Inner Work of Mindful Parenting.* New York: Hyperion, 1997.

Ronna Kabatznick. *The Zen of Eating: Ancient Answers to Modern Weight Problems.* New York: Perigee, 1998.

Louisa Kamps. "Just Hit Refresh." *Elle,* December 22, 2009. Retrieved from http://www.elle.com/life-love/sex-relationships/just-hit-refresh-389417?click=main_sr (Accessed May 18, 2013).

Jonathan S. Kaplan. *Urban Mindfulness: Cultivating Peace, Presence, and Purpose in the Midst of It All.* Oakland, CA: New Harbinger, 2010.

Philip Kapleau. *The Three Pillars of Zen: Teaching, Practice, Enlightenment.* Boston: Beacon Press, 1966.

Tula Karras. "10 Tips for Mindful Living." *Ladies' Home Journal.* Retrieved from http://www.lhj.com/health/stress/relaxation-techniques/10-tips-for-mindful-living/ (Accessed October 1, 2012).

Todd B. Kashdan and Joseph Ciarrochi, eds. *Mindfulness, Acceptance, and Positive Psychology: The Seven Foundations of Well-Being.* Oakland, CA: New Harbinger, 2013.

Stephanie Kaza. *Mindfully Green: A Personal and Spiritual Guide to Whole Earth Thinking.* Boston: Shambhala, 2008.

Jack Kerouac. *The Dharma Bums.* New York: Penguin Books, 1976 [1958].

Dzongsar Jamyang Khyentse. "Not for Happiness." *Shambhala Sun,* 21.3 (January 2013): 34–39.

Cheryl Kimball. *Mindful Horsemanship: Daily Inspirations for Better Communications with Your Horse.* Middleton, NH: Carriage House, 2002.

C.F. Knight. "Mindfulness—An All-Time Necessity." *Bodhi Leaves,* issue 52 (1967).

Carsten Knox. "Raising Baltimore One Child at a Time." *Mindful,* 1.1 (April 2013): 42–51.

Jack Kornfield. *Bringing Home the Dharma: Awakening Right Where You Are.* Boston: Shambhala, 2011.

Jack Kornfield. "Doing the Buddha's Practice." *Shambhala Sun,* 15.6 (July 2007): 38–45.

Jack Kornfield. "Intensive Insight Meditation: A Phenomenological Study." *Journal of Transpersonal Psychology,* 11.1: 41–58.

Jack Kornfield. *Living Buddhist Masters.* Santa Cruz, CA: Unity Press, 1977.

Jack Murray Kornfield. *The Psychology of Mindfulness Meditation.* PhD dissertation, Humanistic Psychology Institute, 1977.

Jack Kornfield. "This Fantastic, Unfolding Experiment." *Buddhadharma: The Practitioner's Quarterly,* 5.4 (Summer 2007).

Jack Kornfield. *The Wise Heart: A Guide to the Universal Teachings of Buddhist Psychology.* New York: Bantam Books, 2008.

Jack Kornfield, Ram Dass, and Mokusen Miyuki. "Psychological Adjustment is Not Liberation." *Zero: Contemporary Buddhist Life and Thought,* 2 (1979): 72–87.

Arnold Kotler, ed. *Engaged Buddhist Reader.* Berkeley, CA: Parallax Press, 1996.

Arnie Kozak. *Wild Chickens and Petty Tyrants: 108 Metaphors for Mindfulness.* Boston: Wisdom Publications, 2009.

Kulananda and Dominic Houlder. *Mindfulness and Money: The Buddhist Path of Abundance.* New York: Broadway Books, 2002.

Sameet M. Kumar. *Grieving Mindfully: A Compassionate and Spiritual Guide to Coping with Loss.* Oakland, CA: New Harbinger Publications, 2005.

Sameet M. Kumar. *The Mindful Path Through Worry and Rumination: Letting Go of Anxious and Depressive Thoughts.* Oakland, CA: New Harbinger, 2009.

George E. La More, Jr. "The Secular Selling of a Religion." *Christian Century,* 92.10 (1975): 1133–1137.

Lorne Lader. "Mindfulness." In *Spiritually Oriented Interventions for Counseling and Psychotherapy,* Jamie D. Aten, Mark R. McMinn, and Everett L. Worthington, Jr., eds. Washington, DC: American Psychological Association, 2011: 229–250.

Ellen J. Langer. *The Power of Mindful Learning.* Reading, MA: Addison-Wesley, 1997.

Elizabeth Lesser. *The New American Spirituality: A Seeker's Guide*. New York: Random House, 1999.

Judy Lief. "The Middle Way of Stress." *Shambhala Sun*, 21.1 (September 2012).

Bruce Lincoln. *Holy Terrors: Thinking About Religion After September 11*. Chicago: University of Chicago Press, 2003.

Donald S. Lopez, Jr. *The Scientific Buddha: His Short and Happy Life*. New Haven: Yale University Press, 2012.

Kate Loring, Halstead Holman, David Sobel, Diana Laurent, Virginia González, and Marian Minor. *Living a Healthy Life with Chronic Conditions: Self-Management of Heart Disease, Arthritis, Diabetes, Depression, Asthma, Bronchitis, Emphysema, and Other Physical and Mental Health Conditions* (4th ed.). Boulder, CO: Bull Publishing, 2012.

Sasha T. Loring. *Eating With Fierce Kindness: A Mindful and Compassionate Guide to Losing Weight*. Oakland, CA: New Harbinger, 2010.

Marsha Lucas. *Rewire Your Brain For Love: Creating Vibrant Relationships Using the Science of Mindfulness*. Carlsbad, CA: Hay House, 2012.

David S. Ludwig and Jon Kabat-Zinn. "Mindfulness in Medicine." *Journal of the American Medical Association*, 300.11 (Sept 17, 2008): 1350–1352.

Elizabeth MacDonald and Dennis Shirley. *The Mindful Teacher*. New York: Teachers College Press, 2009.

Chris Mace. "Mindfulness and the Technology of Healing: Lessons from Western Practice." In *Self and No-Self: Continuing the Dialogue Between Buddhism and Psychotherapy*, Dale Mathers, Melvin E. Miller, and Osamu Ando, eds. London: Routledge, 2009: 132–142.

Chris Mace. *Mindfulness and Mental Health: Therapy, Theory and Science*. London: Routledge, 2007.

Hakyu Taizan Maezumi and Bernard Tetsugen Glassman, eds. *On Zen Practice*. Los Angeles: Zen Center of Los Angeles, 1976.

Vicki Mackenzie. *Why Buddhism? Westerners in Search of Wisdom*. London: Thorsons, 2003.

Barry Magid. *Ordinary Mind: Exploring the Common Ground of Zen and Psychotherapy*. Boston: Wisdom, 2002.

Mark Magill. *Why Is the Buddha Smiling? Mindfulness as a Means of Bringing Calm and Insight to Your Life*. Gloucester, MA: Fair Winds Press, 2003.

Magnolia Grove Monastery. Retrieved from http://magnoliagrovemonastery.org/index.php?option=com_content&view=article&id=145:dom&catid=34:dom&Itemid=89 (Accessed May 10, 2013).

Eric Maisel and Susan Raeburn. *Creative Recovery: A Complete Addiction Treatment Program that Uses Your Natural Creativity*. Boston: Shambhala, 2008.

Tara Jon Manning. *Mindful Knitting: Inviting Contemplative Practice to the Craft*. Boston: Tuttle Publishing, 2004.

Reg McAuliffe. "A Businessman's Dhamma." *Bodhi Leaves*, issue 52 (1967).

Lucia McBee. *Mindfulness-Based Elder Care: A CAM Model for Frail Elders and Their Caregivers*. New York: Springer, 2008.

Donald McCown and Marc S. Micozzi. *New World Mindfulness: From the Founding Fathers, Emerson, and Thoreau to Your Personal Practice*. Rochester, VT: Healing Arts Press, 2012.

Christopher McCurry. *Parenting Your Anxious Child with Mindfulness and Acceptance: A Powerful New Approach to Overcoming Fear, Panic, and Worry Using Acceptance and Commitment Therapy*. Oakland, CA: New Harbinger, 2009.

Suzanna McGee. *Tennis Fitness for the Love of It: A Mindful Approach to Fitness for Injury-free Tennis*. Zuzi Publishing, 2010.

Matthew McKay, Patrick Fanning, and Patricia Zurita Ona. *Mind and Emotions: A Universal Treatment for Emotional Disorders*. Oakland, CA: New Harbinger, 2011.

Melvin McLeod. "For 30 Years the Best of Buddhism in America." *Shambhala Sun*, 17.3: (January 2009).

Melvin McLeod. "A Magazine for Everyone." *Shambhala Sun*, 21.4 (March 2013): 11.

Melvin McLeod, ed. *Mindful Politics: A Buddhist Guide to Making the World a Better Place*. Boston: Wisdom, 2006.

David L. McMahan. *The Making of Buddhist Modernism*. New York: Oxford University Press, 2008.

David L. McMahan. "Meditation, Modern Movements." In *Encyclopedia of Buddhism*, Damien Keown and Charles S. Prebish, eds. London and New York: Routledge, 2007: 502–505.

John R. McRae. *Seeing Through Zen: Encounter, Transformation, and Genealogy in Chinese Chan Buddhism*. Berkeley: University of California Press, 2003.

Mary Jo Meadow, Kevin Culligan, and Daniel Chowing. *Christian Insight Meditation: Following in the Footsteps of John of the Cross*. Boston: Wisdom, 2007.

Mengstupiditis. Retrieved from http://www.mengstupiditis.com (Accessed October 1, 2013).

Franz Metcalf and BJ Gallagher Hateley. *What Would Buddha Do at Work? 101 Answers to Workplace Dilemmas*. Berkeley, CA: Seastone, 2001.

Andrea Miller. "Be Beautiful, Be Yourself: Andrea Miller's Exclusive Interview with Thich Nhat Hanh." *Shambhala Sun*, 20.3 (January 2012).

Andrea Miller "In the Country of the Present Moment." *Shambhala Sun*, 21.3 (January 2013): 40–49.

Andrea Miller. "The Mindful Society." *Shambhala Sun*, 17.1 (September 2008): 56–63, 106.

Andrea Miller. "Real People, Real Practice: Four Inspiring Stories of How Real People Are Integrating Mindfulness into Their Lives." *Shambha Sun*, 19.3 (January 2011): 52–55.

Andrea Miller. "With Mindfulness You're Less Likely to Kill the Person Holding Up the Line." *Shambhala Sun*, 21.3 (January 2013): 25–26.

Andrea Miller and the editors of the *Shambhala Sun. Right Here with You: Bringing Mindful Awareness into Our Relationships*. Boston: Shambhala, 2011.

Karen Maezen Miller. *Momma Zen: Walking the Crooked Path of Motherhood*. Boston: Trumpeter, 2007.

Mindful Clarity. Retrieved from http://www.mindfulclarity.com/About-Us.html (Accessed May 17, 2013).

The Mindful Detox. Retrieved from http:// www.themindfuldetox.com (Accessed February 1, 2013).

The Mindful Doctor. Retrieved from http:// www.themindfuldoctor.com (Accessed February 1, 2013).

The Mindful Judge. Retrieved from http:// www.themindfuljudge.com (Accessed February 1, 2013).

The Mindful Law Professor. Retrieved from http:// www.themindfullawprofessor.com (Accessed February 1, 2013).

The Mindful Law School. Retrieved from http:// www.themindfullawschool.com (Accessed February 1, 2013).

The Mindful Law Student. Retrieved from http:// www.themindfullawstudent.com (Accessed February 1, 2013).

The Mindful Lawyer. Retrieved from http:// www.themindfullawyer.com (Accessed February 1, 2013).

Mindful Living. Retrieved from http:// www.mindfulliving.net (Accessed February 1, 2013).

Mindful Mints. Retrieved from http://www.mindfulmints.com/home.html (Accessed February 25, 2013).

The Mindful Muscle. Retrieved from http://www.themindfulmuscle.com (Accessed February 1, 2013).

The Mindful Parent. Retrieved from http:// www.themindfulparent.org (Accessed February 1, 2013).

The Mindful Physician. Retrieved from http:// www.themindfulphysician.com (Accessed February 1, 2013).

"The Mindful Society." *Shambhala Sun*, 21.3 (January 2013): 75–77.

The Mindful Therapist. Retrieved from http:// www.themindfultherapist.com (Accessed February 1, 2013).

"Mindfulness." *The Golden Lotus*, April–May, 1958: 53–55.

"Mindfulness-Based Stress Reduction—Topic Overview." WebMD, May 23, 2011. Retrieved from http://www.webmd.com/balance/tc/mindfulness-based-stress-red uction-topic-overview (Accessed May 19, 2013).

Mindfulness Bell. Retrieved from https://itunes.apple.com/us/app/mindfulness-bell/ id380816407?mt=8 (Accessed February 22, 2013).

"Mindfulness Goes Corporate." *Mindful*, 1.1 (April 2013): 58.

Mindfulness Research Guide. Retrieved from http://www.mindfulexperience.org/ resources/MRG_pubs_2010.pdf (Accessed October 10, 2012).

Chris Moody. "Mark Sanford Talks Buddhism, His Daily Meditation Practice and Unique Campaign Style." *Yahoo News*, May 6, 2013. Retrieved from http://news.yahoo.com/blogs/ticket/mark-sanford-talks-buddhism-daily-meditation-practice-unique-000939600.html (Accessed May 6, 2013).

The Monastery Store Fall 2012–Winter 2013. Mt. Tremper, NY: Dharma Communications, 2012.

Marcia Montenegro. "Mindfulness Goes to Kindergarten." *Christian Answers for the New Age*. Retrieved from http://www.christiananswersforthenewage.org/Articles_MindfulnessForChildren.html (Accessed January 31, 2013).

R. Laurence Moore. *Selling God: American Religion in the Marketplace of Culture*. New York: Oxford University Press, 1994.

Gerald J. Musante. *The Structure House Weight Loss Plan: Achieve Your Ideal Weight Through a New Relationship with Food*. New York: Simon and Schuster, 2007.

Joseph Naft. "Mindfulness." Inner Horizons. Retrieved from http://www.innerfrontier.org/Practices/Mindfulness.htm (Accessed May 6, 2013).

Bhikkhu Nāṇamoli and Bhikkhu Bodhi, trans. *The Middle Length Discourses of the Buddha: A New Translation of the Majjhima Nikāya*. Boston: Wisdom Publications, 1995.

Lisa Napoli. "Buddhist Meditation: A Management Skill?" *Morning Edition*, September 13, 2012. Retrieved from http://www.npr.org/2012/09/13/161050141/buddhist-meditation-a-management-skill (Accessed May 19, 2013).

National Center for Complementary and Alternative Medicine. Retrieved from http://nccam.nih.gov/health/meditation/overview.htm

D. K. Nauriyal, Michael S. Drummond, and Y.B. Yal, eds. *Buddhist Thought and Applied Psychological Research: Transcending the Boundaries*. London: Routledge, 2006.

J. S. Neki. "Psychotherapy in India: Past, Present, and Future." *American Journal of Psychotherapy*, 29 (1975): 92–100.

Rachel Neumann. *Not Quite Nirvana: A Skeptic's Journey to Mindfulness*. Berkeley, CA: Parallax Press, 2012.

The New York Times Best Sellers. Retrieved from http://www.nytimes.com/best-sellers-books (Accessed December 31, 2013).

Sister Chan Chau Nghiem. "Coming Home." In *Dharma, Color, and Culture: New Voices in Western Buddhism*, Hilda Gutiérrez Baldoquín, ed. Berkeley, CA: Parallax Press, 2004: 117–123.

Ethan Nictern. *One City: A Declaration of Interdependence*. Boston: Wisdom, 2007.

Wes Nisker. *Buddha's Nature: Evolution as a Practical Guide to Enlightenment*. New York: Bantam Books, 1998.

Mandy Oaklander. "Mindfulness Meditation Linked To Improved Brainpower: 3 Ways to Get Smarter and Boost Your Happiness While You're At It." *Prevention*, March 2013. Retrieved from http://www.prevention.com/mind-body/emotional-health/mindfulness-meditation-linked-improved-brainpower (Accessed May 19, 2013).

Henry S. Olcott. *A Buddhist Catechism According to the Canon of the Southern School*. London: Trübner and Company, 1881.

Andrew Olendzki. "Bait and Switch: Attention Needs to Evolve into Mindfulness." *Tricycle: The Buddhist Review*, 32.4 (Summer 2013): 84–85.

Andrew Olendzki. "Meditation, Healing, and Stress Reduction." In *Engaged Buddhism in the West*, Christopher S. Queen, ed. Boston: Wisdom, 2000: 307–327.

Olive Branch Sangha. Retrieved from http://here-and-now.org/wwwArticles/14precepts.html (Accessed May 17, 2013).

OneTaste. http://www.onetaste.us (Accessed March 18, 2009; February 21, 2013; May 18, 2013; October 17, 2013).

"Oprah Talks to Thich Nhat Hanh." *O: The Oprah Magazine*, March 2010. Retrieved from http://www.oprah.com/spirit/Oprah-Talks-to-Thich-Nhat-Hanh (Accessed May 19, 2013).

Susan M. Orsillo and Lizabeth Roemer. *The Mindful Way Through Anxiety: Break Free from Chronic Worry and Reclaim Your Life*. New York: Guilford Press, 2011.

Charles Orzech, trans. "The Scripture on Perfect Wisdom for Humane Kings Who Wish to Protect Their States." In *Chinese Religions in Practice*, Donald S. Lopez, Jr., ed. Princeton: Princeton University Press, 1996: 372–380.

Oxford English Dictionary Online. Retrieved from http://www.oed.com (Accessed July 1, 2013).

Daphne Oz. *Relish: An Adventure in Food, Style, and Everyday Fun*. New York: HarperCollins, 2013.

Parallax Press. Retrieved from http://www.parallax.org(Accessed October 1, 2013).

Maggie Philips. *Reversing Chronic Pain: A 10-Point All-Natural Plan for Lasting Relief*. Berkeley, CA: North Atlantic Books, 2007.

Ed Pilkington. "US Military Struggling to Stop Suicide Epidemic Among War Veterans." *The Guardian*, February 1, 2013. Retrieved from http://www.guardian.co.uk/world/2013/feb/01/us-military-suicide-epidemic-veteran (Accessed February 23, 2013).

Susan Piver. *The Mindful Way Through Pregnancy: Meditation, Yoga, and Journaling for Expectant Mothers*. Boston: Shambhala, 2012.

Plum Village. Retrieved from http://www.plumvillage.org/mindfulness-trainings/3-the-five-mindfulness-trainings.html (Accessed May 17, 2013).

Patrick A. Pranke. "Vipassanā." In *Encyclopedia of Buddhism*, Vol. II, Robert E. Buswell, ed. New York: Thomson Gale, 2004: 889–890.

Charles S. Prebish. *Luminous Passage: The Practice and Study of Buddhism in America*. Berkeley: University of California Press, 1999.

Stephen Prothero. *God Is Not One: The Eight Rival Religions that Run the World—and Why Their Differences Matter*. New York: HarperOne, 2010.

Andy Puddicombe. "10 Tips for Living More Mindfully." *Tricycle: The Buddhist Review*, 21.4 (Summer 2012): 68–71.

Ilana Rabinowitz, ed. *Mountain Are Mountains and Rivers Are Rivers: Applying Eastern Teachings to Everyday Life*. New York: Hyperion, 1999.

Walpola Rahula. *What the Buddha Taught.* Bedford: Gordon Fraser Gallery, 1959.

Valerie Davis Raskin. *Great Sex for Moms: Ten Steps to Nurturing Passion While Raising Kids.* New York: Simon and Schuster, 2002.

Ian Reader and George J. Tanabe, Jr. *Practically Religious: Worldly Benefits and the Common Religion of Japan.* Honolulu: University of Hawaii Press, 1998.

Real World Mindfulness. Retrieved from http://www.real-worldmindfulness.com (Accessed February 23, 2013).

Arthur Remillard. *Southern Civil Religions: Imaging the Good Society in the Post-Reconstruction Era.* Athens, GA: University of Georgia Press, 2011.

T. W. Rhys Davids. *Buddhism: Being a Sketch of the Life and Teachings of Gautama, the Buddha.* London: Society for Promoting Christian Knowledge, 1886.

T. W. Rhys Davids. *Lectures on the Origins and Growth of Religion as Illustrated by Some Points in the History of Indian Buddhism.* London: Williams and Norgate, 1881.

T. W. Rhys Davids. *The Questions of King Milinda [The Sacred Books of the East,* Vol. XXXV]. London: Oxford University, 1890.

T. W. Rhys Davids and C.A.F. Rhys Davids. *Dialogues of the Buddha,* Part II. London: Luzac and Company, 1910.

Lewis Richmond. *Work as a Spiritual Practice: A Practical Buddhist Approach to Inner Growth and Satisfaction on the Job.* New York: Broadway Books, 1999.

David Richo. *How to Be an Adult in Relationships: The Five Keys to Mindful Loving.* Boston: Shambhala, 2002.

Laura Riley. "Take a Mindful Walk." *Parents.* Retrieved from http://www.parents.com/pregnancy/week-by-week/15/mindful-walk/.

Sogyal Rinpoche. *The Tibetan Book of Living and Dying.* San Francisco: HarperSan Francisco, 1992.

James M. Rippe and William Southmayd, with Arthur Pappas, Nancy Clark, and Jon Kabat-Zinn. *The Sports Performance Factors.* New York: Perigee Books, 1986.

Lizabeth Roemer and Susan M. Orsillo. *Mindfulness- and Acceptance-Based Behavioral Therapies in Practice.* New York: Guildford Press, 2009.

Captain T. Rogers. *Buddhaghosha's Parables, Translated from the Burmese, With an Introduction,* Containing Buddha's *Dhammapada, or "Path of Virtue,"* Translated from Pâli by F. Max Müller. London: Trübner and Co., 1870.

Holly Rogers and Margaret Maytan. *Mindfulness for the Next Generation: Helping Emerging Adults Manage Stress and Lead Healthier Lives.* New York: Oxford University Press, 2012.

Scott Rogers. *Mindful Parenting: Meditations, Verses, and Visualizations for a More Joyful Life.* Mindful Living Press, 2005.

Scott L. Rogers. *Mindfulness for Law Students: Using the Power of Mindful Awareness to Achieve Balance and Success in Law School.* Scott L. Rogers, 2009.

Scott L. Rogers. *The Six-Minute Solution: A Mindfulness Primer for Lawyers.* Mindful Living Press, 2009.

David Rome and Hope Martin. "Are You Listening?" In *The Mindfulness Revolution: Leading Psychologists, Scientists, Artists, and Meditation Teachers on the Power of Mindfulness in Daily Life*, edited by Barry Boyce and the editors of *Shambhala Sun*. Boston: Shambhala, 2011: 211–218.

Wade Clark Roof. *Spiritual Marketplace: Baby Boomers and the Remaking of American Religion*. Princeton, NJ: Princeton University Press, 1999.

Elena Rosenbaum. *Being Well (Even When You're Sick): Mindfulness Practice for People with Cancer and Other Serious Illnesses*. Boston: Shambhala, 2012.

Elana Rosenbaum. *Here for Now: Living Well with Cancer Through Mindfulness*. Hardwick, MA: Satya House Publications, 2005.

Donald Rothberg. *The Engaged Spiritual Life: A Buddhist Approach to Transforming Ourselves and the World*. Boston: Beacon Press, 2006.

Denise Roy. *Momfulness: Mothering with Mindfulness, Compassion, and Grace*. San Francisco: John Wiley & Sons, 2007.

Gretchin Rubin. *The Happiness Project, Or, Why I Spent a Year Trying to Sing in the Morning, Clean My Closets, Fight Right, Read Aristotle, and Generally Have More Fun*. New York: Harper, 2009.

Gretchin Rubin. "May's Challenge: Be Mindful." *Woman's Day*. Retrieved from http://www.womansday.com/life/mays-challenge-be-mindful-105804 (Accessed May 19, 2013).

Ron Rubio. *Mind/Body Techniques for Asperger's Syndrome: The Way of the Pathfinder*. London: Jessica Kingsley Publishers, 2008.

Tim Ryan. *A Mindful Nation: How a Simple Practice Can Help Us Reduce Stress, Improve Performance, and Recapture the American Spirit*. Carlsbad, CA: Hay House, 2012.

Sangha Directory. Retrieved from http://www.iamhome.org/directory/index.cgi (Accessed December 23, 2012).

Saki Santorelli. *Heal Thy Self: Lessons on Mindfulness in Medicine*. New York: Bell Tower, 1999.

Mahasi Sayadaw. *Practical Insight Meditation: Basic and Progressive Stages*. Kandy, Sri Lanka: Buddhist Publication Society, 1976.

Leigh Eric Schmidt. *Restless Souls: The Making of American Spirituality*. New York: HarperCollins, 2005.

Deborah Schoeberlein. *Mindful Teaching and Teaching Mindfulness: A Guide for Anyone Who Teaches Anything*. Boston: Wisdom, 2009.

Seth Robert Segall. *Encountering Buddhism: Western Psychotherapy and Buddhist Teachings*. Albany, NY: State University of New York, 2003.

Zindel V. Segal, J. Mark G. Williams, and John D. Teasdale. *Mindfulness-Based Cognitive Therapy for Depression: A New Approach to Preventing Relapse*. New York: Guilford Press, 2002.

E. H. Shattock. *An Experiment in Mindfulness*. London: Rider, 1958.

David Sheff. *Clean: Overcoming Addiction and Ending America's Greatest Tragedy*. Chicago: Houghton Mifflin Harcourt, 2013.

Shauna L. Shapiro and Linda E. Carlson. *The Art and Science of Mindfulness: Integrating Mindfulness into Psychology and the Helping Professions*. Washington, DC: American Psychological Association, 2009.

Brenda Shoshanna. *Jewish Dharma: A Guide to the Practice of Judaism and Zen*. New York: Da Capo Press, 2008.

Daniel J. Siegel. *The Mindful Brain: Reflection and Attunement in the Cultivation of Well-Being*. New York: W.W. Norton, 2007.

Daniel J. Siegel. *The Mindful Therapist: A Clinician's Guide to Mindsight and Neural Integration*. New York: W.W. Norton, 2010.

Daniel J. Siegel. *Mindsight: The New Science of Personal Transformation*. New York: Bantam Books, 2010.

Ronald D. Siegel. "From Me to Us." In *The Mindfulness Revolution: Leading Psychologists, Scientists, Artists, and Meditation Teachers on the Power of Mindfulness in Daily Life*, edited by Barry Boyce and the editors of *Shambhala Sun*. Boston: Shambhala, 2011.

Ronald D. Siegel. *The Mindfulness Solution: Everyday Practices for Everyday Problems*. New York: Guilford Press, 2010: 202–210.

Steve Silberman. "Wise Heart." *Shambhala Sun*, 19.2 (November 2010).

Douglas K. Silsbee. *The Mindful Coach: Seven Roles for Helping People Grow*. Marshall, NC: Ivy River Press, 2004.

Judith Simmer-Brown and Fran Grace, eds. *Meditation and the Classroom: Contemplative Pedagogy for Religious Studies*. Albany, NY: State University of New York Press, 2011.

C. Alexander Simpkins and Annellen M. Simpkins. *Meditation for Therapists and Their Clients*. New York: W.W. Norton, 2009.

Mark Singleton. *Yoga Body: The Origins of Modern Posture Practice*. New York: Oxford University Press, 2010.

Jonathan P. Slater. *Mindful Jewish Living: Compassionate Practice*. New York: Aviv Press, 2004.

Susan L. Smalley and Diana Winston. *Fully Present: The Science, Art, and Practice of Mindfulness*. Philadelphia: Da Capo, 2010.

Susan Smalley and Diana Winston. "Is Mindfulness for You?" In *The Mindfulness Revolution: Leading Psychologists, Scientists, Artists, and Meditation Teachers on the Power of Mindfulness in Daily Life*, edited by Barry Boyce and the editors of *Shambhala Sun*. Boston: Shambhala, 2011: 11–20.

Jeremy Adam Smith. "What's Sex Got to Do with It?" *Mindful*, 1.2 (June 2013).

Jonathan C. Smith. *Relaxation, Meditation, and Mindfulness: Personal-Training Manual*. Jonathan C. Smith, 2005.

Julie Carr Smyth. "'Mindfulness' Grows in Popularity—and Profits." Associated Press, June 11, 2012. Retrieved from http://bigstory.ap.org/article/mindfulness-grows-popularity-and-profits (Accessed October 10, 2012).

So Be Mindful. Retrieved from http:// www.sobemindful.com (Accessed February 1, 2013).

Pavel G. Somov. *Eating the Moment: 141 Mindful Practices to Overcome Overeating One Meal at a Time*. Oakland, CA: New Harbinger, 2008.

Pavel Somov. *Present Perfect: A Mindfulness Approach to Letting Go of Perfectionism and the Need for Control*. Oakland, CA: New Harbinger, 2010.

Jeremy Spiegel. *The Mindful Medical Student: A Psychiatrist's Guide to Staying Where You Are While Becoming Who You Want to Be*. Hanover, NH: Dartmouth College Press, 2009.

Claire Stanley. "Mindfulness for Educators." *Insight Journal*, 28 (Summer 2007): 26–29.

Elizabeth A. Stanley and Amishi P. Jha. "Mind Fitness: Improving Operational Effectiveness and Building Warrior Resilience." *Joint Forces Quarterly*, issue 55 (2009): 147.

Elizabeth A. Stanley and John M. Schaldach. "Mindfulness-based Mind Fitness Training (MMFT)." Mind Fitness Training Institute, 2011.

Elizabeth A. Stanley, John M. Schadach, Anastasia Kiyonaga, and Amishi P. Jha. "Mindfulness-based Mind Fitness Training: A Case Study of a High-Stress Predeployment Military Cohort." *Cognitive and Behavioral Practice*, 18.4 (2011).

Lori Stephens. *The Mindful Dog Owner: What Your Dog Is Teaching You About Living Enlightenment*. Verbatim, 2012.

Jeff Strong and Michael O. Flanagan. *AD/HD for Dummies*. Hoboken, NJ: John Wiley & Sons, 2005.

Michael Stroud. "Mindfulness of Mind." *Shambhala Sun*, 16.4 (March 2008): 47, 112–113.

D. T. Suzuki, Erich Fromm, and Richard De Martino. *Zen Buddhism & Psychoanalysis*. New York: Harper Colophon Books, 1960.

Shunryu Suzuki. *Zen Mind, Beginner's Mind*. New York: Weatherhill, 1970.

Donald K. Swearer. *Secrets of the Lotus: Studies in Buddhist Meditation*. New York: Macmillan Company, 1971.

David Swick. "One Moment at a Time." *Shambhala Sun*, 20.2 (November 2011): 75–76.

Scott H. Symington and Melissa F. Symington. "A Christian Model of Mindfulness: Using Mindfulness Principles to Support Psychological Well-Being, Value-Based Behavior, and the Christian Spiritual Journey." *Journal of Psychology and Christianity*, 31.1 (2012): 71–77.

Chade-Meng Tan. *Search Inside Yourself: The Unexpected Path to Achieving Success, Happiness (and World Peace)*. New York: HarperOne, 2012.

Laurie Tarkin. "Improve Job Satisfaction with Mindfulness." FOX News, January 24, 2013. Retrieved from http://www.foxnews.com/health/2013/01/23/improve-job-satisfaction-with-mindfulness/(Accessed May 18, 2013)

Charles T. Tart. *Living the Mindful Life*. Boston: Shambhala, 1994.

Bron Taylor. *Deep Green Religion: Nature Spirituality and the Planetary Future*. Berkeley: University of California Press, 2009.

Janet Taylor. *Buddhism for Non-Buddhists: A Practical Guide to Ease Suffering and Be Happy*. Kansas City, MI: Janet Taylor, 2012.

Matt Tenney. *From the Brig to the Boardroom: Why Mindfulness is the Ultimate Shortcut to Success*. Createspace, 2012.

Nanamoli Thera. *Mindfulness of Breathing: Ānāpānasati*. Kandy, Sri Lanka: Buddhist Publication Series, 1973.

Nyanaponika Thera, ed. *Pathways of Buddhist Thought: Essays from* The Wheel. London: George Allen and Unwin, 1971.

Nyanaponika Thera. *Satipatthana, The Heart of Buddhist Meditation: A Handbook of Mental Training Based on the Buddha's Way of Mindfulness.* Colombo, Ceylon: The Word of the Buddha Publishing, 1953.

Nyanaponika Thera. *The Vision of Dhamma: The Buddhist Writings of Nyanaponika Thera.* London: Rider, 1986.

Soma Thera. *The Way of Mindfulness: The Satipatthana Sutta and Commentary* (4th ed.). Kandy, Sri Lanka: Buddhist Publication Society, 1975.

Sue Patton Thoelle. *The Mindful Woman: Gentle Practices for Restoring Calm, Finding Balance, and Opening Your Heart.* Oakland, CA: New Harbinger, 2008.

Elizabeth Thoman. "Re-imagining the American Dream." In *Mindfulness in the Marketplace: Compassionate Responses to Consumerism,* Allan Hunt Badiner, ed. Berkeley, CA: Parallax Press, 2002: 119–126.

Mark Thornton. *Meditation in a New York Minute: Super Calm for the Super Busy.* Boulder, CO: Sounds True, 2006.

Chogyam Trungpa. *Cutting Through Spiritual Materialism.* Boston: Shambhala, 1973.

Chogyam Trungpa, ed. *Garuda IV: Foundations of Mindfulness.* Boulder: Vajradhatu, 1976.

Geshe Tashi Tsering. *The Four Noble Truths: The Foundation of Buddhist Thought,* Vol. I. Boston: Wisdom, 2005.

Thomas A Tweed. *The American Encounter with Buddhism, 1844–1912: Victorian Culture and the Limits of Dissent.* Chapel Hill: University of North Carolina Press, 2000.

Thomas A. Tweed. *Crossing and Dwelling: A Theory of Religion.* Cambridge, MA: Harvard University Press, 2006.

UCLA Mindful Awareness Research Center. Retrieved from http://marc.ucla.edu/body.cfm?id=85 (Accessed May 10, 2013)

U.S. Marine Corps. Retrieved from http://www.marines.com (Accessed February 23, 2013).

Vijay Vad. *Stop Pain: Inflammation Relief for an Active Life.* Carlsbad, CA: Hay House, 2010.

Kiera Van Gelder. "My Practice Without Meds." *Buddhadharma: The Practitioner's Quarterly,* 10.3 (Spring 2012).

Brian Victoria. *Zen at War.* New York: Weatherhill, 1998.

Cassandra Vieten. *Mindful Motherhood: Practical Tools for Staying Sane During Pregnancy and Your Child's First Year.* Oakland, CA: New Harbinger, 2009.

B. Alan Wallace, ed. *Buddhism and Science: Breaking New Ground.* New York: Columbia University Press, 2003.

B. Alan Wallace. *Contemplative Science: Where Buddhism and Neuroscience Converge.* New York: Columbia University Press, 2007.

B. Alan Wallace. "A Mindful Balance." *Tricycle: The Buddhist Review,* 17.3 (Spring 2008): 60–63, 100.

Maurice Walsh. "Buddhism in Daily Life." *Bodhi Leaves*, issue 86 (1970).

Maurice Walsh, trans. *The Long Discourses of the Buddha: A Translation of the Dīgha Nikāya*. Boston: Wisdom Publications, 1995.

Robyn D. Walser and Darrah Westrup. *Acceptance and Commitment Therapy for the Treatment of Post-Traumatic Stress Disorder and Trauma-Related Problems: A Practitioner's Guide to Using Mindfulness and Acceptance Strategies*. Oakland, CA: New Harbinger Press, 2007.

Robyn D. Walser and Darrah Westrup. *The Mindful Couple: How Acceptance and Mindfulness Can Lead You to the Love You Want*. Oakland, CA: New Harbinger: 2009.

Peggy Rowe Ward and Larry Ward. *Love's Garden: A Guide to Mindful Relationships*. Berkeley, CA: Parallax Press, 2008.

Henry Clarke Warren. *Buddhism in Translations*. Cambridge, MA: Harvard University Press, 1896.

Stephanie Warsmith. "Plain Township School Stops 'Mindfulness' Program After Some in Community Raise Concerns." *Akron Beacon*, April 15, 2013. Retrieved from http://www.ohio.com/news/plain-township-school-stops-mindfulness-program-after-some-in-community-raise-concerns-1.389761 (Accessed May 17, 2013).

Julie Watson. "Marines Studying Mindfulness-Based Training." Associated Press, January 19, 2013. Retrieved from http://bigstory.ap.org/article/marines-studying-mindfulness-based-training (Accessed February 23, 2013).

Karen Kissel Wegela. *What Really Helps: Using Mindfulness and Compassionate Presence to Help, Support, and Encourage Others*. Boston: Shambhala, 2011.

Andrew Weiss. *Beginning Mindfulness: Learning the Way of Awareness, a Ten-Week Course*. Novato, CA: New World Press, 2004.

Margaret J. Wheatley. *So Far From Home: Lost and Found in Our Brave New World*. San Francisco: Berrett-Koehler Publishers, 2012.

Where's My Zen. Retrieved from http://wheresmyzen.com/program (Accessed February 23, 2013).

Claude Whitmyer, ed. *Mindfulness and Meaningful Work: Explorations in Right Livelihood*. Berkeley, CA: Parallax Press, 1994.

Robert J. Wicks. *Bounce: Living the Resilient Life*. New York: Oxford University Press, 2010.

Angel Kyodo Williams. *Being Black: Zen and the Art of Living with Fearlessness and Grace*. New York: Viking Compass, 2000.

Duncan Ryūken Williams. *The Other Side of Zen: A Social History of Sōtō Zen Buddhism in Tokugawa Japan*. Princeton, NJ: Princeton University Press, 2005.

Mark Williams, Danny Pennman, and Jon Kabat-Zinn. *Mindfulness: An Eight-Week Plan for Finding Peace in a Frantic World*. Emmaus, PA: Rodale, 2011.

Mark Williams, John Teasdale, Zindal Segal, and Jon Kabat-Zinn. *The Mindful Way Through Depression: Freeing Yourself from Chronic Unhappiness*. New York: Guilford Press, 2007.

Lola Williamson. *Transcendent in America: Hindu-Inspired Meditation Movements as New Religion*. New York: New York University Press, 2010.

Val Willingham. "Mindfulness Training Busts Stress." CNN, June 1, 2009. Retrieved from http://www.cnn.com/2009/HEALTH/06/01/mindfulness.training.stress/(Accessed May 18, 2013).

Jan Willis. "Yes, We're Buddhists Too!" *Buddhadharma*, 11.2 (Winter 2011): 42–45.

Jeff Wilson. *Dixie Dharma: Inside a Buddhist Temple in the American South*. Chapel Hill, NC: University of North Carolina Press, 2012.

Jeff Wilson. *Mourning the Unborn Dead: A Buddhist Ritual Comes to America*. New York: Oxford University Press, 2009.

Kimberly Wilson. *Tranquilista: Mastering the Art of Enlightened Work and Mindful Play*. Novato, CA: New World Library, 2010.

F. L. Woodward. *The Book of Kindred Sayings*, Vol. V. London: Pali Text Society, 1956.

Robert Wright. "Mindful Eating and Fast-Food Buddhism." *The Atlantic*, February 10, 2012. Retrieved from http://www.theatlantic.com/health/archive/2012/02/mindful-eating-and-fast-food-buddhism/252896/(Accessed February 11, 2012)

Robert Wuthnow. *After Heaven: Spirituality in America Since the 1950s*. Berkeley: University of California Press, 1998.

Cat Yampbell. "Judging a Book by Its Cover: Publishing Trends in Young Adult Literature." *The Lion and the Unicorn*, 29.3 (September 2005): 348–372.

Philip B. Yampolsky. *The Platform Sutra of the Sixth Patriarch*. New York: Columbia University Press, 1967.

Polly Young-Eisendrath and Shoji Muramoto, eds. *Awakening and Insight: Zen Buddhism and Psychotherapy*. New York: Taylor & Francis, 2002.

Carmen Yuen. *The Cosmos in a Carrot: A Zen Guide to Eating Well*. Berkeley, CA: Parallax Press, 2006.

"Zen Lessons." *Redbook*. Retrieved from http://www.redbookmag.com/health-wellness/advice/zen-lessons-yl-2 (Accessed May 19, 2013).

INDEX